palgrave macmillan law masters

company law

The Ur

Uni

THE UNIVERSITY OF LAW
WITHDRAWN

THE UNIVERSITY OF LAW
WITHDRAWN

The College of Law, Chester

C07308

BUSN
Din
Std

palgrave macmillan law masters

Series editor: **Marise Cremona**

Business Law   Stephen Judge
Company Law   Janet Dine and Marios Koutsias
Constitutional and Administrative Law   John Alder
Contract Law   Ewan McKendrick
Criminal Law   Jonathan Herring
Employment Law   Deborah J Lockton
Evidence   Raymond Emson
Family Law   Kate Standley and Paula Davies
Intellectual Property Law   Tina Hart, Simon Clark and Linda Fazzani
Land Law   Mark Davys
Landlord and Tenant Law   Margaret Wilkie, Peter Luxton and Desmond Kilcoyne
Legal Method   Ian McLeod
Legal Theory   Ian McLeod
Medical Law   Jo Samanta and Ash Samanta
Sports Law   Mark James
Torts   Alastair Mullis and Ken Oliphant
Trusts Law   Charlie Webb and Tim Akkouh

RECEIVED

- 7 NOV 2014

If you would like to comment on this book, or on the series generally, please write to
lawfeedback@palgrave.com.

palgrave macmillan law masters

company law

janet dine

Professor of International Economic Development Law,
Centre for Commercial Law Studies,
Queen Mary, University of London

marios koutsias

Lecturer in EU Commercial Law
University of Essex

Eighth edition

palgrave
macmillan

© Janet Dine 1991, 1994, 1998, 2001 and 2005
© Janet Dine and Marios Koutsias 2007, 2009 and 2014

All rights reserved. No reproduction, copy or transmission of this publication may be made without written permission.

Crown Copyright material is licensed under the Open Government Licence v2.0.

No portion of this publication may be reproduced, copied or transmitted save with written permission or in accordance with the provisions of the Copyright, Designs and Patents Act 1988, or under the terms of any licence permitting limited copying issued by the Copyright Licensing Agency, Saffron House, 6–10 Kirby Street, London EC1N 8TS.

Any person who does any unauthorized act in relation to this publication may be liable to criminal prosecution and civil claims for damages.

The authors have asserted their rights to be identified as the authors of this work in accordance with the Copyright, Designs and Patents Act 1988.

This edition first published 2014 by PALGRAVE MACMILLAN

Palgrave Macmillan in the UK is an imprint of Macmillan Publishers Limited, registered in England, company number 785998, of Houndmills, Basingstoke, Hampshire RG21 6XS

Palgrave Macmillan in the US is a division of St Martin's Press LLC, 175 Fifth Avenue, New York, NY 10010.

Palgrave Macmillan is the global academic imprint of the above companies and has companies and representatives throughout the world.

Palgrave® and Macmillan® are registered trademarks in the United States, the United Kingdom, Europe and other countries.

ISBN: 978–0–230–36207–9

This book is printed on paper suitable for recycling and made from fully managed and sustained forest sources. Logging, pulping and manufacturing processes are expected to conform to the environmental regulations of the country of origin.

A catalogue record for this book is available from the British Library.

Typeset by Cambrian Typesetters, Camberley, Surrey.

Printed and bound in the UK by The Lavenham Press Ltd, Suffolk.

Contents

Company law is a subject with many aspects and with a large ambit of application. It covers issues which relate to the creation of a company, its governance and administration, its relationship with important societal groups, such as employees, creditors, the environment or the local community where a company effectively operates, and issues such as the dissolution of the company after a potential insolvency and takeovers. Therefore, it is an area of law which regulates significant aspects of economic and societal activities. In this sense an understanding of company law is indeed necessary for an understanding of the society within which it operates, as will be demonstrated within the framework of Chapter 2 where the topic of 'Corporate Governance' is analysed in depth.

This book presents the main debates that take place within the context of company law and highlights the provisions that affect how an English company functions. It explains not only the operation of the Companies Act 2006, which is currently the principal legislative tool within the field of English company law, but also the rationale behind the shaping of such a legislative framework within which English companies – private or public – operate.

After a general introduction to the structure and aims of company law, and discussion of the main types of companies in the UK in Chapter 1, the book moves on to an analysis of corporate governance in Chapter 2. As will be explained in Chapter 2, the analysis of this topic is necessary for an understanding not only of the wider context within which corporate activities in the UK take place, but also of the roots of company law in this country.

Chapter 3 explains and analyses the nature and the operation of a company's articles of association. The peculiarity of the nature of the latter is very much related to the contractual nature of the English company, as shown in Chapter 2.

Chapter 4 considers the power to represent the company. Chapter 5 examines shares and shareholders' rights, Chapter 6 the regulation of investment business, with an emphasis on public issue securities, and Chapter 7 capital maintenance, with an analysis of the relevant key terms and legislative framework.

Chapter 8 discusses the specifics of corporate management in the UK, providing the reader with a practical application of the theoretical framework first encountered in Chapter 2.

Chapter 9 analyses the issue of directors' duties, which constitutes an aspect of critical importance for English company law. An understanding of the fundamentals of corporate governance will shed light on the rationale behind the establishment of duties for directors to fulfil and the need to hold them accountable in case of breach.

Chapter 10 complements Chapter 9 with a thorough examination of the remedies available to shareholders against managerial abuse of duties. The relationship between directors and shareholders, which stands at the core of the English company law, is important for understanding both the English company and the system of governance on the basis of which it operates.

Chapter 11 looks at lending money and securing loans, while Chapter 12 provides extensive analysis of a particularly important topic for English company law, namely, takeovers. Chapter 12 adopts a comparative approach between English law and the respective European Union legislation in this regard. The rationale behind this is the fact that takeovers may involve a clear cross-border element, so it is always useful to view such a topic with a more international perspective, albeit with a very clear focus on English law.

Chapter 13 focuses on insolvency and analyses the relevant procedures to be followed, the role of directors at this stage, the nature of the rights of creditors, and the new institutional balances shaped within the company at such a critical stage in its life and existence.

Chapter 14 concludes with an explanation of groups of companies viewed from an international perspective, since again a cross-border element is inherent in their operation. English law will of course be at the very core of this chapter.

Table of cases

Table of legislation

EU Legislation

Chapter 1

Starting a company

Key terms

- **Alter ego** – a device which attributes the acts of important managers to the company itself, so that the company may be sued for compensation or convicted of crimes.
- **Community interest company (CIC)** – this type of company was created by the Companies (Audit, Investigations and Community Enterprise) Act 2004. It is a form of company designed for community enterprises which are not charities.
- **Corporate personality** – the legal fiction that the company is an entity separate from the people actually involved in it.
- **Lifting the veil** – looking at the facts and disregarding the effect of the legal fiction that all companies are completely separate from their shareholders.
- **Private company (Ltd)** – this type of company may not advertise to the public in order to sell shares.
- **Public company (PLC)** – this type of company may offer shares to the public by advertisement.

1.1 Starting a company

The first decision that must be made by those considering incorporation of a business is the type of company that will be suitable.

1.1.1 Unlimited and limited companies

1.1.1(a) Unlimited companies

An unlimited company has the advantage of being a legal entity separate from its members, but lacks the advantage that most people seek from incorporation, that is, the limited liability of the members. Thus, the members of an unlimited liability company will be held responsible for all of the debts of the company without limit. Unlimited companies therefore form only a small proportion of the total number of registered companies.

1.1.1(b) Limited liability companies

'The limited liability corporation is the greatest single discovery of modern times. Even steam and electricity are less important than the limited liability company,' said Professor NM Butler, President of Columbia University (quoted by AL Diamond in Orhnial (ed), *Limited Liability and the Corporation* (Law Society of Canada, 1982) at 42; see also Sealy, *Company Law and Commercial Reality* (Sweet & Maxwell, 1984) at 1).

Why is the limited liability company so important? A huge proportion of the world's wealth is generated by companies, and companies are most often used by people as a tool for running a commercial enterprise. Many of these businesses start in a small way, often by co-operation between a small number of people. If such a commercial undertaking prospers, the persons involved will wish to expand the undertaking, which will generally require an injection of money. This may be achieved by inviting more people to contribute to the capital sum which the business uses to fund its activities. The alternative is to raise a loan. The latter course has the disadvantage of being expensive, because the lender will charge interest. On the other hand, the option of inviting a large number of persons to be involved in a business may have considerable disadvantages. One is that they may disagree with each other as to how the business should best be run. They may even disagree with each other as to who should make the decisions about how the business is to be run. This is partially solved in a company by the necessity of having a formal constitution (the memorandum and articles of association – see Section 1.2.2 below), which sets out the voting and other rights of all the members (shareholders) of a company.

Another disadvantage of expansion of a business is that as the amounts dealt with increase, so too do the risks. The great advantage of the most widely used type of company is that its members enjoy 'limited liability'. This means that if the company becomes unable to pay its debts, the members of that company will not have to contribute towards paying all the company's debts out of their own private funds: they are liable to pay only the amount they have paid, or have promised to pay, for their shares. This means that contributors to the funds of businesses which are run on this limited liability basis may be easier to find. Limited liability is also said to encourage greater boldness and risk-taking within the business community, so that new avenues to increasing commerce are explored.

The advantage of limited liability may lead quite small businesses to use a company, although this may not be advantageous from a tax point of view and does lead to a number of obligations to file accounts and so on, which create a considerable burden for a small concern. Further, if a very small business wishes to raise a loan from a bank, the bank will normally require a personal guarantee from the people running the business. This means that the advantage of limited liability will, practically speaking, be lost.

1.1.1(c) Corporate personality

A further disadvantage of attempting to run a business with a large number of people involved is that considerable difficulties may be experienced when some of those people die, wish to retire or simply leave the business. There may be great difficulties for a person dealing with the business in deciding precisely who is liable to pay him. In a shifting body of debtors, an outsider may experience extreme difficulty in determining which people were actually involved in the business at the time that is relevant to his claim against it. This difficulty is solved by the legal fiction of corporate personality. The idea is that the company is an entity separate from the people actually involved in running it. This fictional 'legal person' owns the property of the business, owes the money that is due to business creditors, and is unchanging even though the people involved in the business come and go. Corporate personality is discussed in further detail in Section 1.5 below.

The UK company law rules were the subject of a Department of Trade and Industry review during 2001–02. Although it was publicised as a 'fundamental review' of company law, the changes that resulted were quite modest in substance. However, the Companies Act 2006 almost completely replaces the previous Companies Act 1985 so that many sections have been slightly changed in substance and bear a different number in the new Act. This is important, because some of the case law will refer to the previous Companies Act 1985 and readers will have to find the relevant section in the Companies Act 2006.

As we examine the company law of the UK, it is useful to consider the purpose behind the various rules and whether they are sufficiently effective in achieving their purpose; also whether they justify the expense which is incurred by companies to ensure that their operations stay within the complicated framework that has grown up.

1.1.2 Public and private companies

The fundamental difference between public and private companies is that only public companies may invite the public to subscribe for shares. Section 755 of the Companies Act 2006 prohibits a private company from offering, allotting or agreeing to allot securities to the public, or acting with a view to their being offered to the public. Section 756 defines 'offer to the public' as including an offer to any section of the public, however selected. However, it is not an offer to the public if it can properly be regarded, in all the circumstances, as:

1. not being calculated to result, directly or indirectly, in securities of the company becoming available to persons other than those receiving the offer; or
2. otherwise being a private concern of the person receiving it and the person making it.

In other words, the offeror and offeree must either be known to each other, or be part of a close network of friends, family or acquaintances for the offer not to constitute an 'offer to the public'.

Public companies are therefore more suitable for inviting investment by large numbers of people. A private company is particularly suitable for running a business in which a small number of people are involved. Professor Len Sealy describes the situation as follows:

> During the nineteenth century (and indeed for a considerable period before that) the formation of almost all companies was followed immediately by an appeal to the public to participate in the new venture by joining as members and subscribing for 'shares' in the 'joint stock' ... The main reason for 'going public' in this way was to raise funds in the large amounts necessary for the enterprises of the period – often massive operations which built a large proportion of the world's railways, laid submarine cables, opened up trade to distant parts and provided the banking, insurance and other services to support such activities. The promoters would publish a 'prospectus', giving information about the undertaking and inviting subscriptions. This process is often referred to as a 'flotation' of the company or, more accurately, of its securities. (Sealy, *Cases and Materials in Company Law*, 6th edn, Butterworths, 1996)

It would now be most unusual for a new enterprise to 'float' immediately. The Stock Exchange controls the rules for flotation of a company, and requires an established business record before it will permit it to occur. Another market, whose requirements are similar but not quite so strict, is the Alternative Investment Market (AIM). (For further discussion, see Section 6.3.)

As one might expect, the regulations governing public companies are more extensive than those governing private companies. In many areas, however, no distinction is made between the two types of company.

1.1.3　Off-the-shelf companies

Ready-made companies may be acquired from enterprises which register a number of companies and hold them dormant until they are purchased by a customer. This may save time when a company is needed quickly for a particular enterprise. There used to be a potential problem in that the objects clause of such a company might not precisely cover the enterprise in question, with the result that such a company would be precluded from carrying on the desired business. Contracts made in pursuance of such an enterprise would be of no effect (see Chapter 4). However, many such companies will be formed in the future with the objects of a general commercial company and with unlimited powers on the basis of section 31 of the Companies Act 2006.

1.1.4　Community interest companies

Community Interest Companies (CICS) are limited companies with special additional features, created for the use of people who want to conduct a business or other activity for the benefit of a community and not purely for private advantage. They were introduced by the Companies (Audit, Investigations and Community Enterprise) Act 2004. The fundamental idea was that this would provide a legal form for those considering creating a social enterprise. This is achieved by a 'community interest test' and 'asset lock', which ensures that the CIC is established for community purposes, and that the assets and profits are dedicated to these purposes. Registration of a company as a CIC has to be approved by the Regulator, who also has a continuing monitoring and enforcement role.

Setting up a CIC is a big step because, once registered, the only ways of changing its form are:

1. dissolving the company so that it ceases to exist altogether; or
2. converting the CIC to a charity and subjecting the company to the more onerous regulatory regime of charity law.

This means that once a company is a CIC, it cannot become an ordinary company. Thus, it is important that before going any further, those considering forming a CIC should take professional advice and examine the list of considerations set out below.

The Department for Business, Innovation and Skills regulates CICs. The basic idea is to have a limited liability company but for a special reason for the community. CICs should have a flexible structure including limited liability, the ability to tailor the management of the company and at some time provide a real benefit for the community. CICs are not focused on profit and if the company is dissolved, the assets of the company should go to the community. Charity status for CICs is not appropriate because of the rigid structures of charity legislation. CICs can be funded by individuals, shareholders or foundations, and some types of CICs can make profits and then pay dividends. However, there are restrictions on dividends and assets and the CIC Regulator can change the caps on dividends and assets.

The office of the Regulator of Community Interests Companies published its Operational Report 2011–2012, saying that the CICs are now part of social enterprise landscape: 'We have CICs in every sector including the arts, education, environment, health, industry and transport.' On 10 December 2013 there were more than 8,000 CICs.

1.2 Formation of a company

Section 7 of the Companies Act 2006 describes the method for forming a company:

A company is formed under this Act by one or more persons—
(a) subscribing their names to a memorandum of association … , and
(b) complying with the requirements of this Act as to registration …

If only it were that simple! That, of course, describes only the basic requirements for forming a company. Many and greater complications will arise when we look at how the company makes decisions and does business in the course of its active life.

1.2.1 Financing a company

The first issue for a business is the way in which the business is to be financed. Limited liability companies have the advantage that the members' liability to contribute to the debts of the company has a fixed limit which is always clear. Traditionally, there were two ways of setting the limit: (i) by issuing shares, or (ii) by taking guarantees from the members that they would contribute up to a fixed amount to the debts of the company when it was wound up or when it needed money in particular circumstances. The first type of company is a company limited by shares, the second is a company limited by guarantee. No new companies limited by guarantee and having a share capital to provide working money may be formed (Companies Act 2006, s 5). This means that a guarantee company formed in the future cannot have any contributions from guarantees. This form is therefore unsuitable for commercial enterprises, although the form has been extensively used to carry out semi-official functions, particularly in the sphere of regulation of the financial services market.

In a company limited by shares, the members know that they will never have to pay more into the company than the full purchase price of their shares. This need not necessarily be paid when they are first purchased. When some money is outstanding on shares, the company may issue a 'call' for the remainder to be paid, but it can never demand more than the full price due to the company for a particular share. Such a company will be registered as a 'company limited by shares'. By section 3(2) of the Companies Act 2006, if the liability of shareholders is limited to the amount, if any, unpaid on the shares held by them, the company is 'limited by shares'. By section 3(3), if the liability is limited to such amount 'as the members undertake to contribute to the assets of the company in the event of its being wound up', it is a 'company limited by guarantee'.

1.2.1(a) Minimum capital requirements for a public company

A private company need have only a very small amount of capital. However, the European Community Second Directive set a minimum amount of capital for a public company. Section 763 of the Companies Act 2006 sets the minimum for UK companies at £50,000 or the euro equivalent, and gives power to the Secretary of State to specify a different sum by statutory instrument. The company is not obliged to have received the full £50,000. However, by section 586, public companies must receive at least one-quarter of the nominal value of the shares. The amount of capital actually contributed could be as little as £12,500, although the company would have a right to make a 'call' on the shareholders demanding payment of the unpaid capital (that is, the outstanding £37,500).

By section 761 of the 2006 Act, it is a criminal offence committed by the public company and any officer of it in default, to do business or to borrow money before the Registrar of Companies has issued a trading certificate to the effect that he is satisfied that the nominal value of the company's allotted share capital is not less than the prescribed minimum, and that he has received a statutory declaration, which must be signed by a director or secretary of the company and must:

1. state that the nominal value of the company's allotted share capital is not less than the authorised minimum;
2. specify the amount, or estimated amount, of the company's preliminary expenses;
3. specify any amount or benefit paid or given, or intended to be paid or given, to any promoter of the company, and the consideration for the payment or benefit (see Chapter 4).

1.2.2 Registration of a company

1.2.2(a) The memorandum of association and the company constitution

It is essential that a company has a memorandum of association, which under section 8 of the Act is:

a memorandum stating that the subscribers—
(a) wish to form a company under this Act, and
(b) agree to become members of the company and, in the case of a company that is to have a share capital, to take at least one share each.

However, the constitution of the company comprises the company's articles of association and any resolutions made under Chapter 3 of the Act, which essentially are 'important' resolutions passed by special majorities or by unanimous agreement. It is important to note that a company must have articles of association, but if none are drafted or not all of the provisions of the 'model articles' are excluded, then those model articles apply by default. The model articles are the default company constitution for limited companies in the UK. Section 20 of Companies Act 2006 clarifies that they form part of the company's articles in the same manner and to the same extent as if articles in the form of those articles had been duly registered (for further detail on the articles of association, see Chapter 3).

The memorandum must be delivered to the Registrar of Companies together with an application for registration. Section 9 sets out the basic requirements which must be included in the application for registration. These are:

- the name of the company;
- whether the registered office is to be in England and Wales, in Wales, in Scotland or Northern Ireland;
- whether liability of the members of the company is to be limited and, if so, whether it is to be limited by shares or guarantee;
- whether it is to be a private or a public limited company.

The application must also contain a statement of proposed officers of the company (s 9(4)(c)).

1.2.2(b) Name

The choice of a name for a company is of considerable importance and subject to a number of restrictions. With exceptions for companies of a charitable or 'social' nature, if the liability of members of the company is to be limited, the company name must end with 'Limited' (permitted abbreviation 'Ltd') if a private company, and 'Public Limited Company' (permitted abbreviation 'PLC' or 'plc') if a public company (or the Welsh equivalents – see further Section 1.2.2(d) below).

By section 53 of the Companies Act 2006, a company may not be registered with a name which, in the opinion of the Secretary of State, would constitute a criminal offence or be offensive, and the Secretary of State's approval is required for the use of a name which would be likely to give the impression that the company is connected with the government or any local authority, or which includes any word or expression specified in regulations made by the Secretary of State (Companies Act 2006, ss 54 and 55). The name must not be the same as any other kept in the index of company names held by the Registrar (Companies Act 2006, s 66).

By sections 77 to 81 of the Act, a company may change its name by special resolution, by any other means provided for by its articles and by a resolution of its directors.

One further restriction on the selection of names is imposed by the rules against using a name so similar to the name used by an existing business as to be likely to mislead the public into confusing the two concerns (so-called 'passing off'). Thus in *Exxon Corporation v Exxon Insurance Consultants International Ltd* [1982] Ch 119, the court granted an injunction restraining the defendants from using the word 'Exxon' in their company's name.

In *Reckitt & Colman Ltd v Borden Inc* [1990] 1 All ER 873, Lord Oliver reaffirmed the test for passing off. The claimant in a passing off action has to:

> establish a goodwill or reputation attached to the goods or services which he supplies in the mind of the purchasing public by association with the identifying 'get-up' (whether it consists simply of a brand name or a trade description, or the individual features of labelling or packaging) under which his particular goods or services are offered to the public, such that the get-up is recognised by the public as distinctive specifically of the [claimant's] goods or services. Second, he must demonstrate a misrepresentation by the defendant to the public (whether or not intentional) leading or likely to lead the public to believe that goods or services offered by him are the goods or services of the [claimant]. ... Third, he must demonstrate that he suffers or ... that he is likely to suffer damage by reason of the erroneous belief engendered by the defendant's misrepresentation that the source of the defendant's goods or services is the same as the source of those offered by the [claimant].

So, the three basic elements of passing off are reputation, misrepresentation and damage to goodwill.

In *Asprey & Garrard Ltd v WRA (Guns) Ltd & Anor* [2001] EWCA Civ 1499, the issue was the defence arising from the use of one's own name in business. Although Mr Asprey was using his own name, that name could be associated with a different retail shop (a famous jewellers), causing confusion. The Court of Appeal stated that in this case the use of the name caused not only confusion but deception as well, as the name had been used as a trade mark. Thus, it is evident that a person cannot carry on business in his own name if he is not honest and he causes deception. The principle is that a person's using his own name in business cannot prevent a passing-off claim by a company already operating under the same or a very similar name.

1.2.2(c) *Share capital*

By section 9(4) of the Companies Act 2006, in the case of a company limited by share capital, the application must state the amount of share capital with which the company proposes to be registered (further details in Chapter 5). This is known as its 'authorised share capital', 'registered share capital' or 'nominal share capital'. It does not represent the amount actually contributed at the time when the company is formed, which may be only part of the share price.

1.2.2(d) *Private or public limited company*

As we have seen, where a company is to be registered as a public company, this must be stated in the application for registration and the words 'public limited company' (or the abbreviation 'PLC' or 'plc') must appear at the end of its name, unless it is Welsh or a CIC (Companies Act 2006, s 58). A private limited company must normally have a name ending in 'Ltd', unless it is a CIC, a charity or otherwise exempted by sections 60, 61 or 62 of the Act.

1.2.3   Incorporation

Section 9 of the Companies Act 2006 requires delivery of the memorandum, the application for registration and a statement of compliance to the Registrar of Companies for England and Wales, if the registered office is to be situated in either England or Wales, and for Scotland if the registered office is to be situated in Scotland. The statement must be signed by or on behalf of the subscribers to the memorandum and the intended address of the company's registered office must be stated.

1.2.4   Duty of the Registrar

Section 14 of the Companies Act 2006 provides that if the Registrar is satisfied that the requirements of the Act have been complied with, he must register the documents delivered to him. Under section 15, he must issue a certificate that the company is incorporated. Section 15(4) provides that the certificate of incorporation is conclusive evidence that the requirements of the Act have been met and the company is duly registered. Thus, the company's existence as such is unchallengeable from the date of the issue of the certificate of incorporation.

By section 16 of the Act:

(1) The registration of a company has the following effects as from the date of incorporation.
(2) The subscribers to the memorandum, together with such other persons as may from time to time become members of the company, are a body corporate by the name stated in the certificate of incorporation.
(3) That body corporate is capable of exercising all the functions of an incorporated company.
(4) The status and registered office of the company are as stated in, or in connection with, the application for registration.
(5) In the case of a company having a share capital, the subscribers to the memorandum become holders of the shares specified in the statement of capital and initial shareholdings.
(6) The persons named in the statement of proposed officers—
    (a) as director, or
    (b) as secretary or joint secretary of the company,
    are deemed to have been appointed to that office.

1.3 Change of status from public to private company and vice versa

A change of status from private to public company is much more common than registration as a public company on initial incorporation. Part 7 of the Companies Act 2006 provides for this change of status from private to public and from public to private status. In both cases the members of the company must pass a special resolution (a resolution passed by at least 75 per cent of the votes cast) to effect the change. In the case of a change from private to public, the Registrar of Companies must be provided with a statutory declaration that the minimum capital requirements for public companies have been satisfied (see Section 1.2.1(a) above) and that the requisite special resolution has been passed (s 90).

If the reverse change of status from public to private is undertaken, the members may find that it is more difficult to sell their shares. There are safeguards in the Act aimed at protecting a minority who object to such a change of status. Under section 98 of the Companies Act 2006, the holders of 5 per cent or more of the nominal value of a public company's shares, any class of the company's issued share capital or 50 members may apply to the court for the cancellation of a special resolution to request re-registration as a private company. The court has an unfettered discretion to cancel or approve the resolution on such terms as it thinks fit (Companies Act 2006, s 98(4) and (5)).

1.4 Groups

The old definition of the parent–subsidiary relationship was to be found in section 736 of the Companies Act 1985. That read:

(1) For the purposes of this Act, a company is deemed to be a subsidiary of another if (but only if)—
   (a) that other either—
      (i) is a member of it and controls the composition of its board of directors, or
      (ii) holds more than half in nominal value of its equity share capital, or
   (b) the first-mentioned company is a subsidiary of any company which is that other's subsidiary.

This definition caused two main difficulties. The first was that it concentrated on the number of shares held (the total of all of the shares together is known as the equity share capital). This ignores the fact that control is exercised through voting rights, which need have no relationship to the number of shares held.

The second difficulty lay with the reference to the control of the board of directors (s 736(1)(a)(i) above). Under the original sections in the 1985 Act, a company was deemed to control the composition of the board of directors if it could appoint or remove the holders of all or a majority of the directorships. If one company could appoint less than a majority of the directors, but those it was able to appoint had extra voting rights so that they could outvote the other directors, then control of the board's activities was effectively achieved, while the arrangement was still outside the scope of the section.

By these and other methods it was possible to avoid the intended effect of the section, which was to treat a group of companies as a single business for various purposes, including accounting purposes. Because of this the Companies Act 1989 introduced new definitions of this relationship. These now appear in the Companies Act 2006, section 1159:

(1) A company is a 'subsidiary' of another company, its 'holding company', if that other company—
   (a) holds a majority of the voting rights in it, or
   (b) is a member of it and has the right to appoint or remove a majority of its board of directors, or
   (c) is a member of it and controls alone, pursuant to an agreement with other shareholders or members, a majority of the voting rights in it,
   or if it is a subsidiary of a company that is itself a subsidiary of that other company.
(2) A company is a 'wholly owned subsidiary' of another company if it has no members except that other and that other's wholly owned subsidiaries or persons acting on behalf of that other or its wholly owned subsidiaries.

The emphasis has shifted from ownership of shares to control of voting rights, which are further defined by the Act. This gives a more realistic picture of a group of companies. (Further details of company groups and multinational companies are to be found in Chapter 14.)

1.5 Corporate personality

1.5.1 Meaning of corporate personality

The essence of a company is that it has a legal personality distinct from the people who compose it. This means that even if the people running the company are continuously changing, the company itself retains its identity, and the business need not be stopped and restarted with every change in the managers or members (shareholders) of the business. If the company is a limited liability company, not only is the money owned by the company regarded as wholly distinct from the money owned by those running the company, but also the members of the company are not liable for the debts of the company (except where the law has made exceptions to this rule in order to prevent fraudulent or unfair practices by those in charge). Members may be called upon to pay only the full price of their shares. After that a creditor must depend on the company's money to satisfy his claim.

This limitation of the liability of the members has led to careful rules being drawn up to attempt to prevent a company from wasting its money (Chapter 7). It is one of the disadvantages of incorporation that a number of formal rules, designed to protect people doing business with companies, have to be complied with. A partnership which consists of people carrying on a business with a view to making profits need comply with many fewer formalities. On the other hand, the members of an ordinary partnership are liable for all the debts incurred by the business they run. (It is possible now to form a limited liability partnership.) If large losses are made, partners in an ordinary partnership must contribute their own money to clear the debts of the business. In practice this may be a distinction without a difference since, where small businesses are concerned, banks will not lend money to a company without first securing guarantees from those running the business, so that if the company cannot pay its debts, such debts will be met from the personal assets of those in charge.

The separate personality of a company creates a range of problems, because although the company is regarded as a person in law, it can only function through the humans who are running the business in which the company is involved. The law must regulate the relationships between a company and its creators and members or shareholders, as well as the relationship between a company and 'outsiders' who do business with the company.

1.5.2   The legal basis for the separate personality doctrine

The case of *Salomon v Salomon* [1897] AC 22 is by no means the first case to depend on the separate legal personality of a company, but it is the most widely discussed in this context. Mr Salomon was a boot and shoe manufacturer who had been trading for over 30 years. He had a thriving business. He also had a large family to provide for. To enable the business to expand, he turned it into a limited liability company. As part of the purchase price he took shares in the company and lent the company money in return for 'debentures', which are paid off preferentially in the event of liquidation (see Chapter 13). The company did not last very long. Almost immediately there was a depression in the boot and shoe trade, and a number of strikes. Mr Salomon tried to keep the company afloat by lending it more money and by transferring his debentures to a Mr Broderip for £5,000, which he handed over to the company on loan. However, liquidation was not long in coming. The sale of the company's assets did not realise enough to pay the creditors. The liquidator claimed that the debentures had been issued fraudulently and were therefore invalid. He also denied that the business had been validly transferred from Mr Salomon to the company. The grounds for both these claims were that the business had been overvalued at £39,000 instead of its true worth of around £10,000, and that the whole transfer to a limited company amounted to a scheme to defeat creditors.

The judge who heard the case first admitted that the transfer had been legally carried out and could not be upset. However, he suggested (*Broderip v Salomon* [1895] 2 Ch 323) that Mr Salomon had employed the company as an agent, and that he was therefore bound to indemnify the agent. He said that the creditors of the company could have sued Mr Salomon despite the existence of the company to which the business had been legally transferred. In the Court of Appeal, Mr Salomon's appeal was dismissed. However, the House of Lords took a different view. Lord MacNaughten said:

> The company is at law a different person altogether from [those forming the company] and, though it may be that after incorporation the business is precisely the same as it was before, and the same persons are managers, and the same hands receive the profits, the company is not in law the agent of the subscribers or trustee for them. Nor are the subscribers as members liable, in any shape or form, except to the extent and in the manner provided by the Act … If the view of the learned judge were sound, it would follow that no common law partnership could register as a company limited by shares without remaining subject to unlimited liability.

Thus was established the complete separation between a company and those involved in its operation. As with many principles of English law, having established first the principle, we must then look at the problems caused by and the exceptions to that principle.

1.5.3   The fundamental importance of separate personality

The invention of the company as separate is vital, as it means that it is free to develop as an instrument of business shaped by both the people involved in its running and those regulating its existence. That different models of companies have come to exist is a direct result of the fact that the company's separate personality sets it apart from the individuals that are running it. Although many people believe that the shareholders of a company are the 'owners' of the company, in fact the shareholders are not the owners of the property of the company. The property of the company is vested in the company itself. The company is a legal fiction; it is a legal person. The shareholders have rights in the company but not ownership of the legal person, the company. The shareholders own shares, and because of that the law and the constitution of the company regulate shareholders' rights. Shareholders' rights are limited by the law, although the articles and the memorandum (the company's constitution – see Chapter 3) may allow shareholders less or more power when the documents founding the company are drafted. The backdrops of the shareholders' rights are the mandatory sections of company law.

In the UK, company law is a contractual model. That means that the shareholders in the company are the paramount stakeholders of the company, although the Companies Act 2006 has softened the hard contractual edge, allowing directors to consider other stakeholders' interests. Other jurisdictions have other models. Those that have developed in different states say a great deal about the society in which they operate. Chapter 2 considers this concept, normally called 'corporate governance', in more detail.

1.5.4 Problems caused by the personality doctrine and exceptions

The first 'personality' problem that may arise is that experienced by those seeking to form a company in order to carry on a business. While they are completing the formalities which will lead to registration of the company and the consequent gain of legal personality for the company, its creators may wish to sign contracts for the benefit of the company when it is formed. The difficulty is that the company does not exist as a legal person until registration and therefore cannot be party to any contract, neither may it employ agents to act on its behalf. The law on such 'pre-incorporation contracts' is explained in Chapter 4.

The second problem is the one under discussion in *Salomon*'s cases (Section 1.5.2 above). A limited liability company can be a very powerful weapon in the hands of someone determined on fraud and on defeating a creditor's rightful claims. Will the courts make no exceptions to the rule that a company is wholly separate from those who manage and control it? A survey of the case law shows that the courts do relax the strict principle of the separateness of the company from time to time. There is general agreement among those who have sought to analyse the relevant cases that the only principle that can be gleaned from the decisions is that the courts will look at the human reality behind the company if the interests of justice provide a compelling reason for doing so. This may sound like an excellent principle, but when the huge variety of fact situations that are likely to arise is considered, such a vague notion makes it extremely difficult to predict what a court will do in any given case. When the existence of the company is disregarded, commentators have referred to it as 'lifting' or 'piercing' of the veil of incorporation. There are a number of cases, discussed in Section 1.5.6 below, which are clearly relevant to the sanctity of the 'veil' of incorporation, but the whole of company law is riddled with examples of the validity of acts depending on the effect they will have on the members of a company. An example would be where the part of the constitution of a company known as the articles of association is changed; that change may be challenged unless it can be justified as being in good faith and for the benefit of the company as a whole. In order to determine the latter, the effect of the decision on the members of the company must be examined.

It is also said that the proper person to sue to redress a wrong done to the company is the company itself. However, there is an exception to this rule to prevent those in charge of the company causing damage to shareholders in a powerless minority, for example by taking the company's property. The examples in Chapter 10 clearly show the difficult task which those seeking to regulate a company have because of the doctrine of legal personality. The company must be given as much independence from its operators as possible, otherwise it would always be subject to interference from a large number of (probably disagreeing) voices and therefore be no less cumbersome than a partnership trying to operate by consensus. On the other hand, the law must always recognise the reality of the fact that the company can do nothing without human operators, and that those human operators may wish to hijack the company for their own ends, to the detriment of others who have money at stake.

1.5.5 Statutory intervention

The personality of the company is recognised and ignored at will by the legislature. Those drafting legislation do not seem to respect the principle as being sacrosanct in itself, and look merely to the end sought to be achieved by particular provisions. This is a highly practical approach. The courts might do well to admit that the only principle running through their decisions is 'justice in the individual case', and thus adopt a similarly pragmatic approach.

1.5.6 Lifting the veil

The separate personality of the company can have some unexpected and sometimes unwelcome effects. In *Neptune (Vehicle Washing Equipment) Ltd v Fitzgerald* [1995] 1 BCLC 352, the defendant was a sole director of a company. Despite this he was obliged to make disclosure of a personal interest in a resolution which he passed purporting to terminate his contract of employment, although the court held that 'it may be that the declaration does not have to be out loud'. Although this sounds strange, it emphasises that the contract was one between the director and the company, so that in his capacity as an official acting in the interests of the company, the director must remind himself of his personal interest before determining a course of action. In *Macaura v Northern Assurance Co* [1925] AC 619, the court refused to ignore the separateness of the company and 'lift the veil', despite the fact that the consequence of so doing was to deny a remedy to someone whose personal fortune had gone up in smoke. Macaura had sold the whole of the timber on his estate to a company. He owned almost all of the shares in the company and the company owed him a great deal of money. Macaura took out an insurance policy on the timber in his own name. When almost all the timber was later destroyed by fire, he claimed under the insurance policy. The House of Lords held that he could not do so. He no longer had any legal interest in the timber and so fell foul of the rule that an insurance policy cannot normally be taken out by someone who has no interest in what is insured.

Sometimes other rules of law may be used to mitigate the effects of the strict application of the doctrine. This was done in *Harrods v Lemon* [1931] 2 KB 157. The estate agents' division of Harrods was acting as agent in the sale of the defendant's house. A purchaser was introduced and subsequently instructed surveyors to examine the house. The surveyors that were instructed were from Harrods' surveyors' department. The survey disclosed defects, as a result of which a reduced price was negotiated. The defendant had been informed prior to this of the fact that Harrods were acting on both sides of the sale. This would normally be a breach of the agency contract between the estate agents' department and the defendant. The defendant, however, agreed to Harrods continuing to act for her. The two departments of Harrods were in fact completely separate. The judge (Avory J) agreed that there had been a technical breach of the agency contract between Harrods and the defendant. Although the two departments were completely separate, the company in fact was one single person in the eyes of the law. However, he also insisted that the defendant should pay Harrods, despite the breach, as she had agreed to their continuing to act despite having full knowledge of the breach.

The following cases provide a prime example of the way the courts will disregard the separate personality of the company if that will achieve a just result, but will equally keep the veil of personality firmly in place where that will benefit someone for whom the court feels sympathy. In *Malyon v Plummer* [1963] 2 All ER 344, a husband and wife had full control of a company. The husband was killed by the defendant in a car accident and the widow was unable to continue the business of the company. An insurance policy had been taken out on the man's life and £2,000 was paid to the company on his death. The shares of the company were therefore more valuable than they had been prior to his death. The plaintiff (widow) had received an inflated salary from the company prior to her husband's death. The court had to assess the future financial situation of the widow in order to set the amount of damages payable to her. It was decided that the excess of the plaintiff's salary over the market value of her services was a benefit derived from the plaintiff's relationship with her husband. It was therefore a benefit lost by his death and only the market value of her services should be taken into account in assessing her future position. This ignores the fact that she was employed by a company which should, in accordance with *Salomon*'s case, have been regarded as an entity completely separate from both husband and wife. It did mean, however, that the widow got more because the compensation was assessed in a way that it included the inflated wage rate. The wage rate should have been assessed by the company, not by the husband because the company should have been completely separate. Similarly, the court held that the insurance money was money which should be regarded as having been paid to the wife as a result of the death of the husband. The shares owned by the wife should therefore be valued at the lower value before the £2,000 was paid.

It is very difficult to see a distinction in principle between *Malyon v Plummer*, where the veil was not just pierced but torn to shreds, and *Lee v Lee's Air Farming* [1916] AC 12, where the emphasis was laid heavily on the separate legal personality of the company. In this case the widow would have lost everything if the *Malyon v Plummer* approach had been adopted. In *Lee*, the appellant's husband was the sole governing director and controlling shareholder of a company. He held all but one of the shares in the company. He flew an aircraft for the company, which had taken out an insurance policy which would entitle his widow to damages if, when he died, he was a 'worker' for the company. He was killed in a flying accident. It was held that the widow was entitled to compensation. Lee's position as sole governing director did not make it impossible for him to be a servant of the company in the capacity of chief pilot, because he and the company were separate and distinct legal entities which could enter and had entered into a valid contractual relationship. The reasoning in *Lee* was followed in *Secretary of State for Trade and Industry v Bottrill* [1999] BCC 177, where the Court of Appeal affirmed that a controlling shareholder could also be an employee of the company for the purposes of claiming under the Employment Rights Act 1996.

The approach in *Lee* was also followed in *Tunstall v Steigman* [1962] QB 593. There, a landlord was unable to terminate a tenancy on the ground that he was going to carry on a business on the premises because the business was to be carried on by a limited company. This was despite the fact that the landlord held all the shares in the company except for two, which were held by her nominees and of which she had sole control. The result in this case would be different if it fell to be decided now, because section 6 of the Law of Property Act 1969 provides that where a landlord has a controlling interest in a company, any business to be carried on by the company shall be treated for the purposes of section 30 of the Landlord and Tenant Act 1954 as a business carried on by him. The case remains useful, however, as an illustration of the way in which the courts have approached the question of corporate personality.

The corporate veil remained firmly in place in *Williams v Natural Life Health Foods Ltd* [1998] 2 All ER 577, where the House of Lords held that a managing director was not liable for negligent advice given by the company. Liability would arise only where personal responsibility for the advice, based on objective factors, had been assumed and there had been reliance on the assumption of responsibility. This had not been established, despite the fact that the director had played a significant part behind the scenes in negotiations leading up to the grant of a franchise which the plaintiff purchased on the faith of financial projections furnished by someone introduced by the director and misrepresented as having relevant expertise. A brochure issued by the director's company had placed particular emphasis on the personal expertise and experience of the director. There were, however, no personal dealings between the managing director and the plaintiff.

1.5.7 Fraud

The ability to hide behind the corporate veil could be a powerful weapon in the hands of those with fraudulent tendencies. The courts have therefore always reserved the right to ignore a company which is formed or used merely to perpetrate a dishonest scheme. In *Salomon*'s cases, both the Court of Appeal and the judge at the first instance thought that they had before them just such a case of fraud. Since there was no evidence of dishonest intent in that case, it seems that these courts were using 'fraud' in a very wide sense. Indeed, they seem to have regarded the formation of the company so that the business could henceforth be carried on with limited liability as sufficient evidence of 'fraud'. To take such a wide view would defeat the whole notion of the separate existence of the company and make it impossible for small private companies to function in any way differently from partnerships. The importance of the decision in *Salomon* in the House of Lords is clear. A mere wish to avail oneself of the benefits of limited liability is not of itself to be regarded as fraudulent.

A different view was taken of the conduct in *Jones v Lipman* [1962] 1 All ER 442. In that case, the first defendant agreed to sell land to the plaintiffs. When he later wished to avoid the sale, he formed a company and transferred the land to it. The court held that the company was a 'cloak' for the first defendant and that he had the power to make the company do as he wished, and therefore the court would order the transfer of land to the plaintiff. In *Trustor AB v Smallbone* [2001] 1 WLR 1177, the defendant, the managing director of Trustor AB, transferred funds from the account of Trustor AB to another company, Introcom Ltd incorporated in Gibraltar, which was owned and controlled by him via a Liechtenstein trust. The board of directors did not authorise such a transaction. A part of these funds had found its way, via Introcom, to the defendant personally. The Court stated that:

> Introcom is liable, as constructive trustee, to account for and repay to Trustor the Trustor moneys that were paid to it … Introcom was the creature of the defendant. He owned and controlled Introcom. The payments out by Introcom of Trustor money were payments made with the knowing assistance of him … the defendant would be liable jointly and severally with Introcom for the repayment of that money with interest thereon. The defendant's joint and several liability would not be confined to the part that he personally received … the defendant is, in my view, clearly liable, jointly and severally with Introcom, for the whole of the sums for which Introcom is accountable.

The defendant was therefore found personally liable to return the funds in question on the basis that Introcom functioned as a façade used by him principally to misappropriate Trustor's funds. He tried to hide behind the corporate veil to escape his obligation to return the misappropriated funds, but the Court held him personally liable.

Similarly, in *Gilford Motor Co v Horne* [1933] Ch 935, the court refused to allow the defendant to avoid an agreement that he would not compete with former employers. He had attempted to do so by competing with them in the guise of a limited company. Even clearer cases were *Re Darby* [1911] 1 KB 95 and *Re H* [1996] 2 BCLC 500. In *Re Darby*, the corporation was simply a device whereby a fraudulent prospectus was issued and the directors of the company pocketed the public's money. The directors were prosecuted for fraud and convicted. The court held that the directors were liable to repay all the money that had been received by them via the company. In *Re H and Others (restraint order: realisable property)* [1996] 2 BCLC 500, two family companies had been used to defraud the Revenue. The assets of the company could be treated as the assets of their fraudulent owners and seized.

Summary

1.1 There are several types of company. The most common company is a limited company, the liability of the members being limited to the amount they have previously agreed. There are some unlimited companies where members are liable to pay the whole of the debts of the company.

Companies may have a share capital or be limited by guarantee. In the former case members buy shares. In the latter case members agree to contribute to the debts of the company up to a certain amount.

Companies may be public companies (PLCs) or private companies (normally having 'Ltd' after their names). Only public companies can offer shares to the public. Public companies are subject to more regulations than private companies; their shares are traded on a recognised stock exchange.

Ready-made companies may be bought.

Community interest companies (CICs) may be created for the use of people who want to conduct a business or other activity for the benefit of a community, and not purely for private advantage

There is a minimum capital requirement for public companies of £50,000.

Summary cont'd

1.2 A company must have a memorandum of association.

The choice of the name of a company is important and subject to a number of restrictions.

Incorporation is achieved after the memorandum and articles are delivered to the Registrar of Companies.

1.3 Companies can change from public to private status and vice versa.

1.4 A group of companies is a number of parent and subsidiary companies where the parent normally exercises control over the subsidiary. The relationship between parent and subsidiary raises a variety of delicate legal issues.

1.5 The doctrine of corporate personality means that the identity of the company stays the same, even if the identities of the managers or members (shareholders) of the business change.

Exercises

1.1 What is the difference between the various types of companies?

1.2 What matters should be considered when choosing a name for a company?

1.3 What information is needed by the Registrar on the incorporation of a company?

1.4 When does a company come into existence?

Further reading

Sealy and Worthington, *Cases and Materials in Company Law*, 10th edn (Oxford University Press, 2013)
Mayson, French and Ryan, *Company Law*, 30th edn (Oxford University Press, 2014)

Chapter 2

Corporate governance

Key terms

- **The nexus of contracts theory** – the company is a private affair based on relationships of a contractual nature.
- **The stakeholder theory** – the company extends to encompass the stakeholders as well as the shareholders.
- **Concession theory** – the company owes a dividend to the society in return for the privileges granted to it by the state.
- **Corporate governance codes** – soft law initiatives aimed at dealing with governance issues on the basis of a 'comply and explain' approach.

2.1 Why corporate governance?

Corporate governance is absolutely fundamental to an understanding of company law, as it not only concerns the institutional setting and the governance arrangements on the basis of which a company operates, but also addresses fundamental questions that define the nature of the companies in question and their raison d'être. Therefore, corporate governance is not only about the institutional architecture of the company, but also about the definition of substantial issues, such as the ownership of the company, its membership, and its very definition and purpose.

Basically, under the title 'corporate governance', we seek to reply to a set of very fundamental questions, such as (among others):

- What is a company?
- Who owns the company?
- Who are its constituents?
- For the interests of whom is the company to be run?
- Who controls the company, and in the pursuit of what goals?

Those questions shape the nature of the companies within a certain jurisdiction and define the character of its corporate governance system. The nature of the institutional system on the basis of which a company is run addresses the aforementioned issues and defines its character.

The chapter will seek to reply to the funadamental question: Who owns and controls the company? It will then focus on the analysis of the main theories that underpin the main corporate governance models; after that, it will present the main categories of corporate governance systems in prominent Western jurisdictions. It will conclude with discussion of the main corporate governance codes adopted in the UK; these deal with aspects of corporate governance on the basis of self-regulation initiatives rather than the hard legislation of the Companies Act 2006, in pursuance of flexibility along with a hands-off approach that grants companies greater scope for discretion.

2.2 Who owns and/or controls the company?

The fundamental questions to be asked at this stage are:

- Who owns the company?
- Who controls the company?

The replies provided to these questions by various jurisdictions have sometimes been distinctly different, something that is due to different prevailing values, distinctive social structures and, in the end, divergent cultural values. Naturally, if all these factors vary, the replies to the aforementioned questions will vary significantly too.

The natural reply to the question 'Who controls the company?' is that it is the owners of the company. But while this seems clear, the reality is in fact quite different. The debate over the ownership and the control of companies emerged in a more lively way in the USA, but the issues with which it was concerned are just as relevant to the UK.

In the USA – and in the UK – the issue of ownership of the company presented no particular controversy as the shareholders were considered to be the exclusive owners of the company: shareholders invest their capital in the corporation by purchasing shares, expecting a return for their investment. Since they buy its shares, they emerge as the capital providers of the company and therefore as its owners. But as companies resorted to the stock market to attract capital by selling their shares to potentially millions of people, their shareholding basis became increasingly dispersed. Therefore, the ability of the shareholders actually and in practice to control the company started to wane significantly for practical reasons.

A large number of shareholders comprising potentially millions of people could not be informed about the everyday running of the company, nor coordinate their actions to monitor the directors and be involved in the day-to-day business of the company. The company is governed in practice by a rather limited number of people – the directors who take all crucial decisions in what they perceive as the best interests of the company. Therefore, it was observed that the shareholders – the so-called 'owners' of the company – had gradually lost control of what they supposedly owned, that is, the company. This is known in company literature as the 'separation of ownership and control'.

2.3 Theories of corporate governance

2.3.1 Introduction

Analysis of the main corporate governance theories is not a theoretical exercise without any practical application; on the contrary, it will be demonstrated that the nature and the character of the institutional structure of companies in different countries are very much linked to the theoretical basis on which the respective system was founded. Each country's company governance system is a product of its history, philosophy, culture and economics. Therefore, the goals which are to be pursued by an English company, the definition of its membership, the relationship between the directors and the shareholders, the constitutional arrangements which define its functions, and the nature of the articles of association as the constitutional document of the company are all understood in the light of an analysis of the theoretical foundations of the corporate governance system which prevails in the UK.

In the UK the prevailing theory is the 'nexus of contracts' theory (see Section 2.3.2 below), which places the shareholders at its very centre, considering the company as a purely private affair founded on the notion of shareholder primacy. That theory leaves its imprint clear on the institutional structure and the organisational architecture of the both the English and the American corporation, by granting exclusive membership and ownership of the company to shareholders.

The stakeholder theory (see Section 2.3.3 below) follows a more inclusive approach. It includes stakeholders such as the employees or the creditors of the company within the corporate planning and definition, and aims at aligning their interests with the interests of shareholders for the benefit of the company and for the maximisation of its profitability. The stakeholder theory underpins the corporate governance models in place in many Continental European countries, with certain variations.

The concession theory (see Section 2.3.4 below), on the other hand, focuses on the granting of the privileges of limited liability and separate corporate personality to the company by the state; therefore, the company is viewed as being obliged to give back a part of its profits to society at large. This entails an institutional framework that will reflect the interests of a greater range of actors; it will include not only the shareholders, but also the employees or the creditors of the company. The employees and the creditors are normally integrated within the institutional setting of the company with a representation at board level. The German corporate governance model and its dual board structure, which entails the participation of the employees among other stakeholders, serves as the most prominent example of a concessionary approach.

Therefore, as is will be demonstrated below, each country has shaped a corporate governance model that suits its distinctive economic model, serves its economic strengths effectively and responds appropriately to its cultural characteristics.

2.3.2   The company as a 'nexus of contracts'

According to this theory, the company is simply a collection of private contractual relationships. Therefore, the company is naturally devoid of any social responsibility and should be left to operate free from any, or at least subject to minimal, regulatory interference by the state.

The company is viewed as a voluntary collaboration of private individuals; namely the shareholders rather than a creation of the state or any other actors, such as the employees for example, who are viewed as an externality. The shareholders are the exclusive members of the company, otherwise known as the 'insiders' of the company, and their interests are synonymous with the interests of the company; the employees, the suppliers, the local community and others comprise the 'outsiders' to the company.

The shareholders enjoy an absolute supremacy with the corporate framework based on a so-called 'residual claim'; this is recognition of the fact that they carry the risk of their investment while receiving no money from the company except dividends in the event of profitability. These are issues that will be examined in detail in the chapters following.

The nexus of contracts theory defines the nature of the English corporate governance system. In this context it is clear that the shareholders are the exclusive members and owners of the company; the interests of the latter coincide with the interests of its shareholders. The internal institutions of the company should reflect this reality, with the exclusion of other actors, such as the employees, from participation on the board of the company. The directors should run the company in its best interests, which effectively means in the best interests of its shareholders. This system is viewed as efficient in terms of shareholders' profit, but the elevation of directors to such a powerful status courts controversy, especially in relation to issues such as their remuneration or bonuses.

2.3.3   The stakeholder theory

The stakeholder theory extends the meaning of 'the company' to encompass all actors who are involved in its operation – the so-called stakeholders. That would include both the internal stakeholders, namely, the employees, and the external stakeholders, such as suppliers, creditors and customers, but also the community in general too. Here, therefore, membership is not granted exclusively to shareholders; external stakeholders find a position within the company's framework and their interests are taken into account when defining the interests of the company.

This theory thus attempts to embrace all the actors – internal and external – who share a sufficient link with the company's activities and whose livelihood, or professional and other development, is dependent on the nature of the corporate decision making. The purpose of the firm is still to create wealth, but the means to achieve this involves engaging with all the actors relevant for the company in its operation, aligning their interests with the the interests of the shareholders.

Despite the fact that the company within this context is defined on more inclusive terms, this may not be reflected at board level, where stakeholders may not be officially represented. Despite that, directors exercise their duties in the best interests of the company, which in this context would include taking into account the interests of stakeholders as well.

Criticism of this theory may be based on the argument that the managers of a company with such a multi-purpose agenda will not focus on what should be the primary focus of the company in any case, which is its profitability, but will be side-tracked instead into achieving the necessary balances between sometimes conflicting interests, thereby undermining the company's fortunes. A great deal of skill will be demanded of the management to carry out such a balancing exercise. For example, if a factory is not profitable in a particular area, the employees may have to be made redundant. For the shareholders, on the one hand, this is the right decision because the company will be more profitable without this factory. For other business in the area, on the other hand, the decision may be particularly detrimental, because the redundant employees will not be able to shop and consume as much as previously as they will not have the same financial resources. The local suppliers would also be impaired by the closure of the factory as they will no longer be required to supply it. The directors have to shape a balance among the stakeholders' interests and decide what the priorities are for the company.

2.3.4   The concession theory

The concession theory views the existence and the operation of the company as a concession granted by the state. Under this theory, the company acquires success as a result of privileges consciously granted to it by the state, namely, limited liability and a separate legal personality. Without these privileges, investment in the company would be an immensely risky business, attracting a limited number of individuals and therefore undermining the venture's success.

The concession theory comes into direct conflict with the nexus of contracts theory (Section 2.3.2 above) as it challenges the nature of the firm as a purely private affair exclusively determined by the will of its shareholders; stakeholders, especially employees and creditors, are given a say in the decision-making process, and they have established interests that should be taken into account at board level.

In this theory the shareholders do not enjoy same position of exclusivity and supremacy as under the nexus of contracts theory, as the institutional structure of the company has to reflect the interests of stakeholders too; the employees and the creditors are officially represented at board level. The definition of 'company' in this context includes not only the shareholders but the stakeholders too. The board of directors includes representatives of shareholders and stakeholders alike. It runs the company in its best interests, which means not only the interests of shareholders but also the interests of the stakeholders. A prominent jurisdiction pioneering the model in question is Germany.

2.4 Systems of corporate governance

2.4.1 The outsider system of corporate governance

The most prominent representatives of the outsider model of corporate governance are the USA and the UK, whose companies and system of corporate governance have been founded upon the nexus of contracts theory. These are jurisdictions that embrace the contractual notion of the company.

The term 'outsider' refers to the source of finance of the public company. Most companies are financed directly by the securities' market, therefore producing a large shareholder basis. The shareholders are viewed as the exclusive members of the company and as its owners. However, as was discussed in Section 2.2 above, the links between ownership of the company and control have waned due to the lack of capacity effectively to monitor the board of directors and therefore the decision-making mechanism on the basis of which the company is run. Within this context one of the distinctive features of the outsider corporate governance system is the so-called 'agency problem', which refers to the relaxation of the monitoring of the directors on the part of the shareholders to such a degree that the former are no longer pursuing the interests of the company and of its shareholders but their own personal interests.

The companies within this context depend more heavily on their board, which is in a position to take decisions swiftly since monitoring from the shareholders is quite lax. Therefore, as a system it allows for a certain flexibility, as the board can act relatively free from the strict control of the shareholders. This model would certainly appear to respond more quickly to external challenges or pressures, precisely because of its ability to restructure itself through swift decision making, even in relation to crucial matters such as the rapid reallocation of labour and capital. It appears to be particularly suitable for countries with a tradition in industries which require exactly that sort of action.

The fact that the world's two leading financial centres are situated in London and New York, in countries that function as the flagship of the outsider model, is not coincidental but a direct result of the historical developments that shaped a certain economic model operating on the basis of open markets, enhanced fluidity and dispersed ownership.

2.4.2 The insider system of corporate governance

The insider system of corporate governance is found in countries whose publicly listed corporations' shareholdings are distributed among a limited number of actors, usually including the government itself, other corporations, the founding families of the corporation, banks, and (more recently) pension and insurance funds. These companies are marked by the close relationships that develop between their shareholders, or at least between the major participants among them, which is greatly facilitated by their rather limited number. The system is usually marked by the existence of blockholders, that is, shareholders with a significant number of shares that effectively put them in an influential position within the company context. As a natural outcome of such concentrated shareholding, ownership and control appear to be closely linked, in sharp contrast to the position in the USA and the UK (see Section 2.4.1 above). The shareholders of the company are often also involved in management.

The limited number of actors involved in the company and the importance and simultaneously comparable size of their shareholdings entails the building of a consensus as a prerequisite for decision making. Stability and consensus with the involvement of all relevant stakeholders emerge as the two foundations upon which planning on a much longer-term basis is carried out. This advantage has enabled long-term planning in sectors of economic activity where it appears to be of particular importance, such as industry and manufacturing. The ability and international prominence of German, Japanese and, to a certain extent, French industry in these very sectors is closely linked with this corporate governance model, which facilitates stability in corporate operation and long-term planning.

2.4.3 The UK corporate governance codes

Apart from the Companies Act 2006, which is the man legislation that regulates the core of the English corporate governance model, the UK employs a wide range of soft-law measures which provide for aspects of its corporate governance system in greater detail. Those texts, known as the Codes, promote a distinctive approach that combines clear elements of self-regulation along with the obligation to explain non-compliance with the principles laid down by them. In this section of the book we shall examine the *main* Codes which have contributed to the shaping of the current corporate governance system in place in the UK.

2.4.3(a) The Cadbury Code

The Committee chaired by Adrian Cadbury produced its report in December 1992 ('the Cadbury Report'). This included a Code of Best Practice which was essentially the first corporate governance code in the UK, the principal recommendations of which were incorporated into the London Stock Exchange Listing Rules. This is a self-regulation measure and not a piece of legislation.

Corporate governance was placed at the heart of the Cadbury Code. The Code established a 'comply or explain' approach; companies were required to state whether they were complying with the Code and to give reasons for any areas of non-compliance. However, no regulator was officially charged with the duty to monitor either compliance with the Code's provisions or any explanation given for non-compliance; adherence to the corporate governance standards set by the Code was basically left to shareholders to monitor.

2.4.3(b) The Greenbury Code

The Greenbury Report was issued in 1995. It was aimed at addressing concerns raised in relation to large pay increases enjoyed by directors in the then recently privatised utility companies. The contrast between managers receiving high salaries and staff being made redundant was alarming, and quite indicative of a situation that needed further attention from the regulators if further controversies were to be prevented.

The elements of transparency on one hand and director accountability on the other hand were placed at the centre of the Report, which significantly enhanced the role of non-executive directors in the corporate context, introducing them for good within the corporate vocabulary and list of actors. The notion and functions of non-executive directors will be discussed further in Chapter 8.

2.4.3(c) The 2003 Combined Higgs, Tyson and Smith Codes

The corporate scandals that rocked the business world in the early years of the new millennium – especially the Enron scandal in the USA, which involved a board operating with very lax control on the part of shareholders – shifted the agenda towards providing institutional safeguards that would function as a firewall to protect British enterprise from scandals of such magnitude and range. The relevant initiatives in the UK took place in parallel with the respective initiatives in the USA, echoing the debates taking place on the other side of the Atlantic. However, despite the similarity in terms of the themes discussed and the subject matter of the debates per se, the nature of the response was quite different. The USA opted for the adoption of a statutory instrument, the Sarbanes Oxley Act of 2002, while the UK remained faithful to a more flexible 'soft law' approach that allowed greater room for discretion, leaving companies the necessary scope to adapt the Codes to their individual situation, nature and risks, without facing the possibility of becoming subject to a 'one size fits all' approach.

The Codes provided for a further increase in the participation of independent non-executive directors on the board, raising the ratio to 50 per cent of the members of the board. Interestingly, they attempted to address the agency problem inherent in the British corporate model (see Section 2.4.2 above) by encouraging the cultivation of links between independent non-executive directors and shareholders.

2.4.3(d) The 2010 UK Corporate Governance Code

The 2010 UK Corporate Governance Code was the next in the line of reports and codes that started in 1992. Despite the evident shift of terminology to a title that sounds more umbrella-like, and the potential initial impression that the UK had now moved towards an even more standardised form of corporate governance regulated by legally binding instruments, the 2010 Code remained faithful to the non-voluntary 'comply and explain' approach introduced by the Cadbury Code (see Section 2.4.3(a)).

The aim of the 2010 Code was to create a structure for the internal operation of a company which would minimise the risk of the company's being mismanaged and which would also improve the way in which the company made its senior management decisions. Bound up in all of this was an implied criticism of the ability of traditional company law to achieve effective corporate governance.

One of the central parameters of the 2010 Code was leadership; the Code stated that every company should be headed by an effective board which was collectively responsible for the long-term success of the company. The Code therefore makes a partial reference to section 172 of the Companies Act 2006 (the duty to promote the success of the company), which is analysed in detail in Chapter 9.

As far as directors' remuneration is concerned, the 2010 Code now includes a supporting principle according to which performance-related elements of executive directors' remuneration should be designed to promote the long-term success of the company. The issue of executive remuneration has in fact emerged at the centre of one of the most heated debates in the UK in the last couple of decades. The financial crisis of 2008–09 and the turbulence in international markets, due partly to the sovereign debt crisis in the European Union of 2010–12 and the insecurity that it creates, in conjunction with a fragile private sector that undermined the return to previously strong growth, have placed the debates in question within a different context.

2.4.3(e) The 2012 UK Corporate Governance Code

The 2012 Code was adopted at the end of 2012 and introduced just a few changes to the 2010 text. The frequency with which Codes are adopted in the UK, and the minimal scope of reforms that each one brings to the already established corporate governance regime of the country, demonstrate the adherence of the business and legal world of the country to a flexible, hands-off approach to corporate governance regulation which is susceptible to constant change and adaptation to the newly emergent trends and needs.

The central principles which form the core of the Code and which embody its principal philosophy remain intact, namely, listed companies are required to report on how they have applied the main principles of the Code and either to confirm that they have complied with the Code's provisions or to provide an explanation for their failure to do so.

Interestingly enough, the 2012 Code hints at addressing the principal problem which stands at the very centre of the English company law, that is, the separation of ownership and control, and the agency problem. To that end, the 2012 Code recognises in its Preface that 'the impact of shareholders in monitoring the Code could and should be enhanced by better interaction between the boards of listed companies and their shareholders'. It appears clear that the strengthening of the link between shareholders and the board emerges as the central aim of the Code; it is of profound significance for the enhancement of the monitoring of the board, and therefore for the improvement of accountability and transparency within the public company.

The Preface to the 2012 Code states that:

> While in law the company is primarily accountable to its shareholders, and the relationship between the company and its shareholders is also the main focus of the Code, companies are encouraged to recognise the contribution made by other providers of capital and to confirm the board's interest in listening to the views of such providers insofar as these are relevant to the company's overall approach to governance.

After affirming its adherence to shareholder primacy as a corollary of the UK corporate governance model, the 2012 Code adopts a cautious approach to the widening of corporate accountability.

Summary

2.1 Corporate governance refers to fundamental issues such as: What is a company? Who owns a company? Who controls the company? How is a company run and for whose interests? It refers to the institutional setting within which those issues are accommodated.

2.2 The shareholders clearly own the company in the UK and in the USA. Whether they can exercise full control of what they own appears to be a more complicated issue.

2.3 In the UK, the shareholders enjoy absolute supremacy, being the only members of the company. Their interests coincide with the interests of the company. The theory underlying the UK corporate governance model is the 'nexus of contracts' theory.

Within this context the notion of the separation of ownership and control is very important. It refers to the increasing inability of the shareholders to control what they supposedly own – the company. The latter is increasingly controlled by the directors of the company.

The 'concession theory' is in complete contrast to the 'nexus of contracts' theory and is applied in jurisdictions such as Germany.

2.4 Corporate governance systems are usually distinguished into two types – the outsider system and the insider system of corporate governance – on the basis of the source of financing for the public company.

The English system of corporate governance is based on the 'nexus of contracts' theory; it is viewed as an outsider system of corporate governance where a separation of ownership and control has taken place.

The UK has adopted consecutive Codes which promote arrangements for the corporate governance of companies on the basis of self-regulation. They are non-legally binding texts which are based on a 'comply or explain' principle. Those companies which do not adhere to the provisions of the Codes must explain the reasons for that non-adherence.

Exercises

2.1 What is corporate governance and why is it important?

2.2 What is the separation of ownership and control?

2.3 What are the main corporate governance theories?

2.4 Which are the main categories of corporate governance systems?

2.5 Explain the theoretical basis and the nature of the English corporate governance system.

2.6 General Motors Plc in 1980 was looking at a net loss in income for the first time since 1921. It was determined by the management that capital expenditure was needed in order for the company to regain its competitive edge and enhance profit. A large five-year capital spending program was planned, involving things like the latest techniques to produce more efficient cars. It was decided that two ageing plants in Detroit should be replaced, and this would mean the termination of 500 jobs. The only site that would meet the company's requirements for the construction of a new plant was a densely settled area of Detroit. An alternative 'green field' site was available in another state in the US. Building on the new Detroit site was more costly ($200 million as against $80 million on the site in the other state). Detroit suffered from significant unemployment, and the building of the new plant in Detroit was supported by local government and the relevant car workers' union. The residents of the area in Detroit where General Motors was considering building were unhappy. The directors had to decide whether it was better to relocate or not. Consider which stakeholders were affected and whether the directors should build the plant in Detroit or in the other state.

Further reading

Bainbridge, *The New Corporate Governance In Theory and Practice* (Oxford University Press, 2010)

Berle and Means, *The Modern Corporation & Private Property* (Harcourt, Brace & World Inc, 1932, 10th printing 2009)

Blair, *Ownership and Control* (The Brooking Institute, Washington, 1995)

Cheffins, *Corporate Ownership and Control, British Business Transformed* (Oxford University Press, 2008)

Clarke, *Theories of Corporate Governance, The Philosophical Foundations of Corporate Governance* (Routledge, 2008)

Dine and Koutsias, *The Nature of Corporate Governance: The Significance of National Cultural Identity* (Edward Elgar, 2013)

Eisenberg, 'The Conception that the Corporation is a Nexus of Contracts and the Dual Nature of the Firm' (1999) 24 *Journal of Corporation Law* 819

Fama, 'Agency Problems and the Theory of the Firm' (1980) 99 *Journal of Political Economy* 288

Fama and Jensen, 'Separation of Ownership and Control' (1983) 26 *Journal of Law and Economics* 301

Keay, *The Corporate Objective* (Edward Elgar, 2011)

Plessis du, Hargovan and Bagaric, *Principles of Contemporary Corporate Governance* (Cambridge University Press, 2011)

Roe, *Political Determinants of Corporate Governance, Political Context, Corporate Impact* (Oxford University Press, 2006)

Solomon, *Corporate Governance and Accountability*, 2nd edn (John Wiley & Sons Ltd, 2009)

Talbot, *Progressive Corporate Governance for the 21st Century* (Routledge, 2013)

Chapter 3

The articles of association

Key terms

▶ **Bona fide for the benefit of the company** – the test used by the courts to determine whether an alteration of the articles of association is valid or is unfair. It has had various meanings over time.
▶ **The articles of association** – the constitutional document of the company of a contractual nature.
▶ **Alteration of the articles** – a mofication of the articles on the basis of a special resolution passed in good faith for the benefit of the company as a whole.

3.1 The nature of the articles of association

3.1.1 The articles as the key constitutional document

The articles of association have replaced the memorandum of association as the key document in the company's constitution (Companies Act 2006, s 18, which requires that a company must have articles of association 'prescribing regulations for the company'). The articles form the constitution of the company. This is the document which provides for the institutional arrangements on the basis of which the company is to operate. The founders of the company are in a position to draft their own articles, but this is not compulsory by any means. Section 20 of the 2006 Act provides for the ability of a limited company not to register any articles, in which case the model articles drawn up by the Secretary of State will apply (see Section 3.1.2 below). If articles are registered they will prevail over the model articles, but only 'in so far as they do not exclude or modify' the model articles (s 20(1)(b)).

The articles will be the chief instrument for regulating the relationship between a shareholder and the company, and the balance of power among shareholders themselves. The voting rights attached to various classes of shares will be one of the most important things set out in most articles of association. Other important matters included in the articles will be:

▶ the powers exercisable by the board (or boards) of directors;
▶ payment of dividends; and
▶ alteration of the capital structure of the company.

A central feature of UK company law is that members are free to make their own rules about the internal affairs of the company, which will form a key part of the company's constitution, provided they do not come into conflict with the provisions of the Act. The articles are basically an agreement of a 'contractual' nature which binds the members among themselves and the company to its provisions. It embodies the freedom of the shareholders to define the terms on the basis of which the company will operate. The wide scope of the discretion granted to the members of the company to determine the content of the agreement on the basis of which the company is to function is indicative of the contractual nature of the UK company (see Chapter 2), which is viewed as a private affair the terms of which are left to the shareholders to determine. Having said that, the 'contractual' nature of the articles bears certain special features which deprive them of classification as a mainstream contract under the basic principles of contract law, as will be analysed in Section 3.2 below – for example, the articles do not require unanimity for their alteration.

3.1.2 Model articles

Under the Companies Act 1985, the model articles for a company limited by shares were called 'Table A'. The incorporators of the company were required to register their own articles of incorporation in a single document when they registered the company. If they refrained from doing so then the relevant model articles 'would form part of the company's articles in the same manner and to the same extent as if articles in the form of those articles had been fully registered'. The 1985 Act further explained that the model articles which were to form the company's articles were those prescribed for a company of that description as in force at the date on which a company was registered. A company might adopt all or any of the provisions of the model articles. Thus, the incorporators could submit a document which stated that the articles of the company were to include the whole or any part of the model articles, together with additional articles. In this way the additions to the model articles might easily be detected.

Under the Companies Act 2006, new model articles apply to all new companies incorporated under the 2006 Act from October 2009. Table A retains its relevance for companies incorporated prior to 1 October 2009 which have chosen not to update their articles. Section 19 of the Companies Act 2006 empowers the Secretary of State to prescribe 'model articles' for companies (see the Companies (Model Articles) Regulations 2008 (SI 2008/3229)).

3.1.3 The articles as an enforceable agreement

One of the most difficult questions to arise concerning the articles of association is the degree to which they form an enforceable agreement between the shareholders and the company itself, and among the shareholders themselves. If the articles were too rigidly binding, management would be restricted in their actions for fear that their decisions would be challenged as having contravened a small (and perhaps relatively unimportant) provision in the articles. On the other hand, the articles are part of the constitution of the company and stand between the shareholders and the otherwise practically unrestricted powers of the management.

The potential misuse of the power to alter articles was well put in the Australian case of *Peters' American Delicacy Company Ltd v Heath* (High Court of Australia) (1939) 61 CLR 457. In that case Dixon CJ said:

> If no restraint were laid upon the power of altering articles of association, it would be possible for a shareholder controlling the necessary voting power so to mould the regulations of a company that its operations would be conducted or its property used so that he would profit either in some other capacity than that of member of the company or, if as member, in a special or peculiar way

inconsistent with conceptions of honesty so widely held or professed that departure from them is described, without further analysis, as fraud. For example, it would be possible to adopt articles requiring that the company should supply him with goods below cost or pay him 99 per cent of its profits for some real or imaginary services or submit to his own determination the question whether he was liable to account to the company for secret profits as a director.

How the law has held the balance between the various power groups whose privileges and duties are governed by the articles is explored in Section 3.2 below.

3.2 The articles as a contract

3.2.1 History

Section 14 of the Companies Act 1985 read as follows:

(1) Subject to the provisions of this Act, the memorandum and articles, when registered, bind the company and its members to the same extent as if they respectively had been signed and sealed by each member, and contained covenants on the part of each member to observe all the provisions of the memorandum and articles.

The precise effect of this provision was always most unclear. First of all, it is a peculiarly drafted provision, as it provides that the members shall be bound as if they had signed and sealed the articles. It makes no mention of the company being bound by the same fiction. This appears to ignore the fact that the company is said to be a legal person separate and distinct from its members (see Chapter 1). The courts have ignored this apparent omission. In *Wood v Odessa Waterworks* (1889) 42 Ch D 636, Stirling J said: 'The articles of association constitute a contract not merely between the shareholders and the company, but between each individual shareholder and every other.'

Further uncertainty is caused by the fact that, unlike an ordinary contract, the 'section 14' contract (ie the articles) might be altered without the consent of one of the parties to it. By section 9 of the Companies Act 1985, a company could alter its articles by special resolution. Thus, if 75 per cent of shareholders present and voting at a meeting determined that the articles were to be altered, that alteration would normally be effective and thus the 'contract' would be altered, as much for the objectors as for those in favour of the alteration. It appears that the *Wood v Odessa* main principles will remain in place under the Companies Act 2006 too.

3.2.2 Companies Act 2006

The ambit of the 2006 reforms is also somewhat unclear. Section 33 of the Companies Act 2006 provides:

(1) The provisions of a company's constitution bind the company and its members to the same extent as if there were covenants on the part of the company and of each member to observe those provisions.

This effectively enacts the decision in *Wood v Odessa Waterworks* (Section 3.2.1 above), but it does not seem to solve other difficulties which arose with the 'contract' in old section 14 of the Companies Act 1985.

3.2.3 What rights are governed by the contract in the articles?

Under the common law, the courts made it clear that the only relationship between members which is governed by the 'contract' in the articles is the dealings which they have with each other because they are shareholders in the company. No contractual relationship outside those confines is created by section 33. This may be illustrated by *London Sack and Bag v Dixon* [1943] 2 All ER 763. This case concerned a dispute between two members of the UK Jute Association. The dispute had arisen out of trading transactions between them, and not as a result of shareholders' rights. It was argued by the appellants that there was a binding submission to arbitration by virtue of the fact that both disputants were members of the association. The articles of the association provided for arbitration in the event of a dispute between members. The court held that the appellants had failed to prove that there had been a binding submission to arbitration. Scott LJ said that the contract, which was created between the members under the predecessor to section 33, did not constitute a contract between them 'about rights of action created entirely outside the company relationship such as trading transactions between members'.

An example from the other side of the line, where shareholders were bound to abide by the articles, was *Rayfield v Hands* [1960] Ch 1. In that case the plaintiff was a shareholder in a company. Article 11 of the articles required him to inform the directors of an intention to transfer shares in the company. The same article provided that the directors 'will take the said shares equally between them at fair value'. The plaintiff notified the directors of his intention of selling the shares but they refused to buy them. The plaintiff's claim for the determination of the fair value of the shares and for an order that the directors should purchase the shares at a fair price succeeded. Vaisey J said that 'the articles of association are simply a contract as between the shareholders inter se in respect of their rights as shareholders'. He also relied on the fact that in this case a small company, somewhat akin to a partnership, had been involved. If he was right to believe that this strengthened the section 33 contract, we can see that this alleged contract affects the 'constitutional' rights of shareholders that are affected by the articles. The contract may be more readily enforced where there are few shareholders.

3.2.4 Outsiders and insiders

Because shareholders are affected by the 'contract' only in their capacity as shareholders, it is clear that outsiders (non-shareholders) cannot be affected by the contract in the articles. Strangely, however, the rights of such outsiders are often set out in the articles. This may be partly because of the special definition of 'outsiders' in these circumstances. The practice has led to a number of cases.

A good illustration of the point is *Eley v Positive Government Security Life Association* (1876) 1 Ex D 88. There, the articles of association contained a clause in which it was stated that the plaintiff should be solicitor to the company and should transact all the legal business. The articles were signed by seven members of the company and duly registered. Later the company employed another solicitor, and the plaintiff brought an action for breach of contract. This action did not succeed. The court held that the articles were a matter between the shareholders among themselves, or between the shareholders and the directors (as representing the company). They did not create any contract between a solicitor and the company. This was so even though the solicitor had become a member of the company some time after the articles had been signed.

This means that there is a subtlety in the definition of an 'outsider' in these circumstances. He is a person unable to enforce the articles or be affected by the contract in the articles. When the person seeking to enforce the articles has effectively two relationships with the company, he may be both an 'outsider', in the sense discussed in *Eley*, and at the same time a shareholder of the company.

This problem was discussed in *Hickman v Kent and Romney Marsh Sheepbreeders* [1915] 1 Ch 881. In that case, the articles contained a clause which provided for a reference to arbitration of any disputes between the company and its members concerning the construction of the articles, or regarding any action to be taken in pursuance of those articles. When the plaintiff issued a writ claiming an injunction to prevent his expulsion from the company, the defendant company asked that the dispute be referred to arbitration. Astbury J cited a number of cases (*Prichard's Case* (1873) LR 8 Ch 956; *Melhado v Porto Alegre Ry Co* (1874) LR 9 CP 503; *Eley v Positive Government Security Life Association* (1876) 1 Ex D 88; and *Browne v La Trinidad* (1888) 37 Ch D 1) and went on to say:

> Now in these four cases the article relied upon purported to give specific contractual rights to persons in some capacity other than that of shareholder, and in none of them were members seeking to enforce or protect rights given to them as members, in common with the other corporators. The actual decisions amount to this. An outsider to whom rights purport to be given by the articles in his capacity as outsider, whether he is or subsequently becomes a member, cannot sue on those articles treating them as contracts between himself and the company to enforce those rights. Those rights are not part of the general regulations of the company applicable alike to all shareholders and can only exist by virtue of some contract between such person and the company, and the subsequent allotment of shares to an outsider in whose favour such an article is inserted does not enable him to sue the company on such article to enforce rights which are … not part of the general rights of the corporators as such.

Having examined a number of other cases (including *Wood v Odessa Waterworks* (1889) 42 Ch D 636; *Salmon v Quinn & Axtens* [1909] AC 442; and *Welton v Saffery* [1987] AC 299), Astbury J found the law clear on the following points:

> [F]irst, that no article can constitute a contract between the company and a third person; secondly, that no right merely purporting to be given by an article to a person, whether a member or not, in a capacity other than that of member, as, for instance, as solicitor, promoter, director, can be enforced against the company; and thirdly, that articles regulating the rights and obligations of the members generally as such do create rights and obligations between them and the company respectively.

The conclusion arrived at by Astbury J was reached after consideration of the case of *Salmon v Quinn & Axtens* (above). In that case, the articles of association gave a veto to Joseph Salmon which could prevent the board of directors from validly making certain decisions. On the occasion in question in this case, Salmon had used his power of veto. Salmon was a managing director, and yet he was able to enforce his right of veto by way of the contract in the articles despite the fact that there was only one other shareholder who held a similar right. This case might be reconciled with *Hickman* on the grounds that every shareholder has the right to enforce the articles of the company, and it is irrelevant and coincidental that the article sought to be enforced in any one case stands to benefit the shareholder bringing the action more than others. In other words, a shareholder who also holds a position as outsider (such as managing director, solicitor, etc) can, wearing his shareholder hat, enforce the contract in the articles, even if the direct result of that enforcement is of benefit to him wearing his outsider hat.

This approach was rejected in *Beattie v Beattie* [1938] Ch 708 (see Case note 1 at the end of the chapter). Sir Wilfred Greene MR said:

> It is to be observed that the real matter which is here being litigated is a dispute between the company and the appellant in his capacity as a director, and when the appellant, relying on this clause, seeks to have that dispute referred to arbitration, it is that dispute and none other which he is seeking to have referred, and by seeking to have it referred he is not, in my judgment, seeking to enforce a right which is common to himself and all other members … He is not seeking to enforce a right to call on the company to arbitrate a dispute which is only accidentally a dispute with himself. He is asking, as a disputant, to have the dispute to which he is a party referred. That is sufficient to differentiate it from the right which is common to all the other members of the company under this article.

The line between shareholders' rights and outsiders' rights remains, despite the anomalous decision in *Salmon v Quinn & Axtens*.

Section 14 of the Companies Act 1985 (with other issues) was the subject of a study by the Law Commission. In *Shareholder Remedies* (Law Commission Report No 246 (available on the Law Commission website at <http://www.lawcom.gov.uk/library>)) the Commission set out the then current law, acknowledging that the law was unclear but recommending against providing a statutory list of situations which fell within the scope of the section. The Law Commission did not suggest an approach which abandoned seeing section 14 of the 1985 Act as a type of contract, and made it clear that it was used in order to protect constitutional rights which belong to a substantial body of shareholders. It did, however, suggest adding further regulations to Table A, with the aim of providing dispute resolution provisions and a means of 'exit' for shareholders in small companies. The Companies Act 2006 seems to have followed this recommendation, leaving us with opposing authorities. The only case above which might be construed as involving an 'entrenched provision' was *Salmon v Quinn & Axtens*, and it does not come squarely within that definition (see Section 3.2.5 below), as the right to veto in that case enabled the veto of certain decisions of the board of directors; it did not involve vetoing a change in articles.

3.2.5 Entrenched provisions

What the 2006 Act has done is provide new law on provisions which are entrenched in the articles. It also provides that where provisions were in a company's memorandum because the company was formed under the 1985 Act or one of its predecessors, they will now be considered to be in the company's articles, and thus subject to the new regime concerning change and entrenchment.

Section 22(1) and (2) of the Companies Act 2006 provides:

(1) A company's articles may contain provision ('Provision for entrenchment') to the effect that specified provisions of the articles may be amended or repealed only if conditions are met, or procedures complied with, that are more restrictive than those applicable in the case of a special resolution.

(2) Provision for entrenchment may only be made—
   (a) in the company's articles on formation, or
   (b) by an amendment of the company's articles agreed to by all members of the company.

The section provides that an agreement of all members is sufficient for alteration even if there is an entrenched provision (s 22(3)). A court or other relevant authority may also alter articles where it has power to do so (s 22(4)).

3.3 The articles as evidence of a contract

Whereas an 'outsider' may not enforce rights which are in the articles by invoking section 33 of the Companies Act 2006 (see Section 3.2.4 above), he may be able to show that he has a contract with the company apart from the articles, although the articles may provide or be evidence of some of the terms of that contract. An example of this is *Re New British Iron Company, ex Parte Beckwith* [1898] 1 Ch 324. In that case, the articles provided (by article 62) that: 'The remuneration of the board shall be an annual sum of £1,000 to be paid out of the funds of the company, which sum shall be divided in such manner as the board from time to time determine.' Wright J said:

> That article is not in itself a contract between the company and the directors; it is only part of the contract constituted by the articles of association between the members of the company inter se. But where on the footing of that article the directors are employed by the company and accept office the terms of article 62 are embodied in and form part of the contract between the company and the directors. Under the articles as thus embodied the directors obtain a contractual right to an annual sum of £1,000 as remuneration.

The same reasoning proved detrimental to the plaintiff in *Read v Astoria Garage (Streatham) Ltd* [1952] 2 All ER 292. The company had adopted the standard form of articles of association set out in the Companies Act in force at the time. The article at the centre of the dispute provided that managing directors could be appointed by a resolution of the directors and for that appointment to be terminated by a resolution of the general meeting. The plaintiff was appointed and dismissed by those procedures. He claimed unfair dismissal, arguing that there was a contract between him and the company, one of the terms of which was that his employment should not be terminated without reasonable notice. The Court of Appeal could find no evidence of a contract between the company and the plaintiff, still less evidence of a contract which contradicted the terms of the articles, so the plaintiff failed.

Still more unfortunate was the plaintiff in *Re Richmond Gate Property Co Ltd* [1965] 1 WLR 335. In that case the court held that the defendant had been employed by the company as managing director. The court looked to the articles to find what remuneration was due, since there was no evidence of a contract term about pay elsewhere. The articles provided that he should be paid such amount 'as the directors may determine'. In fact the directors had made no determination, so nothing was due to him. Furthermore, because he had a contract with the company, he could not recover any money on a 'quantum meruit' claim, which is a claim for money when work has been done without any formal agreement as to the amount that will be paid in respect of that work. It is, in effect, a claim for a 'reasonable amount' for work done.

The facts of the previous two cases considered lead to the question: What would be the situation if a contract had existed, and that contract and the articles contained contradictory clauses? In *Read v Astoria Garage* (see above), Jenkins LJ said:

> a managing director whose appointment is determined by the company in general meeting ... cannot claim to have been wrongfully dismissed unless he can show that an agreement has been entered into between himself and the company, the terms of which are inconsistent with the exercise by the company of the power conferred on it by the article ...

From this it follows that the company can exercise whatever powers the articles specify, but if a contractual right is breached by this exercise of powers, damages must be paid. This was what occurred in *Nelson v James Nelson & Sons Ltd* [1914] 2 KB 770. In that case, the directors tried to terminate the employment of the plaintiff as managing director. He had been appointed as managing director for life, provided that he complied with a number of conditions. It was not alleged that he had broken any of the conditions. The articles gave to the directors power to appoint managing directors and power to 'revoke' such appointments. The court held that the power to revoke appointments did not mean that the directors could do so in such a way that contracts entered into by the company would be broken. That was what had happened here, and therefore the termination of the plaintiff's employment was unlawful and the company was liable in damages for breach of contract.

3.4 Alteration of the articles of association

3.4.1 Requirements for amendment

Section 21 of the Companies Act 2006 provides that a company may amend its articles by special resolution. Special resolutions are discussed in detail in Chapter 8.

By section 25 of the Act, a member will not be bound by alterations made after he has joined the company in so far as they make him liable to pay extra money to the company, unless he has agreed in writing to take more shares than he was obliged to before the alteration.

There are special provisions which apply when the rights attached to classes of shares are to be varied (see Chapter 5 for a detailed analysis of this subject). This cannot be done simply by special resolution. As stated above, the general rule concerning non-variation alterations is that articles may be altered by a special (75 per cent majority) resolution. This rule can put very considerable power in the hands of the majority. The number of shareholders making up such a majority may be very small, perhaps even only one person. Because of this, the courts have found it necessary to control this power. The rule that has been formulated is that an alteration of articles is valid only if it is in good faith (bona fide) and for the benefit of the company as a whole. At first sight this would seem to be a stringent control, but closer examination of the cases (see Section 3.4.2 below) shows a considerable reluctance to intervene in favour of an aggrieved minority, and great confusion as to what is actually meant by 'bona fide for the benefit of the company as a whole'. These cases pre-date the Companies Act 2006 but there is no reason to doubt their continued applicability.

In *Allen v Gold Reefs of West Africa Ltd* [1900] 1 Ch 656 (see Case note 2 at the end of this chapter), Lindley MR said:

> [T]he power conferred by [what is now section 21 of the Act] must, like all other powers, be exercised subject to those general principles of law and equity which are applicable to all powers conferred on majorities and enabling them to bind minorities. It must be exercised, not only in the manner required by law, but also bona fide for the benefit of the company as a whole, and it must not be exceeded. These conditions are always implied, and are seldom, if ever, expressed. But if they are complied with I can discover no ground for judicially putting any other restrictions on the power conferred by the section than those contained in it …

He went on to say that shares were taken on the basis that articles were subject to alteration. It would therefore require very clear evidence of an undertaking by the company to treat a particular shareholder differently – an undertaking that a particular article would not be altered. However, where there was an agreement that would be broken by the alteration of the articles of association, the company would be liable for a breach of contract brought about by the change of article:

> A company cannot break its contracts by altering its articles, but, when dealing with contracts referring to revocable articles, and especially with contracts between a member of the company and the company respecting his shares, care must be taken not to assume that the contract involves as one of its terms an article which is not to be altered. (*per* Lindley MR at 673)

3.4.2 Meaning of bona fide for the benefit of the company

Given that a resolution to alter articles will be regarded as valid if it is passed 'bona fide for the benefit of the company' and invalid if this can be shown not to be the case, do the cases throw light on what is meant by that phrase?

In *Brown v British Abrasive Wheel* [1919] 1 Ch 290, the company needed to raise further capital. The 98 per cent majority were willing to provide this capital if they could buy up the 2 per cent minority. Having failed to effect this by agreement, the 98 per cent majority proposed to change the articles of association to give them power to purchase the shares of the minority. The proposed article provided for the compulsory purchase of the minority's shares on certain terms. However, the majority were prepared to insert any provision as to price which the court thought was fair. Despite this, the court held that the proposed alteration could not be made. Astbury J held that the alteration was not for the benefit of the company as a whole. One reason for this was that there was no direct link between the provision of the extra capital and the alteration of the articles. Although the whole scheme had been to provide the capital after removing the dissentient shareholders, it would in fact have been possible to remove the shareholders and then refuse to provide the capital. Astbury J's judgment seems to determine that two separate criteria must be met:

1. the judgment must be 'within the ordinary principles of justice'; and
2. it must be 'for the benefit of the company as a whole'.

So far as the latter requirement was concerned, the company seems to have been identified with the shareholders and the reality of the whole plan seems to have been overlooked, for the judge ignored the plan to provide capital on the grounds that there was no formal link between this and the alteration. He also said that the alteration would benefit the majority and not the company as a whole, thus ignoring the company's separate existence as a commercial entity in need of further funding.

Brown v British Abrasive Wheel was not followed in the later case of *Sidebottom v Kershaw, Leese & Co Ltd* [1919] 1 Ch 290, and the approach taken by the judge in the *Brown* case was criticised. In *Sidebottom*, an alteration was approved although it provided for the compulsory purchase of shares. One difference between this case and *Brown* is that the ability to purchase the shares was limited to a situation where the shareholder in question was carrying on business in direct competition with the company. The relationship between this article and the benefit of the company was therefore much clearer. In *Sidebottom*, two of the Court of Appeal judges made it clear that they believed that, in *Brown*, Astbury J had been wrong to regard good faith and the company's benefit as two separate ideas. The important question was: Was the alteration for the benefit of the company as a whole?

Settling the important question and determining its meaning proved to be two different things. In *Dafen Tinplate Co Ltd v Llanelly Steel Co (1907) Ltd* [1920] 2 Ch 124, the plaintiff company was a member of the defendant company. The defendant realised that the plaintiff was conducting business in a manner detrimental to its interests. In fact it was buying steel from an alternative source of supply. There was an attempt to buy the plaintiff's shares by agreement but this failed. The defendant company then altered its articles by special resolution to include a power compulsorily to purchase the shares of any member requested to transfer them. It was this alteration which was the subject of the action. The court held that the alteration was too wide to be valid. The altered article would confer too much power on the majority. It went much further than was necessary for the protection of the company. The judge seemed to be using the 'bona fide for the benefit of the company' test in an objective sense, that is, he was judging the situation from the court's point of view.

A different view of the meaning of this important question was taken in *Shuttleworth v Cox Bros & Co (Maidenhead) Ltd* [1927] 2 KB 9. In that case the company had a board of directors appointed for life. The alteration to the articles provided that any one of the board of directors should lose office if his fellow directors requested in writing that he should resign. The alteration was directed at a particular director whose conduct had not been satisfactory. Again the words 'bona fide for the benefit of the company' were interpreted as one condition. This time, however, the Court approached the question from the point of view of the subjective belief of the shareholders. Scrutton LJ said that 'the shareholders must act honestly having regard to and endeavouring to act for the benefit of the company'. Bankes LJ agreed and added:

> By what criterion is the court to ascertain the opinion of the shareholders on this question? The alteration may be so oppressive as to cast suspicion on the honesty of the persons responsible for it, or so extravagant that no reasonable man could really consider it for the benefit of the company. In such cases the court is, I think, entitled to treat the conduct of shareholders as it does the verdict of a jury and to say that the alteration of a company's articles shall not stand if it is such that no reasonable man could consider it for the benefit of the company ... I cannot agree with what seems to have been the view of Peterson J in *Dafen Tinplate Co v Llanelly Steel Co* [see above] ... that whenever the Court and the shareholders may differ in opinion upon what is for the benefit of the company, the view of the court must prevail.

If this passage is right, the court will intervene only in the most extreme cases – when no reasonable man could believe that the alteration could be good for the company. One of the considerations which caused the courts to withdraw from their more interventionist stand is the fact that shares and the right to vote attached to shares are regarded as property rights. It would be unrealistic, in the words of Dixon CJ in *Peters' American Delicacy Company Ltd v Heath* (see Section 3.1.3 above), '[to] suppose that in voting each shareholder is to assume an inhuman altruism and consider only the intangible notion of the benefit of the vague abstraction ... "the company as an institution"'.

A further difficulty is that the alteration of the articles presupposes that there will be conflicting interests to be adjusted. It is therefore very difficult for anyone to determine what will be for the positive benefit of the whole company. It may be that two conflicting rights have been confused. It might be argued that a shareholder has two rights. One is the right to uphold the value of his shareholding. In defence of this right, the shareholder may vote selfishly without any regard to the benefit of the company. If, despite so voting, the right is unfairly damaged, the shareholder will be entitled to compensation under section 994 of the Companies Act 2006 for unfair prejudice. A shareholder defending such a right would not be entitled to set aside a decision of the management or company on such grounds. However, a decision by the company or the management may be struck down if it is not taken bona fide in the interests of the company. This is because decisions which affect the interests of the company must be taken for the benefit of the company as a whole, even if some shareholders are damaged in the process. A decision not taken for the benefit of the company as a whole should be challengeable by shareholders seeking to protect the value of the interests they hold in the company rather than the value of the interest they hold in their shares.

The courts have taken a cautious view and retained their power to prevent manifest abuses while fighting shy of interference in the internal affairs of the company. This caution may be seen as part of the whole approach of the law to the principle of majority rule (see Chapter 2).

Three other cases show the reluctance of the court to intervene. In *Greenhalgh v Arderne Cinemas Ltd* [1951] Ch 286 (see Case note 3 at the end of the chapter), a change in articles which effectively removed the plaintiff's pre-emption rights was approved, despite the reference in the judgment to the factor of discrimination as one which would cause a resolution to be disallowed by the courts. It must be clear that any discrimination between majority and minority shareholders would not be sufficient to cause a resolution to fail the bona fide test, since many alterations of articles will cause adjustments between classes of shareholders from which some will emerge better off than others. An example of this is to be found in *Rights and Issue Investment Trust Ltd v Stylo Shoes Ltd* [1965] Ch 250. In that case the effect of the alteration was (among other things) to halve the voting rights of a number of ordinary shareholders as against the rights held by management. Despite this, the resolution was upheld. The management shares had not been voted and the resolution had been passed by the requisite majority. The court refused to interfere. It seems that if discrimination is to be a ground for interference, it will have to be some very clear, perhaps vindictive, discrimination that is alleged before the court will be moved to upset the normal voting patterns of the company and declare a resolution invalid.

In *Citco Banking Corporation NV v Pusser's Ltd & Anor* (Eastern Caribbean Supreme Court (British Virgin Islands)) [2007] UKPC 13 (28 February 2007), the alteration of the articles was instrumental in the shaping of the balance of power within the company as it gave the company's chairman the voting control of the company. The Privy Council followed the previous judicial pattern to reject any challenge to the validity of the alteration by applying the principles flowing from *Shuttleworth v Cox Bros & Co (Maidenhead) Ltd* (above). Pennycuick J said (at [255]–[256]):

> So far as I am aware there is no principle under which the members of a company acting in accordance with the Companies Act and the constitution of the particular company and subject to any necessary consent on the part of a class affected, cannot, if they are so minded, alter the relative voting powers attached to various classes of shares. Of course, any resolution for the alteration of voting rights must be passed in good faith for the benefit of the company as a whole, but, where it is so, I know of no ground on which such an alteration would be objectionable and no authority has been cited to that effect. So here this alteration in voting powers has been resolved upon by a great majority of those members of the company who have themselves nothing to gain by it so far as their personal interest is concerned and who, so far as one knows, are actuated only by consideration of what is for the benefit of the company as a whole.

These principles, together with the proposition that the burden of proof is upon the person who challenges the validity of the amendment (see *Peters' American Delicacy Company Ltd v Heath* (1939) 61 CLR 457, *per* Latham CJ at 482), appeared to their Lordships to be clearly settled and sufficient for the purpose of deciding this case. Therefore, the court was eager to follow the test formed quite consistently by preceding case law; that involved the recognised freedom of the majority to pursue the constitutional changes it considers necessary for the company on the basis of the bona fide test. As the court noted in this case, 'a shareholder is not debarred from voting or using his voting power to carry a resolution by the circumstance of his having a particular interest in the subject-matter of the vote'.

This is a clear recognition of the fact that shareholders can indeed vote in their best personal interest. This judgment therefore confirmed the already established principles which entail a rather limited willingness of the courts to intervene within the internal corporate life and dictate the institutional solutions. As explained in Chapter 2, the English company based on a contractual model of corporate governance is viewed as a private affair; in this context, any external interventions should be limited to the situations where they are absolutely necessary. The ruling in question clarified the intention of the courts to respect both the recognised ability of the shareholders to vote with their personal interest in mind and the respective ability of the majority to alter the articles of association on the basis of a special resolution. The issue of whether the alteration in question took place bona fide for the benefit of the company as a whole will be dealt with on the basis of the aforementioned parameters along with the application of a test of reasonableness. If reasonable shareholders could consider the amendment to be for the benefit of the company then the alteration in question would be valid, and the courts will avoid doing what they obviously dislike – intervening in the internal affairs of the company.

The freedom of the majority to pass a special resolution and alter the previous constitutional arrangements of the company will find its limits in cases of serious and unfair treatment of minorities. This is a principle that will be interpreted rather narrowly by the courts. In the *Citco* case the court noted that in *Gambotto v WCP Limited* (1995) 182 CLR 432 the High Court of Australia created a new rule for amendments which they characterised as conferring powers of 'expropriation' of the shares of a minority. Such an amendment could be justified only if it was reasonably apprehended that the continued shareholding of the minority was detrimental to the company, its undertaking or the conduct of its affairs, and expropriation was a reasonable means of eliminating or mitigating that detriment. It was not enough in such a case that the amendment was considered by the majority shareholders to be in the interests of the company as a corporate entity, or even that it actually was for the company's benefit. In a joint judgment, Mason CJ, Brennan, Deane and Dawson JJ said (at 446):

> Notwithstanding that a shareholder's membership of a company is subject to alterations of the articles which may affect the rights attaching to the shareholder's shares and the value of those shares, we do not consider that, in the case of an alteration to the articles authorizing the expropriation of shares, it is a sufficient justification of an expropriation that the expropriation, being fair, will advance the interests of the company as a legal and commercial entity or those of the majority, albeit the great majority, of corporators. This approach does not attach sufficient weight to the proprietary nature of a share and, to the extent that English authority might appear to support such an approach, we do not agree with it.

The court obviously did not need to go down that road since the *Citco* case was not one of expropriation, but the reference to the judgment in *Gambotto* was indicative of the potential limits of the ability of the majority to promote an alteration of the articles.

3.4.3 Remedies

The remedies that are available to a successful challenger when an alteration to the articles has been or is about to be made include the following.

3.4.3(a) Injunction

An injunction will be available where the alteration does not pass the bona fide test, but it is doubtful whether it will be available where the objection to the alteration is that it will cause the company to break a contract. In *British Murac Syndicate v Alperton Rubber Co* [1915] 2 Ch 186, there was an agreement separate from the articles, by which the defendant company was obliged to accept two directors nominated by the plaintiff syndicate. Two directors were nominated, but their appointment was not acceptable to the defendant. The defendant company proposed to delete the article that was in the same terms as the external contract. It was held that the company had no power to alter its articles of association for the purpose of committing a breach of contract, and that therefore an injunction would be granted to restrain the holding of the meeting which was to be convened for that purpose.

This case must be contrasted with *Southern Foundries Ltd v Shirlaw* [1940] AC 701. In that case the House of Lords held that the company could alter its articles so as to put itself in a position in which it could break a contract. When such powers were used, however, there would be a breach and the other party to that contract would be entitled to damages. Where there was a contract made in the expectation that a state of affairs would continue, it was not open to the company, by using its power to change articles, so to undermine that contract that it became worthless. While leaving the plaintiff a remedy in damages, this case throws some doubt on the *British Murac* case, since it implies that the change in the articles could not be restrained by injunction. It was only misuse of the new powers inserted by the alteration that could be questioned. Damages were the remedy asked for, so that it is still uncertain if the use of the new powers could have been restrained in respect of this particular member. It may be that in *British Murac* the injunction should not have been aimed at preventing the meeting to alter the regulation but at a future use of the altered regulation in order to break the contract that existed independently of the articles. The exact significance of these two cases is still somewhat uncertain.

3.4.3(b) Damages

There is no doubt that where alteration of the articles, or even use of a power contained in the articles, causes a contract with an outsider to be broken, damages will be awarded. In *Shindler v Northern Raincoat Co Ltd* [1960] 1 WLR 1038, the defendant company agreed to employ the plaintiff as its managing director for 10 years. By using a power in the articles, the plaintiff was dismissed in the first year. He was entitled to damages.

3.4.3(c) Rectification

Rectification would involve an order of the court altering the document (in this case the articles) so that it will read in the way that was originally intended. In the case of articles of association, the courts have held that this is out of the question, because the Registrar approved the document in its original form. It is in that form and no other that the articles become the constitution of the company, binding on the members, so they cannot be altered subsequently by the court (see *Scott v Frank F Scott (London) Ltd* [1940] Ch 794).

Summary

3.1 The articles of association regulate the relationship between the shareholders and the company, and the balance of power among shareholders.

3.2 It is difficult to assess the contractual binding force of the articles as a contract.

Some authorities require the right sought to be enforced under section 33 of the Companies Act 2006 and the articles to be a 'member's right' and not a 'special right'. *Salmon v Quinn & Axtens* appears to contradict this.

3.3 An outsider may be able to show that he has a contract with the company apart from the articles, although the articles may provide or be evidence of some of the terms of that contract.

3.4 An alteration of the articles can be effected by a 75 per cent majority of the shareholders but can be challenged on the ground that the alteration was not 'bona fide for the benefit of the company'.

Exercises

3.1 What are the policy factors behind the decisions on enforcement of the articles of association as a contract?

3.2 What is meant by 'bona fide for the benefit of the company'?

Case notes

1. *Beattie v Beattie* **[1938] Ch 708**

The articles of association contained an arbitration clause. An allegation was made by a shareholder who stated that the defendant had, in his capacity as director, paid himself unjustified remuneration. Sir Wilfred Greene said:

It is to be observed that the real matter which is here being litigated is a dispute between the company and the appellant in his capacity as a director, and when the appellant, relying on this clause, seeks to have that dispute referred to arbitration, it is that dispute and none other which he is seeking to have referred, and by

seeking to have it referred he is not, in my judgment, seeking to enforce a right which is common to himself and all other members.

2. *Allen v Gold Reefs of West Africa Ltd* **[1900] 1 Ch 656**

The case concerned an attempted alteration of the articles of association which would have retrospective effect and alter the obligations of a shareholder towards the company. The court held that, provided the alteration could be seen as 'bona fide for the benefit of the company', the power to alter articles was otherwise unfettered.

3. *Greenhalgh v Arderne Cinemas Ltd* [1951] Ch 286

Evershed MR said:

Certain principles can be safely stated as emerging from [the] authorities. In the first place, I think it is now plain that 'bona fide for the benefit of the company as a whole' means not two things but one thing. It means that the shareholder must proceed upon what, in his honest opinion, is for the benefit of the company as a whole. The second thing is that the phrase 'the company as a whole' does not (at any rate in such a case as the present) mean the company as a commercial entity, distinct from the corporators as a general body. That is to say, the case may be taken of an individual hypothetical member and it may be asked whether what is proposed is, in the honest opinion of those who voted in its favour, for that person's benefit.

I think that the matter can, in practice, be more accurately and precisely stated by looking at the converse and by saying that a special resolution of this kind would be liable to be impeached if the effect of it were to discriminate between the majority shareholders and the minority shareholders, so as to give to the former an advantage of which the latter were deprived.

Further reading

Bourne, *Bourne on Company Law* (Routledge-Cavendish, 2011).

Talbot, *Critical Company Law* (Routledge-Cavendish, 2007).

Chapter 4

The power to represent the company

Key words

▶ **Ultra vires** – acts done by a company which are not authorised by its constitution as set out in its articles of association.

▶ **Objects clause** – the list of activities which a company is authorised to undertake.

▶ **Actual authority** – the 'real' authority which agents of the company have, enabling them to make the company liable for contracts they conclude.

▶ **Ostensible and usual authority** – the authority which a reasonable third party would expect company representatives to have, enabling them to make the company liable for contracts they conclude.

▶ **Promoters** – the persons who are responsible for the company's coming into existence.

▶ **Pre-incorporation contract** – a contract supposedly made on behalf of a company before it has any legal existence.

4.1 Introduction

This chapter deals with the rules regarding the capacity of the directors to bind the company in cases where they may be acting outside their own powers or outside the objects of the company, as well as where someone is acting as if they were a validly appointed director. The chapter will also examine the ability of promoters, ie the persons who are responsible for the company's coming into existence, to bind the company with contracts signed before the company is effectively incorporated.

4.2 Ultra vires: the new law

Before the Companies Act 2006, the memorandum of association was regarded as the most important part of the constitution of the company. This is no longer the case. One problem which caused extensive debate over many years was an issue arising from the setting out of the objects of association in the memorandum. The courts held that the company was unable to create legally binding contracts or act outside the scope of the objects of association as they were set out in the memorandum. The law has now been changed significantly to eliminate this problem. By section 39 of the Companies Act 2006, a company has unlimited capacity to act.

Section 31 of the Companies Act 2006 states as follows:

Statement of company's objects

(1) Unless a company's articles specifically restrict the objects of the company, its objects are unrestricted.

(2) Where a company amends its articles so as to add, remove or alter a statement of the company's objects—

(a) it must give notice to the registrar,
(b) on receipt of the notice, the registrar shall register it, and
(c) the amendment is not effective until entry of that notice on the register.
(3) Any such amendment does not affect any rights or obligations of the company or render defective any legal proceedings by or against it.

This provision now adopts the basic principle that the company will have unlimited objects unless it is specifically stated in its articles that its objects remain restricted. This basic principle applies to companies registered after the Companies Act 2006 came into force. For companies registered before the 2006 Act, the objects clause of the memorandum of association will now be treated as part of the articles and will continue to have a restrictive effect on the objects of the company, unless of course the company is registered as a general commercial one.

Section 31(2) and (3) clarifies the procedure to be followed when the members of the company wish to alter the objects of the company. The amendment of the objects clause comes into effect only from the moment of the registration by the Registrar of Companies of the notice given to it by the company. Any shift in the scope of the objects of the company produces no effect on pre-existing legal obligations, a provision which is consistent with the general spirit of the law which is very much protective of third parties dealing with the company.

Section 39 reads:

A company's capacity
(1) The validity of an act done by a company shall not be called into question on the ground of lack of capacity by reason of anything in the company's constitution.
(2) This section has effect subject to section 42 (companies that are charities).

Charities are excepted from this provision by section 39(2).

The new wording of section 39, in comparison with its predecessor, section 35 of the Companies Act 1985, is a reflection of the change in the status of the articles as the principal constitutional document of a company. Section 35 of the Companies Act 1985 contained the words 'by reason of anything in the company's memorandum', but since the objects clause is now incorporated in the articles, a change of wording was imperative. Section 39 must be viewed in conjunction with section 171 of the Act, which now establishes the obligation of directors to act in accordance with the company's constitution as an independent statutory duty. Therefore, a director acting outside the scope of the objects of the company, if the latter are defined and therefore restricted in the constitution, will now be in breach of the statutory duty enshrined in section 171 and could be found liable. In addition to that, section 260 on the derivative action offers an additional means of protection, as it makes it easier to raise such an action against a director who fails to observe the limitations stemming from the constitution on his ability to act.

Section 40 of the Companies Act 2006 reads as follows:

Power of directors to bind the company
(1) In favour of a person dealing with a company in good faith, the power of the directors to bind the company, or authorise others to do so, is deemed to be free of any limitation under the company's constitution.
(2) For this purpose—
    (a) a person 'deals with' a company if he is a party to any transaction or other act to which the company is a party,
    (b) a person dealing with a company—

    (i)   is not bound to enquire as to any limitation on the powers of the directors to bind the company or authorise others to do so,

    (ii) is presumed to have acted in good faith unless the contrary is proved, and

    (iii) is not to be regarded as acting in bad faith by reason only of his knowing that an act is beyond the powers of the directors under the company's constitution.

(3) The references above to limitations on the directors' powers under the company's constitution include limitations deriving—

    (a) from a resolution of the company or of any class of shareholders, or

    (b) from any agreement between the members of the company or of any class of shareholders.

(4) This section does not affect any right of a member of the company to bring proceedings to restrain the doing of an action that is beyond the powers of the directors. But no such proceedings lie in respect of an act to be done in fulfilment of a legal obligation arising from a previous act of the company.

(5) This section does not affect any liability incurred by the directors, or any other person, by reason of the directors' exceeding their powers.

(6) This section has effect subject to—

section 41 (transactions with directors or their associates), and

section 42 (companies that are charities).

Section 40(2) clarifies that the third party is not bound to enquire as to any limitation on the powers of the director placed by the constitution; and it is also found to be in good faith despite its knowledge that the act in question was beyond the powers of the director as defined by the constitution. At this point, it has to be noted that it is not completely clear what sort of behaviour would amount to the presumption that the third party does not act in good faith, if the active knowledge of the inability of the director to act cannot function as a sufficient indicator. In *Criterion Properties Plc v Stratford UK Properties LLC & Others* [2004] UKHL 28, the House of Lords pointed out that the 'knowing assistance' of the third party to the director in his attempt to breach his duty might be an indication of the former acting in bad faith.

By section 40(4), a shareholder can obtain an injunction to prevent a director acting outside the constitution, provided the act is challenged before a legal obligation has arisen. Further, if the act in question involves a director of the company or its holding company, or a person connected with such a director, the act is voidable by the company. In these circumstances, the company can ask the court to set aside the act. The company's capacity might also be relevant where it seeks to set aside an act alleging that the third party was not acting in 'good faith' (see discussion of s 40, below). It is only in these rare circumstances that any limitations to a company's 'objects' will be of relevance. It should be noted that the objects of the company will be found in the articles of association and any resolutions which form part of the constitution, not in the memorandum which has been downgraded to a simple statement of intent to form a company. In these new circumstances, only a brief discussion of the intricacies of the old law is necessary as the issues could only arise in the limited circumstances set out above, and then only if the company has adopted a restricted list of objects.

There is an exception for acts involving directors or connected persons in section 41. The aforementioned provisions, which abolish ultra vires, have the effect that once an act has been performed on behalf of the company, that act cannot be challenged on the ultra vires basis so as to upset the rights of third parties. The only two situations where third party rights could be called into question are where a director or a connected person is involved, or where the third party is proved to have acted in bad faith. The only other occasion on which the issue could arise is where there is a challenge to directors' acts, either with an injunction in advance of the act, or to allege a breach of duty after the event. However, these remaining provisions mean that, in very rare circumstances, the old, complicated case law might be invoked.

4.3 Ratification

Section 239 of the Companies Act 2006 requires one ordinary resolution for ratification of breaches of duty by directors, but does provide that the votes of any director whose breach is the subject of the resolution and of any connected person (as defined in s 252) do not count in calculating the simple majority which is enough to pass the ordinary resolution.

In the case of a transaction involving a director or connected person, the director or connected person involved and any director who authorised the transaction remain liable under section 41(3):

(a) to account to the company for any gain which he has made directly or indirectly by the transaction, and
(b) to indemnify the company for any loss or damage resulting from the transaction.

The contract will also cease to be voidable (s 41(4)) if:

(a) restitution of any money or other asset which was the subject-matter of the transaction is no longer possible, or
(b) the company is indemnified for any loss or damage resulting from the transaction, or
(c) rights acquired bona fide and for value and without actual notice of the directors' exceeding their powers by a person who is not a party to the transaction would be affected by the avoidance, or
(d) the transaction is affirmed by the company.

Thus, if directors are entering into an agreement in excess of their powers, as the powers are defined by the constitution, and if the other party to the transaction is a director of the company or a connected person or holding company, the transaction which would otherwise be enforceable under section 40 would now be voidable. In simple terms, the third parties on this occasion – namely the parties connected with the director who had exceeded his powers – cannot rely on section 40(1) to enforce the agreement.

It is noteworthy that directors are caught by this section whether or not they know they are exceeding their powers. Others are not affected unless they know that the directors are exceeding their powers (s 41(5)). If someone other than a director of the company or of its holding company, or persons or companies connected or associated with that director, enters into a contract with a company, the contract would normally be fully enforceable even if the directors were acting ultra vires according to the old law.

4.4 Ultra vires – the old law

By section 2(1)(c) of the Companies Act 1985, the memorandum of a company was required to 'state the objects of a company'. This simple requirement has been the object of much heart-searching in the past and gave rise to an enormous body of law. This law needs to be briefly examined in order to form a proper understanding of the present law. It also affords an interesting example of the way in which case law can develop.

It was first apparent that the requirement to state objects would cause problems when the courts held that if a company did an act which was outside the scope of the objects as described in the memorandum, that act would be wholly without legal effect (void). This so-called doctrine of 'ultra vires' is similar to the law concerning public bodies. They are unable to act outside the statutory powers given to them. It was felt that the same should be true of companies. Unfortunately, the law that developed had unhappy results. This is partly because the reason that public bodies should be restricted to the powers given to them by Parliament is in order to safeguard democracy. If a public body takes to itself more power than the elected representatives of the people have chosen to give it, it is setting itself up as more important than the electorate. Similar considerations do not apply when companies are considered. Companies need to respond with a considerable degree of flexibility to changing markets and it is difficult to see who has ever benefited from this doctrine.

4.4.1   Constructive notice

The doctrine of ultra vires only worked in conjunction with the doctrine of constructive notice. By this doctrine, everyone is deemed to know the contents of the memorandum of association of the company with which they are dealing because it is a public document. (This doctrine disappeared on the implementation of the Companies Act 1989 and has no equivalent in the Companies Act 2006.)

4.4.2   Justification of the doctrine

The original justification for the existence of the doctrine was that it would serve as a protection for shareholders and creditors. A company formed for one purpose should not be permitted to pursue other ends which did not have the blessing of the shareholders and creditors, who stood to lose their money if the company indulged in unprofitable adventures. However, as will be seen, the element of protection was lost the moment that the court accepted memoranda with objects clauses so widely drafted that they covered almost every activity. After that, the doctrine was only of use if a party sought to avoid a contract. The determination of where the loss caused by the application of the doctrine should fall appears to have been a matter of mere chance of circumstances.

Apart from providing an expensive parlour game for lawyers, there appeared to be very little point to this doctrine. Reform was attempted on accession to the European Community but it was badly done. The relevant provision of Directive 68/151/EEC is Article 9, which reads:

> Acts done by the organs of the company shall be binding upon it even if those acts are not within the objects of the company, unless such acts exceed the powers that the law confers or allows to be conferred on those organs. However, Member States may provide that the company shall not be bound where such acts are outside the objects of the company if it proves that the third party knew that the act was outside those objects or could not in view of the circumstances be unaware thereof; disclosure of the statutes shall not of itself be sufficient proof thereof.

4.4.3 The old case law

In the limited circumstances where the case law is still relevant, all the old complications may need to be examined by the court. The following is a brief consideration of those difficulties.

One of the early cases was *Ashbury Railway Carriage and Iron Co* (1875) LR 7 HL 653. The memorandum gave the company the power to make and sell railway carriages. The company purported to buy a concession for constructing a railway in Belgium. Later the directors repudiated the contract and were sued. Their defence was that the contract was ultra vires, outside the memorandum and had been of no effect from the first. The court held that a contract made by the directors of such a company on a matter not included in the memorandum of association was not binding on the company. Indeed, the court went further than this and decided that such a contract could not be rendered binding on the company even though it was expressly assented to by all the shareholders. This was because of a principle of agency law that an agent (in this case a director) cannot have more power than the principal (in this case the company). It is possible that this part of the decision would not have been laid down in such absolute terms if it were not for the fact that it was in those days impossible to alter the memorandum of association. Such an alteration was possible after 1890 but was made easier after 1948. However, *Ashbury* and cases like it laid the foundation stones of the doctrine of ultra vires, these being that a contract made in an area not covered by the objects is of no legal effect and that such a contract cannot be made effective by a vote of the shareholders. Although the doctrine could be advantageous to a company where it was used to avoid a contract which had become onerous, it could also be a burden. For example, banks or other companies might be reluctant to deal with a company where the objects of that company were unknown to the contracting partner, where they were narrowly drawn or of uncertain ambit. The courts had decided in *Re Crown Bank* (1890) 44 Ch D 634 that a proper statement of objects had not been made where the objects of the company were expressed in such wide terms as to be (in the words of North J):

> so wide that it might be said to warrant the company in giving up banking business and embarking in a business with the object of establishing a line of balloons between the earth and the moon.

The courts did, however, determine that it was permissible to achieve a similar effect by listing every imaginable kind of business. In *Cotman v Brougham* [1918] AC 514, the company's memorandum had 30 sub-clauses enabling the company to carry on almost any kind of business, and the objects clause concluded with a declaration that every sub-clause should be construed as a substantive clause and not limited or restricted by reference to any other sub-clause or by the name of the company, and that none of such sub-clauses or the objects specified therein should be deemed subsidiary or auxiliary merely to the objects mentioned in the first sub-clause.

The last part of this statement of objects was there to avoid a restriction which the courts had been prone to place on statements of objects. They had construed them according to a 'main objects' rule. This meant that the main object of the company could be determined either from the name of the company or from the first named object on the list of objects. All subsequent statements in the objects clause would then be considered to be powers of the company which could only be validly exercised for the purpose of furthering the 'main' object. In *Cotman v Brougham*, the draftsman had drafted the statement of objects to avoid this rule and also sought to avoid the *Re Crown Bank* restriction by the long list of 30 objects. His attempt was successful. It was held that the memorandum must be construed according to its literal meaning, although the practice of drafting memoranda in this way was criticised.

A further extension of the liberty given to companies came with the acceptance of the 'subjective clause' in *Bell Houses Ltd v City Wall Properties Ltd* [1966] 2 QB 656. In that case, the company's memorandum of association contained the following clause:

> 3(c) To carry on any other trade or business whatsoever which can, in the opinion of the board of directors, be advantageously carried on by [the plaintiff company] in connection with or as ancillary to any of the above businesses or the general business [of the company].

It must be noted that this clause is more restricted than the one found to be an improper statement of objects in *Re Crown Bank*, particularly because it refers to the business already being carried on by the company and requires that the business justified under this clause must be compatible with business permitted by other clauses in the memorandum. If objects as wide as those in *Re Crown Bank* were accepted, the company would be permitted to carry on two competing businesses.

The subjective element in the *Bell Houses* case comes in the reference to the 'opinion of the directors'. With reference to this clause, Danckwerts LJ said in *Bell Houses*:

> On the balance of the authorities it would appear that the opinion of the directors if bona fide can dispose of the matter; and why should it not decide the matter? The shareholders subscribe their money on the basis of the memorandum of association and if that confers the power on the directors to decide whether in their opinion it is proper to undertake particular business in the circumstances specified, why should not their decision be binding?

4.4.4   Objects and powers

We have seen that the memorandum should contain a statement of objects. We have also seen that sometimes the statement of objects would be construed so as to discern a 'main' object and ancillary objects which could only be exercised in order to further the company's main objects.

There are two further complications to this picture. One is that the 'long list' *Cotman v Brougham* approach may list objects and also ancillary objects or powers necessary for the attainment of those objects. The memorandum may then contain a clause that all the clauses and sub-clauses are 'independent objects' and none of them subsidiary to the others. This raises the question as to whether there is any essential distinction between objects and powers, and, if so, what it is and how each may be identified.

The second complication is that all companies are covered by the doctrine of 'implied powers' whereby the law will assume that all powers necessary for the attainment of a lawful objective are possessed by the body seeking to achieve the objective.

In view of these numerous complications it is perhaps unsurprising that the courts seem to have occasionally lost their way in the maze and confused objects and powers.

4.4.5   Ultra vires and objects

Strictly speaking, the doctrine of ultra vires should apply only to objects. However, on numerous occasions, the courts have found that the company has acted outside its powers and held the act to be ultra vires. Many examples of this confusion concerned cases which either involved the company borrowing money in excess of its powers to do so or giving money away. An example of the latter is *Hutton v West Cork Railway Company* (1883) 23 Ch D 654. In that case the company was about to be dissolved. A resolution was passed to the effect that money would be paid by the company to its officials as compensation for loss of office and to other directors who had never received remuneration for their work. The Court of Appeal held that payments of this sort would be invalid. Bowen LJ said:

> Most businesses require liberal dealings. The test … is not whether it is *bona fide*, but whether, as well as being done *bona fide*, it is done within the ordinary scope of the company's business, and whether it is reasonably incidental to the carrying on of the company's business for the company's benefit … a company which always treated its employees with Draconian severity, and never allowed them a single inch more than the strict letter of the bond, would soon find itself deserted – at all events, unless labour was very much more easy to obtain in the market than it often is. The law does not say that there are to be no cakes and ale, but that there are to be no cakes and ale except such as are required for the benefit of the company.

It must be noted that this discussion related to the exercise of a power of the company; giving away money was something which the company had the power to do, but the Court of Appeal suggested in this case that such a gift would be invalid if it were not exercised bona fide for the benefit of the company. Similar restrictions were placed on the exercise of a power to give a gift for the furtherance of scientific education in *Evans v Brunner Mond* [1921] 1 Ch 359. It is noteworthy that in that case the 'power' in question was no different from the implied powers a company would be assumed to have, but in this instance they had been enshrined in the memorandum. Although accepting restrictions similar to those in *Hutton*, in this case the court held that it would be for the benefit of the company to increase the 'reservoir' of trained experts by making a gift which would benefit scientific education.

4.4.6 Knowledge by an outsider that a transaction is outside objects or powers

The ultra vires problem has also frequently arisen where borrowing powers are at issue. In *Re David Payne & Co Ltd* [1904] 2 Ch 608, the court held that where borrowing was for an ultra vires purpose but this was unknown to the lender, the loan could be recovered. In that case, the loan money could have been applied by the directors for intra or ultra vires purposes. The fact that the directors chose to apply the money to ultra vires purposes was a matter for which the directors could be called to account by the shareholders, as being a breach of their duties. It was not a matter which ought to affect the rights of the lender. It would have been different if the lender had notice that the money would be applied for ultra vires purposes. That was the situation in *Re Jon Beauforte (London) Ltd* [1953] Ch 131. The company's memorandum authorised the business of dressmaking. However, at the relevant time, the business carried on was that of veneered panel manufacture. On notepaper which clearly indicated that this was the current business of the company, a supply of coke was ordered. The court held that as the coke supplier had had notice of the fact that the current business of the company was an ultra vires business, the contract for the supply of coke was void and he would therefore not be paid. The validity of the contract in this case depends on the knowledge of the outsider. If he knows that the transaction is outside the powers of the company, the transaction will be unenforceable. We have to remember that the outsider was deemed to have constructive knowledge of the objects of the company under the doctrine of constructive notice (see Section 4.4.1 above), which has now been abolished.

4.4.7   Can borrowing ever be an object?

We have seen that one of the ploys used by draftsmen in order to ensure that a memorandum is as widely drafted as possible, is to insert a clause elevating the long list of clauses to the status of objects. This is added in an attempt to avoid the 'main objects' rule of construction. Despite the finding in *Cotman v Brougham* (see Section 4.4.3) that a memorandum should be read literally, the court held that such an 'elevation' clause was ineffective in the case of borrowing. In *Introductions Ltd v National Provincial Bank Ltd* [1970] Ch 199, there was a provision in the objects clause that the company could 'borrow or raise money in such manner as the company shall think fit'. There was also a clause which expressly declared 'that each of the preceding sub-clauses shall be construed independently of and shall be in no way limited by reference to any other sub-clause and that the objects set out in each sub-clause are independent objects of the company'. Harman LJ said:

> you cannot convert a power into an object merely by saying so ... I agree with the judge that it is a necessarily implied addition to a power to borrow whether express or implied, that you should add 'for the purposes of the company'.

The reason for this restriction is that it makes no commercial sense to have a company with the sole object of 'borrowing'. The judges reasoned from this that borrowing could not be an object or objective but only a power exercised in order to achieve another object.

In that case the judge found that the borrowing was ultra vires, and consequently the contract involved in that borrowing could not be relied on. As we have seen, this goes beyond the original doctrine which held that only actions outside the objects would be void.

4.4.8   1980s cases

Cases decided in the 1980s limited the ultra vires doctrine to a considerable extent. In *Re Halt Garage (1964) Ltd* [1982] 3 All ER 1016, Oliver J was faced with the task of deciding whether payments made to directors just prior to the liquidation of the company were valid, or whether the money could be recovered by the liquidator. There was a power to make payments but the company had been in some financial difficulty at the time when the payments had been made. Oliver J held that if the power to make payments had genuinely been exercised and the payments were not some other transaction in disguise, then they could not be challenged on the grounds that they were ultra vires. The judge refused to accept tests which had been put forward in older authorities which would have resulted in the payments being held to be ultra vires if they were not made in good faith and for the benefit of the company.

Similarly in *Re Horsley & Weight Ltd* [1982] Ch 442, the question was the validity of a pension which had been purchased by the company for a retiring director. The court held that the grant of the pension could fall within a clause of the memorandum which was capable of describing objects, and if that were the case, no question of deciding whether or not the action benefited the company arose – it was valid. The judgment of Buckley LJ contains some interesting observations on what can be considered objects and what can only ever be powers, no matter that the memorandum contains an 'elevation' clause. He said:

> It has now long been a common practice to set out in memoranda of association a great number and variety of 'objects', so called, some of which (for example, to borrow money, to promote the company's interest by advertising its products or services, or to do acts or things conducive to the company's objects) are by their very nature incapable of standing as independent objects which can be pursued in isolation as the sole activity of the company. Such 'objects' must, by reason of their very nature, be interpreted merely as powers incidental to the true objects of the company and must be so treated notwithstanding the presence of a separate objects clause ... *ex hypothesi* an implied power can only legitimately be used in a way which is ancillary or incidental to the pursuit of an authorised object of the company, for it is the practical need to imply the power in order to enable the company effectively to pursue its authorised objects which justifies the implication of the power. So an exercise of an implied power can only be *intra vires* the company if it is ancillary or incidental to the pursuit of an authorised object. So, also, in the case of express 'objects' which upon construction of the memorandum or by their very nature are ancillary to the dominant or main objects of the company, an exercise of any such powers can only be *intra vires* if it is in fact ancillary or incidental to the pursuit of some such dominant or main object.
>
> On the other hand, the doing of an act which is expressed to be, and capable of being, an independent object of the company cannot be *ultra vires*, for it is by definition something which the company is formed to do and so must be *intra vires* ... [counsel] submits that ... a capacity to grant pensions to directors or ex-directors, is of its nature a power enabling the company to act as a good employer in the course of carrying on its business, and as such is an incidental power which must be treated as though it were expressly subject to a limitation that it can only be exercised in circumstances in which the grant of a pension will benefit the company's business. I do not feel able to accept this contention. Paragraph (o) must be read as a whole. In includes not only pensions and other disbursements which will benefit directors, employees and their dependants, but also making grants for charitable, benevolent or public purposes or objects. The objects of a company do not need to be commercial; they can be charitable or philanthropic; indeed they can be whatever the original incorporators wish, provided that they are legal. Nor is there any reason why a company should not part with its funds gratuitously or for non-commercial reasons if to do so is within its declared objects.

This case was affirmed in *Rolled Steel Products v British Steel Corporation* [1985] Ch 246 where Slade LJ, after an extensive review of the authorities, set out the following conclusions:

(1) The basic rule is that a company incorporated under the Companies Acts only has the capacity to do those acts which fall within its objects as set out in its memorandum of association or are reasonably incidental to the attainment or pursuit of those objects. Ultimately, therefore, the question whether a particular transaction is within or outside its capacity must depend on the true construction of the memorandum.

(2) Nevertheless, if a particular act ... is of a category which, on the true construction of the company's memorandum, is capable of being performed as reasonably incidental to the attainment or pursuit of its objects, it will not be rendered *ultra vires* the company merely because in a particular instance its directors, in performing the act in its name, are in truth doing so for purposes other than those set out in its memorandum. Subject to any express restrictions on the relevant power which may be construed in the memorandum, the state of mind or knowledge of the persons managing the company's affairs or of the persons dealing with it is irrelevant in considering questions of corporate capacity.

(3) While due regard must be paid to any express conditions attached to or limitations on powers contained in a company's memorandum (e.g. a power to borrow only up to a specified amount), the court will not ordinarily construe a statement in a memorandum that a particular power is exercisable 'for the purposes of the company' as a condition limiting the company's

corporate capacity to exercise the power; it will regard it as simply imposing a limit on the authority of the directors: see the *David Payne* case [Section 4.4.6].

(4) At least in default of the unanimous consent of all the shareholders ... the directors of a company will not have actual authority from the company to exercise any express or implied power other than for the purposes of the company as set out in its memorandum of association.

(5) A company holds out its directors as having ostensible authority [for a discussion of actual and ostensible authority, see Section 4.5.6] to bind the company to any transaction which falls within the powers expressly or impliedly conferred on it by its memorandum of association. Unless he is put on notice to the contrary, a person dealing in good faith with a company which is carrying on an intra vires business is entitled to assume that its directors are properly exercising such powers for the purposes of the company as set out in the memorandum. Correspondingly, such a person in such circumstances can hold the company to any transactions of this nature.

(6) If, however, a person dealing with a company is on notice that the directors are exercising the relevant power for purposes other than the purposes of the company, he cannot rely on the ostensible authority of the directors and, on ordinary principles of agency, cannot hold the company to the transaction.

The practical effect of these decisions seems to be that if an act could be justified by reference to an object of the company, the transaction could not be challenged. If the act could be justified by reference to a power of the company then the transaction would be valid unless the power was being used as a disguise for another purpose and the outsider was on notice of this. An action may also be valid if it can be justified by reference to an implied power, that is, that it was done bona fide in furthering the objects of a company. This interpretation is supported by *Halifax Building Society v Meridian Housing Association* [1994] 2 BCLC 540, which also makes plain a further area in which the complex case law will still be relevant. Many companies in the 'regulated sector', that is, insurance companies, building societies and friendly societies, have their objects restricted by statute as well as by their rules. This case makes it plain that the old rules will be used to determine the validity of acts of such companies, and this will still be the case for charitable companies. In that case, Mrs Arden J held that a development of mixed offices and residential accommodation was 'reasonably incidental to the pursuit' of the objects of Meridian, which were 'to carry on the industry, business or trade of providing housing or any associated amenities'.

4.5   The power to bind the company

4.5.1   Power of directors to bind the company

Even if an action is within the capacity of the company, it may be outside the powers of the individuals who are involved in the transaction. Rules have been formulated, therefore, to determine in what circumstances a company will be bound, notwithstanding that the individual does not have the power to carry out the transaction in question. A diagrammatic way through these complicated provisions is to be found in Figure 4.1 below.

There are two regimes, under the common law and under the Companies Act 2006. These overlap to a considerable extent. Under the common law, persons outside a company are entitled to assume that internal procedures have been complied with. This is a consequence of *Royal British Bank v Turquand* (1856) 6 E&B 327. That case involved an

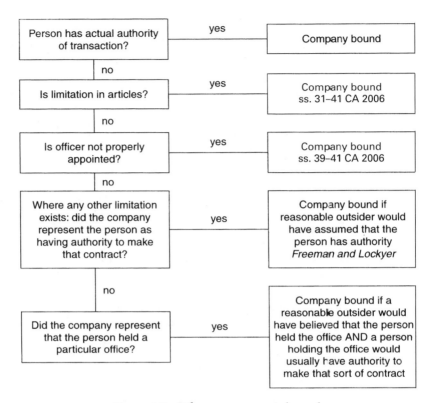

Figure 4.1 When a company is bound

action for the return of money borrowed from the plaintiff by the official manager of a company. The company argued that it was not bound by the actions of the official manager in this case. This was because the company's deed of settlement contained the following clause:

> That the Board of Directors may borrow on mortgage, bond or bill in the name of, and if necessary under the common seal of, the Company such sum or sums of money as shall from time to time, by a resolution passed at a general meeting of the Company, be authorised to be borrowed: provided that the total amount of the sum or sums of money so borrowed shall not at any time exceed two thirds of the total amount on the instalments on the capital of the Company paid up or called for, and actually due and payable at the time of, the passing of such resolution.

No resolution as required by this clause had been passed. The court held that the plaintiff had no knowledge that the resolution had not been passed, and that it did not appear from the face of the public document (the contents of which the plaintiffs were deemed to know) that the borrowing was invalid. The company was therefore bound.

Outsiders are therefore entitled to assume that internal procedures, such as the passing of the resolution in *Turquand's* case, have been complied with. This is now confirmed by sections 40 and 161 of the Companies Act 2006. Section 40 reads:

(1) In favour of a person dealing with a company in good faith, the power of the directors to bind the company, or authorise others to do so, is deemed to be free of any limitation under the company's constitution.

(2) For this purpose—

    (a) a person 'deals with' a company if he is a party to any transaction or other act to which the company is a party,

    (b) a person dealing with a company—

        (i)   is not bound to enquire as to any limitation on the powers of the directors to bind the company or authorise others to do so,

        (ii) is presumed to have acted in good faith unless the contrary is proved, and

        (iii) is not to be regarded as acting in bad faith by reason only of his knowing that an act is beyond the powers of the directors under the company's constitution.

Section 40 is examined in further detail below. Under section 161(1) of the 2006 Act:

The acts of a person acting as a director are valid notwithstanding that it is afterwards discovered—

(a) that there was a defect in his appointment,

(b) that he was disqualified from holding office,

(c) that he had ceased to hold office,

(d) that he was not entitled to vote on the matter in question.

For almost all company law disputes, these provisions will provide comprehensive protection for third parties dealing with a company. The exceptions are as follows:

1. where the third party can be proved to be acting in bad faith (see Section 4.5.5 below);

2. where the transaction involves a director or connected person and where the dealing is not with a 'person acting as director' or a person authorised by an acting director but with some other actor (see Section 4.5.6 below); and

3. where there is scope for argument about the 'usual authority' of any party (see *Panorama Developments v Fidelis Furnishing* in Section 4.5.6 below).

Section 41(2) of the 2006 Act provides the exception to the general rule where the parties to a transaction include the company and either:

    (i)   a director of that company or of its holding company, or

    (ii) a person connected with any such director …

(see Section 8.6.4 for an explanation of these terms). If the parties include such persons (there may be other parties as well) then the situation is as follows:

1. the transaction is voidable at the instance of the company in respect of persons in categories (i) and (ii) above;

2. each of the persons within categories (i) and (ii) above and any director who authorised the transaction is liable to account to the company for any gain made, or indemnify the company for any loss it suffers as a result of the transaction;

3. as regards parties to the transaction other than those in categories (i) and (ii), they remain protected by the provisions of section 40 of the Companies Act 2006, but in that case the court may, if such a person or the company applies, make an order affirming, severing or setting aside the transaction on such terms as appear to the court to be just.

4.5.2 Protection

One thing that is quite clear from section 40 is that it is intended to benefit only an outsider dealing with the company in question. It cannot be used in any way by the company whose action is in question in order to save a transaction. The section could, of course, be used by a company dealing with another company, but only in order to benefit the company whose action is not questionable on constitutional grounds.

4.5.3 Transaction and dealing

The previous law contained an uncertainty about the ambit of the references to 'transaction' and 'dealing'. There was some doubt about whether a gift would be included. This is covered by section 40(2)(a):

> a person 'deals with' a company if he is party to any transaction or other act to which the company is a party.

4.5.4 Decided on by the directors

The law used to require a transaction to be 'decided on by the directors'. It was not clear what degree of delegation was permissible before a transaction became one which was decided on by someone other than 'the directors'. For example, if the directors decided that as a matter of policy they would attempt to move towards making the company environmentally friendly, was it a transaction 'decided on by the directors' when an expensive piece of de-polluting equipment was ordered by a plant manager? A similar problem arose if decisions were taken by a single director. If there was no express delegation of power to him to take decisions in that area, were his acts in pursuance of decisions by the directors? This delegation point is also covered by section 40(1), which provides:

> In favour of a person dealing with a company in good faith, the power of the board of directors to bind the company, or authorise others to do so, shall be deemed to be free of any limitation under the company's constitution.

4.5.5 Good faith

Section 40 applies if the third party is 'dealing with a company in good faith'. The outsider is presumed to be dealing in good faith unless the contrary is proved (s 40(2)(b)(ii)). This means that a company has to prove the absence of good faith if it wishes to avoid being bound. The meaning of the phrase 'good faith' is not clear. In *International Sales and Agencies v Marcus* [1982] 3 All ER 551, Lawson J, referring to the First European Company Law Directive for guidance, came to the conclusion that:

> the defendants had actual knowledge that the payments to them were in breach of duty and trust and were ultra vires the companies … alternatively, at the lowest, that the defendants could not in all the circumstances have been unaware of the unlawful nature of the payments that they received.

In these circumstances the allegation that the defendants were not dealing in good faith had been proved. However, this finding did not help where the lack of good faith was less clear. Could behaviour less blameworthy qualify as bad faith? Did the bad faith relate solely to issues of constitutional irregularity, or would an unconnected allegation be sufficient to prevent recovery? The only guidance we have is that a third party 'is not to be regarded as acting in bad faith by reason only of his knowing that an act is beyond the powers of the directors under the company's constitution' (s 40(2)(b)(iii)). Thus the dealings in *International Sales v Marcus* could be impugned only on the breach of duty and trust ground, not on the ground that they were outside the powers of directors. Presumably the allegation of bad faith would need to show that the directors were breaching their duties in ways which were merely going beyond their powers. Maybe an allegation such as conflict of interest and duty will be necessary.

The following case was decided under the 1985 Act, but, in view of the similarity of the wording of the 1985 provision with that in the Companies Act 2006, may well still be relevant. In *EIC Services Ltd & Another v Phipps & Others* [2004] EWCA Civ 1069, the Court of Appeal clarified the exact scope of section 35A of the Companies Act 1985. According to the Court, 'in the context of the company the term "third parties" naturally refers to persons other than the company and its members' (at [37]). The controversy had been raised after the ruling in *Smith v Henniker-Major & Co* [2002] EWCA Civ 762. In the *EIC* case, a director was assigned a right of action by an inquorate board. A quorum of two directors was required by the articles of association of the company in question but only one director attended. Thus, since the assignment was not valid, the director did not have the standing to engage in the relevant action. The interesting point in the case is that the particular director sought to resort to section 35A. According to section 35A(2)(b), 'a person shall not be regarded as acting in bad faith by reason of only his knowing that an act is beyond the powers of directors under the company's constitution'. The particularity of this case was that the person who should not be regarded in bad faith because he was aware that the director was acting beyond the powers vested to him by the constitution was the director himself. He also sought to resort to section 35A(2)(c) of the 1985 Act, which stated that a person, here the director himself, should be presumed to have acted in good faith unless the opposite was proved. On appeal the decision was taken by a majority. The basic question in accordance with paragraph [118] of the judgment was: Did section 35A enable a director, who had made an honest mistake as to the meaning of a provision in the articles of the company of which he was a director, himself to rely on his own mistake in order to give validity to something which would lack validity were it not for that mistake? To that question Robert Walker LJ gave an affirmative answer and Carnwath LJ and Rimer J a negative answer. Robert Walker LJ believed that a director in such a case could justifiably resort to section 35A, but he supported that the validity of the agreement could still be challenged on the basis of section 322A of the 1985 Act (predecessor to section 41 of the Companies Act 2006), which, however, was not the case in *Smith*. Carnwath and Schiemann LJJ accepted that the word 'person' in the framework of section 35A was wide enough to include a director of a company; however, they both agreed that section 35A inhibited a director who was the author of his own misfortune from profiting vis-à-vis third parties from his own mistake. In contrast, section 322A of the 1985 Act was found to deal with a different problem, namely, with what a company can do vis-à-vis its own director who has overstepped the mark. In practice section 322A prevailed. This case revealed a confusion over the application of the two aforementioned sections and the relevant concepts.

From the interpretation of section 35A of the 1985 Act it is revealed that a validly convened and constituted board of directors may confer authority to a given director to act in a certain way. But this authority is not vested in the director just because he is incorrectly convinced he is in possession of it. The fact that a director can still bind the company in an agreement with a third party even if he does not have actual authority to enter such an agreement, but only ostensible authority, is a different issue, dealt with under the following section on 'Unauthorised agents'.

4.5.6   Unauthorised agents

Despite the reform of the law, a problem remains in that a person purporting to act for a company may actually have no connection whatsoever with that company. In those circumstances it would be wholly unfair to hold the company to a contract purportedly made on its behalf by someone who may be no more than a confidence trickster. If X purports to sell Tower Bridge to Y, should the Tower Bridge Company Ltd (supposing that they own the bridge) be bound? Obviously if there is no connection between X and the Tower Bridge Company Ltd, that course would be wholly unfair. However, if Y reasonably believes that X is authorised, because of the actions of the Tower Bridge Company Ltd, then the company ought to be bound. Although much complicated terminology is used in the cases, the law seems to achieve this result.

In *Freeman & Lockyer v Buckhurst Park Properties Ltd* [1964] 2 QB 480, the plaintiff was a firm of architects and surveyors. The firm was engaged by a person acting as the defendant's managing director. The firm's claim for fees was repudiated on the grounds that the apparent managing director had not been validly appointed. The Court of Appeal upheld the plaintiff's claim. Diplock LJ said:

> It is necessary at the outset to distinguish between an 'actual' authority of an agent on the one hand, and an 'apparent' or 'ostensible' authority on the other. Actual authority and apparent authority are quite independent of one another. Generally they co-exist and coincide, but either may exist without the other and their respective scopes may be different. As I shall endeavour to show, it is on the apparent authority of the agent that the contractor normally relies in the ordinary course of business when entering into contracts.
>
> An actual authority is a legal relationship between principal and agent created by a consensual agreement to which they alone are parties. Its scope is to be ascertained by applying ordinary principles of construction of contracts, including any proper implications from the express words used, the usages of the trade, or the course of business between the parties. To this agreement the contractor is a stranger; he may be totally ignorant of the existence of any authority on the part of the agent. Nevertheless, if the agent does enter into a contract pursuant to the 'actual' authority, it does create contractual rights and liabilities between the principal and the contractor …
>
> An 'apparent' or 'ostensible' authority, on the other hand, is a legal relationship between the principal and the contractor created by a representation, made by the principal to the contractor, intended to be and in fact acted on by the contractor, that the agent has authority to enter on behalf of the principal into a contract of a kind within the scope of the 'apparent' authority, so as to render the principal liable to perform any obligations imposed on him by such a contract … The representation, when acted on by the contractor, by entering into a contract with the agent, operates as an estoppel, preventing the principal from asserting that he is not bound by the contract. It is irrelevant whether the agent had actual authority to enter into the contract.
>
> In ordinary business dealings the contractor at the time of entering into the contract can in the nature of things hardly ever rely on the 'actual' authority of the agent. His information as to the authority must be derived either from the principal or from the agent or from both, for they alone know what the agent's actual authority is. All that the contractor can know is what they tell him,

which may or may not be true ... The representation which creates 'apparent' authority may take a variety of forms of which the commonest is representation by conduct, ie by permitting the agent to act in some way in the conduct of the principal's business with other persons. By doing so the principal represents to anyone who becomes aware that the agent is so acting that the agent has authority to enter on behalf of the principal into contracts with other persons of the kind which an agent so acting in the conduct of his principal's business has normally 'actual' authority to enter into ... [U]nlike a natural person [a company] can only make a representation through an agent, [this] has the consequence that, in order to create an estoppel between the corporation and the contractor, the representation as to the authority of the agent which creates his 'apparent' authority must be made by some person or persons who have 'actual' authority from the corporation to make the representation ... the contractor cannot rely on the agent's own representation as to his actual authority. He can rely only on a representation by a person or persons who have actual authority to manage or conduct that part of the business of the corporation to which the contract relates ... If the foregoing analysis of the relevant law is correct, it can be summarised by stating four conditions which must be fulfilled to entitle a contractor to enforce against a company a contract entered into on behalf of the company by an agent who had no actual authority to do so. It must be shown: (a) that a representation that the agent had authority to enter on behalf of the company into a contract of the kind sought to be enforced was made to the contractor; (b) that such representation was made by a person or persons who had 'actual' authority to manage the business of the company either generally or in respect of those matters to which the contract relates; (c) that he (the contractor) was induced by such representation to enter into the contract, ie that he in fact relied on it; and (d) that under its memorandum or articles of association the company was not deprived of the capacity either to enter into a contract of the kind sought to be enforced or to delegate authority to enter into a contract of that kind to the agent.

The advent of the Companies Act 1989 has almost certainly caused condition (d) to disappear. The outsider will need to show that the other party to the contract appeared, because of some actions by those actually entitled to represent the company, to be empowered to bind the company to the particular transaction in question. This may be because the company in some way represents that he has authority to enter into the particular transaction in question, or because the company make it appear that he holds a particular position or job within the company (often that of managing director). In the latter case, it is necessary for the outsider to go one step further and show that an officer of that kind 'usually' may bind the company to the type of transaction in question, that is, that the company's alleged agent has 'usual' authority. Where a transaction is questioned on the grounds that the company's representative has no power to enter into it (other than because of limitations under the constitution, unless the outsider was acting in bad faith), the relevant questions are:

1. Did the person apparently representing the company have the authority to do so? If so, the contract is enforceable. If not:
2. Did the company lead the outsider to believe that the person apparently representing the company had the power to complete this particular transaction? If so, the contract is enforceable. If not:
3. Did the company lead the outsider to believe that the person apparently representing the company held a particular position in the company? If so and if a person validly appointed to that position would usually be able to complete the type of transaction in question, then the contract is enforceable.

An illustration of the last point made above is to be found in *Panorama Developments Ltd v Fidelis Furnishing Fabrics* [1971] 3 WLR 440. In that case, the company secretary hired cars from the plaintiff pretending that they were for the use of the defendant, but in fact they were for his own use. The Court of Appeal held that the defendant was bound by the contracts. Lord Denning MR said:

> Mr Hames' second point is this: he says that the company is not bound by the letters which were signed by Mr Bayne as 'Company Secretary'. He says that, on the authorities, a company secretary fulfils a very humble role: and that he has no authority to make any contracts or representations on behalf of the company. He refers to *Barnett, Hoares & Co. v South London Tramways Co* (1887) 18 QBD 815, where Esher MR said:
>
> > 'A secretary is a mere servant; his position is that he is to do what he is told, and no person can assume that he has any authority to represent anything at all.'
>
> But times have changed. A company secretary is a much more important person nowadays than he was in 1887. He is an officer of the company with extensive duties and responsibilities. This appears not only in the modern Companies Acts, but also by the role which he plays in the day-to-day business of companies. He is no longer a mere clerk. He regularly makes representations on behalf of the company and enters into contracts on its behalf which come within the day-to-day running of the company's business. So much so that he may be regarded as held out as having authority to do such things on behalf of the company. He is certainly entitled to sign contracts connected with the administrative side of the company's affairs, such as employing staff, and ordering cars, and so forth.

4.6 Promoters

One of the problems caused by the separate legal identity of the company is that prior to registration it has no existence at all. The persons who are responsible for the company's coming into existence are known as 'promoters'. The law imposes duties on them not unlike those owed by directors. This is because the company can be badly cheated at the outset, particularly by those who sell it the assets on which it will found its business.

4.6.1 Who are promoters?

In *Twycross v Grant* (1877) 2 CPD 469, Cockburn CJ said:

> A promoter, I apprehend, is one who undertakes to form a company with reference to a given project and to set it going and who takes the necessary steps to accomplish that purpose. That the defendants were promoters of the company from the beginning can admit of no doubt. They framed the scheme; they not only provisionally framed the company but were, in fact to the end its creators, they found the directors and qualified them, they prepared the prospectus; they paid for printing and advertising and the expenses incidental to bringing the undertaking before the world. In all these respects the directors were passive; without saying that they were in a legal sense the agents of the defendants, they were certainly their instruments.

This passage gives a clear indication of the actions which will be considered important by the courts when they are determining who was and who was not a promoter of a company. No stricter definition of a 'promoter' has been attempted because the situation can vary so widely. Investment of time or money in the enterprise will always be considered important. However, it is possible for a promoter not to have been obviously active. If he is the real 'power behind the throne', he will be held to have been a promoter. This is one case in which the court is committed to looking at the reality of the situation.

Promoters of the type found in the cases are extinct. It is unusual for a newly formed company to make an issue of shares to the public, and impossible to obtain a stock market listing without having been in business for some time. There is also an enormous body of law and regulation aimed at preventing the abuses that in the nineteenth century only the courts could prevent. Private companies do not issue shares to the public. Although they still have promoters in the sense described in the cases, the fact that those promoters are unable to defraud the public makes control of their activities less important. In spite of the obsolescence of this body of law, it is still valid law, so the present tense will be used throughout the following paragraphs to describe it.

4.6.2   Duties of promoters

Promoters are not trustees or agents of the company but they do stand in a special position in relation to the company. This is called a 'fiduciary' relationship, which means that some of the same duties that trustees owe to their beneficiaries will also be owed by promoters to their company.

Promoters are most likely to defraud the company and its future shareholders by selling to the company property that they have previously bought. Because they are usually in control of the company at the outset, they are able to determine the price that is paid. The temptation is to overvalue the property and fail to make disclosure of the overvaluation to an independent person. If that occurs then the company can reverse (rescind) the contract, that is, give back the property and get back the money. The situation differs, depending on when the property was acquired:

▶ *Situation 1 – If property is acquired before promotion commences* (see *Erlanger v New Sombrero Phosphate Co* (1878) 3 App Cas 1218; and *Omnium Electric Palace v Baines* [1914] 1 Ch 332)

If someone who subsequently becomes a promoter acquires property that is resold to the company, he may retain any profit that is made on that property provided he has made the correct disclosures (see 'Disclosure' below). This is so even if the property was acquired with the idea that at some time in the future a company would be formed and the property would be sold to it. The vital factor which needs to be identified is the time at which the promotion commences because different rules apply thereafter.

▶ *Situation 2 – If property is acquired after promotion commences*

If property is acquired by someone who has already become a promoter and that property is subsequently resold to the company, the courts will assume that the property was acquired for the company. Unless it can be proved that this was not the case, the promoter will be unable to make a profit out of that property and the company will have the option of rescinding the contract, or keeping the property and requiring the promoter to account for any profit he has made. This latter option is not open to the company in *Situation 1* above. It was held in *Omnium Electric Palace v Baines* [1914] 1 Ch 332 that proof that the property was not acquired on the company's behalf could consist of proof that the scheme had throughout been that the property should be bought and then resold to the company. The strange result of this seems to be that a profit may be kept if, throughout, the promoter had mercenary intentions. This is, of course, provided that the proper disclosures are made (as in *Situation 1*; and see 'Disclosure' below).

4.6.3 Disclosure

The general rule is that no promoter, whether in *Situation 1* or *Situation 2* above, can make a secret profit. Thus if any property belonging to a promoter is sold to a company, or if a promoter makes a profit on a transaction connected with the company's formation (see *Gluckstein v Barnes* [1900] AC 240), he will not in any event be permitted to keep that profit unless proper disclosure is made of the transaction. The difficulty is that frequently in this situation the same people are the promoters and the first directors. In *Gluckstein v Barnes* and *Erlanger v New Sombrero Phosphate Co* (1878) 3 App Cas 1218, it was suggested that the transaction must have the blessing of an independent board of directors before a promoter would be permitted to keep his profit. This would seem to be far too sweeping since it would invalidate all '*Salomon v Salomon*-type' transactions (see *Salomon v A Salomon & Co Ltd* [1897] AC 22). Nevertheless, the Court was vehement in *Erlanger*. Lord Cairns said:

> I do not say that the owner of property may not promote and form a joint stock company and then sell his property to it, but I do say that if he does he is bound to take care that he sells it to the company through the medium of a board of directors who can and do exercise an independent and intelligent judgment on the transaction.

This strict approach was not followed in *Lagunas Nitrate v Lagunas Syndicate* [1899] 2 Ch 392. In that case the company was formed and directed by a syndicate. The company was specifically formed to purchase part of the property of the syndicate which consisted of nitrate works. The syndicate and the board of directors were composed of the same people. The court held that the company was not entitled to rescission or damages in respect of the contract to purchase the property of the syndicate. Among the reasons given were:

1. At the date of the contract the company knew, because it appeared in its memorandum and articles, that its directors were also the vendors or agents of the vendor syndicate. The mere fact that the directors did not constitute an independent board was not a sufficient ground for setting aside the contract.
2. That there had been no misrepresentation made to, or any material fact concealed from, any of the persons who were members of the company at the date of the contract, those persons being the directors themselves.
3. The defendants as directors had not been guilty of such negligence or breach of trust as would render them liable to the company.

It would seem, then, that disclosure to an independent board or to the present and future shareholders via the articles will be sufficient disclosure. If this is done and the property was acquired before the buyer became a promoter, or was not acquired on behalf of the company, then the profit may be kept by the promoter.

Two other issues are relevant to this discussion: the loss of the right to rescission and the possibility of a remedy in damages.

1. *The loss of the right to rescission*

    Another reason that was given by the Court for the decision in *Lagunas* was that the alteration of the position of the parties as a result of the working of the land had so altered the position of the parties as to make rescission impossible. The remedy of rescission was not available because the contract could not be reversed. The parties could never be put back into the position that they were in before the contract was made. The loss of the remedy is particularly serious in *Situation 1* above. It has been held that where the right to rescission is lost, a company is unable to claim the alternative remedy of demanding that the promoter pay his profits to the company, neither is there a right to damages (see *Gover's Case* [1875] 1 Ch D 182; and *Re Cape Breton* (1885) 29 Ch D 795). In the second situation the company has that alternative.

2. *Claims for damages*

The leading case on damages for fraudulent misrepresentation is *Smith New Court Securities Ltd v Citibank NA and Others* [1996] 4 All ER 769, where the House of Lords ruled that where a plaintiff acquired shares in reliance on a fraudulent misrepresentation, he was entitled to recover the entire loss sustained as a direct consequence of the transaction even where the loss was not foreseeable. Their Lordships held that this would include the full price paid, less any benefit received as a result of the transaction. As a general rule, the benefit received would include the market value of the property acquired at the date of its acquisition, unless:

(a) the misrepresentation continued to operate after the date of acquisition so as to induce the plaintiff to retain the asset; or
(b) the circumstances of the case were such that the plaintiff was, by reason of the fraud, locked into the property.

Further, the plaintiff was entitled to receive consequential losses.

4.6.4   Remuneration of promoters

Promoters do not have a right to remuneration simply because such a right is included in the articles of association (see Chapter 3). Any contract purportedly made with the company before it was formed will equally not be binding on the company (see 'Pre-incorporation contracts' below). To receive remuneration, or even recoup preliminary expenses, the promoter must prove the existence of a binding contract with the company (see *Re National Motor Mail Coach Co* [1908] 2 Ch 515). Section 553 of the Companies Act 2006 is of relevance here, but only permits a company to pay underwriting commission to a promoter if the articles so permit. To enforce a right to this and any other remuneration, the promoter will need to show that the company is contractually bound to pay him.

4.6.5   Pre-incorporation contracts

Until a company is registered it has no existence of any kind. Sometimes promoters wish to enter into contracts which are intended to be for the benefit of the company, and/or the liability under those contracts is intended to be the company's liability. This may be done in order for the public to see, when they are asked to subscribe for shares, that the company is more than just an 'empty shell'. This would be an unusual situation now, when shares are so rarely offered to the public immediately after a company is formed. It may be done simply to 'get things going'. In any event, the promoter must be careful, since it is not possible to act for a non-existent person. The position at common law was confused, but section 51 of the Companies Act 2006 now provides as follows:

51 Pre-incorporation contracts, deeds and obligations

(1) A contract that purports to be made by or on behalf of a company at a time when the company has not been formed has effect, subject to any agreement to the contrary, as one made with the person purporting to act for the company or as agent for it, and he is personally liable on the contract accordingly.

(2) Subsection (1) applies—

(a) to the making of a deed under the law of England and Wales, and Northern Ireland,

(b) to the undertaking of an obligation under the law of Scotland,

as it applies to the making of a contract.

This is unchanged from section 36C of the Companies Act 1985, so that cases under that provision will still be valid.

The promoter is thus personally liable on any pre-incorporation contract. A wide interpretation of the section was adopted in *Phonogram v Lane* [1981] 3 WLR 736. It was held that the company need not actually be in the process of formation for the section to apply and that there need be no representation that the company was already in existence. Further, it was held that the words in the section 'subject to any agreement to the contrary' would prevent the operation of the section only if there was an express agreement that the person who was signing was not to be liable.

However, in other situations a narrow interpretation of the provision was favoured. In *Oshkosh B'Gosh Inc v Dan Marbel Inc Ltd* [1989] BCLC 507, the Court of Appeal held that the section did not apply when the company was in existence at the time when the relevant contracts were made. The promoters were about to buy the company 'off the shelf'. This was held to be the case even though the company had since changed its name. Further, in *Cotronic (UK) Ltd v Dezonie* [1991] BCLC 721, it was held (also by the Court of Appeal) that the provision did not apply when a person purported to make a contract for a company which once existed but has been dissolved.

Since the contract is said to have 'effect' as one entered into by the person purporting to act for the company, it would seem likely that the contract will be enforceable by him as well as against him.

An interesting question was raised in *Braymist Ltd & Others v Wise Finance Company Ltd* [2002] EWCA Civ 127. In this case the solicitor of Braymist signed a contract for the sale of land. The principal point of attention is the fact that Braymist, the vendor, was not in existence at the time the agreement was signed. Later, the other party to the contract refused to go on with it, and the solicitors of Braymist, who also acted as its agents, sought to enforce the contract against the purchaser by virtue of section 36C(1) of the 1985 Act. Thus, the question was whether an agent is not only liable on the contract where his principal is a company in course of formation, but also entitled to sue on it. The Court of Appeal decided that the agent, the solicitor in this case, was not only liable for the contract but could also sue for its breach. The enforcement of the pre-incorporation contract could therefore be pursued by the agent as well.

It is unfortunate that the reform of this area of the law did not go so far as to permit the company to adopt the contract by passing a resolution to that effect in a general meeting. This 'ratification' procedure has been held not to make the company liable (see *Re Northumberland Avenue Hotel Co* (1866) 33 Ch D 16). The company will still not be liable even though all persons concerned act as if the company is bound and large sums of money are spent in the belief that the contract is binding on the company. In certain circumstances a new contract between the original non-promoter party and the company may be deduced from the circumstances, but this will be rare. It is a new contract that is necessary, either expressed or implied. In *Howard v Patent Ivory Co* (1888) 38 Ch D 156, the circumstances were such that a new contract could be inferred. In that case, the contract was made before the company was formed. After formation, the contract was the subject of a resolution passed by the company at a meeting at which the other party to the contract was present. It is significant that the resolution altered the original terms of the agreement. In these circumstances the court could find that there had been a new contract (a novation) formed between the company and the party to the original contract. It is only in this sort of circumstance that a company could be sued on a contract made before its formation by its promoters. It is impossible for a company simply to adopt or ratify a pre-incorporation contract.

Summary

4.1 Under the common law, if an act of a company was not authorised by the objects clause in the memorandum, it was ultra vires the company and of no effect. A director could not bind the company when acting outside of the objects of the company.

4.2 Under the old law, the doctrine of constructive notice applied and everyone was held to know the contents of the memorandum and articles of a company.

4.3 The Companies Act 2006 imperfectly abolishes the doctrine, leaving it open to (a) a shareholder who discovers in advance that an ultra vires action is planned and seeks an injunction, and (b) a member who alleges that there is a breach of duty by a director because he is acting ultra vires, to raise the issue of ultra vires, whereupon the whole of the old case law in relation to a potential breach of duty may become relevant.

4.4 The Companies Act 2006 renders a contract signed by the director outside of the objects of the company valid and absolutely enforceable. The third party is protected unless acting in bad faith. Bad faith in this case is interpreted in very restrictive terms.

4.5 Directors may act within the objects of the company but outside their own personal capacity to act as the company is defined by the company's articles of association. Sections 40 and 161 of the Companies Act 2006 clarify that the third party would be protected in this case too, rendering the contract valid and enforceable. Directors with an actual authority to bind the company will do so even when acting outside the limits set by the articles on their powers.

4.6 Invalidly appointed individuals to directorships or individuals who are not associated with the company may also bind the company into a contract with the third party if the latter is justified in believing that the person in question was acting on behalf of the company within his capacity as a director. A representation on the part of the director would trigger his apparent authority which would result in the enforceability of the contract.

4.7 Matters of directorial liability within the company context are disassociated with the validity of the agreements between the company and the third parties.

4.8 Promoters can sign agreements before the incorporation of the company, but those agreements will bind them personally. The legal person does not exist and therefore it cannot be bound. Should the company decide to pass a novation at its general meeting to adopt the agreement in question, the agreement will bind the company from that point and onwards.

Exercises

4.1 What is an ultra vires contract?

4.2 Is an ultra vires contract valid? And if so, are there any grounds on the basis of which the validity of the contract may be challenged?

4.3 Does the validity of an ultra vires contract impact on the liability of a director for having signed such a contract on behalf of the company?

4.4 Distinguish the various types of authority which may equip a person to make a binding contract on behalf of a company.

4.5 Who are the promoters?

4.6 Can the promoters bind the company with a pre-incorporation contract?

Chapter 5

Shares

Key terms

▶ **Nominal value** – a fixed amount of money which shareholders pay for their shares. They are not allowed to buy a share which is discounted but the share may be more expensive, the extra cost over the nominal value being known as a 'share premium' (Companies Act 2006, s 542).

▶ **Offer to the public** – only public limited companies may offer shares directly to the public.

▶ **Prospectus** – a document containing the information to be made available to those wishing to buy shares (investors).

▶ **Variation of share rights** – note that this is a very technical legal term and there may be all sorts of changes to share rights which do not amount to a legal 'variation'.

▶ **Voting membership** – the number of votes that members (shareholders) are allotted depends on how many shares each member has subscribed to. Each share has a fixed value (nominal value) so therefore the votes can be counted.

5.1 Introduction

A share does not confer on its owner a right to the physical possession of anything. Section 541 of the Companies Act 2006 provides: 'The shares or other interest of a member in a company are personal property ... and are not in the nature of real estate.' A share does, however, confer a number of rights against the company (for example, the limited right to enforce the articles – see Chapter 3). The face value of the share is also a measure of the shareholder's interest in the company. In the event of the distribution of the company's assets, the amount that will come to any particular shareholder will be proportionate to the face value of the shares owned by him. By section 542 of the Companies Act 2006, each share must have a fixed nominal value or the allotment of the share is void.

The interest of the shareowner in the company and his right to uphold the constitution of the company distinguish the shareholder from the owner of a debenture. The holder of a debenture has lent money to the company, so he, as well as a shareholder, has provided money for the company's operations. A debenture holder's rights are, however, restricted to the remedies given to him by his contract of loan with the company. He has no interest in that company.

However, companies have found that to attract different types of investor it is useful to have different types of shares. The various 'classes' of shares all enjoy different rights, which are usually set out in the articles. Where these rights have not been clearly defined, the law lays down rules which fill up the gaps and determine the rights of the different classes of shareholders. Where the company wishes to alter the rights of any of the classes, strict rules have to be complied with. The alteration of such rights is known as a 'variation' of rights.

5.2 Classes of shares

5.2.1 Ordinary shares

The Joint Stock Companies Act 1856 divided the constitution of a company into two documents, the memorandum of association and the articles of association. This changed on 30 September 2009. The provisions of the old memorandum of association for older companies will be incorporated into the articles of the company. The articles are now the key document for the constitution of the company.

Unless the articles or the documents describing the shares when they were issued provide otherwise, ordinary shareholders are entitled to receive dividends when they are declared (they cannot force a declaration), and to be paid a proportion of the company's assets after payment of the creditors when the company is wound up. The amount will be proportionate to the size of their shareholding, and if the amount to be distributed exceeds the nominal value of the company's shares, each shareholder will participate in this 'surplus' in proportion to the nominal value of his shareholding.

An ordinary shareholder will also normally have the right to exercise one vote for each share he holds at the general meetings of the company (see Section 5.3.1).

These rights subsist only if there is nothing to the contrary in the document describing the original issue of the shares, in the articles. The rights otherwise given by law to shareholders are often varied by those documents. For example, it is common for a company to have more than one class of ordinary shareholders with different voting rights.

5.2.2 Preference shares

The holders of preference shares are entitled to have some of a payment out by the company paid to them before the ordinary shareholders are paid. Again, the terms of issue or the memorandum and articles may determine the rights of the holders, but the courts have had to provide a network of rules, which fill possible gaps in the description of the shareholders' rights which appear in these documents. Rules are usually expressed in terms of 'presumptions', that is, the courts will presume that a particular right does or does not attach to a share unless it can be shown that this cannot be the case because of the way in which the shares are described in one of the documents mentioned. The alternatives are that the preference shares can be preferred over the ordinary shares in respect of:

1. dividend; or
2. return of capital; or
3. both dividend and return of capital.

In all these cases matters are further complicated by the fact that the preferences may be 'cumulative' or 'non-cumulative'. A cumulative right means that if the dividend in one year was less than the shareholder was entitled to expect, the arrears must be made up in a subsequent year before the ordinary shareholders receive anything. Unlike the ordinary shareholders, the preference shareholders do know what sum they should receive because the dividend due to a preference shareholder is generally expressed as a fixed percentage of the par value of the share. The par value is a nominal value of a share which is used in valuing the assets of the company if the shareholder has not contributed all of the price of his share. It is now unusual to defer the contribution so there was a debate in the Company Law Review Steering Group suggesting that shares of no par value should be compulsory for private companies and optional for public companies (Company Law for the Competitive Economy: Company Formulation and Capital Maintenance (URN 99/1145) (London: DTI, 1999)). However, the difficulties of *redefining* the rights of third parties (including creditors) stopped this reform.

5.2.2(a) Preference as to dividend

There is a presumption that a fixed preferential dividend is cumulative, that is, arrears from previous years must be made good before any amount is paid to the ordinary shareholders. The presumption may be rebutted by the terms of the documents describing shareholders' rights. The right to have any money paid to them by way of dividend becomes a right only when the directors exercise their discretion to pay a dividend at all. Neither the preference shareholders nor the ordinary shareholders can force the declaration of a dividend, even when the company is doing well.

When the company goes into liquidation, a difficult question which sometimes needs to be settled is whether the preference shareholders are entitled to arrears of dividend before anyone else is paid. A number of cases have determined that unless there is an express right to the arrears in the documents, the preference shareholders are not entitled to have these arrears made up (see, for example, *Re Crichton's Oil* [1902] 2 Ch 86; and *Re Wood Skinner & Co* [1944] Ch 323). The 'express' right need not be very clear, however, as the presumption that they will not be made up is easy to displace.

The other presumption that applies here is that the rights stated in any of the relevant documents are exhaustive. The preference shareholders will have a right to what is expressly stated but no more.

5.2.2(b) Capital

Just because preference shareholders have a right to be paid dividends before ordinary shareholders does not give them automatic preference when the company is being wound up and the capital of the company is being distributed among the shareholders. A further question that arises is whether the preference shareholders are entitled to participate on an equal footing with the ordinary shareholders if there is a surplus after:

1. the preference shareholders have had their capital returned (if they have a preference as to return of capital); and
2. the ordinary shareholders have had their capital returned.

If after those two operations there is still a surplus for distribution, there is a question as to whether the preference shareholders may participate in the distribution of the surplus. These two dilemmas are solved, first, by the presumption that all shareholders should be treated equally, so that unless there is a specific right spelled out in the documents giving the preference shareholders a preference as to the repayment of capital, they have no such preference. Secondly, where a preference as far as the repayment of capital is expressed, the rights set out in the document describe the totality of the rights as far as capital is concerned. The description of rights is said to be 'exhaustive'. Where a preference as to capital is given to preference shareholders, they will therefore not participate in any surplus remaining after capital has been repaid unless an express right to do so is written into the issue documents, the memorandum or the articles.

5.3 Voting rights

5.3.1 Voting rights and non-voting shares

The allocation of voting rights is a matter for the constitution of the company and will be found in the company's articles of association. The articles may provide for one vote per share, or may provide for as complicated a structure of voting rights as may be desired. The shareholders will vote on a resolution. In an ordinary resolution, the majority of the votes will determine the issue and the resolution will be passed. If it is a special resolution, it will be passed only if 75 per cent vote for the resolution. The Companies Act 2006 determines some situations where a special resolution is compulsory, but the articles of a particular company may decide the voting pattern for a particular issue unless it is restricted by the law.

The idea of non-voting shares has been attacked from time to time. An example of the case against non-voting shares is to be found in a 'Note of Dissent' to the Jenkins Committee Report. The report was set up by the government to 'report upon the provisions and working of the Companies Act 1948' and other legislation. The 'Note of Dissent' was signed by Mr L Brown, Sir George Erskine and Professor LCB Gower (London: Board of Trade, June 1962):

> Feeling as we do, that the development of non-voting equity shares is undesirable both in principle and practice, we find ourselves unable to concur in the failure to make stronger recommendations for their control …
>
> 2. In our opinion the growth of non-voting and restricted voting shares (a) strikes at the basic principle on which our Company Law is based, (b) is inconsistent with the principles underlying our Report and the Reports of earlier Company Law Committees and (c) is undesirable.
>
> 3. The business corporation is a device for enabling an expert body of directors to manage other people's property for them. Since these managers are looking after other people's money it is thought that they should not be totally free from any control or supervision and the obvious persons to exercise some control are the persons whose property is being managed. Hence the basic principle adopted by British Company Law (and, indeed, the laws of most countries) is that ultimate control over the directors should be exercised by the shareholders. This control cannot be exercised in detail and from day to day, but shareholders retain the ultimate sanction in that it is they who 'hire and fire' the directorate.
>
> When the directors own the majority of the equity they are free from outside control, but here they are managing their own money. Hence the interests of the directors and the shareholders are unlikely to conflict, and self-interest should be a sufficient curb and spur (subject to certain legal rules to protect the minority against oppression). When, however, the directors have no financial stake in the prosperity of the company, or only a minority interest, outside control operates.
>
> [Paragraphs 4 and 5 showed that the thrust of most Company Law reports was to increase effective shareholder control.]
>
> 6. In recent years, however, control by shareholders has been stultified in two ways: firstly in a few cases by cross-holdings and circular-holdings within a group of companies [see Chapter 1], and secondly by non-voting equity shares. …
>
> 7. It is said that shareholder control is ineffective because of the indifference of shareholders. Everyone would probably agree that shareholders are apathetic while all goes well. But, while all goes well, there is no reason why they should not be apathetic; their intervention is only required when things go ill. No doubt it is true that the small individual shareholder has little power even

then, but, as we point out … the institutional investor has considerable influence; and even non-institutional shareholders are collectively powerful so long as they have votes. It can hardly be doubted that the possibility that a take-over bidder will obtain control by acquiring those votes has caused directors to pay greater heed to the interests of shareholders.

8. It is also said that shareholder control is inefficient, since directors, as a class, know better what is good for business and for the shareholders than the shareholders themselves. In the normal case this is usually true. But if shareholder control is destroyed and nothing put in its place we have to go still further and say that business efficiency is best ensured by allowing the directors to function free from any outside control, except that of the Courts in the event of fraud or misfeasance, and by making themselves irremovable, without their own consent, however inefficient they may prove to be.

Despite this cogent criticism (albeit in an old report), nothing has been done to curb the use of non-voting shares. Indeed, the Stock Exchange accepts non-voting shares, provided it is made clear at the outset that this is what they are. However, the London Stock Exchange and the financial press do not like the idea of non-voting shares.

Preference shareholders may have restricted voting rights, but they often have a right to vote on issues when their dividend is a certain amount in arrears. By statute they have voting rights when the company is trying a 'variation' of their rights. However, we shall see that 'variation' has in this context a special and narrow definition (see Section 5.4 et seq).

5.3.2   The exercise of voting powers

Normally each member at a meeting has one vote which is exercised by a show of hands. However, many companies allow members to have a number of votes. The number of the votes is decided by the articles, and the number of votes is proportional to the shares held by the member. Normally each member votes in favour of or against a resolution by raising a hand.

Show of hands and poll (Companies Act 2006, ss 282–284)

Exceptionally, a member can cast more than one vote if he is appointed as a proxy for absent members. If a poll vote is decided on, each voting member has a vote for each share, a written record is made of each voter's vote and the numbers for and against the motion are counted.

The difference between the systems can be stark, because in a show of hands, each individual votes once; however, in a poll, each member will often have multiple votes and each vote will be counted in a poll. It is extremely important to know which system will be used in any particular meeting. The company may not exclude the right to demand a poll, except on the question of who is to chair a meeting and whether the meeting is to be adjourned (Companies Act 2006, s 321(1)). The Model Articles (SI 2008 / 3229) state that a show of hands is the normal system, unless there is a demand for a poll (art 42 for private companies; art 34 for public companies). An ordinary resolution will be carried by a simple majority; a special resolution will pass if a 75% majority of voting members agree (see Chapters 1 and 3).

5.3.3   Joint shares

Shares can be split into joint shares. The joint holders of the share have certain rights. The most important right is to the right to vote in meetings. The Companies Act 2006, section 286 enacts a default rule providing that only the most senior member can vote. Seniority is determined by the order of the names in the company's register. Joint holders therefore have a right to instruct the company to determine the order in which their names are to appear in the register (*Re TH Saunders and Co Ltd* [1908] 1 Ch 415). This can be changed by the articles.

5.3.4 Restrictions on the right to vote

There are three important restrictions imposed by the courts on the exercise of the right to vote. First, the vote must be exercised in a way that is 'bona fide for the benefit of the company as a whole' in situations where the courts permit a challenge to a resolution on that basis (this question principally arises where there is an attempt to alter the articles – see Section 3.4 et seq above). Secondly, where the member voting belongs to more than one class of shareholder, and he is exercising a vote in the context of a 'class vote', he may not vote with his holdings in another class principally in mind. Both of these principles are aptly illustrated by *Re Holder's Investment Trust Ltd* [1971] 1 WLR 583. In that case, the court was considering an unopposed petition for the confirmation by the court of a reduction of capital. Megarry J said:

> The resolution was carried by the requisite majority because nearly 90 per cent of the preference shares are vested in the trustees of three trusts set up by Mr William Hill, and they voted in favour of the resolution. These trustees ... also hold some 52 per cent of the ordinary stocks and shares ... [Counsel] contends that the extraordinary resolution of the preference shareholders was not valid and effectual because the supporting trustees did not exercise their votes in the way that they ought to have done, namely, in the interests of preference shareholders as a whole. Instead, being owners of much ordinary stock and many shares as well, they voted in such a way as to benefit the totality of the stocks and shares that they held ... In the British America case [*British America Nickel Corporation Ltd v MJ O'Brien Ltd* [1937] AC 707], Viscount Haldane, in speaking for a strong board of the Judicial Committee, referred to ... 'a general principle, which is applicable to all authorities conferred on majorities of classes enabling them to bind minorities; namely, that the power given must be exercised for the purpose of benefiting the class as a whole, and not merely individual members only' ... I have to see whether the majority was honestly endeavouring to decide and act for the benefit of the class as a whole, rather than with a view to the interests of some of the class and against that of others ... [The] exchange of letters seems to me to make it perfectly clear that the advice sought, the advice given, and the advice acted upon, was all on the basis of what was for the benefit of the trusts as a whole, having regard to their large holdings of the equity capital ... From first to last I can see no evidence that trustees ever applied their minds to what under company law was the right question, or that they ever had the bona fide belief that is requisite for an effectual sanction of the reduction. Accordingly, in my judgment there has been no effectual sanction for the modification of class rights.

The third restriction is in relation to ratification of a breach of duty by directors, when the director concerned and any connected person may not vote (Companies Act 2006, s 239) (see Section 9.5). Ratification means that the company cannot sue that director because he was in breach of one of his duties to the company. Unless authorisation can be given by directors under the Companies Act 2006, section 175(5) (where the constitution allows the ratification by the directors), the ratification can only be effected by the members by a resolution (s 239(2)). The same applies to ratification of acts of a former director or a shadow director (s 239(5)(b) and (c)).

A director has a duty to avoid conflicts of interests (Companies Act, 2006, s 175; see Section 9.2.2), but this duty does not extend to voting. In *Peters' American Delicacy Co Ltd v Heath* (1939) 61 CLR 457, Dixon J said (at 504):

The shareholders are not trustees for one another, and, unlike directors, they occupy no fiduciary position and are under no fiduciary duties. They vote in respect of their shares, which are property, and the right to vote is attached to the share itself as an incident of property to be enjoyed and exercised for the owners' personal advantage.

A director who has shares therefore wears two hats in the company: one as a fiduciary owing duties to the company, and one as an individual who can vote selfishly if he wants to.

5.4 Variation of class rights

If a company wishes to vary the rights attaching to a class of shares or act contrary to the interests of a class of shareholders, special rules must be observed.

5.4.1 Class rights

The protection of the special regime extends to 'rights attached to any class of shares', and it is only when these rights are under threat that it applies. A question as to the meaning of the phrase 'class of shares' arose in *Cumbrian Newspapers Group Ltd v Cumberland & Westmorland Herald Newspaper & Printing Co Ltd* [1987] Ch 1. In that case, a wide definition of the phrase was adopted. Scott J said:

> In my judgment, if specific rights are given to certain members in their capacity as members or shareholders, then those members become a class. The shares those members hold for the time being, and without which they would not be members of the class, would represent, in my view, a 'class of shares'.

Section 629 of the Companies Act 2006 broadly follows this definition. It reads:

(1) For the purposes of the Companies Acts shares are of one class if the rights attached to them are in all respects uniform.
(2) For this purpose the rights attached to shares are not regarded as different from those attached to other shares by reason only that they do not carry the same rights to dividends in the twelve months immediately following their allotment.

In the *Cumbrian Newspapers* case, the right in issue was a right given to the plaintiff under the defendant's articles, including a pre-emptive right regarding the transfer of any shares in the defendant and the right to nominate a director to the board of the defendant so long as it held 10 per cent of the issued ordinary shares of the defendant. These rights were held to be class rights, alterable only in accordance with the special procedure set out in (then) section 125 of the Companies Act 1985 (now section 630 of the 2006 Act). This decision means that where particular rights are granted to an individual shareholder, they would not be alterable without the consent of that shareholder. In those circumstances the individual concerned would constitute a class of one. It might in some cases be possible to say that the right had not been granted to the individual 'in his capacity as shareholder' but in some other capacity. If that is not so, provisions very common in the articles of private companies will become, for all practicable purposes, unalterable. For the time being it is clear that 'class rights' are to be widely defined.

5.4.2 Variation of class rights

5.4.2(a) Meaning of 'variation'

The special procedures apply to the variation of class rights (Companies Act 2006, s 630(6)). The courts have, in general, taken a narrow view of what is meant by variation of class rights. In general, there will be a variation if the alteration directly affects the way the rights are described, but not if the value of the shareholding has been altered in some other way, for example by varying the rights of another class of shares.

The attitude of the courts can be understood properly only by examining some of the relevant cases. In *Greenhalgh v Arderne Cinemas Ltd* [1946] 1 All ER 512, the company, by resolution, subdivided some 10s (50p) ordinary shares into five 2s (10p) ordinary shares. The votes created by this were used to pass a resolution for increasing the capital of the company. The effect of this was explained by Greene MR as follows:

> As a result of those two resolutions, if they are valid, the voting power of the appellant, which previously gave him a satisfactory measure of voting control, is liable to be completely swamped by the votes of the other ordinary shareholders.

Despite this, the resolution was held not to have varied the rights of the appellant:

> [T]he effect of this resolution is, of course, to alter the position of the ... 2s shareholders. Instead of Greenhalgh finding himself in a position of control, he finds himself in a position where control has gone, and to that extent the rights of the ... 2s shareholders are affected, as a matter of business. As a matter of law, I am quite unable to hold that, as a result of the transaction, the rights are varied; they remain what they always were – a right to have one vote per share pari passu with the ordinary shares for the time being issued which include the new 2s ordinary shares resulting from the subdivision.

In *Re Old Silkstone Collieries* [1954] Ch 169, it was held that a reduction of capital by repaying preference shareholders, so that they would lose their right to any compensation due to them under the government's compensation scheme, did constitute a variation of their rights. However, by no means will every elimination of a class of shares constitute a variation. Where capital is repaid in accordance with the par value of the shares, and no well-defined right is taken away, the special procedure need not be invoked. The most usual occasion when the special procedure will not be invoked is where there is a clearly defined right to participate in surplus assets on a winding up (see Section 5.2.2(b)).

The protection intended by the statute has not been forthcoming in the following cases:

- In *Re Mackenzie & Co Ltd* [1916] 2 Ch 450, where a reduction of capital was carried out by the cancellation of paid-up capital in two cases to an equal extent. The practical result was to reduce the amount payable under the fixed preferential dividend to the preference shareholders, while the ordinary shareholders could share the larger remainder of any declared dividend. Because the percentage of the dividend was not affected, that is the actual description of the rights, on the face of it, was not altered, there was held to be no variation.
- In *Re Schweppes Ltd* [1914] 1 Ch 322, an issue of shares ranking equally with existing shares was held not to be a variation.
- In the *Greenhalgh* case (above), subdivision of shares and consequent dilution of voting rights was held not to be a variation.

- In *White v Bristol Aeroplane Company* [1953] Ch 65, an issue of bonus shares to one class which greatly increased its voting power as opposed to another class was held not to be a variation.
- In *Dimbula Valley (Ceylon) Tea Co v Laurie* [1961] Ch 353, an issue of bonus shares to one class which would substantially reduce the amount it would receive when participating in surplus assets on a winding up was held not to be a variation.

Thus, it is only in the most obvious cases, usually when the rights attaching to shares have been altered by alteration of the actual wording describing those rights, that the special protection afforded by section 630 will come into play. This seems to be an unnecessarily technical and legalistic approach to interpretation of legislation. It seems particularly strange when deciding what is meant by a law operating in the business sphere, that a hard distinction should be drawn between 'affecting rights as a matter of business' and 'varying rights as a matter of law'. One reason for this cautious approach which may be discerned from the cases is the fear that by using a wide definition of 'variation' the courts would be allowing one class a veto over a scheme which might benefit the company as a whole. It would seem, however, that in this instance the courts have been rather overcautious.

5.4.2(b) Where there is a true 'variation'

Once it has been determined that a class right will be varied by a scheme put forward by a company, the correct procedure depends on the provisions of sections 630–634 of the Companies Act 2006, which represent a very welcome simplification of the complex regime under the 1985 Act. Section 630(2) and (4) provides:

> **630 Variation of class rights: companies having a share capital**
> (2) Rights attached to a class of a company's shares may only be varied—
>   (a) in accordance with provision in the company's articles for the variation of those rights, or
>   (b) where the company's articles contain no such provision, if the holders of shares of that class consent to the variation in accordance with this section.
> (3) …
> (4) The consent required for the purposes of this section on the part of the holders of a class of a company's shares is—
>   (a) consent in writing from the holders of at least three-quarters in nominal value of the issued shares of that class …
>   (b) a special resolution passed at a separate general meeting of the holders of that class sanctioning the resolution.

Similar provisions apply to a company without a share capital, and in both cases there is a right to object to the variation (Companies Act 2006, ss 633 and 634). If holders of more than 15 per cent of the shares object to the variation then, provided they did not vote for it, they may apply to the court to cancel the variation (s 633(2)) (see below).

5.4.2(c) Statutory right to object

Section 630(5) of the Companies Act 2006 gives a right to apply to the court to have a variation cancelled. The right to apply is surprisingly limited. One inbuilt limitation is the very narrow definition of 'variation' which was discussed above (see Section 5.4.2(a)). As well as that, the statute requires that the application must be made by the holders of not less than 15 per cent of the issued shares of the class of shares whose rights are being varied, provided that they did not consent to or vote for the alteration. An application must be made to the court within 21 days after the variation was apparently made, and may be made by one of the shareholders who must be appointed in writing (Companies Act 2006, s 633(4)). If such an application is made, the variation has no effect until it is confirmed by the court. On hearing the application the court has a discretion to disallow the variation if it is satisfied, having regard to all the circumstances of the case, that the variation would unfairly prejudice the shareholders of the class represented by the applicant.

The narrow ambit of this minority right may account for the fact that the courts have indicated that a minority shareholder affected by a variation would have a common law right to challenge a variation on the grounds that the resolution to achieve it was not passed in good faith (see *Carruth v Imperial Chemical Industries Ltd* [1937] AC 707 at 756, 765). There would be no necessity for the holders of 15 per cent of the shares of the class to agree on such a claim The matter could also come before the court in an action under sections 994 et seq for unfairly prejudiced shareholders (see Section 10.2.4 et seq).

Summary

5.1 Shares confer on a shareowner a number of rights in a company.

5.2 Shares are often divided into different classes, ordinary and preference shares being commonplace.

The rights attaching to shares are usually to be found in the articles of association. Any lacunae in the description of share rights are made good by various presumptions of law.

5.3 Shares may or may not have voting rights.

5.4 Changing class rights will be considered a 'variation' only if the description of the rights is changed.

Where there is a true variation, the correct procedure must be followed or the variation will be open to challenge. The procedure is largely set out in section 630 of the Companies Act 2006.

Exercises

5.1 What are the arguments for and against non-voting shares?

5.2 Are the courts too restrictive in their definition of variations?

5.3 What are the usual differences between ordinary and preference shares?

Further reading

Sealy, '"Bona Fide" and "proper purposes" on corporate decisions' (1989) 15 *Mon LR* 265
French, Mayson and Ryan, *Company Law*, ch 14, see 14.14.1 et seq (the book is updated annually)

Chapter 6

Buying and trading shares and the regulation of investment business

Key terms

- **Authorised person** – person permitted to carry on investment business in the UK.
- **Regulated business** – business regulated by the Financial Conduct Authority (FCA) and the Prudential Regulation Authority (PRA).

6.1 Introduction

There is now an enormous amount of regulation which affects the way that 'investment business' is carried on. As investment business includes dealing in shares and debentures, the regulatory framework has an effect not only on companies or firms which are involved in investment businesses, but also on companies whose shares are being dealt with.

The Financial Services Act 1986 provided a framework within which there was originally to be a degree of self-regulation. In 1997 a system for regulation of investment business was introduced. The whole financial services industry (including the banks) was to be regulated by a 'super regulator', the Financial Services Authority (FSA). The Financial Services and Markets Act (FSMA) 2000 (now amended by the Financial Services Act 2012) was the foundation of the legislation for the FSA. In 1998 the Bank of England Act transferred banking supervision from the Bank of England to the FSA. During a period dating between 2012–18 the government will transfer the powers of regulating the financial industry back to the Bank of England. During this process there are now two regulator agencies backed by the Bank of England. The regulators are the Financial Conduct Authority (FCA) and the Prudential Regulation Authority (PRA). In this chapter we will consider the implications of the rather complex legislative and regulatory framework. The regulators are responsible for over 20,000 financial services firms and supervising about 3,000 listed companies. Not surprisingly, this is a difficult task involving a mix of compulsory rules and soft law (codes, frameworks, targets etc). The reason that the government decided to revisit the financial regulatory system was because of the terrible economic recession of 2007.

6.2 Reforming the regulatory framework

The financial crisis powerfully demonstrated the need for a new approach to financial regulation. Major reforms therefore have been and continue to be under way, with the aim of establishing a UK regulatory framework that is more focused on the issues that matter and better equipped to deliver financial stability. Many analysts believe that the financial crisis was partly the fault of the lax regulation of the financial sector, and theoretically this reform will make the system sound and secure for investors, companies and the taxpayer. We start with the reason why we need investment in our companies.

6.3 Public issue of securities: buying and trading shares

6.3.1 The finance of the company

Companies need capital for investing in their plant, factories, machinery and materials. A western state's economy depends on individuals investing in shares so that companies will have enough capital to start and expand their businesses. We have seen in Chapter 2 (see Section 2.4.1) that the UK has an outsider system of corporate governance. The term 'outsider' refers to the source of finance of the public company. Most companies are financed directly by the securities market, therefore producing a large shareholder base. Individuals may invest in a company by buying shares, but in large companies the individual shareholder will not be able to exercise significant power in the company because of the small number of his votes. In the UK our corporate governance system is focused on institutional shareholders who can vote a large number of their shares and therefore can overwhelm individual shareholders. Individual shareholders thus cannot change a company's policies because they have very limited power. Often an institutional investor is a fund or a company which has only one business, which is to sell or buy shares in other companies, harvesting the dividends for their members. A good example is a company that invests shares for employees for their pension funds. The institutional investors are powerful because they hold a large number of shares – about 75% of shares in public companies in the UK are held by institutional shareholders.

6.3.2 Offering shares to the public: private companies

By section 755 of the Companies Act 2006, it is an offence for a private limited company to offer shares to the public. The result is that only public limited companies (PLCs) can offer shares to the public. Section 756(2)–(4) explains what is meant by 'offer to the public':

(2) An offer to the public includes an offer to any section of the public, however selected.
(3) An offer is not regarded as an offer to the public if it can properly be regarded in all the circumstances, as—
  (a) not being calculated to result, directly or indirectly, in securities of the company becoming available to persons other than those receiving the offer; or
  (b) otherwise being a private concern of the person receiving it and the person making it.
(4) An offer is to be regarded (unless the contrary is proved) as being a private concern of the person receiving it and the person making it if—
  (a) it is made to a person already connected with the company and, where it is made on terms allowing that person to renounce his rights, the rights may only be renounced in favour of another person connected with the company; or
  (b) it is an offer to subscribe for securities to be held under an employees' share scheme …

Section 756(5) sets out the definition of a 'person already connected with a company' (s 756(4)(a) above), which includes family members, civil partners, debenture holders and trustees. The offer must therefore be made to persons within a very restricted range, most of whom will be known to each other.

Theoretically it is possible for a company to start life as a public company, but in fact a company is now always registered first as a private company. It will then be converted to a public company when more money than can be supplied by the members needs to be found to fund an expansion of the business. This will require the raising of money by issuing shares.

6.3.3   Shares

For a discussion of the nature of rights in shares, see Section 5.1. Here we are concerned with the way in which shares come into the hands of the shareholders, and the rules governing issuing shares to the public. Later in this chapter we will provide an overview of the regulatory framework that now governs the carrying on of 'investment business'. Here we are considering the buying of shares. Section 6.5 will detail the regulatory framework in the UK.

6.3.3(a) Direct offers, offers for sale, issuing houses

A direct offer of shares to the public is now an unusual method of proceeding, although still possible. If it were to be used, investors would subscribe for shares which would be allotted directly by the company.

A more common method of issuing shares is by an offer for sale. Here all of the shares are taken by an 'issuing house' which then offers them to the public for purchase. This means that the issuing house, and not the company, will take responsibility for the risk that all the shares may not be sold. It will therefore be the issuing house which will need to take out insurance against this risk. We have seen that the system of corporate governance in the UK is an outsider system (Section 2.4.1); this means that the bulk of the shares in public companies are owned by investors who are not particularly focused on the management of the company, rather they are focused on profit. Many of them will be institutional investors, including pension funds and other funds. These investors are often incorporated, themselves owing duties to their shareholders. Investors need information to decide whether their investment will be profitable for their stakeholders. This section considers the way that offers to the public are regulated.

6.3.3(b) Rights offers and public offers

If a company wishes to raise money from existing shareholders, it may seek to do so via a 'restricted rights offer'. This is an offer of more shares made to existing shareholders and capable of acceptance only by existing shareholders. If the shareholder is able to pass the offer on to others, the issue is described as a 'rights issue'. In the case of a rights issue, the shares will usually be offered in a renounceable letter of right. If the shareholder to whom the offer is addressed does not wish to avail himself of it, he may renounce his right to do so in favour of another person.

A 'public offer' is an invitation to the public at large to buy the shares. When shares are bought for the first time, this is called a 'subscription'; the shares are subscribed for and the buyer is known as a subscriber.

6.3.3(c) Placing

An alternative way of disposing of shares and raising money is to sell (at the time of first sale of a share, this is known as an 'allotment') the entire issue to an 'issuing house', which will find buyers other than by an offer to the public at large. It is said to 'place' the shares with its clients, hence this method is known as a 'placing' of shares. This type of placing is now also referred to (in the Listing Rules) (see Section 6.4 below) as 'selective marketing'.

6.3.3(d) Pre-emption rights

Sections 560 to 577 of the Companies Act 2006 set out a procedure which must be followed if the company already has shareholders who own ordinary (equity) shares. Those shareholders have the right to be offered a proportion of any new securities which correspond to the proportion of 'relevant shares' (ordinary shares) already held by them. The shares must be offered on the same terms as, or on more favourable terms than, the eventual offer to the public. The definition of 'relevant shares' excludes shares which have a right to participate in a distribution only up to a specified amount (non-participating preference shares) (see Section 5.2.2).

The offer may be made in hard copy or electronic form (Companies Act 2006, s 562). The shareholders then have at least 21 days (s 562(5)) in which to accept the offer. This right applies to public and private companies, but it may be excluded by the articles of a private company (s 567). Private companies must not contravene the ban on offering shares to the public. Private companies may thus make restricted rights offers only in respect of equity securities (ordinary shares) provided the offer is limited to their own shareholders or employees.

In both a private and a public company, pre-emptive rights may be overridden by a general authority given to directors under section 551 of the Companies Act 2006 if confirmed by the articles or a special resolution (s 570) (see below).

6.3.3(e) Authority to issue shares

Section 551 of the Companies Act 2006 requires directors who issue shares to have been authorised to do so either by the company's articles or by a resolution of the company. Authority may be given for a particular occasion or it may be a general power. The authority must state the maximum amount of shares which may be allotted under it. It must also state the date on which it will expire. This is to be not more than five years from the date of the incorporation where an authority was included in the articles. In any other case it is not more than five years from the date on which the authority is given by resolution.

Where directors have a general authority under section 551, they may be given power by the articles or by special resolution to allot shares as if the pre-emption rights granted by section 561 (see above) did not exist. Pre-emption rights also do not apply where the shares are to be wholly or partly paid for otherwise than in cash. This provision makes a large hole in the idea of the protection of the existing shareholders, since only a small part of the consideration needs to be otherwise than in cash.

6.3.3(f) Directors' duties

Directors must use their powers to issue shares bona fide for the benefit of the company (*Percival v Wright* [1902] 2 Ch 421). The court will examine the reason for the issue, and if the 'primary purpose' was not to raise capital, the issue will be an abuse of the directors' powers (*Howard Smith Ltd v Ampol Petroleum Ltd* [1974] AC 821). Directors may purchase shares from existing shareholders but must not do so on favourable terms (see *Alexander v Automatic Telephone Co* [1990] 2 Ch 56) unless the terms have been publicised.

6.3.3(g) The structure of the rules

The rules relating to the issue of shares to the public are in a kind of pyramid: at the top are the European regulations, here the Prospectus Directive; lower is the Financial Services and Market Act 2000, which has been amended by the Financial Services Act 2012; lower again are the regulators, the Financial Conduct Authority (FCA) and the Prudential Regulation Authority (PRA) which itself is governed by the Bank of England. At the bottom of the pyramid are the statutory instruments drafted and passed by the FCA and the PRA. The next section considers the Prospective Directive.

6.3.4 The Prospectus Directive

6.3.4(a) Requirements under the Directive

The Prospectus Directive (2003/71/EC) focuses on the provision of information to investors. Its central aim is to put investors into a position to make a correct assessment of the risk in investing in transferable securities by the provision of full appropriate information concerning those securities and the issuers of such securities. The correct functioning of the securities market on the basis of confidence in transferable securities stands at the core of the Directive. The Directive applies to securities that are offered to the public or admitted to trading on a regulated market in a Member State.

The prospectus must contain all information that is necessary to enable investors to make an informed assessment of the assets and liabilities, financial position, profit and losses, and prospects of the issuer and of any guarantor, and of the rights attaching to such securities. This information must be presented in a comprehensible form. Civil liability (not criminal sanctions) will attach to the persons who have tabled the summary only if the summary is misleading, inaccurate or inconsistent with the other parts of the prospectus. Responsibility for the information given in a prospectus attaches at least to the issuer or its administrative, management or supervisory bodies, the offeror, the person asking for the admission to trading on a regulated market or the guarantor, as the case may be. They must all be clearly identified in the prospectus. No prospectus shall be published until it has been approved by the competent authority of the home Member State. In the UK the relevant regulator is the FCA. The competent authority must normally issue a decision on the approval of the prospectus within 10 working days of the submission of the draft prospectus. Once approved, the prospectus must be filed with the competent authority of the home Member State and made available to the public by the issuer, offeror or person asking for admission to trading on a regulated market as soon as practicable. A significant change brought about by this Directive is that, from now on, this approval is to have EU scope.

Subsequently, Commission Regulation (EC) No 809/2004 laid down the arrangements for implementing Directive 2003/71/EC as regards both the format of the prospectus and the documents relating to the information to be included in the prospectus.

The Prospectus Directive 2003/71/EC has been amended by Directive 2010/73/EC on the transparency requirements in relation to information about issues whose securities are admitted to trading on a regulated market. This is a small amendment, mostly relaxing some of the amounts in the regulations. A more significant amendment was passed later which deals with the aftermath of the financial crisis. This is contained in Directive 2010/78/EC:

Whereas:

(1) The financial crisis in 2007 and 2008 exposed important shortcomings in financial supervision, both in particular cases and in relation to the financial system as a whole. Nationally based supervisory models have lagged behind financial globalisation and the integrated and interconnected reality of European financial markets, in which many financial institutions operate across borders. The crisis exposed shortcomings in the areas of cooperation, coordination, consistent application of Union law and trust between national competent authorities

(2) In several resolutions before and during the financial crisis, the European Parliament has called for a move towards more integrated European supervision, in order to ensure a true level playing field for all actors at Union level and reflect the increasing integration of financial markets in the Union (in its resolutions of 13 April 2000 on the Commission communication on implementing the framework for financial markets: Action Plan, of 21 November 2002 on prudential supervision rules in the European Union, of 11 July 2007 on financial services policy (2005 to 2010) – White Paper, of 23 September 2008 with recommendations to the Commission on hedge funds and private equity, and of 9 October 2008 with recommendations to the Commission on Lamfalussy follow-up: future structure of supervision, and in its positions of 22 April 2009 on the amended proposal for a directive of the European Parliament and of the Council on the taking-up and pursuit of the business of Insurance and Reinsurance (Solvency II) and of 23 April 2009 on the proposal for a regulation of the European Parliament and of the Council on Credit Rating Agencies).

(3) In November 2008, the Commission mandated a High-Level Group chaired by Jacques de Larosière to make recommendations on how to strengthen European supervisory arrangements with a view to better protecting the citizen and rebuilding trust in the financial system. In its final report presented on 25 February 2009 (the 'de Larosière Report'), the High-Level Group recommended that the supervisory framework be strengthened to reduce the risk and severity of future financial crises. It recommended far-reaching reforms to the supervisory structure of the financial sector within the Union. The de Larosière Report also recommended that a European System of Financial Supervisors (ESFS) be created, comprising three European Supervisory Authorities (ESA) – one for each of the banking, the securities and the insurance and occupational pensions sectors – and a European Systemic Risk Council.

(4) In its Communication of 4 March 2009 entitled 'Driving European Recovery', the Commission proposed to put forward draft legislation creating the ESFS and in its Communication of 27 May 2009 entitled 'European Financial Supervision', it provided more details of the possible architecture of that new supervisory framework.

(5) In its conclusions following its meeting on 18 and 19 June 2009, the European Council recommended that a European System of Financial Supervisors, comprising three new ESA, be established. The system should be aimed at upgrading the quality and consistency of national supervision, strengthening oversight of cross-border groups, establishing a European single rule book applicable to all financial institutions in the internal market. It emphasised that the ESA should also have supervisory powers for credit rating agencies and invited the Commission to prepare concrete proposals on how the ESFS could play a strong role in crisis situations.

This means that the regulators in the UK must cooperate with the European authorities, specifically in the context of prospectuses.

6.3.4(b) *The Directive and its implementation in the UK*

The UK legislative framework for public offers and admission of securities to trading on regulated markets consists of the following:

- the Prospectus Regulations 2012 (SI 2012/1538); and
- the FSMA 2000, Part VI.

The Regulations, which amended the FSMA 2000, cover the production of prospectuses for offers to the public of non-listed securities. Section 85(1) of the FSMA 2000 reveals the central principle underlining the Regulations: it is unlawful for transferable securities to which this subsection applies to be offered to the public in the United Kingdom unless an approved prospectus has been made available to the public before the offer is made. For this purpose, 'transferable securities' are taken to be shares in companies and other securities equivalent to shares in companies, and bonds and other forms of securitised debt.

If an approved prospectus is required, the prospectus must be submitted to the FCA for approval with a fee. The FCA has 10 working days to give its approval if the issuer has securities admitted to trading on a regulated market and has previously offered securities to the public, and 20 working days if not. Although not all of the reform is yet complete, there is now some clarity in the regulatory system.

The issue of shares in a company applying for a Stock Exchange Listing is governed by the Financial Services and Markets Act 2000 (FSMA 2000), the Financial Services Act 20012, the rules of the FCA and PRA, the rules which apply to listing particulars (see below) and the rules in the Prospectus Regulations 2012.

In the case of both an application for listing and an issue of a prospectus, there will be a very wide duty of disclosure (FSMA 2000, s 80(1) and (2); Prospectus Regulations 2012, reg 2). In both cases, supplementary documents must be issued if there is a change of circumstances (FSMA 2000, s 81); and in both cases the provision for compensation for misleading information is very wide (FSMA 2000, ss 82 and 90).

6.4　Admission to Stock Exchange listing

Where the shares are to be listed on the Stock Exchange, the company must comply with the FCA rules, which set out a number of conditions to be fulfilled by an applicant. These can be found in the FCA's Handbook, the Prospectus Rules. This is confusing because the Prospectus Regulations 2012 are only an amendment to the FSMA 2000; the FCA Handbook has more comprehensive rules on prospectuses (see <http://fshandbook.info/FS/html/FCA/PR>). The FCA has published a Handbook which includes a sourcebook setting out compulsory rules, and a 'manual' which contains provisions relevant to the regulatory relationship which the regulators have with firms, such as supervision, enforcement and levying fees. The PRA rules are very similar, using the two layers of regulation and also using a sourcebook and a manual. The FCA's rules contain Principles of Business (see below) (the PRA has less extensive rules):

The Principles

1	Integrity	A *firm* must conduct its business with integrity.
2	Skill, care and diligence	A *firm* must conduct its business with due skill, care and diligence.
3	Management and control	A *firm* must take reasonable care to organise and control its affairs responsibly and effectively, with adequate risk management systems.
4	Financial prudence	A *firm* must maintain adequate financial resources.
5	Market conduct	A *firm* must observe proper standards of market conduct.
6	Customers' interests	A *firm* must pay due regard to the interests of its *customers* and treat them fairly.
7	Communications with clients	A *firm* must pay due regard to the information needs of its *clients*, and communicate information to them in a way which is clear, fair and not misleading.

8	Conflicts of interest	A *firm* must manage conflicts of interest fairly, both between itself and its *customers* and between a *customer* and another *client*.
9	Customers: relationships of trust	A *firm* must take reasonable care to ensure the suitability of its advice and discretionary decisions for any *customer* who is entitled to rely upon its judgment.
10	Clients' assets	A *firm* must arrange adequate protection for *clients'* assets when it is responsible for them.
11	Relations with regulators	A *firm* must deal with its regulators in an open and cooperative way, and must disclose to the *appropriate regulator* appropriately anything relating to the *firm* of which that regulator would reasonably expect notice.

Note: The PRA applies Principles 1 to 4, 8 and 11 only.

Of course this is soft law, so it is unlikely to end up in the courts, and it is clear that some of the principles are vague, for example (3) 'a firm must take care to organise and control its affairs'; or (5) 'a firm must maintain adequate financial resources'. These appear to be pious expectations; the compulsory regulations of the Prospectus Rules are more detailed. Any financial services firm must be authorised by the FCA or the PRA to carry on a business that involves financial services. If a company wants to offer shares to the public, it must write a prospectus. The FSMA 2000 and the FCA regulate the conditions in which a prospectus can be issued.

The conditions can be found in the FSMA 2000. The FCA intends to implement new listing requirements in May 2014. At present, among the conditions are the following:

1. The applicant must be a public company.
2. The expected market value of securities for which listing is sought must be at least £700,000 in the case of shares. Securities of a lower value may be admitted provided that the Committee of the Stock Exchange is satisfied that adequate marketability can be expected. These limits do not apply where the issue is of more shares of a class already listed.
3. The securities must be freely transferable.
4. A company must have published or filed accounts in accordance with its national law for five years preceding its application for listing. The Committee has a discretion to accept a shorter period provided that it is satisfied:
   (a) that it is desirable in the interests of the company or of investors; and
   (b) investors will have the necessary information available to arrive at an informed judgement on the company and the securities for which listing is sought.
5. At least 25 per cent of any class of shares must at the time of admission be in the hands of the public (that is, persons who are not associated with the directors or major shareholders).
6. The Bank of England controls sterling issues in excess of £1 million in value. In such cases application must be made to the government broker for a date known as 'impact day' when the size and terms of the issue are to be made known.
7. All offer documents (including listing particulars) must be lodged in final form 48 hours before the Committee is to hear the application.
8. No offer documents may be made public until they have received the approval of the Department for Business, Innovation and Skills.

6.4.1 Contents of listing particulars

The required contents for listing particulars form a long list. Included in the mandatory contents are:

1. details of the company and details of any group or company of which it is a part;
2. details of the shares which are to be issued;
3. considerable financial detail of the company and group, including an accountant's report for the last five completed financial years;
4. details of the persons forming the management of the company;
5. a description of the recent developments and prospects of the company and its group.

6.4.2 Continuing obligations

Companies that wish to obtain a listing on the Stock Exchange must comply with continuing obligations imposed by the Listing Rules. These require a listed company to notify to the FCA any information necessary to enable holders of the company's listed securities and the public to assess the performance of the company. The obligation requires a company to make an announcement where, to the knowledge of the company directors, there is a change in the company's financial position, the performance of its business or in the company's expectation of its performance, where knowledge of that change is likely to lead to a substantial movement in the price of the company's listed securities. No guidance is given as to the meaning of 'substantial movement', which will therefore depend on the individual track record of the particular company.

6.4.3 Remedies for defective listing particulars

The remedies available where listing particulars are defective consist of remedies available under the common law and statutory remedies contained in sections 90 and 91 of the FSMA 2000. The common law remedies are discussed below.

Section 80 of the FSMA 2000 contains a general duty of disclosure. It reads:

(1) Listing particulars submitted to the competent authority under section 79 must contain all such information as investors and their professional advisers would reasonably require, and reasonably expect to find there, for the purpose of making an informed assessment of—
   (a) the assets and liabilities, financial position, profits and losses, and prospects of the issuer of the securities; and
   (b) the rights attaching to the securities.
(2) That information is required in addition to any information required by—
   (a) listing rules, or
   (b) the competent authority,
   as a condition of the admission of the securities to the official list.

The information must be within the knowledge of any person responsible for the preparation of the particulars, or it must be information which 'it would be reasonable for him to obtain by making enquiries' (s 80(3)(b)). In determining what information should be included, the type of investment and the type of persons likely to acquire such investments are to be taken into account (s 80(4)). Presumably the more unsophisticated the potential purchasers of the securities, the more information should be included, although section 80(4)(c) tends to limit the range of information to be made available by requiring that, in determining the information to be included in listing particulars, regard shall be had 'to the fact that certain matters may reasonably be expected to be within the knowledge of professional advisers of any kind which those persons may reasonably be expected to consult'. Section 81 of the FSMA 2000 requires any significant change or new matter which would be relevant to be the subject of supplementary listing particulars to be submitted to the FCA for approval and then published.

Given the long list of matters which must be included and the general duty of disclosure, the remedy afforded by section 90 of the FSMA 2000 is very wide. Section 90 states:

(1) Any person responsible for listing particulars is liable to pay compensation to a person who has—
   (a) acquired securities to which the particulars apply; and
   (b) suffered loss in respect of them as a result of—
      (i) any untrue or misleading statement in the particulars; or
      (ii) the omission from the particulars of any matter required to be included in section 80 or 81.
(2) Subsection (1) is subject to exemptions provided by Schedule 10.
(3) If listing particulars are required to include information about the absence of a particular matter, the omission from the particulars of that information is to be treated as a statement in the listing particulars that there is no such matter.
(4) Any person who fails to comply with section 81 is liable to pay compensation to any person who has—
   (a) acquired securities of the kind in question; and
   (b) suffered loss in respect of them as a result of the failure.
(5) Subsection (4) is subject to exemptions provided by Schedule 10.
(6) This section does not affect any liability which may be incurred apart from this section.
(7) References in this section to the acquisition by a person of securities include reference to his contracting to acquire them or any interest in them.
(8) No person shall, by reason of being a promoter of a company or otherwise, incur any liability for failing to disclose information which he would not be required to disclose in listing particulars in respect of a company's securities—
   (a) if he were responsible for those particulars; or
   (b) if he is responsible for them, which he is entitled to omit by virtue of section 82.
(9) The reference in subsection (8) to a person incurring liability includes a reference to any other person being entitled as against that person to be granted any civil remedy or to rescind or repudiate an agreement.
(10) 'Listing particulars', in subsection (1) and Schedule 10, include supplementary listing particulars.

Schedule 10 contains exemptions from liability if, at the time when the listing particulars were submitted, the person responsible for the listing particulars believed, after making reasonable enquiries, that the statement was true and not misleading or that the omission was proper and:

1. he continued in that belief until the time when the securities were acquired; or
2. the securities were acquired before it was reasonably practicable to bring a correction to the attention of persons likely to acquire the securities in question; or
3. before the securities were acquired he had taken all such steps as it was reasonable for him to have taken to secure that a correction was brought to the attention of those persons; or

4. he continued in that belief until after the commencement of dealings in the securities following their admission to the Official List and securities were acquired after such a lapse of time that they ought in the circumstances to be reasonably excused.

It is important to note that it is for the 'person responsible' to satisfy the court of the exemptions – once a breach of the rules is established, that person bears the burden of proof.

Schedule 10 contains other exemptions, for example an exemption relating to statements made on the authority of an expert. A person responsible for particulars will not be liable if he believed on reasonable grounds that the expert was competent and had consented to the inclusion of the statement (FSMA 2000, Sch 10, para 2). Similarly, there will be no responsibility for the accurate and fair reproduction of a statement made by an official person or contained in a public official document (FSMA 2000, Sch 10, para 5). The full list of exemptions in Schedule 10 is set out in the Legislation at the end of the chapter, together with the list of persons who are responsible for listing particulars.

Several points must be noted about the remedy for defective listing particulars:

1. It applies to omissions as well as positive misstatements.
2. The claimant need only show that he has acquired the securities and suffered loss as a result of the untrue or misleading statement or omission. After that the burden lies on the persons responsible for listing particulars to exculpate themselves. This reversal of the usual burden of proof could assist a claimant considerably.
3. The remedy is available to first-time purchasers of shares when they are initially issued (subscribers) and to later purchasers.
4. This remedy is available as well as the common law remedies discussed below in relation to liabilities for misleading prospectuses. In view of the width of the statutory remedy, however, it would be rare for the common law remedies to be more beneficial to a claimant.

6.4.4 Liabilities for misstatements in prospectuses and listing particulars

As well as the statutory remedies mentioned above, the issue of a misleading prospectus could also give rise to actions by oppressed minority shareholders, either by way of sections 994 to 996 of the Companies Act 2006 or via a derivative action. Further, the directors may well be in breach of their duties to the company and be liable for such breaches. Criminal penalties under section 91 of the FSMA 2000 and the Fraud Act 2006 might apply.

In the past, a problem was caused by *Houldsworth v City of Glasgow Bank* (1880) 5 App Cas 317. In that case, the question discussed was whether a person holding shares in a company was entitled to receive damages from that company. It was held that because of the shareholder's special relationship with the company, it was not open to him to remain a member of the company and claim damages from the company for fraudulently inducing him to buy stock.

Following that decision, it was clear that where the company was the defendant in an action for fraud, no damages could be awarded to a member of the company. Rescission was the only remedy available to him. Following the implementation of section 131 of the Companies Act 1989, however, members have an unrestricted right to claim damages from a company. Section 131 of the 1989 Act introduced section 111A into the Companies Act 1985, which provides that a person is not to be debarred from obtaining damages or other compensation from a company simply because he holds or has held shares in the company, or has any right to apply or subscribe for shares or to be included in the company's register in respect of shares.

The measure of damages for intentional wrongdoing was determined by the House of Lords in *Smith New Court Securities v Scrimgeour Vickers (Asset Management) Ltd and Another* (1996) *The Times*, 22 November. The House of Lords decided that an intentional wrongdoer in an action for fraudulent misrepresentation would be liable for all loss (including consequential loss) flowing directly from the fraudulent misrepresentation and could not benefit from any issues as to foreseeability. The plaintiff was entitled to be put into the position he would have been in if no misrepresentation had been made.

A number of claims seeking damages for negligence and deceit have left the law in some confusion. Thus in *Al-Nakib Investments (Jersey) Ltd v Longcroft* [1990] 1 WLR 1390, a prospectus, which was issued specifically to enable shareholders to consider the rights offer, was held not to give rise to a duty of care between the issuers and people who subsequently purchased shares on the market. No duty would arise unless the person responsible for the prospectus was aware, or ought to have known, that the recipient would rely on it for the specific purpose of entering into a particular transaction. However, in *Possfund Custodian Trustee v Diamond* [1996] 2 BCLC 665, Lightman J in the Chancery Court refused to strike out an action for deceit and negligence by purchasers subsequent to the original subscribers. He held that it was arguable that persons responsible for the issue of a company's share prospectus owed a duty of care to, and could be liable for damages to, subsequent purchasers of shares on the unlisted securities market, provided that the purchaser could establish that he had reasonably relied on representations made in the prospectus and reasonably believed that the representor intended him to act on them, and that there existed a sufficient direct connection between the purchaser and the representor to render the imposition of such a duty fair, just and reasonable. He also felt that *Al-Nakib* should be reviewed by a higher court. That has not happened, so the extent of the duty owed by issuers to subsequent purchasers remains uncertain.

6.5 Market abuse

6.5.1 Market abuse and insider dealing

There are two main categories of market abuse:

1. insider dealing; and
2. market manipulation.

The practice of 'insider dealing' or 'insider trading' occurs when a person with information gained from being in a privileged position makes use of that information for his own gain or to enable another to gain. Market manipulation occurs when false or misleading information about the supply, demand or value of financial instruments is spread, creating a false market.

Strict control of these forms of market abuse was the central objective of Directive 2003/6/EC of 28 January 2003 on insider dealing and market manipulation (market abuse), which was implemented in the UK by Part VIII of the FSMA 2000. This effectively penalises insider dealing and market manipulation, requires insiders to declare their trading and places an obligation on companies to publish all information which may affect the value of their publicly traded shares. An injunction restraining the relevant activity may be issued if the FCA detects behaviour constituting market abuse by an individual. Section 123 of the FSMA 2000 permits the FCA to impose a financial penalty or publicly censure the individual in cases of abuse. However, the penalty itself does not render the transaction in question void or unenforceable in accordance with section 131 of the 2000 Act.

6.5.2 Market abuse and granting security over shares

On 8 December 2008 it was announced that one of the directors of Carphone Warehouse Group plc had resigned from the directorship of the company after disclosure of the fact that he had pledged his shares to secure personal loans. On 9 January 2009 the FSA clarified that persons discharging managerial responsibilities, such as the directors of listed companies, are required to inform their companies of any grant of security over their shares. The FSA recognised, however, that the rules in question remained unclear for both practitioners and companies, and it therefore granted a moratorium of two weeks ending on 23 January 2009, during which there could be no action against directors who had engaged in such practices. From that point onwards, though, directors have an obligation to disclose the pledging of shares as security for personal loans. What the FSA did was to clarify the application and essence of a set of rules, including the operation of Disclosure and Transparency Rule (DTR) 3.1 and the Model Code with regard to using shares as security. DTR 3.1 requires persons discharging managerial responsibilities, such as directors, to disclose 'transactions' conducted on their own account in shares of the issuer, or derivatives or any other financial instrument relating to those shares. The FSA clarified that it considered the grants of security over shares to fall within the scope and ambit of the regulated 'transactions'. This interpretation signalled a change in the approach adopted up to that point, as the term 'transactions' was deemed not to include the granting of security over shares.

The FSA specifically stated its intention to let the granting of security over shares fall within the definition of the term 'transactions' and therefore within the scope of protection afforded by DTR 3.1. The rules on this issue are not clear because the FCA has not issued a decisive rule, the Handbook being drafted during 2014–2018. The FCA rules mean not only that directors are required to notify such transactions to their companies, but also that the companies in question must on their part notify the market as soon as possible.

6.6 The new regulatory system for banks and financial firms

This chapter has considered the Prospectus Rules and listings; reform of this system has been partly implemented. This reform also affects financial firms, banks and providers of financial services. We have seen that there was a significant recession starting in 2007–08. Many commentators believed that the system of regulating financial services had become lax, allowing extreme risk taking, especially by the big banks. This led to a bail-out of some of the UK banks by the UK taxpayers. The government therefore reformed the financial authorities: the Financial Services Authority (FSA) was abolished and two new agencies were created. In 2013 the Financial Conduct Authority (FCA) and the Prudential Regulation Authority (PRA) started their work. The legislative framework was similar (the Financial Services and Market Act 2000), but this was amended by the Financial Services Act 2012. This section considers the new regime from the position of financial services firms. The FCA and the PRA regulate by statutory instrument. The Financial Services Act 2012 created an independent Financial Policy Committee (FPC – see Section 6.6.1 below) at the Bank of England, and the Financial Services Authority (FSA) has ceased to exist in its current form with its responsibilities transferred to two new bodies. The Prudential Regulation Authority (PRA – see Section 6.6.2 below) will be a part of the Bank of England, focusing on prudential issues. The Financial Conduct Authority (FCA), a separate body, will be responsible for business and market conduct. The reforms transfer responsibility for the supervision of financial market infrastructure to the Bank from the FSA.

The reforms took effect on 1 April 2013.

6.6.1 Financial Policy Committee

On 1 April 2013 the new legislation established a Financial Policy Committee (FPC) charged with the primary objective of identifying, monitoring and taking action to remove or reduce systemic risks with a view to protecting and enhancing the resilience of the UK financial system. The FPC will have a secondary objective to support the economic policy of the government.

Previously, in February 2011, the Bank of England's Court of Directors created an interim FPC to undertake, as far as possible, the future statutory role of FPC. Although lacking the statutory powers of direction and recommendation, the interim FPC aimed to contribute to financial stability by identifying, monitoring and publicising risks to the financial system and advising action to reduce and mitigate them.

The interim FPC held its first policy meeting in June 2011, and has met on a quarterly basis since then. The Committee publishes a record of its formal meetings, and is responsible for the Bank of England's bi-annual Financial Stability Report.

6.6.2 Prudential Regulation Authority

The Prudential Regulation Authority (PRA) is responsible for the supervision of banks, building societies and credit unions, insurers and major investment firms. In total the PRA regulates around 1,700 financial firms. The PRA's role is defined in terms of two statutory objectives: (i) to promote the safety and soundness of these firms; and (ii) specifically for insurers, to contribute to the securing of an appropriate degree of protection for policyholders.

In promoting safety and soundness, the PRA focuses primarily on the harm that firms can cause to the stability of the UK financial system. A stable financial system is one in which firms continue to provide critical financial services to the economy – a precondition for a healthy and successful economy.

The PRA works alongside the FCA, creating a 'twin peaks' regulatory structure in the UK. The FCA is responsible for promoting competition, ensuring that financial markets function well and that financial firms conduct their business so that consumers get a fair deal.

Supervision is still divided into industry sectors, for example, banks are supervised separately from investment businesses. Although officially the FCA is a single body, there are still different regimes of supervision for different parts of the financial services industry.

Sections 2 to 6 of the FSMA 2000 set out four objectives:

▶ to maintain confidence in the financial system;
▶ to promote public understanding of that system;
▶ to secure 'the appropriate degree of protection for consumers'; and
▶ to reduce the extent to which it is possible for a financial services business to be used for a purpose connected with financial crime.

The decisions of the FCA are subject to judicial review following the case law which concerned its predecessor, the Securities and Investment Board (SIB), with regard to setting the limits of its powers (see *R v SIB* [1995] 2 BCLC 76, [1996] 2 BCLC 342), but in *Melton Medes v SIB* (1994) *The Times*, 27 July, the Chancery Court held that no action for breach of statutory duty would lie against a regulatory body.

6.7 Carrying on a regulated activity

Section 19 of the FSMA 2000 contains the 'general prohibitions':

(1) No person may carry on a regulated activity in the United Kingdom or purport to do so, unless he is—
(a) an authorised person; or
(b) an exempt person.

6.7.1 Meaning of 'regulated activity'

Before considering in more detail the way a person becomes 'authorised' or 'exempt' (see Section 6.7.2 below), it is useful to know what is meant by a 'regulated activity'. Regulated activities are described in Part I of Schedule 2 to the FSMA 2000. They include:

1. dealing in investments;
2. arranging deals in investments;
3. managing investments;
4. advising on investments;
5. deposit taking;

6. establishing collective investment schemes;
7. using computer-based systems for giving investment instructions.

The definitions follow the same pattern as under the predecessor to the FSMA 2000, the Financial Services Act 1986. The approach adopted by that Act was to include an enormous range of activities within the scope of the restriction and then try to exempt from the Act operations which could be seen as 'commercial' rather than 'investment' transactions. Obviously there is a very fine line between the two, and considerable difficulty has been experienced in drawing the line. An example of this may be seen in the treatment of 'futures' contracts. Essentially these are contracts to buy a commodity at some time in the future. At one end of the scale these contracts are clearly investment contracts. This is when there is never any intention for one of the parties to the contract to deliver to the other any of the actual commodity involved, while at the same time it is clear that the right to the quantity of the commodity acquired will be sold on to another buyer quickly, perhaps even before the commodity exists or has been extracted from the ground (for example, wheat before it has grown, oil before extraction). At the other end of the scale, the Financial Services Act was never meant to regulate a contract between two parties to buy and sell a quantity of a commodity. There are many shades in between. If a cargo of oil is purchased with the buyer intending to take delivery, but the buyer's circumstances change and he resells that cargo, has this become an investment rather than a commercial contract? The treatment of futures in the statute is important, not because it will be of wide importance in company law but because it is indicative of the whole approach of the statute which embraces all and then seeks to exclude.

Something of the immense complexity of the system should be apparent from the foregoing discussion. Under the FSMA 2000 the matters of most immediate concern to all companies are contained in Schedule 2, Parts I and II: 'Dealing in investments: Buying and selling and subscribing: … accepting deposits … shares or stocks in a company … debentures … bonds … options.'

The FSA identified four main types of risk:

1. prudential risk – the risk of the collapse of a firm 'because of incompetent management or a lack of capital';
2. bad faith risk – fraudulent or negligent conduct on the part of the selling firms;
3. complexity/unsuitability risk – that consumers end up with an unsuitable or impossible-to-understand product;
4. performance risk – 'the risk that the investments do not deliver hoped-for returns'.

There is no reason that the FCA and the PRA will change this structure significantly.

The FSA did not believe that it was part of its role to protect consumers against performance risk, other than to raise awareness that it is inherent in the market. On the other risks, it made a distinction between consumers and counterparties. Counterparties are professionals who may be assumed to be much more aware of the workings of the financial markets. Consumers were supposed to need higher levels of protection.

The most important part of the FSA's processes was a system of risk analysis. We do not know whether this system of risk will be significantly changed by the FCA and the PRA. The risk was scored taking into account probability and impact factors (see Figure 6.1).

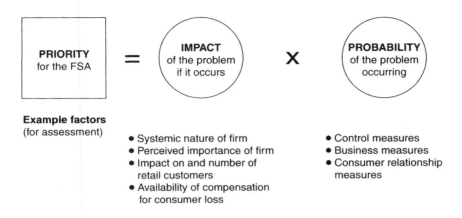

Figure 6.1 Risk assessment and prioritisation: firm-specific approach

Probability factors take into consideration the likelihood of the risk happening. Impact factors assess the 'scale and significance' of the harm done should the risk occur (see further 'Assessing firm-specific risks: impact and probability factors' at the end of this chapter). The FSA used a spectrum of supervision from maintaining a continuous relationship with firms that have a high-impact risk rating to 'remote monitoring' of low-impact firms. Firms in the latter category had a regular relationship with the FSA, and had to submit periodic returns for automated analysis, and to inform the FSA of any major strategic developments.

Having assessed the risks, the FSA deployed its 'regulatory toolkit' to counter the risks. Figures 6.2 and 6.3 set out the contents of the regulatory toolkit and illustrate how the FSA used this range of tools in response to particular situations. Figure 6.2 shows the ways in which the FSA might expect to act where risks arose as a result of a new product being marketed direct to the public. This approach might be appropriate, for example, in the early stages of the introduction of new products. The figure illustrates how in this case the emphasis is on consumer-oriented and industry-wide activities (such as consumer education, disclosure and market monitoring) rather than on firm-specific activities. Figure 6.3 shows how the FSA used a different range of tools in response to a particular problem within a specific firm or group. It takes as an example a major bank with a significant capital markets operation, which includes trading for its own account in derivative products. As a result of identified control and management weaknesses, the bank is vulnerable to major trading losses through errors, mismarking, etc. The example shows how the FSA's response in such situations would be likely to focus on the tools which are directed at individual firms, rather than those which are directed at consumers, at all banks, or at all firms engaged in proprietary trading.

The tools listed at the bottom of Figures 6.2 and 6.3 are illustrative only and do not represent the full range available to the FSA. For example, in the situation described in Figure 6.3, the FSA might well have wished to commission work from the firm's external auditors, in addition to using the tools illustrated. Moreover, in both examples some of the tools are described in fairly high-level terms, whereas in practice careful consideration would need to be given, for example, to whether disciplinary action might be appropriate or precisely which issues are to be addressed in the course of a visit to a firm.

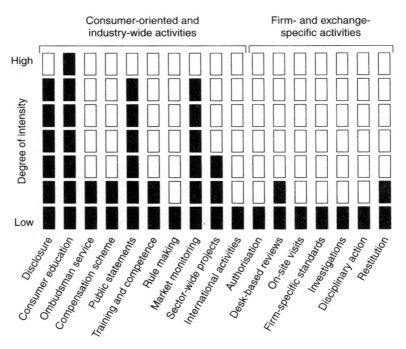

Figure 6.2 Response to risks arising from a new product being marketed direct to the public

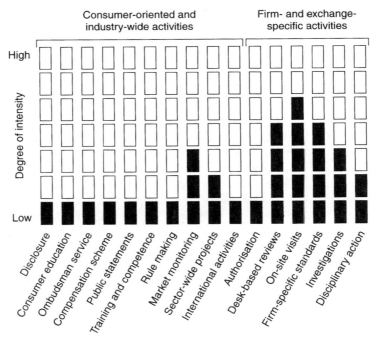

Figure 6.3 Choice of regulatory response: firm-specific approach

6.7.2 Authorisation provisions

Authorisation is to carry out specific activities. It may be obtained:

1. by permission directly from the FCA to carry out one or more regulated activities in the UK (FSMA 2000, s 31);
2. by obtaining authorisation from the European Economic Area state in which it has its headquarters (FSMA 2000, s 31);
3. by using its authorisation under the previous regime (FSMA 2000, ss 426 and 427).

An authorised person's carrying on a regulated activity outside the terms of the permission does not make that person guilty of an offence or the transaction void or unenforceable (FSMA 2000, s 20), but it does make that person subject to a wide range of disciplinary procedures available to the FCA (FSMA 2000, ss 20 and 66). A person breaching the general prohibition – that is, an unauthorised person carrying on regulated activity – is guilty of a criminal offence (FSMA 2000, s 23). Similarly, a false claim to be authorised or exempt is a criminal offence (s 24). The FCA has the power to withdraw authorisation (s 33). Clearly this is a very drastic remedy, and both this action and the use of disciplinary powers will be subject to the provisions of the Human Rights Act 1998 (see Section 6.9 below).

Section 41 of and Schedule 6 to the FSMA 2000 set out the 'threshold conditions' for authorisation. That is, the applicant must:

- have an appropriate legal status
- carry on business in the UK
- not have 'close links' with an entity which would prevent effective supervision by the FCA (for example, be a subsidiary of a parent outside the EEA)
- have adequate resources, and
- 'be a fit and proper person'.

The FCA has a similar structure: the business Principles.

6.8 Complaints

6.8.1 The Financial Services and Markets Tribunal

The Financial Services and Markets Tribunal, set up by section 132 of the FSMA 2000, was an important part of the new regulatory scheme. Many decisions of the FSA came under its scrutiny, including decisions to authorise (or not), to vary or withdraw authorisation, disciplinary measures and the imposition of financial penalties for market abuse. An appeal from a final decision of the Tribunal may be made, with leave, to the Court of Appeal and ultimately the Supreme Court, but only on a point of law (FSMA 2000, s 137).

6.8.2 The Financial Ombudsman

The rather complex provisions that have emerged on this topic have created voluntary and compulsory schemes for access to the Ombudsman. The compulsory scheme is confined to authorised firms, whereas the voluntary scheme may be joined by regulated or unregulated firms. Under the compulsory scheme, the Ombudsman must determine the case as he thinks 'fair and reasonable in all the circumstances' and is not confined to finding breaches of rules or Codes of Conduct. He must provide a written statement of his decision. If the complainant accepts it, the determination becomes final and binding. If not, he may take the matter to court. The respondent firm has no right of appeal even on a matter of law (FSMA 2000, s 228).

The Ombudsman scheme is separate from the compensation scheme which is required in the event of the insolvency of a firm. This scheme is run by the Financial Services Compensation Scheme (FSCS). The FCA will make rules enabling the FSCS to assess and pay compensation for claims in respect of regulated activities of defaulting authorised firms, and raise levies on authorised persons to create the fund to make this possible.

6.9 The Human Rights Act 1998

In 1998 the UK government incorporated the European Convention on Human Rights into the law of the UK by the Human Rights Act 1998. Courts are now bound to construe legislation so far as possible in a way which is compatible with the Convention and will make a public declaration of incompatibility where legislation contravenes the Convention.

The European Court of Human Rights, in interpreting the Convention, has insisted that its protection will be extended to those undertaking private commercial activities (*Pudas v Sweden* (1988) 10 EHRR 380). Most importantly, this protection includes the right to a fair and public hearing within a reasonable time by an independent tribunal established by law (Art 6(1) of the Convention, applying to civil and criminal proceedings). More extensive rights apply to criminal proceedings and the Court in Strasbourg does not accept that states can escape from those obligations merely by defining punitive procedures as civil proceedings (*Engel v Netherlands* (1976) 1 EHRR 647).

6.10 The Markets in Financial Instruments Directive 2004/39/EC and the new Markets in Financial Instruments Directive 2014

The Markets in Financial Instruments Directive (2004/39/EC) replaced the Investment Services Directive adopted in 1993. The 2004 Directive is the cornerstone of the Commission's Financial Services Action Plan, and represented the most far-reaching change in financial regulation since the 1993 Directive, as it affects most aspects of the function of financial institutions, including those left unregulated by the 1993 Directive. It sets out the regulatory framework for investment services and financial markets across the EU. Its basic aim is naturally the further integration of the capital markets of the Union through increased cross-border trading. It attempts to achieve that by providing a safety-net of protection for investors.

The adoption of the 2004 Directive, which changed the landscape in the financial markets, was deemed necessary as the previous Investment Services Directive 1993 failed to deal with the relevant challenges in an effective manner, rendering its reform and substitution by a subsequent piece of EU legislation necessary. The 'passport' system which stood at the core of the 1993 Directive was a way of harmonising the conduct of investment firms, but it was not as effective as initially presumed. The Markets in

Financial Instruments Directive broadened the scope of the 'passport' system for investment firms, as it provides for the harmonised conduct of business and harmonised control requirements for investment firms. Barriers to cross-border trading were still in place, discouraging the integration of European investment services. In addition to that, the protection afforded to investors needed to be further enhanced so as to attract new investors to the capital markets of the EU. A new piece of legislation was deemed imperative because new financial instruments, such as derivatives (derivatives are a way of gambling between commodities or currencies), had to be brought under the umbrella and within the ambit of the EU legislation.

Furthermore, the 2004 Directive increased the extent to which home state rules govern cross-border business by extending the 'home state' rule that allows companies offering their services in another Member State to adhere to the rules of the home state in which they are based, facilitating cross-border exchanges and contacts. For example, the conduct of business regulation will be an issue to be determined on the basis of the 'home state' rules, reflecting the greater level of harmonisation that the Directive aims at achieving.

The Markets in Financial Instruments Directive came into force in November 2007 and the FSMA 2000 was revised accordingly. After the financial crisis, further EU legislation was deemed to be necessary. In 2014 the Markets in Financial Instruments Directive will be passed. The European Commission says that this Directive will help efficiently regulate derivatives and high frequency trading (see <http://europa.eu/rapid/press-release_IP-11-1219_en.htm?locale=en>). High frequency trading is a way of selling and buying in markets in seconds, often done by computers rather than individuals. The European Commission's press release explains the reason for the Directive:

> In recent years, financial markets have changed enormously. New trading venues and products have come onto the scene and technological developments such as high frequency trading have altered the landscape. Drawing lessons from the 2008 financial crisis, the G20 agreed at the 2009 Pittsburgh summit on the need to improve the transparency and oversight of less regulated markets – including derivatives markets – and to address the issue of excessive price volatility in commodity derivatives markets.

On 15 April 2014 the European Parliament adopted the Directive. It is very likely that it will be passed.

Summary

6.1 No investment business may be carried on in the UK unless the person conducting the business is an exempt or authorised person under the Financial Services and Markets Act 2000.

6.2 The Financial Conduct Authority and the Prudential Regulation Authority regulate all investment business and the conduct of banks. The FCA is also responsible for the Listing Rules. A number of European Directives seek to provide firms with a 'passport' permitting them to operate throughout the EU.

Exercises

6.1 Under its risk assessment scheme, how would the PRA regulate a small investment bank operating in the City of London but with high-risk business outside the European Economic Area?

6.2 Why is it important to devote so much energy to regulating financial services?

6.3 Consider the range of remedies available to a person who suffers loss as a result of misstatements in listing particulars/prospectuses.

6.4 Find a prospectus in one of the broadsheet newspapers. Does the quantity of information that needs to be disclosed make it unreadable?

Assessing firm-specific risks: impact and probability factors

▶ **Impact factors (from FSA risk analysis documents)**

For firm-specific risks, the first step is to assess the impact were a particular event to occur.

Impact relates to the damage that a regulatory problem within a firm (collapse or lapse of conduct) would cause to the FSA's objectives. While a firm may have a high probability of a regulatory problem, if it is low impact (for example, a small firm conducting little retail business), the overall risk posed to the objectives is likely to be low.

The impact of an event will be assessed by reference to the following criteria:

- ▶ systemic significance of the firm (that is, the impact which the collapse of the firm would have on the Findustry as a whole);
- ▶ perceived importance of the firm (impact of the firm's collapse on public perception of the market and thereby on market confidence);
- ▶ retail customer base (number and nature of customers, nature of customers' exposure to firm);
- ▶ availability of compensation or redress for consumer loss.

In assessing impact, we will [the FSA] also take into account the cumulative effect of problems in a number of similar firms, even though, considered individually, the firms concerned might be graded low-impact.

▶ **Probability factors**

For firm-specific risks, the probability of a problem occurring is assessed under three headings:

1 *Business risk*
The risk arising from the underlying nature of the industry, the external context, and the firm's business decisions and strategy. High business risk on its own may not pose a threat to the stability of a firm, if the controls are sound. However, the firm could collapse if its capital or controls are inadequate for the business risks it faces. Business risk relates to:

- ▶ capital adequacy (ability to absorb volatility/loss);
- ▶ volatility of balance sheet (risk of portfolio of assets and liabilities, exposure to external risks);

> ▶ volatility and growth of earnings (historical trends and patterns, mix of business, sources of income);
> ▶ strategy (change in business, sustainability of earnings).

2 *Control risk*
The risk that a firm cannot or will not assess, understand and respond appropriately to the risks it faces. High control risk means that the firm's controls are not adequate in the light of its business risk. Control risk subdivides into consideration of:

> ▶ internal systems and controls (information flow, decision-making processes, risk management, etc);
> ▶ board, management and staff (skill, competence, fitness and propriety, etc);
> ▶ controls culture (adherence to internal controls, compliance record, etc).

3 *Consumer relationship risk*
The risk that the firm will cause damage to consumers by failing to provide suitable products and services. In this respect firms operating exclusively in wholesale markets will typically be lower risk. A medium/high impact firm with a medium/high risk grading could constitute a threat to the consumer protection objective. A substantial problem of this nature could also affect market confidence. This risk is assessed by reference to:

> ▶ nature of customers and products (focusing on any mismatch between customer sophistication and product sold);
> ▶ marketing, selling and advice practices (focusing on sales force incentives, compliance culture, record-keeping).

Key resources

A new approach to financial regulation: securing stability and protecting consumers, HM Treasury, 27 January 2012

Draft memorandum of understanding on crisis management, HM Treasury, January 2012

White Paper: A new approach to financial regulation: the blueprint for reform, HM Treasury, 16 June 2011

A new approach to financial regulation: building a stronger system, HM Treasury, 17 February 2011

A new approach to financial regulation: judgement, focus and stability, HM Treasury, 26 July 2010

FSMA 2000, Schedule 10

SCHEDULE 10

COMPENSATION: EXEMPTIONS

Statements believed to be true

1(1) In this paragraph 'statement' means—
  (a) any untrue or misleading statement in listing particulars; or
  (b) the omission from listing particulars of any matter required to be included by section 80 or 81.
  (2) A person does not incur any liability under section 90(1) for loss caused by a

statement if he satisfies the court that, at the time when the listing particulars were submitted to the competent authority, he reasonably believed (having made such enquiries, if any, as were reasonable) that—
  (a) the statement was true and not misleading, or
  (b) he matter whose omission caused the loss was properly omitted,
and that one or more of the conditions set out in sub-paragraph (3) are satisfied.

(3) The conditions are that—
  (a) the continued in his belief until the time when the securities in question were acquired;
  (b) they were acquired before it was reasonably practicable to bring a correction to the attention of persons likely to acquire them;
  (c) before the securities were acquired, he had taken all such steps as it was reasonable for him to have taken to secure that a correction was brought to the attention of those persons;
  (d) he continued in his belief until after the commencement of dealings in the securities following their admission to the official list and they were acquired after such a lapse of time that he ought in the circumstances to be reasonably excused.

Statements by experts

2(1) In this paragraph 'statement' means a statement included in listing particulars which—
  (a) purports to be made by, or on the authority of, another person as an expert; and
  (b) is stated to be included in the listing particulars with that other person's consent.

(2) A person does not incur any liability under section 90(1) for loss in respect of any securities caused by a statement if he satisfies the court that, at the time when the listing particulars were submitted to the competent authority, he reasonably believed that the other person—
  (a) was competent to make or authorise the statement, and
  (b) had consented to its inclusion in the form and context in which it was included,
and that one or more of the conditions set out in sub-paragraph (3) are satisfied.

(3) The conditions are that—
  (a) he continued in his belief until the time when the securities were acquired;
  (b) they were acquired before it was reasonably practicable to bring the fact that the expert was not competent, or had not consented, to

the attention of persons likely to acquire the securities in question;
  (c) before the securities were acquired he had taken all such steps as it was reasonable for him to have taken to secure that that fact was brought to the attention of those persons;
  (d) he continued in his belief until after the commencement of dealings in the securities following their admission to the official list and they were acquired after such a lapse of time that he ought in the circumstances to be reasonably excused.

Corrections of statements

3(1) In this paragraph 'statement' has the same meaning as in paragraph 1.

(2) A person does not incur liability under section 90(1) for loss caused by a statement if he satisfies the court—
  (a) that before the securities in question were acquired a correction had been published in a manner calculated to bring it to the attention of persons likely to acquire the securities; or
  (b) that he took all such steps as it was reasonable for him to take to secure such publication and reasonably believed that it had taken place before the securities were acquired.

(3) Nothing in this paragraph is to be taken as affecting paragraph 1.

Corrections of statements by experts

4(1) In this paragraph 'statement' has the same meaning as in paragraph 2.

(2) A person does not incur liability under section 90(1) for loss caused by a statement if he satisfies the court—
  (a) that before the securities in question were acquired, the fact that the expert was not competent or had not consented had been published in a manner calculated to bring it to the attention of persons likely to acquire the securities; or
  (b) that he took all such steps as it was reasonable for him to take to secure such publication and reasonably believed that it had taken place before the securities were acquired.

(3) Nothing in this paragraph is to be taken as affecting paragraph 2.

Official statements

5   A person does not incur any liability under section 90(1) for loss resulting from—
    (a) a statement made by an official person which is included in the listing particulars, or
    (b) a statement contained in a public official document which is included in the listing particulars,
    if he satisfies the court that the statement is accurately and fairly reproduced.

False or misleading information known about

6   A person does not incur any liability under section 90(1) or (4) if he satisfies the court that the person suffering the loss acquired the securities in question with knowledge—
    (a) that the statement was false or misleading,
    (b) of the omitted matter, or
    (c) of the change or new matter,
    as the case may be.

Belief that supplementary listing particulars not called for

7   A person does not incur any liability under section 90(4) if he satisfies the court that he reasonably believed that the change or new matter in question was not such as to call for supplementary listing particulars.

Meaning of 'expert'

8   'Expert' includes any engineer, valuer, accountant or other person whose profession, qualifications or experience give authority to a statement made by him.

Further reading

Michael Blair, George Walker and Robert Purves, *Financial Services Law*, 3rd edn (Oxford University Press, 2014).

Chapter 7

Maintenance of capital

Key terms

- **Capital maintenance** – a system which tries to make the company financially secure by law.
- **Dividends** – payments out of company profits made to shareholders at the discretion of directors. The amount that the directors can pay shareholders after deducting expenses including tax.
- **Reduction or increase of capital** – changing the capital sum in the company.
- **Bonus shares** – the company pays shares to the members without charge.
- **Group accounts** – links between companies in an enterprise. Sometimes the accounts are put together to give a fair and true understanding of the assets of the enterprise.

7.1 Introduction

The principal concern of the law in this area is that the company should get full value for the shares it issues and that, having received the money, that money should be kept within the company. Because the members of a company are in control of it, in theory they could make the company transfer all its assets to them. In particular, therefore, money should not be returned to the members of the company, leaving the company's creditors with an empty shell to rely on when their bills are due to be paid. In this area the original common law rules have, to a considerable extent, been overtaken by statutory rules, many of them introduced by the Companies Acts 1980 and 1981 as a direct result of the then European Community's company law harmonisation program. These rules are now part of the Companies Act 2006.

The harmonisation of company law at EU level has been a divisive problem for many years, not least in the rules about capital maintenance. The real problem is that there are two systems for safeguarding creditors and shareholders. The American and UK philosophy, on the one hand, is to safeguard creditors and shareholders by making sure that directors are decent and professional. If something fraudulent occurs, the courts will be able to crack down on bad conduct retrospectively. Many Continental jurisdictions have exactly the opposite system, preferring rules which are supposed to stop infringements by management before shareholders and creditors are damaged. The German system is often cited in this regard, having a set of capital maintenance rules which is comprehensive and extremely complicated. The harmonisation of these different systems has not been well understood and the resulting Directives have sometimes represented a compromise, which means that the domestic rules are occasionally unclear.

There are three other difficulties in this regard: the speed of electronic transactions; the *Centros* case (*Centros Ltd v Erhvervs-og Selskabsstyrelsen* (case C-212/97) [2000] Ch 446), which showed that the EU harmonisation of company law was difficult because of the differences of philosophy between Member States (see Chapter 2); and the enlargement of the EU:

1. Capital maintenance rules can work only if accountants know what assets are in the company. However, the speed of transactions means that it is extremely difficult to know whether a company is solvent or not at a particular moment in time. A number of scandals in the western world have involved a catastrophic insolvency. An example is the Enron bankruptcy which happened extremely suddenly.

> Enron imploded with breathtaking speed in the early 2000s, going virtually overnight from being the nation's seventh-largest company to a bankrupt shell synonymous with corporate greed and deceit. Kenneth Lay and Jeffrey Skilling were at the helm as the company collapsed, taking the jobs and savings of thousands along with it. Lay helped create Enron in 1985 as a natural gas provider and presided as it grew into an energy-trading behemoth worth some $68 billion in 2000. Skilling joined in 1990 and, as he rose, pushed an aggressive growth strategy that, in retrospect, relied on shady accounting to reflect chimerical profits. In 2001, Skilling briefly became the company's CEO while Lay moved to chairman; Skilling abruptly resigned months later as the energy giant neared the breaking point, later cashing out nearly $60 million in stock. The company filed for Chapter 11 [the company was insolvent] on December 2, 2001. (see Bethany McLean and Peter Elkind, *The Smartest Guys in the Room*, Penguin, 2003)

2. In the EU the Member States had two opposing systems of incorporating companies: 'the company seat system' and the 'incorporation system'. The former system was intended to allow governments more control over companies in their territories, by monitoring the management in a particular place. Under this system, companies must maintain an office or a 'seat' where the management is found and where its business is conducted; the personal law of a company is the law of the state where the company's centre of administration is established. As we have seen above, Germany prefers a system which manages businesses via strict regulation. It is perhaps not surprising that Germany was the architect of the 'company seat theory', nor that the UK fiercely opposes it. In the UK, companies are incorporated by registration and the business may be founded anywhere; a corporation operates under the law in force where it has been incorporated.

The argument hotted up when the *Centros* case was decided. Two Danish individuals incorporated Centros Ltd under UK company law. The company was intended to trade only in Denmark. The incorporators clearly stated that they had established the entity under UK company law solely to avoid the minimum capital requirement for Danish limited liability companies. The Danish Commercial Registry considered this to be an unlawful circumvention of the Danish minimum capitalisation rules and so refused to register the company's branch office in Denmark. The problem for the EU and its Treaty provisions was the compatibility with the provisions on freedom of establishment (now Articles 49–55 TFEU). The European Court of Justice (ECJ) had to decide whether it was compatible with freedom of establishment to refuse registration of a branch of a lawfully founded company that had its registered office in another Member State, but one in which the company did not itself carry on any business. The ECJ ruled that where a company exercises its freedom of establishment under the Treaty, the Member States are prohibited from discriminating against the company on the ground that it was formed in accordance with the law of another Member State in which it has its registered office but where it does not carry on any business. Secondly, a state is not authorised to restrict freedom of establishment on the ground of protecting creditors or preventing fraud if there are other ways of countering fraud or protecting creditors. This argument has been important in the long dispute between EU Member States about company employee participation, because companies incorporated in states where there are no employee participation systems can nevertheless do business without employee participation. The UK system of corporate governance does not include any meaningful employee participation in the management affairs in the company; any rights of employees come from labour law not via company law. (See Section 2.2–2.3.3.)

3. Of course the enlargement of the EU has made this complexity worse. Each EU Member State has a different set of legislation and regulations, and therefore disputes between countries about which regulations are crucial for the public interest is inevitable. This is not only a matter of dispute between Germany and the UK – so far the EU has not been able to solve these issues properly.

7.2 The fundamental rule and subsequent modifications

7.2.1 The fundamental rule

The basic common law rule was that it was illegal for a company to acquire its own shares. The reasoning was that the capital of a company could be discovered by adding up the amounts paid for the shares it had issued. If those shares had been purchased by the company itself, no money in respect of those shares would have flowed into the company's coffers. Thus, a creditor would be relying on illusory prosperity if he relied on the value of shares issued when giving credit to the company. The rule was established in the case of *Trevor v Whitworth* (1887) 12 App Cas 409 and is therefore often referred to as 'the rule in *Trevor v Whitworth*'. In that case Lord Watson said: 'It is inconsistent with the essential nature of a company that it should become a member of itself. It cannot be registered as a shareholder to the effect of becoming a debtor to itself for calls ...' This emphasises the difficulties that would arise if a company were able to buy its own shares. If they were not fully paid, the company would be liable to pay itself money when the 'call' to pay the outstanding amount was made.

Nevertheless, this 'blanket' prohibition was felt to be too restrictive. Subsequent attempts to modify it and to define when it is permissible to pay money out to the shareholders have, however, led to a very complex system of rules. We shall deal first with the basis on which payment of money to members is permitted, since understanding this will help to make sense of the rules governing prohibited payments.

7.2.2 Payment of money to members

One of the difficulties of understanding these rules is that the law tends to treat the capital of a company as a fixed amount kept in a piggy bank. The reality is quite different – the money contributed by the shareholders is used in the business, and used to buy a continually changing set of assets. These assets will go up or down in value. It is unlikely that their value will remain static. Consequently the rules designed to draw a sharp distinction between the capital of a company and profits available for distribution to members are based on a false view of the way companies work. The distinction is particularly false where the company is a small private company and the members are all directors or employees. Payments to such people are not governed by the rules on 'distributions' to members and count as ordinary trading debts. If not otherwise controlled, it would be open to the members of such companies to pay the assets of the company to themselves by way of remuneration. If the company has resolved to pay such salaries, the court will not usually enquire as to whether such a payment was reasonable, that is, the size of the payment will not normally invalidate it in civil proceedings (see *Re Halt Garage (1964) Ltd* [1982] 3 All ER 1016).

In *Progress Property Co v Moorgarth Group Ltd Co* [2011] 1 WLR 1, the claimant company sold all of the shares it held in a wholly owned subsidiary to the defendant company. Both companies were controlled by the same man. However, because the transaction was part of a deal to refinance his companies, the claimant and the defendant were represented by separate solicitors; there had been an independent professional valuation of the shares. All the parties had misunderstood some details of the valuation. The shares were alleged to be worth about £4 million more than the amount paid. The Supreme Court decided that there was a genuine commercial sale even though there were mistakes in the valuation. The valuation was an error, not fraud. The Supreme Court decided that the transaction was not illegal and tainted by rules about an illegal return of capital. However, it has been held that unreasonable payments of this nature can amount to theft of the company's property even when the alleged thieves are the sole owners and directors of the company (see the House of Lords decision in *R v Gomez* [1992] 3 WLR 1067).

Other controls on such practices are contained in the Insolvency Act 1986. Section 238 of that Act gives a liquidator of a company a power to apply to the court for an order cancelling the effect of a gift of the company's property made in the two years preceding commencement of a company's winding up, if the company was insolvent (see Chapter 13 for the definition of 'insolvent') at the time of the gift or if the gift made the company insolvent. The provision also applies to a transaction with a person in which the consideration given by the person was significantly less valuable than the consideration provided by the company.

Furthermore, large payments to member-directors while the company is struggling have been considered as one reason, amongst others, for issuing a disqualification order against a director, preventing him from acting as a director. This power is given to the court by the Company Directors Disqualification Act 1986.

7.3 Distributions

7.3.1 Distributions not to exceed profits

By far the majority of companies exist to make profits for their shareholders. There must therefore be a system by which those profits can be distributed to the shareholders. As explained in Section 7.2.1 above, the law seeks to permit distribution of profits alone, leaving intact a quantity of assets, known as 'capital', which is to be kept in the company as a source to which creditors can look for payment of their bills and, at the end of the company's life, as the fund out of which the shareholders will be repaid the amount they put into the company when they bought their shares. Thus, although the power to distribute money to the shareholders is implied, there need not be a specific clause in the articles permitting a distribution. The rule is that the distributions of a company should not exceed its realised profits. Capital, which includes amounts held in the share premium and capital redemption reserve, must remain intact.

7.3.2 Exceptions to rules governing distributions

By section 829 of the Companies Act 2006, the statutory rules governing distributions apply to 'every description of distribution of a company's assets to its members, whether in cash or otherwise', with the following exceptions (s 829(2)):

(a) an issue of shares as fully or partly paid bonus shares;
(b) the reduction of share capital—
   (i) by extinguishing or reducing the liability of any of the members on any of the company's shares in respect of share capital not paid up, or
   (ii) by repaying paid-up share capital;
(c) the redemption or purchase of any of the company's own shares out of capital ... or out of unrealised profits [in accordance with the Act, see Section 7.3.4(c) below];
(d) a distribution of assets to member of the company on its winding up.

The exceptions will be examined in more detail in Section 7.3.4 below. The next step is to examine the rules surrounding the most common method of distribution of profits to the members of a company, which is by paying a dividend to members.

7.3.3 Dividends

7.3.3(a) Profits available for the purpose

The definitions of 'profit' and 'dividends' are complicated. The Companies Act 2006 sets out a complex array of rules to make sure that creditors are protected from the management and shareholders. As well as this, the directors have complete discretion to manage the company where it is profitable. The shareholders are not able to insist on getting money from the company via a distribution (a dividend). The directors might use any profit for research or for opening a new plant, rather than distributing it to shareholders. In a public company, this is a risky strategy by the directors because the shareholders might sell their shares, leaving the company starved of investment. Other shareholders might buy the shares, but if there are no dividends in sight, the shares will be less valuable.

The company's profits available for this purpose are set out in section 830(2) of the Companies Act 2006:

(2) A company's profits available for distribution are its accumulated, realised profits, so far as not previously utilised by distribution or capitalisation, less its accumulated, realised losses, so far as not previously written off in a reduction or reorganisation of capital duly made.

7.3.3(b) Realised and unrealised profits and losses

The notion of restricting the amount available for distributions to realised profits was introduced into UK law by the Companies Act 1980 in accordance with the provisions of the EC Fourth Directive. The Companies Act 2006 reiterated the rules (see Part 23, ss 829–853). It means that companies must examine their accounts and separate out any amounts which are due to the revaluation of assets. Before this provision came into force, it was considered permissible to pay a dividend where assets had increased in value even when that asset had not been sold so that the value had not been 'realised'. Realisation means turning an asset into cash. The *realised profits* of a company for a financial year are the profits on its sales of assets – that is, the amount by which income from the sale of its assets exceeds associated expenses. An *unrealised profit* will occur when assets have risen in value: when, for example, the buildings owned by the company have increased in value but those buildings have not been sold. Similarly, a *realised loss* occurs when expenses associated with sales for a particular year exceed revenue derived from those sales, while an *unrealised loss* will occur where assets fall in value but they have not yet been sold at a loss.

As a general rule, expenses must be recorded in accounts when they are incurred, not when they are actually paid for. Similarly, income from sales of goods or supply of services must generally be recorded at the time of sale or supply rather than when the money is actually received, provided that there is an amount fixed at that time and provided also that there is a reasonable possibility of eventual collection of the debt. It is interesting to note that one of the ways in which the Enron company inflated its 'profits' was to record as income money which it would receive only over a long period (sometimes as much as 20 years). This, of course, did not give a 'true and fair view' of the company's assets (see Section 7.6.5 below). At the end of the year, some money appearing in the income side of the accounts will not have been received by the company. These bad debts must be reflected in the accounts. This is done by calculating the percentage of the total trade debts which the company's past experience shows will not be paid. In a new concern, the pattern of business in the industry would provide first estimates.

If a company is about to incur a future liability which cannot be precisely quantified, it can set aside a fund called a 'provision'.

7.3.3(c) Public companies

As well as the restrictions discussed above, public companies are subject to further restrictions contained in section 831 of the Companies Act 2006. By that section:

> (1) A public company may only make a distribution—
>> (a) if the amount of its net assets is not less than the aggregate of its called-up share capital and undistributable reserves, and
>> (b) if, and to the extent that, the distribution does not reduce the amount of those assets to less than that aggregate.

The 'undistributable reserves' are:

1. the share premium account – this contains any amount paid for a share over and above its par or face value;
2. the capital redemption reserve – this contains an amount equivalent to the value of shares legally redeemed (see Section 7.3.4(c) below);
3. accumulated unrealised profits less accumulated unrealised losses; and
4. any other reserve which the company is forbidden to distribute under its articles or any rule of law.

One of the important differences between public and private companies is highlighted here, in that a public company must write off its unrealised losses against realised and unrealised profits before it can make a distribution out of the balance of its realised profits. A private company need not do this.

7.3.3(d) Members' liability

Section 847 of the Companies Act 2006 makes a member liable to repay a distribution he has received if, at the time of the distribution, he knew or had reasonable grounds for knowing that it was being paid in contravention of the Act.

7.3.4 Other permitted payments to members

We saw in Section 7.3.2 above that the rules concerning distributions do not apply to certain other payments to members. These are (Companies Act 2006, s 829):

1. the return of capital or distribution of surplus assets on a winding up;
2. the return of capital to members in a properly authorised reduction of capital (including the cancellation or reduction of liability on partly-paid shares);
3. the issue of fully or partly-paid bonus shares;
4. the purchase or redemption of the company's own shares.

The return of capital and assets on a winding up are covered by rules explained in Chapter 13. The rules relating to the other types of payment out are discussed in Sections 7.3.4(a)–7.3.4(d) below.

7.3.4(a) Reductions of capital

The provisions regarding the reduction of capital are set out in sections 641 to 657 of the Companies Act 2006. The reduction of a company's capital was traditionally regarded as a matter to be strictly controlled since it reduced the fund available for creditors.

Statutory framework for reduction of capital

Section 641(1)–(3) of the 2006 Act sets out the framework for reduction of capital:

> (1) A limited company having a share capital may reduce its share capital—
>   (a) in the case of a private company limited by shares, by special resolution supported by a solvency statement;
>   (b) in any case by special resolution confirmed by the court.
> (2) A company may not reduce its capital under subsection 1(a) if as a result of the reduction there would no longer be any member of the company holding shares other than redeemable shares.
> (3) Subject to that, a company may reduce its share capital under this section in any way.

Section 641(4) sets out particular situations where the power may be used. They are:

1. to reduce members' liability to pay uncalled capital; or
2. to reflect a diminution of the company's assets.

In a private company, a reduction of capital and the return of capital to a member or members may be necessary when a company changes hands on the death or retirement of a person who was chiefly concerned in the running of the business. Until 1981 this could be done only by special resolution and confirmation by the court. Now private companies in particular have other choices (see Section 7.4.1(b) below). In *Carruth v Imperial Chemical Industries Ltd* [1937] AC 707, it was held that it was proper to reduce the nominal value of one class of the company's shares so as to reflect the low price at which they were traded on the Stock Exchange.

Confirmation by the court

This regime is available to both public and private companies, although private companies will try to steer clear of it because of the expense. The court has refused to determine whether a reduction of capital is commercially sensible. However, the court will attempt to ensure that the reduction is not unfair. In *British and American Trustee & Finance Corporation Ltd v Couper* [1894] AC 229, Lord Herschell LC said:

> There can be no doubt that any scheme which does not provide for uniform treatment of shareholders whose rights are similar, would be most narrowly scrutinised by the Court, and that no such scheme ought to be confirmed unless the Court be satisfied that it will not work unjustly or inequitably.

In that case, the Court had already ascertained that no interests of creditors would be affected by the reduction. It is clear, then, that two important considerations which will influence the court when deciding whether to sanction a reduction are:

1. whether and to what extent the interests of creditors will be affected; and
2. whether the reduction deals with different classes of shareholders fairly and equitably.

A third consideration referred to by the House of Lords judges in *Ex parte Westburn Sugar Refiners Ltd* [1951] AC 625 was 'the public interest'. This was not very clearly defined, but the concern seems to have been to ensure that sufficient capital was retained in the company to safeguard the interests of those 'who may in future form connections with the company as creditors or shareholders'. Political considerations, such as whether the reduction was in response to and likely to defeat the purpose behind nationalisation of an industry, were held to be irrelevant. It seems, then, that in this case a vague third requirement applied:

3. that the reduction should not be contrary to the public interest.

The validity of this consideration was doubted by Harman J, in *Re Jupiter House Investments (Cambridge) Ltd* [1985] BCLC 222, who considered it of more importance that 'the causes of the reduction should have been properly put to shareholders so that they were able to exercise an informed choice and that the reason for the reduction is supported by evidence before the court'.

Despite these requirements it has been held that it is permissible to carry out a reduction of capital by extinguishing entirely a class of members. This was done in *British and American Trustee & Finance Corporation Ltd v Couper* (above) and in *Re Saltdean Estate Co Ltd* [1968] 1 WLR 1844. In *Re Saltdean Estate Co Ltd*, the company's preference shareholders were eliminated by returning the capital paid by them plus a premium of 50 per cent. It was further held in that case that the expulsion of the preference shareholders did not amount to a variation of their rights. In these circumstances 'variation' of rights is a very technical concept (explained in Section 5.4). Where a reduction of capital does involve a variation of the rights of one or more classes of shareholders, the special procedures explained in Chapter 5 must be followed as well as gaining the approval of the court for the reduction of capital.

Interests of creditors

The Companies Act 2006 provides a special procedure where the interests of creditors are likely to be affected adversely by a reduction of capital. If the reduction involves either a diminution of a member's liability to pay future calls on shares or repayment of capital to members, the special procedure comes into operation, subject to a discretion which the court has to dispense with it (ss 645 and 646). By section 645(4), the court may direct that this special procedure should be adopted in the case of any other type of reduction, but it was held in *Re Meux's Brewery Co Ltd* [1919] 1 Ch 28 that where a company is not parting with a means of paying its creditors, the creditors must show a very strong reason why they should be heard in objection to the company's petition seeking approval for the reduction.

The special procedure involves drawing up a list of the creditors of the company. Section 647 makes it an offence to conceal the company's creditors or misrepresent their claims. The creditors that must be included are those who could prove for their claims if the company went into liquidation as at a date fixed by the court. The court may make an order confirming the reduction only when it is satisfied that every creditor on the list has either been paid in full or has positively consented to the reduction (s 648(2)). The court may dispense with the consent of a creditor if it is satisfied that the company has made provision for paying him. In the case of a disputed claim, the court must be satisfied that adequate provision has been made (s 646(5)). Any creditor on the list is entitled to be heard by the court in opposition to the proposed reduction.

Procedure

If the court sanctions the reduction, the order approving the reduction must be registered with the court. The reduction does not take effect until the registration has been carried out. The court then certifies the registration and his certificate is conclusive evidence that all the requirements of the Act have been complied with (s 649).

7.3.4(b) Bonus shares

Bonus shares are shares which are issued with the value paid out of the profits of the company. They are wholly paid for by the company (Companies Act 2006, s 582) rather than by the member, and yet they confer a right on the member to participate in a share-out of capital in the event of the liquidation of the company; they represent a transfer of capital from the company to the member. This transfer would be prohibited by the rule against return of capital to members were it not permitted by the Companies Act 2006. Bonus shares are allotted to existing members of a company. A decision to issue bonus shares paid for by capital (a capitalisation issue) is to be taken by the directors on the authority of an ordinary resolution of its members (see Model Articles, art 78 for public companies; art 36 for private companies).

7.3.4(c) Redeemable shares and the forfeiture of shares

Other permitted methods for the transfer of capital from the company to its members are by way of redeemable shares and the forfeiture of shares. The articles of the company may allow the company to forfeit a share if the shareholder has defaulted on his contract to pay the call due on his share (Companies Act 2006, s 659(2)(c)). The Model Articles for a public company deal with this situation in arts 58–61. The courts have always interpreted any provision for the forfeiture of property strictly (see *Johnson v Little's Iron Agency* (1877) 5 ChD 687).

By section 684 of the Companies Act 2006, a company may issue shares which are redeemable. This is another way of reducing the capital of a company. For a public company this is permitted only if authorisation for such a class of shares is contained in the articles. By section 685 the directors may determine the terms of redemption if so authorised by the articles or by a resolution of the company. Where they are not authorised, the terms of redemption must be stated in the company's articles. A private company may pay for redeemable shares out of capital. Public companies may use only distributable profits or the proceeds of a share issue made for the purposes of the redemption. When the temporary membership of the company conferred as a result of issue of these shares comes to an end, the shares are cancelled and the nominal value of the shares is repaid to the member. Sometimes a redemption bonus will be paid as well as the nominal value of the shares.

Normally the company is obliged to maintain a fund which must not be diminished by the repayment of redeemable shares. In the case of a public company, the repayment to a member on the redemption of a redeemable share will not represent a reduction of this core capital fund, as it can redeem redeemable shares only out of profits or the proceeds of a further issue of shares. However, a private company can, by adopting the procedure set out in the Act, redeem shares out of existing capital. The members of a private company may adopt a special resolution to enable its shares to be redeemed without the capital accounts being increased in exact proportion to the payments out. This could be of great value to a private company, particularly where the head of a small company was hoping to take his capital out of the company and retire. However, the legislature has hedged about the ability to reduce capital in this way with so many restrictions that the procedure is not as valuable as it otherwise might be.

Only a fully paid-up share may be redeemed (Companies Act 2006, s 686(1)). When a redeemable share is redeemed, it must be cancelled. The nominal value of the share is deducted from the share capital account. In a public company this reduction would be compensated by the transfer from the profit and loss account of an amount equivalent to the amount written off the share capital account. An alternative would be to issue new shares. However, the members of a private company may use the redemption of shares to reduce capital by adopting a resolution not to make up the amount in this way. There is a limit set to the extent to which a reduction in this way may be made. The amount set is called the 'permissible capital payment' (Companies Act 2006, s 710). This is calculated so that a company must transfer the proceeds of new issues of shares and all distributable profits to the capital account which is to be reduced. The payment out of capital must be approved by special resolution of the company (s 716). The persons holding the shares proposed for redemption may not vote in favour of the resolution to redeem the shares (s 717). There are complex rules relating to the calculation of available profits (s 712) and the directors' statement (s 714).

Not more than a week before a resolution to make a payment out of capital is adopted by a company, the directors must make a statutory declaration of the size of the permissible capital payment (Companies Act 2006, s 714). The directors' declaration must state:

1. that the company will be able to pay its other debts immediately after the redemption is made; and

2. that the company will continue in business for the whole of the year following the redemption and for the whole of that year will be able to pay its debts.

A director who makes such a declaration without reasonable grounds for the opinion expressed in the declaration will be liable to a criminal penalty (s 715). If the company goes into insolvent liquidation within a year of making a redemption out of capital, the member whose shares were redeemed and the directors who made the declaration are liable to repay the amount paid out of capital in so far as this is necessary to pay the company's debts.

There are extensive provisions requiring an auditor's report and requiring publicity of the redemption. Indeed these are so extensive that it prompted Dr Sealy to call for the replacement of the 20 sections involved in the 1985 Act with the single section used to achieve the same result in Canada (see Sealy, *Company Law and Commercial Reality* in 'Further reading' below). Sadly, the opportunity to streamline the system in the 2006 Act has not been taken.

7.3.4(d) Purchase of own shares

Having seen in Section 7.2.1 above that there was a general rule which prohibited the purchase by a company of its own shares, we now have to look at the exceptions which statutes have made to this rule. These exceptions are now so wide that it could be said that there is a general rule that a company may purchase its own shares; it is in the exceptional case that this manoeuvre is forbidden. However, although there are many situations in which it is permissible for a company to purchase its own shares, the correct procedure must be followed otherwise the purchase will be illegal. The strictness of the rules, and the prohibition on using this method to reduce the capital of a public company, support the traditional view that the general prohibition still stands; it is only in exceptional cases that such a purchase is permitted.

The general prohibition and exceptions

The general prohibition is now contained in section 658(1) of the Companies Act 2006:

> (1) A limited company must not acquire its own shares, whether by purchase, subscription or otherwise, except in accordance with the provisions of this Part.

This is backed by criminal penalties both for the company and any individual involved. The general rule is immediately followed by a list of exceptions in section 659:

> (1) A limited company may acquire any of its own fully paid shares otherwise than for valuable consideration.
> (2) Section 658 does not prohibit—
>   (a) the acquisition of shares in a reduction of capital duly made;
>   (b) the purchase of shares in pursuance of an order of the court under [various sections];
>   (c) the forfeiture of shares …

7.4 Illegal transactions

The procedures discussed in this chapter so far are the legal methods by which a company may come to own its own shares. We now have to consider transactions which fall on the other side of the line and are prohibited.

7.4.1   Financial assistance for the purchase of shares

7.4.1(a) The general prohibition on public companies

Section 678 of the Companies Act 2006 prohibits a public company or its subsidiary from giving financial assistance, either directly or indirectly, for the purpose of the acquisition of its shares. The significant change brought in by the 2006 Act is that section 678 applies to public companies only. Section 679 extends the prohibition to assistance by a public company for the acquisition of shares in its private holding company, but private companies escape the provisions.

'Financial assistance' is defined by section 677 of the 2006 Act, and includes the widest imaginable range of transactions, including:

- gifts
- guarantees
- loans

One problem that the courts have encountered concerns the involvement of the company in the illegal transaction. It is a general principle of English law that a claimant must not base a claim for compensation on an illegal act in which he was involved: 'No person should profit from his own wrong.' In the case of illegal payments being made out of company funds for the purchase of shares in that company, the company, as a separate legal person, is in law involved. The rules could therefore lead to the conclusion that the company (which in fact was the victim of this transaction) could not recover compensation because in law it was a party to the wrongful transaction. This difficulty was resolved in the case of *Selangor United Rubber Estates v Craddock* [1968] 1 WLR 1555. Craddock made a bid for the shares of the plaintiff company. The bid was made through an agent. Craddock got the money from a bank. Money from the plaintiff company was then transferred to the bank and lent to Craddock, who used it to repay the bank. The company sought to recover the money from Craddock, claiming that because he had wrongfully been in possession of money which in fact belonged to the company, he held that money on trust for the company. Between themselves, that would make Craddock a trustee and the company the person entitled to benefit, 'the beneficiary', who could call for payment of the money in trust at any time. Ungoed Thomas J said:

> I appreciate that, in the ordinary case of a claim by a beneficiary against a trustee for an illegal breach of trust, the beneficiary is not a party to the illegality; but that, when directors act for a company in an illegal act with a stranger [in this case Craddock], the company is itself a party to the transaction and therefore the illegality. The company, therefore, could not rely on the transaction as 'the source of civil rights' and, therefore, for example, it could not successfully sue the stranger with regard to rights which it was claimed the transaction conferred ... The plaintiff's claim, however, for breach of trust is not made by it as a party to that transaction, or in reliance on any right which that transaction is alleged to confer, but against the directors and constructive trustees for perpetrating that transaction and making the plaintiff company party to it in breach of trust owing to the plaintiff company.

The essence of the passage is that the company, being more sinned against than sinning, can recover the money. The wrong has been done to the company by its directors and their cronies and not by the company, even though it was perforce a party to the illegal transaction.

The major difficulty in this area in the past has not been the legal problems involved so much as the immense complexity of the arrangements that must be unravelled to discover if they contravene the section. The exclusion of private companies from the prohibition is a great step forward, as cases such as the following will have relevance only where a public company is involved, and public companies are assumed to have sophisticated legal advice. In *Belmont Finance Corporation v Williams Furniture Ltd (No 2)* [1980] 1 All ER 393, the Court of Appeal accepted previous authority to the effect that a purchase of property at an inflated price in order to put the seller in funds to buy shares would contravene the predecessor section to section 151 of the Companies Act 1985 (now section 678 of the Companies Act 2006). In the *Belmont* case itself, the judgments went further. Buckley LJ accepted that both parties to the transaction in question had honestly believed that they were entering into commercial transactions in which they were getting value for money. However, he went on to say that:

> it was certainly not a transaction in the ordinary course of Belmont's business or for the purposes of that business as it subsisted at the date of the agreement. It was an exceptional and artificial transaction and not in any sense an ordinary commercial transaction entered into for its own sake in the commercial interests of Belmont. It was part of a comparatively complex scheme for enabling Mr Grosscurth and his associates to acquire Belmont at no cash cost to themselves.

The transaction was therefore caught by the prohibition against providing assistance, even though both parties believed that it was a transaction for full value. It was significant to Buckley LJ that '[i]t was not a transaction whereby Belmont acquired anything which Belmont genuinely needed or wanted for its own purposes'.

This decision was difficult to apply to complex transactions, since the legality of those transactions depended wholly on whether the property which one party believed was being bought or sold was in the judgment of the court something which the company would have found of equal value if the share deal had not been related. Section 54 of the Companies Act 1948, under which the above case was decided, was repealed by the Companies Act 1981 and replaced by section 151 of the Companies Act 1985. Section 153 of the Companies Act 1985 sought to exempt transactions such as that in *Belmont* from the ambit of the section. The provisions of that section are repeated in the Companies Act 2006, but the *Belmont* transactions would not be caught by the 2006 regime as they concerned a private company.

Section 678(2) of the Companies Act 2006 exempts from the ambit of the general prohibition those transactions which in fact give assistance if:

(a) the company's principal purpose in giving the assistance is not to give it for the purpose of any such acquisition, or

(b) the giving of the assistance for that purpose is only an incidental part of some larger purpose of the company, and the assistance is given in good faith in the interests of the company.

This provision was discussed at length in *Brady v Brady* [1989] 1 AC 755. That case arose from a complicated scheme to divide a business between two brothers who were unable to agree to work together amicably. Because the businesses had assets of unequal value, some complicated moves were made in order to achieve a fair distribution between the two brothers of the assets of what had been a family firm. In the course of this, a transaction occurred which undoubtedly resulted in the original company (Brady) giving assistance to one of the new companies, Motoreal Ltd, in the acquisition by Motoreal of the shares in Brady. It was admitted that the assistance had been given, but it was argued that the transaction was saved by the exceptions set out in section 153 (now section 678(2)). Lord Oliver found that the first part of section 153 could not apply. In this case the sole purpose and therefore the principal purpose of the assistance had been to enable the acquisition of shares. Consequently the company could not come within the 'principal purpose' exception in paragraph (a) above. The company could escape only if it could show that the assistance was part of 'some larger purpose' of the company and that it had been given in good faith and in the interests of the company (paragraph (b) above). Lord Oliver confessed that he found the concept of 'larger purpose' difficult to grasp but was anxious not to give it too wide a meaning as this would enable wholesale evasion of the rule in section 151. He went on to say:

> [T]here has always to be borne in mind the mischief against which s 151 is aimed. In particular, if the section is not, effectively, to be deprived of any useful application, it is important to distinguish between a purpose and the reason why a purpose is formed. The ultimate reason for forming the purpose of financing an acquisition may, and in most cases probably will, be more important to those making the decision than the immediate transaction itself. But 'larger' is not the same thing as 'more important' nor is 'reason' the same as 'purpose'. If one postulates the case of a bidder for control of a public company financing his bid from the company's own funds – the obvious mischief at which the section is aimed – the immediate purpose which it is sought to achieve is that of completing the purchase and vesting control of the company in the bidder. The reasons why that course is considered desirable may be many and varied. The company may have fallen on hard times so that a change of management is considered necessary to avert disaster. It may merely be thought, and no doubt would be thought by the purchaser and the directors whom he nominates once he has control, that the business of the company will be more profitable under his management than it was heretofore. These may be excellent reasons but they cannot, in my judgment, constitute a 'larger purpose' of which the provision of assistance is merely an incident. The purpose and the only purpose of the financial assistance is and remains that of enabling the shares to be acquired and the financial or commercial advantages flowing from the acquisition, whilst they may form the reason for forming the purpose of providing the assistance are a by-product of it rather than an independent purpose of which the assistance can properly be considered to be an incident.

The problem with this approach is that in seeking to avoid a construction which would permit wholesale evasion of the prohibition in section 678(1), such a narrow view of the exception was taken that it is difficult to envisage a deliberate scheme which would escape prohibition. If the financial assistance were provided by accident it might perhaps escape, but that seems an unlikely scenario. So long as the provision of assistance is deliberately with a view to the purchase of shares, it will have been given for that 'purpose', according to Lord Oliver's formulation. The reason driving the whole arrangement would not be regarded as a larger purpose. In *Brady* the scheme was held to have contravened section 682(1) but was saved by virtue of the fact that it could be validly carried out under other sections of the 1985 Act.

A fairly liberal approach to construction seems to have been adopted in *Acatos and Hutcheson plc v Watson* [1995] 1 BCLC 218, [1995] BCC 441, where the court held that the purchase of another company whose sole asset was a substantial holding of shares in the first company was not precluded by the rules against a company acquiring its own shares.

Note that these transactions would be exempt from the 2006 regime as they involved private companies. The interpretation of the courts will still be valid if public companies are involved in similar transactions.

7.4.1(b) Exceptions

We have already examined some of the exceptions to the rule against a company giving financial assistance for the purchase of its own shares in some detail (see Section 7.4.1(a) above). A complete list may, however, be of value. Section 681 of the Companies Act 2006 contains a list of transactions wholly outside the operation of section 678. They are:

1. a distribution of a company's assets by way of a dividend lawfully made, including a distribution made in the course of winding up the company;
2. the allotment of bonus shares;
3. any reduction of capital made under the Act;
4. a redemption or purchase of any shares made in accordance with the relevant sections of the Act;
5. anything done by way of a court-approved compromise or arrangement with members or creditors;
6. anything done under an arrangement made in pursuance of section 110 of the Insolvency Act 1986, that is a reconstruction linked to a voluntary winding up (see Chapter 13);
7. anything done under an arrangement made between a company and its creditors which is binding on the creditors by virtue of Part I of the Insolvency Act 1986 (see Chapter 13).

More exceptions appear in section 682, but a public company is permitted to take advantage of these only if the transaction does not reduce the company's net assets, or, to the extent that those assets are reduced, the assistance is provided out of distributable profits. Three exceptions concern employee share schemes. The other exempts the lending of money in the ordinary course of its business by a company whose ordinary business includes moneylending.

7.5 Serious loss of capital by a public company

Section 656 of the Companies Act 2006 contains a measure first introduced into UK law as a supposed implementation of the EC Second Directive (63/21 of 18 December 1962) on company law. The Directive requires a meeting to be convened in the situation where the net assets of a public company are half or less of its called-up share capital, 'to consider whether any, and if so what, steps should be taken to deal with the situation'. The meeting must be convened not less than 28 days after the day on which a director learns that the company has lost capital to this extent. It must take place within 56 days of that day. The section is silent as to what happens if the meeting decides to do nothing. The section seems to have no other purpose than notifying the shareholders of the situation. Criminal sanctions attach to the failure of a director to call the meeting, but no civil consequences flow from contravention of the section.

7.6 Accounts

An important feature of company law is the requirement of an annual meeting to consider the accounts of the company. The directors must prepare annual accounts and present them to the members. The accounts are then filed at Companies House. In *Caparo Industries plc v Dickman* [1990] 2 AC 605, Lord Jauncey of Tullichettle said (at p 662):

> the purpose of annual accounts, so far as members are concerned, is to enable them to question the past management of the company, to exercise their voting rights, if so advised, and influence future policy and management.

The Financial Reporting Council (FRC) is the regulator of accountancy, auditing and financial reporting. Financial results are required to be presented in a balance sheet and profit and loss account. The amount that a company has available for distribution must in principle be determined from its most recent accounts that have been laid before a general meeting. The directors must state in the balance sheet the total amount they recommend should be distributed as a dividend. This will happen only after consideration of accounts drawn up according to strict rules (Companies Act 2006, ss 380–484).

7.6.1 Company accounts

It is a fundamental principle of both EU and UK company law that annual accounts should be provided and circulated to members. The accounts are useful for members so that they can judge the state of the enterprise in which they have invested and assess the performance of its directors. It may also be useful to creditors seeking reassurance that their debts will be paid.

Much legislative energy has been expended in attempting to compel companies to paint as accurate a picture as possible in their accounts. It is now a fundamental principle that, overall, the accounts must give a 'true and fair view' of the economic state of the company (see Section 7.6.5 below). A major difficulty is the valuation of the fixed assets of a company. If the value that is entered into the accounts is the value at the time of acquisition, this could have been radically altered by inflation over a number of years. On the other hand, if a current valuation is entered, this will vary according to the method used in arriving at the valuation and also according to whether the asset is valued at the sum it would raise if sold, or valued as part of the company as a going concern.

7.6.2 Financial Reporting Council

The FRC is theoretically an independent regulator. It intends to foster investment by regulating corporate governance in the UK. It issues the UK Corporate Governance and Stewardship Code (see Section 2.4.3). It also sets standards on auditing. It operates independent disciplinary arrangements for accountants (see www.frc.org.uk). Accounting requirements of company law are harmonised in the European Economic Area (EEA) by Directives 78/660/EEC and 83/349/EEC, the Fourth and Seventh Company Law Directives. The European Commission has proposed replacing these with a single new Directive (COM (2011) 684).

7.6.3 The obligation to prepare accounts

The Companies Act 2006, section 386 provides:

(1) Every company must keep adequate accounting records.
(2) Adequate accounting records means records that are sufficient—

(a) to show and explain the company's transactions,
(b) to disclose with reasonable accuracy, at any time, the financial position of the company at that time, and
(c) to enable the directors to ensure that any accounts required to be prepared comply with the requirements of this Act [and relevant regulations].
(3) Accounting records must, in particular, contain—
(a) entries from day to day of all sums of money received and expended by the company, and the matters in respect of which the receipt and expenditure takes place,
(b) a record of the assets and liabilities of the company.

The section also provides that a company dealing in goods must keep records of stock. A failure to keep accounting records amounts to an offence (s 387).

7.6.4 Keeping the records

By section 388 of the 2006 Act, the accounting records must be kept at a company's registered office or 'such other place as the directors think fit'. There are safeguards which require records to be available in the UK. The records must be open to inspection by the company's officers at all times. Private companies must keep their records for three years from the date at which they are made; public companies for six years.

7.6.5 Duty to prepare individual company accounts and 'true and fair view'

A key section in the 2006 Act is section 393, which continues the obligation on directors to approve accounts only if they give a 'true and fair view' of the assets of the company or group of companies. Sections 394 to 396 require the directors of every company to prepare for each financial year a balance sheet and profit and loss account, giving a true and fair view of the state of affairs of the company.

7.6.6 Small companies and small groups

Small companies and small groups are identified by sections 381 to 385 of the Companies Act 2006. Only private companies qualify. In the case of an individual company, a small company is one which satisfies two or more of the following requirements (s 382(3)):

1. Aggregate turnover not more that £5.6 million net or £6.72 million gross.
2. Aggregate balance sheet total not more than £2.8 million net or £3.36 million gross.
3. Aggregate number of employees not more than 50.

A parent of a group qualifies as a small company if the group meets the same requirements (s 383(4)). By section 477 of the Act, such companies are excluded from the obligation to have an audit of their accounts.

7.6.7 Medium-sized companies

A medium-sized company is not exempted from audit but has fewer filing requirements for its accounts. By section 465 of the 2006 Act, a medium-sized company exists if in any year it meets two or more of the 'following requirements' (s 465(3)):

1. Turnover not more than £22.8 million.
2. Balance sheet total not more than £11.4 million.
3. Number of employees not more than 250.

7.6.8   Group accounts

Where companies are operating together, a fairer picture of the financial health of the enterprise as a whole will be given by 'consolidated' or 'group' accounts. Small companies are exempt from this requirement (Companies Act 2006, s 398). Accordingly, section 399 provides that if at the end of a financial year a company is a parent company, the directors have an additional duty to prepare group accounts, which must give a true and fair view of the state of affairs of the parent and its subsidiaries at the end of the year, and also a true and fair view of the profit and loss of the undertakings included in the consolidation during that year.

Considerable difficulty has been experienced in devising a law which adequately requires consolidation of accounts. The problem is partly one of devising a satisfactory definition of 'parent' and 'subsidiary'. By section 1159(1) of the Companies Act 2006:

> (1) A company is a 'subsidiary' of another company, its 'holding company', if that other company—
>   (a) holds a majority of the voting rights in it, or
>   (b) is a member of it and has the right to appoint or remove a majority of its board of directors, or
>   (c) is a member of it and controls alone, pursuant to an agreement with other members, a majority of the voting rights in it,
>   or if it is a subsidiary of a company that is itself a subsidiary of that other company.

The duty extends also to groups which may include a partnership or unincorporated association carrying on a business, which are known as 'undertakings' (s 1161).

By section 1162(2), an undertaking is a parent undertaking in relation to another undertaking, a subsidiary undertaking, if:

> (a) it holds a majority of the voting rights in the undertaking, or
> (b) it is a member of the undertaking and has the right to appoint or remove a majority of its board of directors, or
> (c) it has the right to exercise a dominant influence over the undertaking—
>   (i) by virtue of provisions contained in the undertaking's memorandum or articles, or
>   (ii) by virtue of a control contract, or
> (d) it is a member of the undertaking and controls alone, pursuant to an agreement with other shareholders or members, a majority of the voting rights in the undertaking.

In the accounts of both single companies and groups, information about employee numbers and costs must be given (s 411), as well as information about directors' benefits (ss 412 and 413).

The company's auditors must have reported on the accounts before a distribution can lawfully be made. By sections 475 to 484 of the 2006 Act, if the report of the auditors contains any qualification concerning the way in which profits, losses, assets, liabilities, provisions, share capital or reserves have been dealt with in the accounts, they must state whether or not, in their opinion, the legality of the proposed distribution would be affected by the matters stated in the qualification. Their statement on this point must be presented to the members with the accounts.

An alternative justification for a distribution is on the basis of interim accounts more recent than the last annual accounts available. In the case of a private company, no rules concerning the method of preparation of those accounts appear in the statute. So far as public companies are concerned, such interim accounts must be prepared as nearly as possible in the manner in which annual accounts are prepared. No auditor's report is required but such accounts must be filed with the Registrar.

7.6.9 Directors' report

By section 415 of the Companies Act 2006, the directors must prepare a directors' report for each financial year of the company. Section 416 sets out the general contents of the report, which include the names of the directors and the principal activities of the company. Section 417 contains much more detail, requiring a 'business review'. By section 417(2), the purpose of the business review is to inform members of the company and help them assess how the directors have performed their duty under section 172. To that end it must:

1. contain a fair review of the company's business (s 417(3)(a)); and
2. provide a balanced and comprehensive analysis of the position of the company's business at the end of that year, consistent with the size and complexity of the business (s 417(4)(b)).

Quoted companies alone are required, 'to the extent necessary for an understanding of the development, performance or position of the company', to include:

(a) the main trends and factors likely to affect the future development, performance and position of the company's business; and
(b) information about—
    (i) environmental matters (including the impact of the company's business on the environment),
    (ii) the company's employees, and
    (iii) social and community issues,
    including information about any policies of the company in relation to those matters and the effectiveness of those policies … (s 417(5))

7.7 Conclusion

We have seen the immensely elaborate attempts that the law makes with the purpose of trying to preserve a fund in order to protect the interests of creditors. The necessity for such an elaborate scheme must be a matter of some doubt, particularly in view of the extent of directors' duties which would also prohibit unreasonable use of capital (see Section 9.1). For a discussion of this area of law see the contribution by Sterling noted in 'Further reading' below, and note that the reform of this area of the law is under active discussion. However, the UK has limited room for reform, as it is obliged to conform with its obligations under the EC Second Directive. As discussed, these obligations include a duty to prohibit the purchase by a company of its own shares and the provision of financial assistance for such a purchase.

Summary

7.1 The law seeks to ensure that companies get full value for their shares and that a fund of money remains in the company so that creditors have something to rely on.

7.2 A basic rule is that a company cannot acquire its own shares. This is subject to a number of exceptions.

7.3 Money may be returned to members by way of an authorised distribution.

7.4 Dividends are paid out of profits available for the purpose.

7.5 If a company wishes to reduce its capital it must comply with strict controls.

7.6 In very restricted circumstances redeemable shares may be issued and a company permitted to purchase its own shares.

7.7 The rules about maintenance of capital are reinforced by the rule that a company may not provide financial assistance for the purchase of its own shares. This rule is also subject to exceptions.

Exercises

7.1 Are the above rules instrumental in ensuring a fund is available for creditors of the company?

7.2 Are the rules unnecessarily complicated?

7.3 Are there more exceptions than rules in this area?

7.4 In a world where millions of pounds, dollars or euros can be transmitted (and won or lost) within seconds, are the complex accounting rules a method of shutting the stable door after the horse may have bolted?

Further Reading

Dine, Koutsias and Blecher, *Company Law in the New Europe* (Edward Elgar, 2007)

Haaker, 'The Future of European Creditor Protection and Capital Maintenance from a German Perspective' (2012) 13 *German Law Journal* 637–58, available at <http://ssrn.com/abstract=2120514>

Mclean, Bethany and Elkind, *The Smartest Guys in the Room* (Penguin, 2003)

Sealy, *Company Law and Commercial Reality* (Sweet & Maxwell, 1986)

Sterling, 'Financial assistance by a company for the purchase of its shares' (1987) 8 *Company Law* 99

Chapter 8

The management of the company

Key terms

- **Ordinary, special and written resolutions** – the decision-making mechanism of the company.
- **Director** – a 'director' includes any person occupying the position of director.
- **Shadow director** – means a person in accordance with whose directions or instructions the directors of the company are accustomed to act.
- **De facto** – the de facto director is a person who, despite the fact that he lacks valid appointment to a directorship, acts as if he is a de jure director.
- **Shareholder agreements** – agreements between shareholders on how they are going to vote about company matters; the participation of directors is subject to a bona fide test.
- **Shareholder meetings and the board of directors** – the institutional setting of the company.

8.1 Introduction

A great deal has been written about 'corporate governance'. The debate ranges across many of the issues covered in this book because it involves looking at the best way to run a company. It considers what is the best model of company to adopt (see Chapter 2), the best way to control directors (see Chapter 9), whether or not the German dual board pattern should be adopted (see Chapter 2), and whether and to what extent the company owes 'social duties' to employees, the environment and the state generally. The different categories of corporate governance models and the theories that underpin them were presented in detail in Chapter 2 of this book.

This chapter will focus on the practicalities of corporate governance, emphasising the institutions of governance of companies in the UK: the directors and their authority to act on behalf of the company, the types of directors, the shareholders' meetings and the voting arrangements, such as the different types of resolutions, along with details in relation to the everyday running of the company. In other words, this chapter will present a map of the company and its internal structure. It will shed light on its decision-making mechanism, along with the institutional procedures on the basis of which the company operates. The chapter will examine all the significant aspects of the management of the company such as the meeting of shareholders, the board of directors, voting procedures, proxies, quotas and resolutions, among others.

Theoretically, the general meeting of the body of shareholders has considerable power to make decisions which affect the management of the company by using the votes attached to their shares. This apparently independent power is subject to a number of practical qualifications. Others will appear throughout the chapter. First, a qualification of considerable importance is the right of shareholders to appoint a proxy.

8.2 Proxy voting

8.2.1 Appointment of proxies

Section 324 of the Companies Act 2006 confers a right on a shareholder to appoint a proxy to attend meetings and vote instead of him at those meetings. The proxy need not be a member. In the case of a private company, the proxy has the same right to speak at the meeting as the member would have had. The articles of association will normally have regulations governing the form in which proxies may be made (see the Model Articles (SI 2008/3229)).

Section 324 also provides that a proxy may exercise all or any of the member's rights. This is particularly important, because directors will often suggest to shareholders that they are well informed about the business transactions and other ramifications of the enterprise so that shareholders should appoint them as their proxies. Of course this means that the directors become more powerful in the company.

8.2.2 Solicitation of proxies

Two important elements which affect the balance of power between management and shareholders are:

1. the management may themselves hold a considerable number of the shares; and
2. the directors may employ the company's money in soliciting proxies on behalf of its policies.

In *Peel v London and North Western Rly Co* [1907] 1 Ch 5, the court held that the company was bound to explain its policy to shareholders, and was entitled to solicit votes in support of that policy at the company's expense. If an officer of the company issues invitations to appoint a proxy, those invitations must go to all members entitled to notice of the meeting or a criminal offence will be committed by him.

The ability of the directors to issue reasoned circulars accompanied by proxy forms means that many issues affecting a company will be determined before the meeting is held and determined in favour of the management.

8.3 Meetings

8.3.1 Formality of procedure

It has been established for some time that agreement of all the members to a course of conduct is sufficient to bind the company, even when no formal meeting has been held. In *Cane v Jones* [1981] 1 WLR 1451, this principle applied even in the case where the articles had in effect been altered. The informality principle now has statutory force: section 288 of the Companies Act 2006 provides that, in the case of a private company, a written resolution which is passed (s 296(4)) by the required majority signifying consent is as effective as a resolution passed at a meeting. There are two exceptions to this general power:

1. resolutions under section 168 removing a director before his term of office has expired; and
2. resolutions under section 510 to remove an auditor before the expiration of his term of office.

See Section 8.4 for an analysis of resolutions.

8.3.2 General meeting

Private companies are not required to hold an annual general meeting; under section 336 of the Companies Act 2006, this requirement is imposed only on public companies (see Section 8.3.3 below). Instead, sections 302 and 303 of the 2006 Act permit directors to call general meetings. Section 303 permits members to require directors to hold a general meeting if those members represent 10 per cent of the paid-up capital of the company or, if there is no share capital, 10 per cent of the voting rights, unless the last meeting was held more than a year ago, in which case the required percentage is 5 per cent. If the members require the directors to call a meeting, this must happen within 21 days. The meeting must be convened within that time limit, not necessarily held within it (see *Re Windward Islands (Enterprises) UK Ltd* [1983] BCLC 293). If the directors fail to convene a meeting within the 21 days, those requesting the meeting may do so. The expense will fall on the company (ss 305 and 306).

By section 306, the court has a reserve power to call a meeting if 'for any reason it is impracticable' to call the meeting otherwise. An application to the court to order a meeting under this section may be made by any director or any member entitled to vote at the meeting. In *Re El Sombrero Ltd* [1958] Ch 900 the court, considering the predecessor to section 306 (Companies Act 1985, s 371), held that to decide when the holding of a meeting was 'impracticable', the court must, in the words of Wynn-Parry J, 'examine the circumstances of the particular case and answer the question whether, as a practical matter, the desired meeting of the company can be conducted, there being no doubt, of course, that it can be convened and held'. In that case the order was granted, the facts of the case being an illustration of the circumstances in which the power to order a meeting to be held is very useful. In *Re El Sombero Ltd* there were three shareholders, two of these being directors. A quorum of three was required for a meeting. The non-director shareholder, who held a majority of the shares, wished to convene a meeting to remove the directors. They refused to attend a meeting, thus preventing a quorum from being achieved. However, the Court of Appeal held that it would be wrong to use the reserve power to call a meeting and determine its quorum if the effect of that would be to override class rights which were embedded in a shareholder agreement.

In *Harman and Another v BML Group Ltd* [1994] 2 BCLC 674, the capital of the company was divided into A and B shares, the B shares being registered in the name of B. H and M held a majority of the A shares. Under an agreement signed by all the shareholders, it was provided that a meeting of shareholders would not be quorate unless a B shareholder or proxy were present. H and M applied for an order under the predecessor to section 306 that a meeting of the company be summoned. The judge ordered that a meeting should be summoned, ruling that any two members of the company would constitute a quorum. The Court of Appeal held that this was not a proper use of the provision.

8.3.3 Annual general meeting

A public company must hold an annual general meeting (AGM) (Companies Act 2006, s 336). This must be held in addition to any other meetings that are convened. Section 336(1) provides that:

> Every public company must hold a general meeting as its annual general meeting in each period of 6 months from the date when its annual accounts are dated.

Section 336(3) and (4) provides criminal penalties for all officers in default if the meeting is not held.

The 2006 Act does not specify in any detail the business to be transacted by the AGM. This usually consists of:

1. the adoption of the annual accounts;
2. the reading of the auditor's report and the appointment of auditors for the future;
3. the directors' report, which will include the directors' recommendation of the dividend to be paid to shareholders – a resolution will be proposed that the amount recommended be paid by way of dividend;
4. appointment of directors where some are retiring;
5. a resolution to pay the auditors;
6. a resolution to pay the directors.

8.3.4 Notice of meetings

The information disclosed in notices of meetings must be sufficient to enable the shareholder to exercise an informed judgement. The courts will require full disclosure of any benefits which directors will reap from proposed resolutions. In *Baillie v Oriental Telephone and Electric Company Ltd* [1915] 1 Ch 503, the notice did not disclose the fact that the directors stood to gain substantially from the passing of certain resolutions. Lord Cozens-Hardy MR said:

> I feel no difficulty in saying that special resolutions obtained by means of a notice which did not substantially put the shareholders in the position to know what they were voting about cannot be supported, and in so far as these special resolutions were passed on the faith and footing of such a notice the defendants cannot act upon them.

8.3.5 Class meetings

If there is a reason to convene a meeting of a particular class of shareholder, for example to consider the variation of share rights (see Chapter 5), only the holders of the shares of the particular class should be present. In *Carruth v Imperial Chemical Industries Ltd* [1937] AC 707, Lord Russell of Killowen said:

> Prima facie a separate meeting of a class should be a meeting attended only by members of the class, in order that the discussion of the matters which the meeting has to consider may be carried on unhampered by the presence of others who are not interested to view those matters from the same angle as that of the class; and if the presence of outsiders was retained in spite of the ascertained wish of the constituents of the meeting for their exclusion, it would not, I think, be possible to say that a separate meeting of the class had been duly held.

8.3.6 Quorum

Section 318 of the Companies Act 2006 provides that a single member is sufficient for a valid meeting in the case of a single member company. In all other cases, two members are sufficient unless they both represent the same person as a proxy (see Section 8.2.1 above) or they represent the same corporation. However, the section is expressly subject to contrary provision in the articles. The quorum of meetings may also be contained in shareholder agreements (see *Harman and Another v BML Group Ltd* [1994] 2 BCLC 674 and Section 8.5.3 below).

Except in the case of a single member company, no single member can constitute a quorum even if representing several shareholders (see *Re MJ Shanley Contracting Ltd* (1979) 124 SJ 239). This rule is displaced when the meeting is called by the court or BIS.

8.3.7 The Shareholders' Rights Directive

Certain changes in the area were introduced by the Shareholders' Rights Directive (Directive 2007/36/EC), which was adopted in July 2007. The Member States of the EU were granted a two-year deadline to incorporate the Directive into their national legal order (3 August 2009). The Directive regulates the exercise of certain rights of shareholders in listed companies. More specifically, the Directive sets certain requirements for the exercise of shareholder rights attached to voting shares in relation to the general meetings of companies which have their registered office in a Member State and whose shares are traded in a regulated market operating in a Member State. The basic aim of the Directive is to improve corporate governance in European companies traded on regulated markets by enabling shareholders to exercise their voting rights across borders. It aims at setting up a common framework by removing the existing obstacles that shareholders deal with when voting at company meetings. The Directive is promoting minimum standards of harmonisation across the EU and more generally across the EEA. As it is a tool of minimum harmonisation, Member States are allowed to introduce additional measures so as to facilitate further the exercise of the rights referred to in the Directive. Despite the fact that the UK already has an array of provisions which promote standards relative to those of the Directive, further changes appear necessary so as to fully comply with the provisions of the Directive.

It has to be noted that the Directive allows the convocation of meetings by notice of 14 days only 'where the company offers the facility for shareholders to vote by electronic means accessible to all shareholders' and where such a decision is upheld by 'a majority of not less than two thirds of the votes attaching to the shares or the subscribed capital represented' and this resolution is renewed annually. According to Article 5(4) of the Directive, Member States are now under the obligation to ensure that the company shall make available to its shareholders on its Internet site the convocation of the general meeting and the documents to be submitted to it; these acts have to take place 21 days prior to the meeting. The 2006 Act will have to be reshaped accordingly.

Furthermore, Article 7 of the Directive effectively abolishes 'share blocking' and introduces a record date in all Member States which may not be more than 30 days before the general meeting. The record date is the specified date prior to the general meeting on which the shareholders who are to participate in it and to vote in respect of their shares shall be determined with respect to the shares held. 'Share blocking' normally meant that after this date the shares involved could not be traded. However, Article 7 now clearly states that 'the rights of a shareholder to sell or otherwise transfer his shares during the period between the record date and the general meeting to which it applies are not subject to any restriction to which they are not subject at other times'; this provision effectively abolishes share blocking. The truth is that share blocking is not a common practice in the UK; however, there is nothing in the Companies Act 2006 to prevent it. This is something that will need to be changed in light of the Directive.

In addition, Article 8 of the Directive entails the abolition of the existing obstacles on electronic participation in the general meeting including electronic voting. Under Article 8:

> the use of electronic means for the purpose of enabling shareholders to participate in the general meeting may be made subject only to such requirements and constraints as are necessary to ensure the identification of shareholders and the security of the electronic communication, and only to the extent that they are proportionate to achieving those objectives.

This provision covers what is already a common practice among UK quoted companies, but for reasons of legal clarity it might appear necessary to amend the current legislation to ensure that the standard introduced by the Directive is expressly provided for by the 2006 Act.

Article 9 of the Directive expressly provides for the right of 'every shareholder to ask questions related to items on the agenda of the general meeting' and the obligation of 'the company to answer the questions put to it by shareholders'. There is nothing in the 2006 Act discouraging such a practice; however, the 2006 Act might need to be amended so as expressly to include a concrete obligation on behalf of the companies concerned to 'answer the questions put to them by shareholders'.

Moreover, Article 10 promotes the abolition of existing constraints on the eligibility of people to act as proxy holder and of excessive formal requirements for the appointment of the proxy holder. More specifically, according to the relevant text, 'apart from the requirement that the proxy holder possess legal capacity, Member States shall abolish any legal rule which restricts, or allows companies to restrict, the eligibility of persons to be appointed as proxy holders'.

In addition, Article 12 allows companies to offer their shareholders the possibility to vote by correspondence in advance of the general meeting. In the UK the aforementioned right exists, but only in so far as the shareholders appoint a proxy by correspondence or electronically to vote on their behalf. The role of the proxy at this point now appears redundant, as the Directive grants shareholders the right to vote by correspondence without the intervention of any other party; the clarification of such a possibility will require changes to the 2006 Act.

8.4 Resolutions

The decisions in a company are made either by voting on resolutions at a meeting, or by voting on written resolutions. Public companies only have the option of passing resolutions at meetings (Companies Act 2006, s 281(2)). The usual decision-making process is by an ordinary resolution, which requires a simple majority of votes to pass (s 282). The company's articles may require a higher majority, however, and the Companies Act 2006 imposes a higher majority in certain cases, such as where a resolution concerns amendment of the articles (s 21).

8.4.1 Special resolutions

Special resolutions are more often required. The alteration of articles by special resolution is dealt with in Chapter 3 and serves as the main example where a special resolution is required. Section 283 of the 2006 Act provides:

> A special resolution of the members (or of a class of the members) of a company means a resolution passed by a majority of not less than 75 per cent.

In the case of a written resolution, it must have been proposed as a special resolution.

8.4.2 Unanimous consent

The members of the company do not have to meet if they all agree to a particular course of conduct, unless the course of conduct is illegal or there is a provision in the articles forbidding this method of proceeding. In the latter case it would seem that the unanimous consent of the shareholders can effect an alteration in the articles, so that the effectiveness of such a prohibition must be in some doubt (see *Cane v Jones* [1981] 1 WLR 1451).

8.5 Voting

8.5.1 Methods of voting

The voting rights of the shareholders will normally be set out in the articles. The usual method of voting is to take a show of hands. In this case, each member will have one vote. However, in some circumstances a member, dissatisfied with the outcome of a show of hands, may call for a 'poll'. The standard article provides that on a poll 'every member shall have one vote for every share of which he is the holder'.

It can clearly be seen that the outcome of a vote on a poll may radically differ from that on a show of hands. The right to demand a poll is therefore of considerable importance. The circumstances in which a poll may be demanded may appear in the articles. However, the Companies Act 2006 provides a 'minimum standard' for the articles. Under section 321:

(1) A provision contained in a company's articles is void in so far as it would have the effect of excluding the right to demand a poll at a general meeting on any question other than—
   (a) the election of the chairman of the meeting; or
   (b) the adjournment of the meeting.
(2) A provision of a company's articles is void in so far as it would have the effect of making ineffective a demand for a poll on any such question which is made—
   (a) by not less than 5 members having the right to vote on the resolution; or
   (b) by a member or members representing not less than 10 per cent of the total voting rights of all the members having the right to vote on the resolution (excluding any voting rights attached to any shares in the company held as treasury shares); or
   (c) by a member or members holding shares in the company conferring a right to vote on the resolution, being shares on which an aggregate sum has been paid up equal to not less than 10 per cent of the total sum paid up on all the shares conferring that right (excluding shares in the company conferring a right to vote on the resolution which are held as treasury shares).

8.5.2   Exercise of voting rights

There is considerable weight of authority to support the proposition that a shareholder may exercise his right to vote as he pleases and does not have any duty to take into account the interests of others or of the company. In *Pender v Lushington* (1877) 6 Ch D 70, Jessel MR said:

> [A] man may be actuated in giving his vote by interests entirely adverse to the interests of the company as a whole. He may think it more for his particular interest that a certain course may be taken which may be in the opinion of others very adverse to the interests of the company as a whole, but he cannot be restrained from giving his vote in what way he pleases because he is influenced by that motive.

(See also *North West Transportation v Beatty* (1887) 12 App Cas 589.)

An inroad into this principle appeared to be made by the judgment in the case of *Clemens v Clemens Bros Ltd* [1976] 2 All ER 268. There, a challenge was made to a resolution to issue further shares to directors. This would have had the effect of substantially reducing (from 45 per cent to below 25 per cent) the voting power of the plaintiff. Foster J said:

> I think that one thing which emerges from the cases to which I have referred is that in such a case as the present Miss Clemens is not entitled to exercise her majority vote in whatever way she pleases. The difficulty is in finding a principle, and obviously expressions such as 'bona fide for the benefit of the company as a whole', 'fraud on a minority' and 'oppressive' do not assist in formulating such a principle.
>
> I have come to the conclusion that it would be unwise to try to produce a principle, since the circumstances of each case are infinitely varied. It would not, I think, assist to say more than that in my judgment Miss Clemens is not entitled as of right to exercise her votes as an ordinary shareholder in any way she pleases … I cannot escape the conclusion that the resolutions have been framed so as to put into the hands of Miss Clemens and her fellow directors complete control of the company and to deprive the plaintiff of her existing rights as a shareholder with more than 25 per cent of the votes … They are specifically and carefully designed to ensure not only that the plaintiff can never get control of the company but to deprive her of what has been called her negative control. Whether I say that these proposals are oppressive to the plaintiff or that no one could honestly believe that they are for her benefit matters not. A court of equity will in my judgment regard these considerations as sufficient to prevent the consequences arising from Miss Clemens using her legal right to vote in the way she has and it would be right for a court of equity to prevent such consequences taking effect.

This passage is clearly irreconcilable with the traditional view above. The right to vote as a shareholder pleases derives from the idea that the right to vote is a property right which should not be subject to equitable restraints. It is possible to reconcile the two cases by arguing that a shareholder has the right to vote to protect the value of shares in any way he wishes, but the best interests of the company can override that right and a decision contrary to these best interests will not be upheld.

8.5.3   Shareholder agreements

Shareholders are free to agree among themselves how they will vote on particular issues. These agreements may be enforced by mandatory injunction (*Puddephatt v Leith* [1916] 1 Ch 200). Such agreements may substantially affect the balance of power among the various groups of shareholders, and anyone seeking to understand how any particular company functions would need to know of the existence and content of such agreements.

The agreements may supplement the articles of association and contain quite fundamental rights (see *Harman and Another v BML Group Ltd* [1994] 2 BCLC 674 – Section 8.3.2).

In *Russell v Northern Bank Development Corporation Ltd* [1992] BCLC 1016, the House of Lords held that an agreement between four shareholders of a private company not to vote in favour of an increase in share capital unless they had first agreed to do so in writing was valid and enforceable. However, the part of the agreement which purported to bind the company was void, because it was an attempt to fetter the company's statutory power to alter its articles.

8.6 Management of the company

8.6.1 Introduction

We saw in Chapter 2 that one of the advantages of incorporation was to create a legal person separate from its members which could operate at a distance from those members. Used properly this enables (though not obliges) companies to be run by specialists. The members may simply regard the company as a form of investment for their money. The persons actually concerned in the running of the company are known as the directors. Even if they have not been appointed officially, the law will in many instances treat these individuals in the same way as directors because they will qualify as 'shadow directors' (this term is discussed more fully in Section 8.6.3 below). If the members wish one person to be particularly concerned with the everyday running of the business, that person should be appointed as managing director (see further Section 8.6.10 below).

If the shareholders are not content to have their money managed on their behalf by the directors but wish to have a say in the way that the company is run, the chances are quite high that they will come into conflict with the 'professional' management in the form of the directors. Berle and Means found (see 'Further reading') that where ownership of shares in large American corporations was widely dispersed, no individual or group was in a position to control the corporation; instead management was in control. Large institutional investors such as pension funds and insurance companies are in a position to exercise control over management. However, such control seems usually to be exercised in an informal way rather than through the formal mechanisms of meetings, which are where, according to the company's constitution, decisions will be taken. Most meetings of public companies are poorly attended. The UK government's policy of encouraging small shareholdings (in, for example, privatised industries) would seem likely to exacerbate this problem, as the difficulty and expense of attending a meeting when the shareholder has only a small sum at stake will not be undertaken. In large public companies the management are in control of business decisions and are out of control in the sense that they are not effectively accountable to other organs of the company. This perception may have fuelled the debate about the benefits of a two-tier structure of management, with a supervisory board of directors overseeing the directors involved in day-to-day business decisions. Such a system is an option that a company could adopt under the European Company Statute Directive. In any event, under those proposals there would be a 'supervisory' element to the board structure. It was also instrumental in starting the committee enquiry which eventually reported as the Cadbury Committee on the Financial Aspects of Corporate Governance. This produced a Code, which relied heavily on the appointment of non-executive directors. This body was followed by the Hampel Committee on Corporate Governance and eventually by the issue of a 'Combined Code' which is embedded in the rules of the London Stock Exchange. All listed companies are obliged to comply with the Combined Code or give reasons for not doing so. An important part of the Combined Code is the requirement of a 'sound system of internal control' to manage 'significant risks'. The Code is revised annually, the latest revision was in 2012.

The board of directors must consider:

1. the nature and extent of the risks facing the company;
2. the likelihood of the risks materialising;
3. the company's ability to reduce the impact of such risks if they do materialise;
4. costs relative to benefits.

The Code is now supplemented by the Companies Act 2006 provisions on directors' duties (see Chapter 9 for a detailed analysis of directors' duties).

In the case of small companies, the system of agreement at formal meetings may also be unreal. Decisions may well be made by the few people who actually run the business, meeting informally day by day. If there are any other shareholders, they may take no interest in the business at all.

Others are interested in the way that the company is run as well. Employees have a very considerable interest in the decisions that are made in the course of managing the business. Creditors are also concerned, particularly when the company has fallen upon hard times. Each of these groups has some claim to be consulted, or at least to have their interests considered when management decisions are made. In this chapter we shall examine the way that each of these interest groups may influence decisions about the way a company is managed.

With the reservations expressed above in mind, we turn to examination of the rules governing the appointment and removal of officers of the company, managing directors and shadow directors, directors' meetings, the general meeting, the relationship between managers and shareholders, and the influence of employees and creditors.

8.6.2   Appointment of directors

Section 154(1) of the Companies Act 2006 provides that every private company must have at least one director. Section 154(2) requires public companies to have at least two directors. By section 155, a company must have at least one director who is a natural person.

The term 'director' is not fully defined, section 250 of the Act merely stating that a '"director" includes any person occupying the position of director, by whatever name called' (but see Companies Act 2006, s 251 and the discussion of 'shadow directors' at Section 8.6.3 below), nor is there much positive guidance in the legislation as to how a director should act. There is a considerable body of both statute and case law which will show directors what they must not do, but except in general terms (see Chapter 9) there is little guidance on how the company should be managed. Much of the structure of management will appear in the articles of association which will often adopt at least parts of the Model Articles, although modifications may be made to accommodate peculiarities relating to the particular company.

The first directors of any company are the directors named in the memorandum and articles of association of the company to the Registrar of Companies when the company is formed.

Until the subscribers to the memorandum have made appointments, the company cannot act except by a decision of the general meeting (which is made by a majority at a meeting of subscribers, or in writing by all the subscribers without a meeting: *John Morley Building Co v Barras* [1891] 2 Ch 386; and *Re Great Northern Salt and Chemical Works Co* (1890) 44 Ch D 472).

8.6.3 Shadow directors and de facto directors

The definition of 'director' in section 250 of the Companies Act 2006 includes 'any person occupying the position of director, by whatever name called' (see Section 8.6.2 above), and that includes both shadow directors and de facto directors.

Section 251 of the Act defines 'shadow director'. That is a term used in the statute where there is a possibility that someone responsible for misfeasance could escape liability where he had not officially been appointed as a director but was really in charge of the business. Section 251 provides:

> (1) In the Companies Acts 'shadow director', in relation to a company, means a person in accordance with whose directions or instructions the directors of the company are accustomed to act.

Therefore, the shadow director is the person, usually hidden in the background, who pulls the strings and dictates the implemented policies to the de jure directors. The person in question, although not visible and perceivable as such by the outsiders, is in fact in a position to exercise an overwhelming degree of influence on the de jure directors to such an extent that many of what appear to be the directors' own decisions bear the distinctive stamp of the shadow director. Therefore, the connecting link between the de jure directors and the shadow director is the influence that the latter consistently exercises on the former, and consequently on the decision making of the company.

The de facto director is a person who, despite the fact that he lacks valid appointment to a directorship, acts as if he is a de jure director. The lack of existence of a valid appointment is an element shared with the shadow director; however, the distinctive factor that distinguishes a de facto director from a shadow director is the element of visibility. Outsiders perceive the de facto director as a validly appointed director, as he or she openly acts as the person responsible for carrying out those tasks integral to the director's routine. The de facto director is not the force behind the de jure director, dictating his decisions, but the person who visibly substitutes for the de jure director in the public eye.

The definition of the term 'director' to encompass to a certain extent both the shadow and the de facto directors has a clear impact on directors' duties. Section 250 provides the legal basis on which a shadow or a de facto director could be found liable for a breach of duty, albeit on the basis of different preconditions and to a different extent. A thorough analysis of the issues in question is included in Chapter 9, which focuses on directors' duties.

8.6.4 Persons associated with a director

The director may find himself in breach of duty when he enters into a transaction with an individual or company with whom he is connected. Therefore, in order to prevent evasion of duties by the use of members of a director's family or a company controlled by a director, statute often extends a prohibition relating to a transaction to 'connected persons' or 'associated companies'. By section 252(2) of the Companies Act 2006, the persons 'connected with' a director are:

(a) members of the director's family ... ;
(b) a body corporate with which the director is connected ... ;
(c) a person acting in his capacity as trustee of a trust—
  (i)   the beneficiaries of which include the director or a person ... connected with him, or
  (ii) the terms of which confer a power on the trustees that may be exercised for the benefit of the director or any such person,
  other than a trust for the purposes of an employees' share scheme or a pension scheme;
(d) a person acting in his capacity as partner—
  (i)   of the director, or
  (ii) of a person ... connected with that director;
(e) a firm that is a legal person under the law by which it is governed and in which—
  (i)   the director is a partner,
  (ii) a partner is a [connected person], or
  (iii) a partner is a firm in which the director is a partner or in which there is a partner who [is a connected person].

The members of a director's family are listed in section 253:

1. the director's spouse or civil partner;
2. any person (whether of a different sex or the same sex) with whom the director lives as a partner in an enduring family relationship;
3. the director's children or step-children;
4. any children or step-children of a partner who live with the director and are under the age of 18;
5. the director's parents.

8.6.5 Age of directors

Section 157 of the Companies Act 2006 sets 16 as the minimum age for a director. The Secretary of State may make provision by regulations for cases in which a person who has not attained the age of 16 years may be appointed a director of a company according to section 158.

8.6.6 Remuneration of directors

Directors are in a curious position, as their appointment does not entitle them to be paid, even if they in fact do work for the company (see *Re George Newman and Co* [1895] 1 Ch 674). However, the articles of association may provide for directors' pay. This will not benefit a director unless he is in a position to enforce any provision in his favour in the articles by using section 33 of the Companies Act 2006 (see Chapter 3). Usually the right to be paid will arise from a contract of employment made with the company. Some of the terms of that contract may be discoverable by looking at the articles where, for example, the amount that directors are to be paid may be specified. The situation which arises then is clearly set out in *Re New British Iron Company, ex parte Beckwith* [1898] 1 Ch 324, where the articles of association contained the following provision:

> 62: The remuneration of the board shall be an annual sum of £1,000 to be paid out of the funds of the company, which sum shall be divided in such manner as the board shall from time to time determine.

Wright J said:

> Article 62 fixes the remuneration of the directors at the annual sum of £1,000. That article is not in itself a contract between the company and the directors; it is only part of the contract constituted by the articles of association between the members of the company inter se. But where on the footing of that article the directors are employed by the company and accept office the terms of article 62 are embodied in and form part of the contract between the company and the directors. Under the article as thus embodied the directors obtain a contractual right to an annual sum of £1,000 as remuneration.

In *Re Richmond Gate Property Co Ltd* [1965] 1 WLR 335, the articles provided that the directors were to be paid such remuneration as the board of directors determined by resolution. The company was wound up before a resolution settling the amount to be paid had been passed. The directors were entitled to nothing under the employment contract. Plowman J said:

> [A] contract exists between [the applicant] and the company for payment to him of remuneration as managing director, and that remuneration depends on Article 108 of Table A [the equivalent article is Article 84 of Table A to the Companies Act 1985], and is to be such amount 'as the directors may determine'; in other words, the managing director is at the mercy of the board, he gets what they determine to pay him, and if they do not determine to pay him anything he does not get anything. That is his contract with the company, and those are the terms on which he accepts office.

It was argued in that case that the directors should be entitled to be paid for work which they had actually done under a claim known as a 'quantum meruit' claim. It was held, however, that because there was a contract of employment, such a claim was excluded.

Considerable public disquiet concerning large pay rises awarded to directors of public companies led the Confederation of British Industry to set up a committee chaired by Sir Richard Greenbury to consider the remuneration of directors. The committee drew up a Code of Best Practice (contained in its 1995 report) which was subsequently echoed in the Combined Code. A company listed on the Stock Exchange must state in its annual report and accounts whether it has complied with the Code. The 'best practice' provisions require the directors of a listed company to set up a remuneration committee, consisting exclusively of non-executive directors, to determine the company's policy on executive directors' pay and specific packages for each executive director. This attempt to inject some objectivity into the level of pay does not seem to have had a significant impact. Neither does the 'advisory vote' which shareholders are now entitled to exercise on directors' pay, although there is some evidence of withdrawal of huge pay rises where the company has been doing particularly badly.

8.6.7   Removal of a director

Section 168 of the Companies Act 2006 provides:

> (1) A company may by ordinary resolution … remove a director before the expiration of his period of office, notwithstanding anything in any agreement between it and him.

This replaces section 303 of the Companies Act 1985 which included the words 'notwithstanding anything in its articles'.

This sweeping power apparently given to the general meeting to remove a director is nonetheless subject to two very significant qualifications. One appears in statutory form in section 168(5) of the Companies Act 2006, which expressly preserves the right of a director dismissed in accordance with section 168 to damages for any breach of contract of employment that has occurred. The rule is that the director may be dismissed, but because he has been dismissed by the company that is also the other party to his employment contract, he will be entitled to damages on the principle expressed in *Stirling v Maitland* (1864) 5 B&S 840, where Cockburn LJ said:

> [I]f a party enters into an arrangement which can only take effect by the continuance of a certain existing set of circumstances, there is an implied engagement on his part that he shall do nothing of his own motion to put an end to that state of circumstances under which alone the arrangement can be operative.

Thus, a director's employment contract can continue to operate only while the company refrains from dismissing him by passing a resolution under section 168 of the Companies Act 2006. If such a resolution is passed, it is effective to dismiss him, but it is at the same time a breach of contract and damages for that breach must be paid. The same principle applies where the company is in breach of such a contract by alteration of its articles. See *Southern Foundries Ltd v Shirlaw* [1940] AC 701; *Shindler v Northern Raincoat Co Ltd* [1960] 1 WLR 1038; *Nelson v James Nelson & Sons Ltd* [1914] 2 KB 770; and *Read v Astoria Garage (Streatham) Ltd* [1952] 2 All ER 292 (see Chapter 3).

A provision which may in some cases alleviate this liability is to be found in section 188 of the 2006 Act. This provides that a director may not be employed for a period exceeding two years unless there is prior approval of the contract by the general meeting. Any term included in a director's employment contract which contravenes this prohibition is void to the extent that the two-year term is exceeded. Unless the general meeting so approves, this will limit the damages payable to the amount owed to the director for what remains of the two-year period at the time of his dismissal. The director will also be under a duty to 'mitigate' the damage, that is, to take any reasonable steps available to him to limit the amount payable to him. Whatever the length of the contract, it is common practice for directors to have 'rolling' contracts which renew themselves daily. Thus each day, the contract stretches two years into the future.

The second qualification to the power to remove a director by using section 168 arises because of the strange decision in *Bushell v Faith* [1970] AC 1099, which appears to retain its relevance in the regime created by the Companies Act 2006. In that case, the articles of a private company provided:

> [I]n the event of a resolution being proposed at any general meeting for the removal from office of any director any shares held by that director shall on a poll in respect of such resolution carry the right of three votes per share.

Since only three persons were involved (a brother and two sisters), the situation was that if an ordinary resolution were to be passed under the predecessor section to section 168 of the Companies Act 2006 (Companies Act 1948, s 184), the sisters would be able to outvote the brother 2:1, and he would be able to be removed as a director. If his special voting right were to be taken into account, however, the same resolution would be defeated 3:2. This meant that the director in question was effectively irremovable. It was argued that such a 'weighted voting provision' was inconsistent with the predecessor to section 168, since that section had been intended to prevent entrenchment of directors by inserting provisions in the articles. The relevant section (now s 168) therefore contained the words 'notwithstanding anything in the articles'. Lord Upjohn said:

> My Lords, when construing an Act of Parliament it is a canon of construction that its provisions must be construed in the light of the mischief which the Act was designed to meet. In this case the mischief was well known; it was a common practice, especially in the case of private companies, to provide in the articles that a director should be irremovable or only removable by an extraordinary resolution; in the former case the articles would have to be altered by special resolution before the director could be removed and of course in either case a three-quarters' majority would be required. In many cases this would be impossible, so the Act provided that notwithstanding anything in the articles an ordinary resolution would suffice to remove a director.

Despite the identification of the 'mischief' at which the section was aimed, and the admission that the device used in the case made the director irremovable, the House of Lords came to the conclusion that it was permissible to have this type of weighted voting provision and that it was not in conflict with the predecessor to section 168. This was said to be because no restriction had been placed on the company's right to specify the voting rights of particular shares. There is much to be said for the dissenting judgment of Lord Morris of Borth-y-Gest:

> Some shares may, however, carry a greater voting power than others. On a resolution to remove a director shares will therefore carry the voting power that they possess. But this does not, in my view, warrant a device such as Article 9 introduces. Its unconcealed effect is to make a director irremovable. If the question is posed whether the shares of the respondent possess any added voting weight the answer must be that they possess none whatever beyond, if valid, an ad hoc weight for the special purpose of circumventing [now s 168]. If Article 9 were writ large it would set out that a director is not to be removed against his will and that in order to achieve this and to thwart the express provision of [now s 168] the voting power of any director threatened with removal is to be deemed to be greater than it actually is. The learned judge thought that to sanction this would be to make a mockery of the law. I think so too.

It has to be noted, though, that this kind of weighted voting would be totally unacceptable in large public companies, and that the London Stock Exchange would refuse the listing to any public company with articles that provide for such weighted voting rights.

Note that an effect similar to that of *Bushell v Faith* may be achieved using shareholder agreements (discussed in Section 8.5.3 above). The application of *Bushell v Faith* is in doubt following the omission of 'notwithstanding anything in the articles' from section 168. However, this will depend on the interpretation of section 33 as to whether the constitution is an 'agreement' between the director and the company.

Under section 169 of the 2006 Act, a director has the right to protest against removal, and he is entitled to be heard at the meeting called to remove him.

8.6.8 Disqualification of directors

A person subject to a disqualification order made under the Company Directors Disqualification Act 1986 may not act as a director (see Chapter 9). The articles may contain other situations which will require a director to vacate office. Article 18 of the Model Articles provides for the following cases where a director's appointment is terminated:

> A person ceases to be a director as soon as—
> (a) that person ceases to be a director by virtue of any provision of the Companies Act 2006 or is prohibited from being a director by law;
> (b) a bankruptcy order is made against that person;
> (c) a composition is made with that person's creditors generally in satisfaction of that person's debts;
> (d) a registered medical practitioner who is treating that person gives a written opinion to the company stating that that person has become physically or mentally incapable of acting as a director and may remain so for more than three months;
> (e) by reason of that person's mental health, a court makes an order which wholly or partly prevents that person from personally exercising any powers or rights which that person would otherwise have;
> (f) notification is received by the company from the director that the director is resigning from office, and such resignation has taken effect in accordance with its terms.

8.6.9 Directors' meetings

The rules governing directors' meetings are usually to be found in the articles of association.

One clear rule is that notice must be given to all directors of a meeting (see *Re Portuguese Copper Mines* (1889) 42 Ch D 160), unless a particular director is abroad and unable to be reached by notice (see *Halifax Sugar Refining Co v Franklyn* (1890) 59 LJ Ch 591). Sections 248 and 249 of the 2006 Act provide that minutes of directors' meetings must be taken and may be used as evidence of the proceedings at those meetings. Note that the Companies Act 2006 requires a director (including a director of a single member company) to declare transactions in which he has an interest (s 182) and provides that it is a criminal offence not to do so (s 183).

8.6.10 Managing director

It is usual to include in the articles of association a power for the directors to appoint one or more of their number to be the managing director or directors, and permitting the delegation of such powers as are necessary for him or them to manage the business. It will be the business of such an appointee to be closely involved in the day-to-day running of the business. He will be an 'executive' director. Others on the board may consider themselves to be 'non-executive' directors and to be chiefly concerned with matters of policy rather than the nitty-gritty of the management of the company.

If the managing director is removed from office before his contract of employment expires, this will entitle him to damages for breach of contract (see *Nelson v James Nelson & Sons Ltd* [1914] 2 KB 770) under the doctrine discussed in Section 8.6.7 above in relation to section 168, that is, that the one party to a contract must not do anything which prevents the other party from completing his side of the bargain. There is thus some difficulty between the rule often to be found in the articles, that the delegation of powers by the board may be revoked, and the commission of a breach of contract by the company, which may, by such a revocation, be preventing the managing director from continuing to carry out his employment. A case in which the relationship between these two rules arose is *Harold Houldsworth & Co (Wakefield) Ltd v Caddies* [1955] 1 WLR 352. The decision is of limited use as a precedent for the future, as it is generally considered to have turned on the construction of the particular contract of employment in that case. Under that contract, Caddies had been appointed managing director of Houldsworth (the parent company). The contract provided that he should perform the duties and exercise the powers in relation to the business of the company and the business of its existing subsidiaries, 'which may from time to time be assigned to or vested in him by the board of directors of the company'. At first Caddies managed Houldsworth and a subsidiary. However, a dispute arose between Caddies and his fellow directors. The board of directors instructed Caddies thereafter to confine his attentions to the subsidiary alone. The House of Lords held that this was not a breach of the contract of employment. If the contract had not contained the clause giving such wide discretion to the board to define Caddies's job 'from time to time', the action would have been a breach of contract.

8.6.11 Relationship between the board of directors and the general meeting

For companies registered prior to 1 July 1985, the relationship between these two organs was usually governed by an article similar or identical to Article 80 of Table A annexed to the Companies Act 1948. This read:

> The business of the company shall be managed by the directors who may pay all expenses incurred in promoting and registering the company, and may exercise all such powers of the company as are not, by the Act, or by these regulations, required to be exercised by the company in general meeting, subject, nevertheless, to any of these regulations, to the provisions of the Act and to such regulations, being not inconsistent with the aforesaid regulations or provisions as may be prescribed by the company in general meeting; but no regulations made by the company in general meeting shall invalidate any prior act of the directors which would have been valid if that regulation had not been made.

This appeared to reserve to the general meeting a power to make regulations to govern the conduct of directors. The scope of this power was most uncertain until the judges determined the balance of power issue firmly in favour of the directors to the detriment of the powers of the general meeting. Thus in *Automatic Self Cleansing Filter Syndicate Company Ltd v Cunningham* [1906] 2 Ch 34, the Court of Appeal held that a resolution passed by a simple majority of shareholders (an ordinary resolution) was not effective. The resolution purported to order the directors to go ahead with an agreement to sell the whole of the assets of the company. The directors believed that this was an unwise course. Warrington J said:

> The effect of this resolution, if acted upon, would be to compel the directors to sell the whole of the assets of the company, not on such terms and conditions as they think fit, but upon such terms and conditions as a simple majority of the shareholders think fit. But it does not rest there. Article 96 provides that the management of the business and control of the company are to be vested in the directors. Now that article, which is for the protection of a minority of the shareholders, can only be altered by a special resolution, that is to say, by a resolution passed by a three-fourths' majority, at a meeting called for the purpose, and confirmed at a subsequent meeting. If that provision could be revoked by a resolution of the shareholders passed by a

simple majority, I can see no reason for the provision which is to be found in Article 81 that the directors can only be removed by a special resolution. It seems to me that if a majority of shareholders can, on a matter which is vested in the directors, overrule the discretion of the directors, there might just as well be no provision at all in the articles as to the removal of directors by special resolution. Moreover, pressed to its logical conclusion, the result would be that when a majority of the shareholders disagree with the policy of the directors, though they cannot remove the directors except by special resolution, they might carry on the whole of the business of the company as they pleased, and thus, though not able to remove the directors, overrule every act which the board might otherwise do. It seems to me on the true construction of these articles that the management of the business and control of the company are vested in the directors, and consequently that the control of the company as to any particular matter, or the management of any particular transaction or any particular part of the business of the company, can only be removed from the board by an alteration of the articles, such alteration, of course, requiring a special resolution.

This approach was adopted in *Breckland Group Holdings Ltd v London and Suffolk Properties Ltd* [1989] BCLC 100, where the court held that the conduct of the business of the company was vested in the board of directors, and the shareholders in general meeting could not intervene to adopt unauthorised proceedings.

It seems to have been the case that the general meeting could not interfere in management decisions by way of an ordinary resolution, even under the 1948 Companies Act.

The justification for the insistence that there should be no interference in director-control save by a special resolution was well expressed in *Gramophone and Typewriter Ltd v Stanley* [1908] 2 KB 89. Buckley LJ said:

> The directors are not servants to obey directions given by the shareholders as individuals; they are agents appointed by and bound to serve the shareholders as their principals. They are persons who may by the regulations be entrusted with the control of the business, and if so entrusted they can be dispossessed from that control only by the statutory majority which can alter the articles.

When coupled with the knowledge that a very few persons can hold a large number of the shares in a company, that directors can be entrenched by *Bushell v Faith* clauses and that shareholders with small stakes in a company rarely take an interest in meetings, it can be seen that 'shareholder democracy' is an extremely hollow concept, and the directors will often have complete freedom from control in managing the business.

8.6.12 Where the board of directors ceases to function

The analysis in Section 8.6.11 above holds good for the situation where the board of directors is a functioning organ of the company. If for some reason the directors are unable or unwilling to exercise their powers of management, those powers revert to and are exercisable by the company in general meeting. In *Alexander Ward & Co Ltd v Samyang Navigation Co Ltd* [1975] 2 All ER 424, the House of Lords held that the company could act through its two shareholders to recover its debts. This was possible despite an article in the company's constitution which read as follows:

> The business of the Company shall be managed by the Directors, who … may exercise all such powers of the company as are not by the [Hong Kong] Ordinance or by these Articles required to be exercised by the Company in General Meeting.

The company had no directors at the relevant time. Lord Hailsham said:

In my opinion, at the relevant time the company was fully competent either to lay attestments or to raise proceedings in the Scottish courts. The company could have done so either by appointing directors, or, as I think, by authorising proceedings in general meeting, which in the absence of an effective board, has a residual authority to use the company's powers. It had not taken, and did not take the steps necessary to give authority to perform the necessary actions. But it was competent to have done so, and in my view it was therefore a competent principal . . . So far as regards the powers of general meeting, in Gower, *Modern Company Law* (3rd edn, 1969), pp 136–37 it is stated:

> 'It seems that if for some reason the board cannot or will not exercise the powers vested in them, the general meeting has been held effective where there was a deadlock on the board, where an effective quorum could not be obtained, where the directors are disqualified from voting, or, more obviously, where the directors have purported to borrow in excess of the amount authorised by the articles.'

Moreover, although the general meeting cannot restrain the directors from conducting actions in the name of the company, it still seems to be the law (as laid down in *Marshall's Valve Gear Co v Manning Wardle & Co* [1909] 1 Ch 267) that the general meeting can commence proceedings on behalf of the company if the directors fail to do so. In that case counsel attempted to draw a distinction between the cases supposed in this passage, where the directors were for some reason unable or unwilling to act, and the instant case where there were no directors. I see no difference in the distinction ...

8.6.13 The company secretary

Sections 270 and 271 of the Companies Act 2006 provide that private companies need not have a secretary but that public companies must have one. The increased importance of the company secretary was recognised by Lord Denning in *Panorama Developments Ltd v Fidelis Furnishing Fabrics* [1971] 3 WLR 440 (see Section 4.5.6 above). In that case, it was held that a company secretary had the power to make certain contracts on behalf of the company. Contracts to hire cars were held to be binding on the company, despite the fact that the company secretary in question had hired the cars ostensibly for the company but in fact for his own use.

The increased importance of company secretaries is also recognised by section 273 of the Companies Act 2006. This applies only to public companies and imposes a duty on the directors of such companies to:

> take all reasonable steps to secure that the secretary (or each joint secretary) of the company—
> (a) is a person who appears to them to have the requisite knowledge and experience to discharge the functions of secretary of the company ...

There follows a list of acceptable qualifications for the post, which include membership of a number of accountants' professional organisations and legal qualifications (s 273(2) and (3)). However, these qualifications are not exclusive, as section 273(2)(d) also provides that the secretary may be 'a person who, by virtue of his holding or having held any other position or his being a member of any other body, appears to the directors to be capable of discharging the functions of secretary of the company'.

The secretary is responsible for making sure that the documents that a company must send to the Registrar are accurate and are sent on time. With the increasing complexity of requirements to make disclosure of company affairs in this way, the role has become considerably more complex and important.

8.7 Employees

8.7.1 Old law

By section 309 of the Companies Act 1985:

> (1) The matters to which the directors of a company are to have regard in the performance of their functions include the interests of a company's employees in general, as well as the interests of its members.

8.7.2 New law

Section 309 of the 1985 Act has been replaced by section 172 of the Companies Act 2006:

> A director of a company must act in the way he considers, in good faith, would be most likely to promote the success of the company for the benefit of its members as a whole, and in doing so have regard (amongst other matters) to—
>
> …
>
> (b) the interests of the company's employees.

The effect of this replacement is completely unclear and directors' duties generally are discussed in Chapter 9. However, it is arguable that the new version represents a dilution of the rights of employees to be considered, first because they are included in a list of other matters to be considered, and secondly because the duty comes explicitly with a 'filter' which promotes the interests of the members as of paramount consideration. This is an enactment of the understanding at common law, but it nevertheless is a clear and explicit statement that employees' interests are relevant only in so far as considering that their interests promote the interests of the shareholders.

In both the 1985 Act and the 2006 Act, the duty imposed on directors has no effective enforcement mechanism. If there was an alleged failure to take account of employees' interests, the failure would theoretically have to be enforced by the company voting in general meeting to bring an action against the directors. It seems unlikely that there would be enough employee shareholders or a sufficient number of altruistic shareholders in order to achieve the necessary majority. Even if it were possible, proof that employees' interests had not been considered might be extremely difficult to determine. See Chapter 9 for a more detailed analysis of this issue.

Summary

8.1 The voting power of shareholders may be more apparent than real. One limitation in practice is the power of management to solicit proxy votes.

8.2 There are a number of technical rules concerning the conduct of meetings, but it is doubtful if there is a general principle that a shareholder must use his vote otherwise than in his own selfish interest, except in the case of a director who may not vote to ratify his own actions.

8.3 Ordinary resolutions passed at meetings of shareholders require a simple majority. Special resolutions require a 75 per cent majority.

The power of shareholders over management is probably less than it would appear from the legal framework.

8.4 A public company must have at least two directors.

Appointment as a director does not as such entitle the appointee to payment.

Section 168 of the Companies Act 2006 provides for the removal of directors, but this power does not prevent the director from gaining compensation for loss of office if he is dismissed in breach of contract.

A managing director may be appointed to manage the day-to-day affairs of the company.

The general meeting may not interfere in the general conduct of business by the directors unless the board of directors is unable or unwilling to exercise its usual functions.

The secretary of a company, particularly of a public company, is to be regarded as 'more than a mere clerk' and as being capable of committing the company to binding contracts in his sphere of competence.

8.5 The directors must have regard to the interests of employees but there is no effective method of enforcing this obligation.

Exercises

8.1 Explain the functions of the main institutions of the company.

8.2 Distinguish between the various types of resolutions.

8.3 What are the shareholders' agreements?

8.4 How many categories of directors are there? How are they defined?

8.5 Distinguish the various types of authority which may equip a person to make a binding contract on behalf of a company.

8.6 Explain the different types of directors. Does the distinction in question have any effect on the duties they owe to the company?

8.7 Are the employees members of the company? Can they force the company to take their interests into account in its decision-making process?

Further reading

Berle and Means, *The Modern Corporation and Private Property* (New York: Transaction Publishers, 1932)

Cheffins, *Company Law: Theory, Structure and Operation* (Clarendon, 1997)

Florence, *Ownership, Control and Success of Large Companies* (Sweet & Maxwell, 1961)

Lowry and Reisberg, *Pettet's Company Law: Company Law and Corporate Finance* (Pearson, 2012)

Talbot, *Critical Company Law* (Routledge-Cavendish, 2008)

Chapter 9

Directors' duties

Key terms

- **Duty of care and skill** – duty related to a director's demonstrating a certain level of skill while performing his duties.
- **Fiduciary duties** – duties which are strict because they reflect the powerful position of directors who have full legal powers to deal with other people's property.
- **Phoenix companies** – new companies trading with the same personnel and a very similar name to a failed company. The ability to disqualify directors was introduced partly as a response to the misuse of companies by starting one company, defaulting on that company's debts, winding up the company, then duping the public by immediately beginning to trade using a similarly-named company.
- **Unfit** – one of the key disqualification provisions requires the disqualification of an 'unfit' director. The meaning of this term is still rather uncertain.

9.1 Introduction

9.1.1 Formulating a standard of conduct

A director of a company will often be dealing with other people's property, not only in the legal sense that he will be in charge of the property of the company, but also in the sense that the company may have shareholders who have put money into the company by buying shares but who have little or no control over what the directors do. Their investment will be lost if the company becomes insolvent. Also, if goods or services are supplied to a company on credit, the directors will be dealing with money to which the creditors have a claim until they are paid in full. It is obviously necessary to control the behaviour of someone in such a position of power and to impose upon him a standard of conduct which will protect people who stand to lose if the director is either incompetent or dishonest. There are three major difficulties, however, in imposing such a standard:

1. The extent of directors' involvement with a company varies considerably. It is now becoming recognised practice to separate the members of a board of directors into 'executive' and 'non-executive' members. The executive directors will be very closely involved with the day-to-day affairs of the company, and the amount of knowledge that they might be expected to have about the internal affairs of the company will far exceed that of the non-executive members, whose job it is to take an overall view of the running of the company, lend what expertise they have to the making of policy decisions and sound warning bells if anything suspicious comes to their notice. This separation was not common practice in the past and is by no means universal now. The law has sought to impose a standard of conduct on all directors regardless of their degree of involvement with the company. To formulate a standard of conduct which would be fair to all types of director has proved difficult.

2. There are also different types of company. Companies vary, from huge multinational giants to a small family business run by one person who has decided that the business would best be managed in corporate form. This substantial difference in the size and complexity of companies has caused difficulty in formulating a standard by which the performance of all company directors may be judged. There had been considerable reluctance, until legislation (much of it EU Directive-driven), to attempt to impose different directors' duties depending on the type of company. Now, in statutes, the distinction is often drawn between directors of public companies and directors of private companies. This distinction is sometimes criticised because there can be large and complex private companies as well as small and relatively simple public companies. Nevertheless, if a distinction is to be made, the public/private distinction seems to work as well as any.

   The case law in this area is still very important. Although the Companies Act 2006 codified directors' duties, the law cannot provide all of the answers on complicated situations, so the decisions of the courts remain crucial. In the case law on directors' duties, no formal distinction is normally made between different types of companies. Rather, the cases impose a sliding scale of responsibility which depends on what might reasonably be expected of someone in that position. A complex body of both case and statute law has grown up. Not all of it is satisfactory, as we shall see.

3. The third difficulty in formulating a standard of behaviour for directors is to be found in the nature of the decisions that they make. Most of these decisions will be business decisions about which contracts it would be best for the company to enter into. It is very difficult for a court of law looking at events with hindsight to judge whether that decision was commercially foolish at the time it was made. It may have turned out badly for the company, but that may be because of factors which could not be foreseen by the directors when the decision was made. The courts do not wish to encourage directors to become too cautious by imposing too high a duty of care. They must therefore respect decisions which they believe were made in good faith even though they may have been commercially disastrous for the company as things turned out. The difference in the sizes and complexity of companies, and the differences in the degree of involvement of the directors in question, coupled with the unique economic circumstances surrounding each decision, make it difficult for the court to build up a body of precedents. This is unlike judging the performance of other professions where often similarly qualified persons have had similar decisions to make.

9.1.2 Duty owed to the company

It is important to remember that directors owe their duties to that legal person 'the company', rather than to shareholders or potential shareholders. This is particularly significant when the enforcement of those duties is in question, because the general rule is that directors' duties can be enforced only by the company (ie suing directors). The principle may be illustrated by the facts of *Percival v Wright* [1902] 2 Ch 421. In that case, shareholders wrote to the secretary of a company asking if he knew anyone likely to buy their shares. The chairman and two other directors purchased the shares at £2 10s (£2.50) per share. The shareholders subsequently discovered that, prior to the negotiations for the sale of the shares, the chairman and directors had been approached by a third party. The third party wished to purchase the company and was offering a price which would mean that each share would be valued at well over £2 10s. The shareholders asked for the sale of the shares to be set aside by the court on the grounds that the chairman and directors had been in breach of a duty to the shareholders. Swinfen-Eady J refused to set aside the sale and firmly rejected the idea that there was any duty owed by the chairman and directors to the shareholders. Their duties were owed to the company.

This situation may well now be caught by the section 994 remedy (petition by company member – see Chapter 10). However, the fundamental principle that directors owe their duty to the company is unchanged. This principle may cause difficulties where there are several companies acting as a group. Normally one company is seen as the 'parent' company and will hold a majority of the shares in its subsidiary companies. The exact relationship between parent and subsidiary is discussed elsewhere (see Chapter 14). In these circumstances directors may be appointed to the board of the subsidiary by the parent company. It is very tempting for them to look after the interests of the parent company and ignore the interests of the subsidiary. That they must not do so is clearly illustrated by the case of *Scottish Co-operative Wholesale Society Ltd v Meyer* [1959] AC 324, where Lord Denning emphasised that the duty of directors was owed to the particular company which had appointed them.

This is another area of law where reform is actively being considered. Many companies do act with group interests in mind, and it seems sensible to bring the law more into accord with commercial practice.

In *Hawkes v Cuddy & Ors* [2009] EWCA Civ 291, one of the principal questions raised was: 'What duties does a nominee director of a company owe to firstly the company and secondly his appointor?' The issue was, therefore, whether the director of the company owed a duty not only to the legal entity that is the company but also to his nominator. The Court noted that the fact that a director of a company has been nominated to that office by a shareholder does not, of itself, impose any duty on the director owed to his nominator. The director may owe duties to his nominator if he is an employee or officer of the nominator, or by reason of a formal or informal agreement with his nominator, but such duties do not arise out of his nomination but out of a separate agreement or office. Such duties cannot, however, detract from his duty to the company of which he is a director.

9.1.3 Section 250 and the definition of 'director'

Since the issue in question concerns the duties that directors owe to the company, the actual and precise definition of the term 'director' is naturally of paramount importance for the application of the law in question. As explained in Chapter 8, the definition of the term 'director' is not as straightforward as might initially be thought. The term 'director' includes not only a person validly or legally appointed to the position – otherwise known as a de jure director – but also de facto or shadow directors.

The aforementioned concepts were explained in Chapter 8, but additional analysis will be included here as it is necessary for the understanding of the issues in question. Section 250 of the Companies Act 2006 states that in the Companies Acts, 'director' includes any person occupying the position of director, 'by whatever name called'. This definition, albeit unorthodox at first glance, is expressed in a very appropriate way so as to encompass all forms of directorship, whether de jure, de facto or shadow.

Section 251 defines 'shadow director'. This a term used in the statute where there is a possibility that someone responsible for misfeasance could escape liability where he had not officially been appointed as a director but was really in charge of the business. Section 251 reads:

(1) In the Companies Acts 'shadow director', in relation to a company, means a person in accordance with whose directions or instructions the directors of the company are accustomed to act.
(2) A person is not to be regarded as a shadow director by reason only that the directors act on advice given by him in a professional capacity.

The exception in section 251(2) prevents a person who is giving advice only as, for example, a solicitor to the company, from being regarded as a shadow director, and thus sharing some of the responsibilities of true directors, merely because the directors usually act on his advice. Shadow directors are creatures of statute and so will be under a duty to the company only where such a duty is specifically imposed by statute. This is applicable where responsibilities might easily be evaded by someone who was the real 'power behind the throne' but was not officially a director. Examples of the imposition of duties on shadow directors may be found in the Chapters 8 and 13 concerning the statutory liability of directors and the insolvency of a company respectively.

The definition of 'shadow director' has now been considered by the courts. In *Re Hydrodan (Corby) Ltd* [1994] BCC 161, Millett J made it clear that a shadow director is different from a de facto director, that is, a person acting as a director without valid appointment. He said that there are four steps to establishing whether someone was a shadow director. These are:

1. the identity of the appointed and acting directors must be established;
2. it must be established that the alleged shadow director directed those directors as to their actions in relation to the company;
3. it must be established that the directors followed those directions; and
4. it must be established that the directors were accustomed to follow directions from the alleged shadow director.

Those factors were not established in *Re Unisoft Group Ltd (No 2)* [1994] BCC 766, where it was held that compliance by one of a number of directors with the directions of an outsider could not make that outsider a shadow director. Only if the whole board or a governing majority was accustomed to act on the directions of the outsider would he become a shadow director.

As far as shadow directors are concerned, section 170(5) of the 2006 Act states that '[t]he general duties apply to shadow directors where, and to the extent that, the corresponding common law rules or equitable principles so apply'. Therefore, the decision as to whether the general duties apply to a particular alleged shadow director lies with the judges, who are to decide the question on the basis of precedent. In *Ultraframe (UK) Ltd v Fielding* [2005] EWHC 1638 (Ch), Lewison J held that where the governing majority of the board was accustomed to act at the direction of a person then that person was capable of being a shadow director. Despite that, the court went on to hold that the characterisation of a person as a shadow director did not automatically impose all the same fiduciary duties on that person as were imposed on de jure and de facto directors. Thus, it is for the judge to examine the particular circumstances and facts which would suggest the existence of a fiduciary relationship in order for shadow directors to come under the same duties as de jure and de facto directors.

There is no respective statutory provision for de facto directors. In *Secretary of State for Trade and Industry v Hall* [2006] EWHC 1995 (Ch), [2009] BCC 190, the court stated that the definition of 'de facto director' required positive action by an individual which showed that he was acting as if he was a director. In *Holland (Respondent) v The Commissioners for Her Majesty's Revenue and Customs (Appellant) and another* [2010] UKSC 51, the court invoked the definition of the term 'director' by the Companies Act 2006. The court added that persons who are not directors de jure may nevertheless be treated as directors de facto. It defined 'de facto director' as a person who assumes to act as a director. He is held out as a director by the company, and claims and purports to be a director, although never actually or validly appointed as such. To establish that a person was a de facto director of a company, it is necessary to plead and prove that he undertook functions in relation to the company which could properly be discharged only by a director. It is not sufficient to show that he was concerned in the management of the company's affairs or undertook tasks in relation to its business which can properly be performed by a manager below board level. The court stated that in order for a person to be deemed a de facto director, it is necessary to be a part of a corporate governance structure and assume a position which entails a role capable of bearing fiduciary duties. In this case the court stated that the first mention in the case law of 'de facto directors' appears to have been in *Mangles v Grand Collier Dock Co* (1840) 10 Sim 519, a case involving the formation of a dock company by private Act of Parliament. Sir Lancelot Shadwell V-C said (at 535) that the Act assumed that persons by whom a call was made had to be directors de facto, and that all that Parliament meant was that if the call were made by persons appearing to be directors, it should not be necessary to prove their appointment.

9.1.4 What is the company?

In Chapter 2 various different models of companies were described. The model chosen makes a difference to the way in which directors exercise their duties to the company, because the interests which are seen as making up the company vary with the model chosen. To say that the directors owe a duty to the company is clear, but it makes no sense if the company is regarded as a legal personality or piece of paper alone. The directors must take note of the interests of the human beings who are actively involved in the company's affairs. Which persons are entitled to have their interests regarded? The three categories of person are:

1. the members of the company;
2. the employees of the company; and
3. the creditors of the company.

Each of these categories is examined further below.

9.1.4(a) Members

Clearly the members' interests are of very considerable importance, although that also raises the problem of whether a dissenting minority of members has a right to have its interests taken into account. This question is examined in more detail in Chapters 8 and 3 concerning shareholders' rights and the alteration of the articles of association respectively.

It may be stated here that in the UK it is absolutely clear that the shareholders constitute the only members of the company. This is a further reflection of the contractual basis of English company law. The company is viewed as a contract to which the shareholders are the signatory parties. The shareholders offer the necessary capital to the company with the purchase of its shares and therefore assume the right to become parties to the contractual agreement which is the company. English company law remains faithful to the contractual understanding of the legal phenomenon of the company; the Companies Act 2006 has confirmed the enlightened shareholder approach in the drafting of section 172 which is analysed in Section 9.2.1(a) below. The Companies Act 2006 has not broken with the previous English legislative and judicial tradition which views the shareholders as the exclusive insiders while considering the other actors which do share a link with the company as externalities. The drafting of section 172, albeit inclusive of a variety of factors the interests of which are to be taken into account by directors during the decision-making process, does not mark a significant shift towards the adoption of a more stakeholder orientated approach. The principle of shareholder primacy that grants to the shareholders the privilege of the exclusive membership of the company continues to stand at the foundation of English company law.

9.1.4(b) Employees

By section 172 of the Companies Act 2006 (Section 9.2.1 below), company directors are 'to have regard' to the interests of employees as well as to the interests of members. However, this duty to have regard to employees' interests is expressed to be part of the general duty owed by directors to the company. It can therefore be enforced only by the company. The employees would have no standing to complain to the court that their interests had not been considered. This duty has no enforcing 'teeth' and may be seen as mere 'window dressing'.

9.1.4(c) Creditors

Creditors also have their money tied up in the company. It is logical to expect their interests to be important to the directors in making a decision, and section 172 of the Companies Act 2006 recognises this (see Section 9.2.1 below). In *Lonrho v Shell Petroleum* [1980] 1 WLR 627 this factor was acknowledged by Lord Diplock, who said (at 634) that 'it is the duty of the board to consider ... the best interests of the company. These are not exclusively those of its shareholders but may include those of its creditors'.

The Court of Appeal confirmed this view in *The Liquidator of the Property of West Mercia Safetywear Ltd v Dodd and Another* [1988] BCLC 250. However, in that case the interests of the company were said to include the interests of creditors because the company was insolvent at the relevant time. In *Lonrho*, insolvency was not an issue. Neither was insolvency an issue in *Winkworth v Edward Baron* [1987] BCLC 193, where Lord Templeman referred to a duty owed directly to creditors. In *Brady v Brady* [1989] 1 AC 755, Nourse LJ regarded the interests of the company as synonymous with the interests of the creditors where the company was insolvent or 'doubtfully solvent'. It seems clear:

1. Where the company is insolvent, the interests of creditors and the interests of the company coincide to a considerable degree (see *Standard Chartered Bank v Walker* [1992] 1 WLR 561).
2. Where a company is approaching insolvency, the interests of the creditors are important where an assessment is made of whether the directors acted in the interests

of the company. (What is not clear is precisely at what stage in the slide into insolvency the creditors' interests become paramount, or what test is to be applied to determine the directors' appreciation of the insolvency. If they ought to have known of the insolvency but did not, are they still liable? The cases provide no clear answer.)

3. In the case of a solvent company, the interests of creditors should still be considered, but it is unclear what weight the directors should give to consideration of those interests.

9.1.4(d) Conclusion

In *Modern Company Law for a Competitive Economy: Developing the Framework* (March 2000), the DTI Company Law Review Committee proposed an 'inclusive approach' to the issue 'in whose interests should the company be run?', arguing that 'the overall objective of wealth generation and competitiveness for the benefit of all' can best be achieved through a duty on directors requiring them to have regard to the long- and short-term interests of the company and 'all the relationships on which the company depends'. This formula contains unworkable contradictions which are only partly solved by the fact that the aim is stated as 'achieving company success for the benefit of shareholders as a whole'. It seems clear that shareholders are still to be viewed as the paramount interest but, as we have discussed, long- and short-term interests may well be wholly at odds with each other; there is no such thing as 'shareholders as a whole'.

Nevertheless this approach was enacted. The Companies Act 2006 also contains a somewhat mysterious reference to the pre-existing law. Thus section 170(3) and (4) reads as follows:

(3) The general duties are based on certain common law rules and equitable principles as they apply in relation to directors and have effect in place of those rules and principles as regards the duties owed to a company by a director.

(4) The general duties shall be interpreted and applied in the same way as common law rules or equitable principles, and regard shall be had to the corresponding common law rules and equitable principles in interpreting and applying the general duties.

These subsections indicate that the common law rules developed by the courts will be of considerable significance in interpreting the statutory rules. However, the extent to which the statutory rules change the common law is less clear and will need to be developed by the courts on a case-by-case basis. The text of this chapter looks at the statute and the common law rules together, to try to give an indication of likely interpretations. The common law duties were divided into 'fiduciary' duties (see Section 9.2), which reflected the position of the director as a guardian of the interests of the company and those concerned in it (principally the shareholders), and duties of care and skill. The statute follows a similar layout, with a separate section setting out the 'duty to act with reasonable care, skill and diligence' (see Section 9.3).

9.2   The fiduciary duties of directors

It was traditional under the common law to give a list of the breaches of fiduciary duties of directors under headings such as:

- misappropriation of company property;
- exercise of powers for an improper purpose;

- fettering discretion; and
- permitting interest and duty to conflict.

While no one would dispute that these are all areas where directors have been found to be in breach of duty, the listing of the duties in this way tended to obscure the fundamental point that a director was under one overriding duty, to act bona fide in the interests of the company. The list of duties that grew out of the case law was in fact a list of situations where a director was most likely to be in breach of his fundamental duty. Thus, for example, if a director found himself in a position where he had a conflict of interests, he was in dire peril of being found to be in breach of his overriding duty to act bona fide for the benefit of the company.

The Companies Act 2006 seems partially to accept this reasoning by articulating a general duty *to promote the success of the company*. However, the statute also sets out a list of other duties which are formulations of the pre-existing case law. The duty to promote the success of the company is not separate from the list of duties, neither is it the first duty to be mentioned. Although it appears to be an overriding duty, it is not obviously identified as such.

Regarding all duties as on the same level tends to obscure the debate about the possibility that behaviour that does come under one of these headings may be excused by the company voting to that effect in general meeting. It is difficult to accept the ratification (excusing) of something which is the breach of a fundamental duty. It is easier to see how, if a director places himself in one of the perilous situations but his behaviour has not breached the fundamental duty of acting bona fide, such behaviour may be regarded as acceptable by the company. Behaviour which is not bona fide for the benefit of the company cannot be condoned unless 'the company' (in the wide sense explained in Section 9.1.4 above – members, creditors and possibly employees) agrees. Thus, where sole shareholders and directors took money from a company, this was nevertheless held to be theft despite the fact that they clearly had the agreement of all the members (themselves) to do so (*Re Attorney-General's Reference (No 2 of 1982)* [1984] 2 WLR 447; and *R v Phillipou* [1989] Crim LR 559 and 585). These cases were affirmed by the House of Lords in *R v Gomez* [1992] 3 WLR 1067. The distinction between the overriding duty of good faith and the effect of putting oneself in one of the perilous situations varies with the seriousness with which the particular behaviour is viewed. Thus, it will be a most unusual situation where there has been a 'misappropriation of company property' but the directors can nevertheless be held to have acted bona fide for the benefit of the company and therefore can be excused by a majority of shareholders against the wishes of the minority. As we have seen, where dishonesty is proved, not even the unanimous consent of the shareholders will suffice to excuse the behaviour. However, where there is much more equivocal behaviour, such as using powers given for one purpose to achieve a different object, it is much easier for the court to accept that the directors are acting bona fide and thus may be excused by the company.

9.2.1 The duty under section 172 to promote the success of the company

9.2.1(a) The subjective test

The duty to promote the success of the company, which appears to be a fundamental one, is set out in section 172 of the Companies Act 2006:

172 Duty to promote the success of the company

(1) A director of a company must act in the way he considers, in good faith, would be most likely to promote the success of the company for the benefit of its members as a whole and in doing so have regard (amongst other matters) to—

 (a) the likely consequences of any decision in the long term,

 (b) the interests of the company's employees,

 (c) the need to foster the company's business relationships with suppliers, customers and others,

 (d) the impact of the company's operations on the community and the environment,

 (e) the desirability of the company maintaining a reputation for high standards of business conduct, and

 (f) the need to act fairly as between members of the company.

(2) Where or to the extent that the purposes of the company consist of or include purposes other than the benefit of the members, subsection (1) has effect as if the reference to promoting the success of the company for the benefit of its members were to achieving those purposes.

(3) The duty imposed by this section has effect subject to any enactment or rule of law requiring directors, in certain circumstances, to consider or act in the interests of creditors of the company.

In section 172(1) a variety of issues is raised and attempted to be clarified. According to the wording of this subsection, 'the director must act in the way *he* considers … would be most likely to promote the success of the company' (emphasis added). Therefore, the law provides for a principally subjective test to determine whether a given director has effectively pursued the success of the company or failed to do so. The good faith test remains the main standard against which his actions will be judged. Were the acts of the director performed in good faith for the benefit of the company as a whole? If the reply to the question is positive, the court is more likely to find a director acting in accordance with his statutory duties. Therefore, directors are bound to act bona fide in what they subjectively consider is in the interests of the company (*Regentcress v Cohen* [2001] 2 BCLC 80). The court will not attempt to determine whether the decision in question has objectively been the best at a given moment for the company. In *Regentcress plc v Cohen*, Jonathan Parker J stated:

> [T]he question is not whether, viewed objectively by the court, the particular act or omission … was in fact in the interests of the company … but whether [the director] honestly believed that his act was in the interests of the company. The issue is as to the director's state of mind. No doubt, where it is clear that the act … resulted in substantial detriment to the company, the director will have a harder task persuading the court that he honestly believed it to be in the company's interests; but that does not detract from the subjective nature of the test.

Despite that, an additional element of control on directors' scope of action is likely to be detected in an element of reasonableness that the court might require in order to exempt a director from liability. If a director acts reasonably in the way he considers to promote the success of the company, it appears that the courts will be reluctant to find him in breach of section 172(1). However, this is one of the areas in the Companies Act 2006 which remains confusingly vague and needs further clarification, as the judgment in *Item Software (UK) v Fassihi* [2004] EWCA Civ 1244 proved. In that case, the court supported the proposition that if there is no basis on which a director could claim that he acted reasonably while aiming at promoting the success of the company (in this case he refused to disclose important information to the company) then he is to be found in a breach of duty. But it is unclear what would have happened if a reasonable director giving the necessary consideration concluded that the action was likely to promote the success of the company. There is the need to analyse future case law to provide more solid and clear replies to such questions. What is clear at this stage is that the law grants the directors a wide scope of power, on the one hand, to determine what 'success' entails in the context of their own company and, on the other hand, to perform all the acts they consider necessary to promote the success of the company. In general it may validly be suggested that the 'success of the company' will most significantly entail an increase of the financial value of the company. However, the means to achieve this end remains an issue left to directors to define.

In this context, in *Re Genosyis Technology Management Ltd Wallach and another v Secretary of State for Trade & Industry* [2006] EWHC 989 Ch, the two directors entered into an agreement with a third party on the basis of which the company resigned from a claim of £1.25 million to gain only £166,000. Even in the event of the acceptance of the directors' honest belief that the agreement in question was in the best interests of the company, the court clarified that they had no reasonable grounds for believing so and therefore they were found to be in breach of their duties. In *Primlake Ltd v Matthews Associates & Ors* [2006] EWHC 1227 (Ch), the director paid considerable amounts of money to the de facto director in the knowledge that the latter was not entitled to them; the court stated that the director in question could not have had an honest belief that the transfers of money were in the best interests of the company. In *Simtel Communications Ltd v Rebak and others* [2006] EWHC 572 (QB), the court stated that the director acted in breach of his duty to act bona fide in the interests of the company because an intelligent and honest man in the position of Mr Rebak – the director in question – could not, in the whole of the circumstances, have reasonably believed that the transactions in question were for the benefit of the company.

9.2.1(b) Section 172: The members 'as a whole'

The success of the company may be viewed in relation to its members 'as a whole'. The primacy of the company, which is a fundamental principle of English company law, finds its place in the Companies Act 2006. Directors owe their duties to the company; from that it may be deduced that if the interests of the company as a separate entity come into conflict with the interests of some members, the company's interests are still the main priority of the directors. Apart from that, the emphasis given to the phrase 'as a whole' is very important, as it creates another obligation that needs to be taken into account when directors make their decisions; favouring a section of shareholders to the detriment of the collective body of the company's members can now bring the director to a point where he may be found liable for a breach of duty. This is of particular importance, as favouring majority shareholders against the minority ones, or directors who simultaneously happen to be shareholders against other members of the company, may theoretically at least be treated as a breach of directors' duties.

Section 172 introduces a novel element as it specifically includes a range of different actors to whom directors are to 'have regard' when they take their decisions, that is:

- the company's employees;
- suppliers and customers;
- the community; and
- the environment.

Although including additional actors when taking a decision to promote the success of the company is a positive development, it is doubtful whether this provision will bring any far-reaching shift in the nature of decision making within the company. It is important to note that the aforementioned actors remain outside the company and are still defined as persons 'other than the company'. Shareholders retain their status as the exclusive 'members of the company'. In addition to that, the duty of directors to have regard to the interests of other stakeholders is still owed to the company and only to it. The importance of this statement is twofold. First, the interests of stakeholders other than the shareholders may be taken into account in so far as they are deemed compatible with the interests of the company. If they happen to conflict with the interests of the company then priority is to be given to the interests of the latter. Secondly, if the duty imposed by section 172 to have regard to other actors' interests is breached, it is again for the company (which, as explained above, basically means the shareholders) to act. Therefore, the only litigants are still the majority shareholders, a minority shareholder raising either a derivative action or acting in accordance with section 994, and a liquidator acting on behalf of an insolvent company. And it is very unlikely that the shareholders will act against the directors for having breached their duty to the outsiders, especially if the directors have been effective in pursuing the interests of the members of the company. For these reasons, this provision, although a positive development, is most likely not going to produce any dramatic change in the directors' duties landscape. The case law so far confirms the validity of such a view.

The formulation in relation to employees under the 2006 Act may be weaker than that previously provided by section 309 of the Companies Act 1985 because of the explicit primacy of members' interests. Directors are required to consider the listed matters only in so far as they benefit and are compatible with interests of the shareholders; this approach adopted by section 172 is known as the 'enlightened shareholder value', which is in contrast with the so-called 'pluralist' or 'stakeholder' approach favouring the introduction of a duty to consider the interests of all stakeholders when acting for the benefit of the company. Therefore, section 172 is absolutely consistent with the contractual nature of the company and reflecting the reality in question.

9.2.2 The categories of fiduciary duties

The general duties set out in sections 171 to 177 of the Companies Act 2006 are owed by a director of a company to the company. We have examined the duty under section 172 in detail in Section 9.2.1 above. The remaining duties are:

- the duty to act within powers (s 171)
- the duty to exercise independent judgment (s 173)
- the duty to avoid conflicts of interest (s 175)
- the duty not to accept benefits from third parties (s 176)
- the duty to declare interest in proposed transaction or arrangement (s 177).

Each if these duties is discussed in further detail in Sections 9.2.2(a)–9.2.2(e) below.

9.2.2(a) Duty to act within powers

This duty has two aspects. Section 171 provides:

A director of a company must—
(a) act in accordance with the company's constitution, and
(b) only exercise powers for the purpose for which they are conferred.

We have seen that the consequence of acting outside the constitution will not affect third parties. The courts have also decided that certain powers of the directors were given to them for a particular purpose. If the directors use them to achieve a different object, the court will intervene to prevent this if it is requested to do so. This is one area, however, where the courts are very often happy to permit the majority to excuse the action of the directors, so that this is perhaps an area where a director is in the least danger of being found to be in breach of his fundamental duty. A good example is the power to issue shares. The courts have determined that where directors have this power, the purpose for which it was bestowed was to raise capital. It is a power which can easily be used to fend off a takeover or to prevent directors from being removed from office. This can be done by diluting the voting capacity of a hostile element of shareholders by the issue of new shares. *Punt v Symonds & Co* [1903] 2 Ch 506 and *Piercy v S Mills & Co Ltd* [1920] 1 Ch 77 are good examples of this type of manoeuvring. A slightly more complicated problem arose in the case of *Howard Smith Ltd v Ampol Petroleum Ltd* [1974] AC 821. There, a company was threatened with a takeover by two associates who between them held 55 per cent of the company's shares. The company needed more capital but proposed to obtain it by issuing over four million shares to members other than the takeover bidders. This allotment would have reduced the takeover bidders to a minority in the company and was held to be a misuse of the directors' powers. The case was complicated by the fact that the issue had been made for two purposes: (i) to raise capital (the proper purpose) and (ii) to defeat the takeover (an improper purpose). The court reached the conclusion that directors would be acting within their powers if the dominant or substantial purpose of the exercise of those powers was proper. Lord Wilberforce, giving the advice of the Privy Council, said (at 835):

> In their Lordship's opinion it is necessary to start with a consideration of the powers whose exercise is in question ... Having ascertained, on a fair view, the nature of this power, and having defined as can best be done in the light of modern conditions the, or some, limits within which it may be exercised, it is then necessary for the court, if a particular exercise of it is challenged, to examine the substantial purpose for which it was exercised, and to reach a conclusion whether that purpose was proper or not. In doing so it will be necessary to give credit to the bona fide opinion of the directors, if such is found to exist, and will respect their judgment as to matters of management; having done this, the ultimate conclusion has to be as to the side of a fairly broad line on which the case falls.

Lord Wilberforce also emphasised that the court would not simply accept a statement by directors that they acted for a particular purpose. He said (at 832):

> [When] a dispute arises whether directors of a company made a particular decision for one purpose or another, or whether, there being more than one purpose, one or another purpose was the substantial or primary purpose, the court, in their Lordships' opinion, is entitled to look at the situation objectively in order to estimate how critical or pressing, or substantial or, per contra, insubstantial an alleged requirement may have been. If it finds that a particular requirement, though real, was not urgent, or critical, at the relevant time, it may have reason to doubt, or discount, the assertions of individuals that they acted solely in order to deal with it, particularly when the action they took was unusual or even extreme.

In *Criterion Properties Plc v Stratford UK Properties LLC* [2004] UKHL 28, two companies were parties to a joint venture which was governed by a partnership agreement. This agreement was accepted as valid and enforceable. In 2000 a supplementary agreement was signed, aimed at amending the initial one. The effect of the new supplementary agreement was to protect Stratford UK Properties LLC against a potential takeover and change of management by the introduction of a 'poison pill' device. (These are tactics employed by the target company aimed at making the takeover more difficult or costly. They usually involve the issuing of new shares to the current shareholders that sometimes grant enhanced voting rights to them or the right to a hefty premium after the takeover has taken place. As a result the company evolves into a less attractive target for the bidder.) The second supplementary agreement was signed on behalf of Stratford UK Properties LLC by one of its directors without the approval of the entire board of directors. That managing director had come to an agreement with an important shareholder within the company context that required the company to buy out his shareholding at a high price if there was a change of control in the company or a removal of a director from the board. In April 2001 the managing director was dismissed because the board of directors had learnt for the first time about the existence of the second supplementary agreement. The company also asked the court to set the agreement aside because it was signed for an improper purpose. The agreement, according to the claims, had not been a proper use of directors' powers and could not be enforced against the company. The agreement had as a result that Stratford UK Properties LLC would have to endure a heavy financial burden in the case of a breach of its terms (that is, in the case of a potential takeover or a removal of a director from the board). Thus, a potential bidder would have been discouraged from trying to acquire it. The House of Lords in this case chose to view the case from an angle different from that of the 'proper purpose' argument, and focused more on the argument related to the nature of the authority of the managing director in question who had entered into the agreement on behalf of the company. The agreement would be set aside and the company would not be found bound to that only if the director was not under any authority (actual or ostensible) to sign the agreement. The House stated that in order to resolve this issue the principles relevant to consider were those of agency. Their Lordships further recommended that the relevant 'authority' issues should be dealt with at a separate trial, especially in the light of the fact that they were not addressed during the proceedings in the lower courts.

In *Re Looe Fish Ltd* [1993] BCC 368, the failure by a director to exercise the power of allotment of shares for the purpose for which it was conferred led to disqualification under section 8 of the Company Directors Disqualification Act 1986. See also *Bishopgate Investment Management (in liquidation) v Maxwell* [1993] BCC 120.

9.2.2(b) Duty to exercise independent judgment

Section 173 of the Companies Act 2006 reads:

> (1) A director of a company must exercise independent judgment.
> (2) This duty is not infringed by his acting—
>   (a) in accordance with an agreement duly entered into by the company that restricts the future exercise of discretion by its directors, or
>   (b) in a way authorised by the company's constitution.

This is a statutory restatement of the common law duty which prevented a director from 'fettering his discretion', which was probably merely another way in which directors might have had an interest in conflict with their duty to the company. If directors bound themselves by agreement to act in a particular way, they would have had a personal interest in fulfilling that agreement. This was in conflict with their duty to be able to act always in the best interests of the company.

The issue here is the one of 'shareholder agreements'. Shareholders are free to agree among themselves on how they are going to vote on certain issues; these decisions can affect crucial aspects of the company's policies as well as the balance of power within the company. The shareholders are free to agree to coordinate their actions and to grant or to refuse their consent to proposals put forward by the company. This is due to the ability that shareholders have to pursue their own personal interests. Within the corporate context, shareholders are free to let their personal interest dictate their decisions and determine their approval or disapproval of the company's decision. Their right to participate in the company while pursuing their own personal interests grants them the discretion necessary to become parties to such agreements.

Problems start to occur when directors become parties to such agreements too; the distinctive factor that renders the participation of directors deeply problematic is the fact that in contrast to shareholders, directors are not free to pursue their personal interests but are under a clear duty to promote the success of the company on the basis of section 172 of the 2006 Act. The duty imposed upon them to work in the interests of the company as a whole serves as a clear limitation on their ability to act in the pursuance of their personal interests. Therefore, their participation in a shareholders' agreement will be problematic from a legal point of view, as they will be bound, under the agreement, to act in a certain way that may indeed conflict with the duty to promote the success of the company as a whole. That will consequently lead to a breach of duty. The participation of directors in a shareholders' agreement was dealt with in the following case; the court has provided us with the test on the basis of which the issue of directors' liability is to be determined.

The issue was discussed in *Fulham Football Club and Others v Cabra Estates Plc* [1994] 1 BCLC 363. The directors of Fulham Football Club (the company) agreed with the respondents to support planning applications for the development of land leased by the company and oppose different plans proposed by the local council. Large sums of money were paid to the company as a result of that agreement. A number of planning applications failed and enquiries were held, and the issue in the case was whether the undertakings by the directors applied to new planning applications by the respondents and others, whether the undertakings had been improper in fettering the discretion of the directors and whether the agreement was subject to an implied term that the directors would not be required to do anything contrary to their fiduciary duties. The Court of Appeal held that the agreement was valid, was not an improper fettering of discretion and was not subject to the suggested implied term. The company had gained substantially from the agreement. The test to be applied was: 'Was the contract as a whole bona fide for the benefit of the company?' If it was, the directors were entitled to bind themselves to do anything necessary to carry it out.

There are two additional elements in section 173(1): first, a director must exercise judgment; and, secondly, he must exercise that judgment independently. Prima facie, this rule would catch those directors who play no active role in the management of the company, leaving the decision making to others. By analogy, this would impact on de jure directors who fail to engage actively in their duties to such a degree as to allow for the existence of shadow directors. Arguably, if a director is to exercise independent judgment then there will be no scope for shadow directors. However, the government has confirmed in debate in Parliament that a director will not be in breach of this duty if he exercises his own judgment in deciding whether to follow someone else's judgment on a matter. That is the case when he independently decides to rely on another person's expertise and opinion, as long as this is not a pattern that leads to the introduction of a constantly influential behind-the-scenes shadow director who will end up dictating the company's policies.

9.2.2(c) Duty to avoid conflicts of interest

Here the Companies Act 2006 has taken a new approach to two situations which were dealt with together under the case law. Section 175 provides:

(1) A director of a company must avoid a situation in which he has, or can have, a direct or indirect interest that conflicts, or possibly may conflict, with the interests of the company.
(2) This applies in particular to the exploitation of any property, information or opportunity (and it is immaterial whether the company could take advantage of the property, information or opportunity).
(3) This duty does not apply to a conflict of interest arising in relation to a transaction or arrangement with the company.
(4) This duty is not infringed—
   (a) if the situation cannot reasonably be regarded as likely to give rise to a conflict of interest; or
   (b) if the matter has been authorised by the directors.

The matter may be authorised by the directors if it is possible under the constitution and the interested director does not vote on the matter.

Section 170(2) extends the duty:

(2) A person who ceases to be a director continues to be subject—
   (a) to the duty in section 175 … as regards the exploitation of any property, information or opportunity of which he became aware at a time when he was a director …
   To that extent those duties apply to a former director as to a director, subject to any necessary adaptations.

This is one area where it is unclear if the statute changes the (already uncertain) case law.

The preceding case law covered various situations where benefits were siphoned away from the company by directors. This may happen in a more sophisticated way than merely taking money from the company. An example is *Menier v Hooper's Telegraph Works* (1874) LR 9 Ch D 350. In that case, Hooper's company was a substantial shareholder in the European Telegraph company, and had contracted with it to make and lay a cable to South America under certain concessions granted to the European company by the foreign governments concerned. Menier, a minority shareholder in the European company, claimed that Hooper's company had used its votes to procure the diversion of this business to a third company, to cause the abandonment of proceedings brought by the European company to assert its right to the concessions and to have the European company wound up. James LJ said:

> Hooper's company have obtained certain advantages by dealing with something which was the property of the whole company. The minority of the shareholders say in effect that the majority has divided the assets of the company, more or less, between themselves, to the exclusion of the minority. I think it would be a shocking thing if that could be done, because if so the majority might divide the whole assets of the company, and pass a resolution that everything must be given to them, and that the minority should have nothing to do with it.

The court upheld Menier's claim (at 353).

Similarly, in *Cook v Deeks* [1916] 1 AC 554, the directors of a company were involved in negotiating a series of construction contracts with the Canadian Pacific Railway. The last of the series of contracts was negotiated in the same way as the others, but when the negotiations were complete, the directors took the contracts in their own names. It was held that because the directors were acting for the company at the time of the negotiations, the benefit of the contracts belonged to the company. The directors could not therefore take the benefit of those contracts for themselves.

Where there is a conflict of interest and duty, there is clearly a breach of duty, but it remains unclear whether such breaches may be ratified. The more serious the courts judge the conflict to be, the less likely are they to permit a majority of the company to ratify the actions of the directors, particularly where there is a dissenting minority.

An example of a situation in which duty and interest may be in conflict is *Scottish Co-operative Wholesale Society Ltd v Meyer* [1959] AC 324, where three directors were both directors of a parent company and directors of a subsidiary of that parent. As soon as the interests of these two companies conflicted, the directors were unable to fulfil their duty to both companies.

Under case law, the situation in which a director contracts with his company was dealt with under the same heading. It is now separate, under section 176 (see Section 9.2.2(d) below), but the general rule remains that a director is in peril of being in breach of his overriding duty if he makes a contract in which he has a personal interest with his company. In *Aberdeen Railway Co v Blaikie Bros* (1854) 1 Macq 461 (HL), Lord Cranworth said 'it is a rule of universal application that no one, having [fiduciary] duties to discharge, shall be allowed to enter into engagements in which he has or can have a personal interest conflicting or which possibly may conflict with the interests of those whom he is bound to protect'. This rule has been referred to as the 'self-dealing' rule (see *Movitex Ltd v Bulfield and Others* [1988] BCLC 104 in Section 9.5 below). It is by no means absolute, and this is an area where the company will readily be able to ratify acts done in breach of the general rule, provided there has been sufficient disclosure and the directors are apparently acting honestly. This is also an area where the duty itself may be modified in advance of any action by directors. This may be done by redefining the duties in the articles of association (see *Movitex*, above).

The most difficult area in which interest and duty often conflict is where a director is alleged to have profited personally from an opportunity or information which came to him in his capacity as director. A famous case where this type of situation was in issue was *Regal (Hastings) Ltd v Gulliver* [1942] 1 All ER 378. There, the directors of the appellant company, which owned a cinema, were anxious to acquire two other cinemas. A subsidiary company was formed for the purpose of acquiring the additional cinemas. Its capital was 5,000 shares with a par value of £1. A lease of two cinemas was offered, provided that the subsidiary company's capital was paid up. It was the directors' intention that the appellant company should own all the shares in the subsidiary company. However, the appellant company could afford to invest only £2,000. Accordingly, the directors and the company solicitor each took 500 shares, and three investors found by the chairman also took 500 shares each. Subsequently the shares in the company and the subsidiary were sold, and the new shareholders of the company sought to make the directors, the solicitor and the chairman liable to account to the company for the profit made in respect of the subsidiary company's shares. The House of Lords held that the directors were liable to account to the company for their profit. It is notable that this is a case where the company was unable to make use of the opportunity, which was then taken advantage of by the directors.

When does the duty under section 175, to avoid conflicts of interests, cease to exist? When addressing this question the courts have shaped two lines of cases, examined below:

1. the *Industrial Developments v Cooley* line of cases; and
2. the *Island Export Finance Ltd v Umunna and Another* line of cases.

The *Industrial Developments v Cooley* line of cases

The first line of cases is represented by a number of rulings on the basis of the decision in *Industrial Developments v Cooley* [1972] 1 WLR 443. In that case the defendant was managing director of the plaintiff company. While serving in that capacity he became aware of information that would have been valuable to the company, but instead of passing it on to the company he kept it to himself. He also obtained his release from the company by dishonest representations and for the purpose of obtaining a lucrative contract for himself. The plaintiff company could not have obtained the contract because the other party to the contract was opposed to the 'set-up' of the plaintiff company and the group of which it was a part. Despite this, and despite the fact that the defendant had made it clear to the other party to the contract that he was dealing with him on a personal basis and not in the capacity of managing director of the plaintiff, the court held that the defendant must account to the plaintiff company for the profits that had been made from the contract.

Consistent with this line of reasoning, the court ruled in *Gencor ACP Ltd v Dalby* [2000] 2 BCLC 734 that a director cannot escape liability on the basis of a defence that his company would not have taken advantage of a particular business opportunity. However, he can escape liability if he manages to obtain the consent of the company's shareholders for his actions.

Similarly, in *CMS Dolphin Ltd v Simonet* [2002] BCC 600, an advertising company claimed that its former managing director was in breach of his fiduciary duty to act bona fide for the benefit of the company as a whole and of his duty of fidelity stemming from his employment contract. The rationale behind the company's claims had its basis in the fact that the director resigned from the company and created a new one to which he transferred the principal clients and business from the company. The court held that the power of the director to resign was not a fiduciary power, and that a fiduciary obligation towards the company does not continue to exist and operate beyond the end of the relationship which gave rise to it. The former director of a company is not precluded from releasing himself from the company and using his personal skill and knowledge to compete with the company. However, the exploitation on the part of the director of a maturing business opportunity of the company was regarded as a misuse of the company's property, in relation to which a fiduciary duty did exist. The director took advantage of information to which he had access because of his previous position and status in the company, which he chose to misuse. He thus breached his duty to act bona fide for the benefit of the company and was personally liable towards the company for the profits he made. In addition to that, the director in question was found to be in breach of contract and he gave no notice of his resignation. Therefore, the duties stemming from his contract had continued to exist and the diversion of clients and business to his own company was found to be a breach of them. He was found liable for damages towards the company.

In *Bhullar v Bhullar* [2003] EWCA Civ 424, following a breakdown in the relations of the two families who comprised the company in question, it was decided that no further properties should be bought by the company. One of the directors had subsequently bought property situated next to the company's existing investment properties on his own behalf at a quite advantageous price. The judge found him in breach of his fiduciary duty, although the company did not, because of the circumstances, seek to take advantage of property opportunities at that point. According to the Court of Appeal, the director had brought himself to a situation where his personal interest had conflicted with the duty he owed to the company. By buying this property, he had gained a personal interest which might potentially come into conflict with the interests of the company. Thus, interestingly enough, the director was found in breach of duty even where the company could not, or would not, benefit from the opportunity in question. The issue was that the director had obtained access to information that was very useful from a commercial point of view. He was under a fiduciary duty to communicate it to the company. Whether the company would have acquired the property was irrelevant. What matters was that information relevant to the company was not passed to it by the director in question, who was consequently found to be in breach of his duty towards the company and therefore liable to account for his profits. *Cooley* was applied in this case as well.

In *Item Software (UK) v Fassihi* [2004] EWCA Civ 1244, the appellant appealed against a decision which found him to be in a breach of duty. He and another person (C) were the only directors of a company (A) dealing with distributing software produced by another company (B). The two companies entered into formal discussions for the renegotiating of the terms of their cooperation, but the director commenced private talks with B, interested in creating his own company. He later encouraged C to change the terms of the contract, and subsequently B took the decision to terminate it. The company A sought damages for a breach of a fiduciary duty and the director was dismissed. The Court stated that the director was under a fiduciary duty to disclose his own wrongdoing to the company; since he had failed to do so, he was in breach of that duty. This was found to be a part of the broad and well-established duty to act bona fide for the benefit of the company as a whole. Further, the director was not justified in believing that it was in the company's best interest to keep his actions secret from it, since those actions had such an adverse effect on the company's interests. In *Towers v Premier Waste Management Ltd* [2011] EWCA Civ 923, the director of a company accepted a free loan of equipment from a customer without disclosing the transaction to the company and without seeking approval by it. The Court stated that the director had breached his duties by accepting personal benefits from one of the company's customers as he did not disclose the benefits to his fellow directors, nor seek or obtain their approval on behalf of the company. The Court clarified that a director's liability for disloyalty in office does not depend on proof of fault or proof that a conflict of interest has in fact caused the company loss, as previously stated in *Foster Bryant Surveying Ltd v Bryant* [2007] EWCA Civ 200. A director's potential conflict of interest may arise in connection with a business opportunity. If a director obtains the opportunity for himself, he will be liable to the company for breach of duty, regardless of the fact that he acted in good faith or that the company could not, or would not, take advantage of the opportunity.

The defences raised against the breach of duty claim in *Towers* failed to convince the Court. More specifically, the absence of evidence that the company would have taken the opportunity on its own, or had in fact suffered any loss, or that the director in question had any corrupt motive or that, if there had been no free loan, the director would have hired that sort of equipment in the market, along with the fact that the value of the benefit to the director was small, were not found either convincing or relevant; none of those matters supported the contention that there was no breach of the duty of loyalty or no breach of the 'no conflict' duty. Therefore, the court also appeared to reject any *de minimis* rule applying at this point. Even the proof that the benefit which the director derived from the transaction was indeed minimal and the fact that the company did not suffer any loss would not prevent the director in question being found in breach of the duty under section 175. The ambit of the provision in question appears to be very wide, and the court seems to have interpreted the particular rule with the intention of encompassing an impressively wide range of directorial behaviours.

The *Island Export Finance Ltd v Umunna and Another* line of cases

A contrasting case is *Island Export Finance Ltd v Umunna and Another* [1986] BCLC 460. The ruling in this case constitutes a different approach taken by the court in relation to the issue in question. The position of the court in this case departs from the principles adopted in *Industrial Development* and its subsequent rulings (above) to such a degree that we may refer to 'two lines of cases'.

In the *Island Export Finance* case, the defendant was managing director of the plaintiff company. He secured for the company a contract for postal caller boxes in The Cameroons. He subsequently resigned from the company, solely because of his dissatisfaction with it. At the time of his resignation the company was not seeking any further contracts for postal caller boxes. The defendant then procured two such contracts for his own company. The court held that there had been no breach of duty. It accepted that a duty could continue after resignation, but the facts in this case pointed to there having been no breach. The facts singled out as particularly important in coming to this conclusion were:

1. The company had only a vague hope of further contracts rather than an expectation, and it was not actively seeking new contracts at the time of the defendant's resignation. This would now appear to be irrelevant under section 175(2) (above).
2. The resignation was not prompted or influenced by the director's desire to obtain the contracts for himself.
3. The information about the contracts was not confidential information, since it merely amounted to knowledge of the existence of a particular market. To prevent directors using such information would conflict with public policy on the restraint of trade.

Another action which failed was *Framlington Group Plc and Another v Anderson and Others* [1995] 1 BCLC 475. There, the defendants were directors of and employees of the plaintiff company. The defendants were free, if they left the employment of the plaintiff, to set up or join a competing business and to take with them the plaintiff's clients. They were all private client fund managers. R plc offered jobs to all three defendants. At the same time R plc negotiated a transfer of funds from the plaintiff company. This negotiation was carried out by other members of the plaintiff company and the defendants were told not to get involved. The defendants did not inform the plaintiff company of the employment packages they had negotiated. The plaintiff claimed that the benefits received by the defendants from R plc were secret profits and should be paid to the company. The court held in favour of the defendants. The fact of the negotiations on employment had been known to the plaintiff company, which had taken deliberate steps to keep the two negotiations separate and had told the defendants that they were not concerned with the detail of the employment package which was being negotiated.

A potential third way?

A case which throws some further doubt on the continuance of directors' duties after resignation was *British Midland Tool Ltd v Midland International Tooling Ltd* [2003] 2 BCLC 523. In that case there was a conspiracy by four directors to set up a new company and poach employees and business from the plaintiff company. One of the directors resigned, but he was actively engaged in the conspiracy with the remaining directors for some months. The three directors who continued in office were found to be in breach of their duties, but the director who resigned was held not to have breached his duty to the company he had left. Hart J said (at [89]): 'A director is free to resign his directorship at any time notwithstanding the damage that the resignation may itself cause the company: see *CMS Dolphin Ltd v Simonet* [2001] 2 BCLC 704 at [95] per Lawrence Collins J.' This ruling was astonishing, as the behaviour of the director who was cleared of any liability amounted to a clear breach of the duty enshrined in section 175 as the director in question, despite his resignation, participated actively in the efforts to set up a new competing business while diverting employees and customers from his previous company to the newly founded one.

Therefore, the court can interpret the real facts of each case in such a way as to fit in within each line of cases, with the *British Midland Tool Ltd* one adding yet another significant, as well as confusing, aspect to the field in question.

When should a director resign to avoid a breach of section 175?

In the *British Midland Tool Ltd* case (above), the court stated that by resigning his directorship the director would put an end to his fiduciary obligations to the company so far as concerned any future activity by himself (provided that it did not involve the exploitation of confidential information or business opportunities available to him by virtue of his directorship). Falconer J, in *Balston Ltd v Headline Filters Ltd* [1990] FSR 385, was of a different opinion, stating that 'a director who wishes to engage in a competing business and not disclose his intentions to the company ought, in my judgement, to resign his office as soon as his intention has been irrevocably formed and he has launched himself in the actual taking of preparatory steps'. In *Shepherds Investments Ltd v Walters* [2006] EWHC 836, [2007] IRLR 110, it was nevertheless stated that the point at which a director should resign to pursue new business opportunities strictly depends on the facts of each case, without any general rule applying:

> [T]he precise point at which preparations for the establishment of a competing business by a director become unlawful will turn on the facts of any particular case. In each case, the touchstone for what, one the one hand, is permissible, and what, on the other hand, is impermissible unless consent is obtained from the company or employer after full disclosure, is what, in the case of a director, will be in breach of the fiduciary duties to which I have referred, or, in the case of an employee, will be in breach of the obligation of fidelity. It is obvious, for example, that merely making a decision to set up a competing business at some point in the future and discussing such an idea with friends and family would not of themselves be in conflict with the best interests of the company and the employer. The consulting of lawyers and other professionals may, depending on all the circumstances, equally be consistent with a director's fiduciary duties and the employee's obligation of loyalty. At the other end of the spectrum, it is plain that soliciting

customers of the company and the employer or the actual carrying on of a trade by a competing business would be in breach of the duties of the director and the obligations of the employee. It is the wide range of activity and decision making between the two ends of the spectrum which will be fact sensitive in every case.

In *Foster Bryant Surveying Ltd v Bryant & Another* [2007] EWCA Civ 200, it was supported that a decision should be taken on the basis of the particular circumstances, taking into account factors such as the personal freedom to compete on the one hand and the misuse of a company's secrets and business opportunities on the other.

In *Bhullar & Ors v Bullar & Another* [2003] EWCA Civ 424 it was said:

[I]n a case such as the present, where a fiduciary has exploited a commercial opportunity for his own benefit, the relevant question … is not whether the party to whom the duty is owed (the Company, in the instant case) had some kind of beneficial interest in the opportunity: … that would be too formalistic and restrictive an approach. Rather, the question is simply whether the fiduciary's exploitation of the opportunity is such as to attract the application of the rule. As Lord Upjohn made clear in *Phipps v Boardman*, flexibility of application is of the essence of the rule. Thus, at ibid p 123, he said: 'Rules of equity have to be applied to such a great diversity of circumstances that they can be stated only in the most general terms and applied with particular attention to the exact circumstances of each case.'

In *Bhullar* the judges found the approach taken in *Cooley* (above) the most appropriate:

Like the defendant in *Industrial Development Consultants Ltd v Cooley*, the appellants in the instant case had, at the material time, one capacity and one capacity only in which they were carrying on business, namely as directors of the Company. In that capacity, they were in a fiduciary relationship with the Company. At the material time, the Company was still trading, albeit that negotiations (ultimately unsuccessful) for a division of its assets and business were on foot … Whether the Company could or would have taken that opportunity, had it been made aware of it, is not to the point: the existence of the opportunity was information which it was relevant for the Company to know, and it follows that the appellants were under a duty to communicate it to the Company. The anxiety which the appellants plainly felt as to the propriety of purchasing the Property through Silvercrest without first disclosing their intentions to their co-directors – anxiety which led Inderjit to seek legal advice from the Company solicitor – is … eloquent of the existence of a possible conflict of duty and interest … 'reasonable men looking at the facts would think there was a real sensible possibility of conflict'.

In *In Plus Group Ltd v Pyke* [2002] EWCA Civ 370 at [89], Judge Levy stated that 'it is not a breach of a fiduciary duty of a director to work for a competing company in circumstances where he has been excluded effectively from the company of which he is a director'. In this case, P and M founded a number of companies and held 50 per cent each as directors and shareholders. Their relationship broke down and the companies in question did not provide any further remuneration to P, who could not have any access to the companies' finances. A customer of one of the companies stopped placing any contracts with it and instead, six months after the relationship broke down, P started doing subcontract work for this customer. The company in question that lost the client and the related business alleged that this was a clear breach of P's duty not to bring himself into a situation of conflict of interests. However, the appeal was dismissed on the grounds that while the duty to act bona fide for the benefit of the company as a whole in its specific application of the non-conflict rule is well established and generally accepted, a fact-specific analysis had to be made. While the Court acknowledged that there was a well-established duty to act in a certain way, each case should be dealt on an individual basis on the grounds of the specific facts. P was not found in breach of duty on this point, although there remained the claim of bringing himself into a situation of conflicting interests. However, since he was found to be effectively expelled from the everyday life and functions of the companies involved, he could not have made use of any of the company's assets and did not obtain relevant information as a part of his post as a director of the companies in question. Therefore, he was not found to have breached the duty towards the company: 'The defendant's role as a director of the claimants was throughout the relevant period entirely nominal … in the concrete sense that he was entirely excluded from all decision making and all participation in the claimant company's affairs. For all the influence he had, he might as well have resigned' (at [90]); 'The unusual circumstances of the instant case seem to … lead inescapably to the conclusion that the claim based on fiduciary duty fails … had P resigned as a director in late 1996 or early 1997 his resignation would have done no more than reflect what has in practice already happened' (at [94]).

In *Thomas Marshall (Exports) Ltd v Guinle* [1979] Ch 227, Megarry VC sought to identify the type of information that would be protected by the courts, in as much as they would prevent the disclosure of such information or prevent anyone owing a duty to the company that was entitled to the benefit of the information from profiting from it. He said (at 248):

> First, I think that the information must be information the release of which the owner believes would be injurious to him or of advantage to his rivals or others. Second, I think the owner must believe that the information is confidential or secret, ie, that it is not already in the public domain. It may be that some or all of his rivals already have the information: but as long as the owner believes it to be confidential I think he is entitled to try and protect it. Third, I think that the owner's belief under the two previous heads must be reasonable. Fourth, I think that the information must be judged in the light of the usage and practices of the particular industry or trade concerned. It may be the information which does not satisfy all these requirements may be entitled to protection as confidential information or trade secrets: but I think that any information which does satisfy them must be of a type which is entitled to protection.

Conclusion

From the statute and cases the following principles emerge:

1. A director is in danger of being in breach of his fundamental duty to the company if he places himself in a position where one of his private interests comes into conflict with the company's interests.
2. This duty continues after resignation.
3. Use of information or opportunity which comes to the director because of his position in the company will very likely be a breach of his duty to the company even if he tries to disassociate himself from the company by:
   (a) saying he is acting in a private capacity on this occasion; or
   (b) resigning for the purpose of exploiting the information or opportunity.
   Here the statute and case law may differ, although the statute refers to 'necessary adaptations' for directors who have left office and the ambit is therefore unclear.
4. Confidential information includes those categories described by Megarry VC in *Thomas Marshall*, but that definition was not exclusive, so other information may be included.

As in other areas of 'duty', it must be remembered that breaches may be excused by the majority on the same principles.

9.2.2(d) Duty not to accept benefits from third parties

Section 176 of the Companies Act 2006 introduces a duty not to accept benefits in return for a particular action. It reads:

> (1) A director of a company must not accept a benefit from a third party conferred by reason of—
>   (a) his being a director, or
>   (b) his doing (or not doing) anything as director.

This would seem to be a reflection of the general duty not to allow duty and interest to conflict (see Section 9.2.2(c) above). It incorporates in a statutory form the so called 'non profit' rule. Benefits cover both monetary and non-monetary benefits, such as money, presents, trips or other forms of contribution. The director may escape liability if the acceptance of such a benefit cannot reasonably be regarded as likely to give rise to a conflict of interest. However, accepting the benefit will certainly bring him into a grey area where he could be found liable on the basis of section 176.

The duty under section 176 is extended by section 170(2) of the 2006 Act:

> (2) A person who ceases to be a director continues to be subject—
>   (a) …
>   (b) to the duty in section 176 … as regards things done or omitted by him before he ceased to be a director.

To that extent those duties apply to a former director as to a director, subject to any necessary adaptations.

9.2.2(e) Duty to declare interest in proposed transaction or arrangement

Under section 177 of the Companies Act 2006:

> (1) If a director of a company is in any way, directly or indirectly, interested in a proposed transaction or arrangement with the company, he must declare the nature and extent of that interest to the other directors.
> …
> (4) Any declaration required by this section must be made before the company enters into the transaction or arrangement.

Section 177 in a way involves an aspect of the duty provided for by section 175 (see Section 9.2.2(c) above), as it will involve a situation marked by a conflict of interests. The director will engage in one way or another with a transaction with the company, creating the conditions necessary for a conflict of interests to take place. In this context it is useful to bear in mind that both duties may now continue to exist even after a director ceases to hold office.

Section 177 of the Act reflects section 317 of the 1985 Act in that it requires a director to disclose his interest to the board of the company when a transaction is proposed between a director and his company. However, it goes further than the requirement under the 1985 Act by requiring a director to declare the nature and the extent of the interest to the other directors. Disclosure also extends to a person connected with the director, for example his wife and children. The requirement for disclosure is dispensed with in circumstances where the interest cannot reasonably be regarded as likely to give rise to a conflict of interest.

As stated in Section 9.1.4(d) above, section 170(3) and (4) makes it clear that the statutory general duties are to be interpreted and applied in the same way as the common law rules and equitable principles. This means that this section, as with the rest of the provisions on directors' duties, will be interpreted on the basis of the previous case law, which remains relevant even after the passing of the Companies Act 2006.

9.3 Duty to exercise reasonable care, skill and diligence

The duty to exercise reasonable care, skill and diligence is an independent duty on its own; it does not form a part of the aforementioned list of fiduciary duties. The courts have produced extensive case law which explains the parameters on the basis of which the duty is to apply.

The difference in the degree of involvement of directors may be illustrated by the facts of the old case known as *The Marquis of Bute's Case* [1892] 2 Ch 100. The Marquis of Bute became president of the Cardiff Savings Bank when he was six months old, having inherited the office from his father. He attended only one board meeting of the bank in 38 years. However, he was held not liable for irregularities which occurred in the lending operations of the bank. The judge held that he could not be considered liable as he knew nothing about what was going on. There was no hint that he ought to have kept himself informed.

Similarly, in *Dovey v Cory* [1901] AC 477, the director was able to escape liability for malpractice which had occurred, on the grounds that he had relied on information given to him by the chairman and general manager of the company. The standard applied here seems to be somewhat stricter than that in *The Marquis of Bute's Case* since the Court held that the reliance on the chairman and general manager was reasonable and that the director had not been negligent. The standard in this case was one of negligence, that is, the director must have acted as a reasonable man. If a reasonable man would have been suspicious of the information that was given and would have investigated further, a director who failed to do so could well have been liable for the loss caused by the irregularity. This may well be a higher standard than that imposed in the previous case where there seems to be no suggestion that a 'reasonable man' test should be used to judge the Marquis's inaction.

A case in which these issues were fully explored is *Re City Equitable Fire Insurance* [1925] Ch 407. That case is still generally regarded as important in this area, although the courts have moved away from the subjective standards imposed in *Re City Equitable Fire Insurance* to a more objective standard (see below). In *Re City Equitable Fire Insurance* the judge set out three important rules:

1. A director need not exhibit in the performance of his duties a greater degree of skill than may reasonably be expected from a person of his knowledge and experience.
2. A director is not bound to give continuous attention to the affairs of his company. His duties are of an intermittent nature to be performed at periodical board meetings and at meetings of any committee of the board on which he happens to be placed. He is not, however, bound to attend all such meetings, though he ought to attend whenever in the circumstances he is reasonably able to do so.
3. In respect of all duties that, having regard to the exigencies of business and the articles of association, may properly be left to some other official, a director is, in the absence of grounds for suspicion, justified in trusting that official to perform such duties honestly.

These rules were affirmed in *Dorchester Finance Co Ltd v Stebbing* [1989] BCLC 498, where it was also held that there was no difference in the duties owed by executive and non-executive directors.

Notable aspects of these rules are as follows:

- *Rule 1*. The standard is not that of a 'reasonable professional director' but refers to the reasonable man with the skill and experience actually possessed by the particular director in question. This has two effects. If someone like the baby Marquis of Bute is appointed to the board of a company, he will presumably be held not liable for irregularities, as a small baby has extremely limited skill and experience. This may be fair from the baby's point of view, but the standard does little to protect the public. However, leaving such extreme examples aside, the standard is capable of working quite well and of having sufficient flexibility to be valuable in different types of companies for judging the behaviour of different types of directors. Larger and more complex businesses are more likely to employ highly qualified and experienced directors to run affairs. Under the test in Rule 1, such people will have a higher standard of skill expected of them. Thus the more complex the operation, the more the interests of those with money at stake will be protected. The test is therefore seriously inadequate only where a very inappropriate appointment has been made, whether the operation is large or small.
- *Rule 2*. Similar considerations apply to Rule 2, since the duty is to attend meetings and give attention to company affairs 'whenever in the circumstances [the director] is reasonably able to do so'. In the case of a full-time, salaried director of a large company, it is obviously reasonable to expect his working life to be devoted to the affairs of the company. The standard will vary to take into account different types of director, so that a non-executive director will not be bound to give the affairs of the company as much of his time as would an executive director.
- *Rule 3*. At first sight this seems to benefit a director who absents himself or who fails to keep himself informed on company matters so that he will not be aware of any 'grounds for suspicion' and thus can safely leave the running of the company to others. However, if this rule is taken in conjunction with the other two rules, it will be seen that the director is obliged (by Rules 1 and 2) to take proper part in the affairs of the company, so that unless his appointment has been manifestly foolish (as in the case of the baby Marquis), the rules will work together to provide a sliding scale of responsibility which will weigh heaviest on those most able to do the job and whose expectations of reward from the job are probably highest.

In extreme cases, however, the rules will not protect those with money at stake. For many years there was a call for an objective standard of competence to be imposed so that directors could not do the job if they were dishonest or foolish (or six months old). The DTI Company Law Review Committee accepted that an objective standard had been adopted into the general law by analogy with section 214 of the Insolvency Act 1986 (see *Modern Company Law for a Competitive Economy: Developing the Framework*, March 2000). In *Re D'Jan of London Ltd* [1993] BCC 646, Hoffman LJ stated that the common law duty of care owed by directors was accurately stated in section 214 of the Insolvency Act 1986.

The Companies Act 2006 adopts this objective standard. Section 174 reads:

174 Duty to exercise reasonable care, skill and diligence
(1) A director of a company must exercise reasonable care, skill and diligence.
(2) This means the care, skill and diligence that would be exercised by a reasonably diligent person with—
    (a) the general knowledge, skill and experience that may reasonably be expected of a person carrying out the functions carried out by the director in relation to the company, and
    (b) the general knowledge, skill and experience that the director has.

Section 174 therefore contains a test against which a breach of duty of care and skill is to be determined. This test has an objective (section 174(2)(a)) and a subjective component (section 174(2)(b)). The former assesses the directorial behaviour on the basis of the knowledge, skill and experience that may reasonably be expected from any person carrying out the functions of a director. It presupposes a level of skill and knowledge naturally expected of any person holding such an office; that would determine whether the director in question exhibited the skills expected by an individual at such a role or failed the first part of the test. The latter means that there is a base level of reasonable expectation which appears to be related to the type of company in which the director finds himself as well as to his personal qualifications, characteristics and experience. Where the director is particularly experienced, he will not be permitted to perform to a lower standard. An example might be if an executive director of a large public company retires and takes a directorship in a small family firm. He would be expected to perform to a high standard because of his past experience. Both requirements have to be met cumulatively for a director to escape liability on the basis of section 174.

The statute strikes a good balance, as imposition of too high a standard might pose the same problems as have been experienced in the USA, where the imposition of huge liabilities on the board of directors for negligence (see *Smith v Van Gorkom* 488 A 2d 858 (1985) (Supreme Court of Delaware)) led to the adoption by a number of States of legislation permitting the elimination of the liability of directors for various breaches of duty. The imposition of liability for negligence proved too strict in view of the huge sums of money involved and led to a distinct reluctance to join boards as non-executive (outside) directors. An example of such a law is the Delaware Corporation Law, § 102(b)(7), which was adopted on 1 July 1986 and reads:

> [T]he certificate of incorporation may also contain any or all of the following matters:
>
> (7) A provision eliminating or limiting the personal liability of a director to the corporation or its stockholders for monetary damages for breach of fiduciary duty as director, provided that such provision shall not eliminate or limit the liability of a director, (i) for any breach of the director's duty of loyalty to the corporation or its stockholders; (ii) for acts or omissions not in good faith or which involve intentional misconduct or knowing violation of the law; (iii) under § 174 of this title [relating to limitations on distributions to stockholders]; or (iv) for any transaction from which the directors derived an improper personal benefit. No such provision shall eliminate or limit the liability of a director for any act or omission occurring prior to the date when such provision became effective …

9.4   Consequences of a breach of duty

Section 178 of the Companies Act 2006 refers to the preceding common law concerning the consequences of a breach of duty. A director may be prevented from doing an action in breach of his duties by an injunction, and if he has profited from the breach he will be obliged to pay the company any money that he has made because of the breach (*Regal*

Hastings Ltd v. Gulliver – Section 9.2.2(c) above). A director may become a constructive trustee of money which has been mishandled. As well as these remedies, breach of directors' duties may be the foundation of actions open to shareholders or the company. Section 183 of the 2006 Act makes it a criminal offence to fail to declare an interest in a transaction with the company.

9.5 Are the prohibitions absolute?

We have seen already that the answer to this question is 'no'. The behaviour may be forgiven by the company with a varying degree of ease depending on how serious a view the court takes of it. The behaviour may be ratified under section 239 of the Companies Act 2006, and the statutory statement regarding ratification retains the common law uncertainty about the limits of ratification. Section 239(7) provides that:

> This section does not affect any other enactment or rule of law imposing additional requirements for valid ratification or any rule of law as to acts that are incapable of being ratified by the company.

At common law, breaches such as use of powers for an improper purpose were regarded as unlikely to breach the bona fide rule and could normally be condoned by a majority of the general meeting. At the other end of the scale, theft or fraud could not be condoned unless all those affected agreed to the behaviour.

A further point to note under this head is that the prohibitions may themselves be redefined by the company in advance. This clearly points to the difference between the fundamental duty and the prohibitions or disabilities as they were called in one case (*Movitex Ltd v Bulfield and Others* [1988] BCLC 104). It would be unthinkable for the court to permit an insertion in the articles of a clause allowing the directors to act in bad faith against the interests of the company. The courts have, however, permitted the articles of association to remove or redefine what would otherwise be disabilities or prohibitions.

An example of the way the system works is to be found in *Movitex* (above). There it was held that the true explanation of what was urged by counsel for the company to be the 'self-dealing' duty, or in other words the duty not to allow oneself to be in a position where duty and interest conflict, was that a director was, because of his position, unable (under a disability) to act in certain ways because it was likely that his behaviour would be seen as a breach of his fundamental duty of good faith. The company could nevertheless agree in advance that certain types of behaviour would not automatically be regarded as breach of the fundamental duty. Thus the articles (which allowed self-dealing transactions in certain circumstances) had not exempted the director from a duty; they had relieved the director from a prohibition or disability he would normally be under. This rule is variously reflected in the statute in relation to each of the listed duties.

In *Franbar Holdings Ltd v Patel & Ors* [2008] EWHC 1534 (Ch) the court stated that the words of Sir Richard Baggalay, delivering the advice of the Privy Council in *North-West Transportation Company v Beatty* (1887) 12 App Cas 589, 594, describing the circumstances in which a company cannot ratify breaches of duty by its directors, remain good law: '... provided such affirmance or adoption is not brought about by unfair or improper means, and is not illegal or fraudulent or oppressive towards those shareholders who oppose it.'

9.6 Specific duties of directors

The general duties of directors discussed in Sections 9.2 and 9.3 above are reinforced by specific statutory duties spelt out in the Companies Act 2006. These replace very complicated provisions under the 1985 Act, many of which were introduced as a result of financial scandals. The government of the day wished to be seen to be 'doing something' to remedy the situation.

The scheme of the 2006 Act is to require members' approval of certain transactions with directors. These are:

1. directors' service contracts of more than two years (ss 188 and 189);
2. substantial property transactions with directors (ss 190–196);
3. loans, quasi-loans and credit transactions (ss 197–214);
4. payments for loss of office (ss 215–222).

The sections mentioned contain definitions of the transactions and exceptions, and set out the legal consequences if they are infringed. This simplification is very welcome.

9.7 Disqualification of directors

Under the Company Directors Disqualification Act 1986, section 6, the courts must disqualify a director from managing a company if he has been a director of a company which has become insolvent (either while he was acting for it or later) and the court finds that his conduct 'makes him unfit to be concerned in the management of a company'. By section 6(4), the minimum period of disqualification is two years and the maximum is 15 years.

Although this legislation raises many questions, the major issue relevant to the standard of directors' duties is what is meant by 'unfitness'. Unfitness also seems to have an objective content, and this will be discussed in detail in Section 9.7.2(b) below. There are other grounds for disqualification which must be examined too (see Section 9.7.1 below). In *Official Receiver v Brady and Others* [1999] BCLC 258, it was held that companies, as well as individuals, could be subject to disqualification orders.

9.7.1 Reasons for disqualification

Under sections 2 to 5 of the Company Directors Disqualification Act 1986, a court may make a disqualification order against a person for the following reasons.

9.7.1(a) Conviction of indictable offence

A disqualification order may be made where a person is convicted of an indictable offence in connection with the promotion, formation, management or liquidation of a company, or with the receivership or management of a company's property (s 2). The offence need only be capable of being prosecuted on indictment; the relevant conviction could be obtained in a magistrates' court. Actual misconduct of a company's affairs need not be proved. In *Re Georgiou* (1988) 4 BCC 322, the offence was carrying on an unauthorised insurance business. There was no allegation that it was a badly managed insurance business. In *R v Goodman* [1994] BCLC 349, a chairman and major shareholder of a public company 'gave' his shares to a friend who sold them three days before it became public knowledge that the company was in trouble. He was later convicted of insider dealing and disqualified for 10 years under section 2 of the Company Directors Disqualification Act 1986. He appealed on the grounds that the insider trading was not an offence committed in connection with the management of a company. It was held that it was. The correct test was whether the offence had some relevant factual connection with the management of the company, not whether it had been committed in the course of managing the company (such as not filing returns). Here there was a clear connection.

There is no minimum period of disqualification under section 2 and disqualification is discretionary. If the offence is dealt with by a magistrates' court, the maximum disqualification period is five years. If the offence is dealt with on indictment, the maximum period is 15 years.

9.7.1(b) Persistent default

A disqualification order may be made if a person appears to the court to have been persistently in default in relation to any requirement under the companies' legislation for the filing, delivery or sending of any return, account or other document, or the giving of any notice with or to the Registrar of Companies (s 3). There is a presumption that a person has been 'persistently in default' if he has been convicted of a default, or has been required by court order to make good a default, three times in the preceding five years (s 3(2) and (3)). This does not prevent an application for an order being made under this section when neither of those matters can be shown. In *Re Arctic Engineering Ltd* [1986] 1 WLR 686, 'persistently' was held to require some degree of continuance or repetition. There is no need to show a wilful disregard of statutory requirements, although the absence of fault will be important when the exercise of the discretion not to disqualify is in question.

Under section 3, any court having jurisdiction to wind up the company has jurisdiction to make the order. Section 5 gives jurisdiction in precisely the same circumstances to a magistrates' court. This will usually be the court which actually convicts the director. Under both sections disqualification is discretionary and there is a maximum period of five years.

9.7.1(c) Fraud discovered in the course of winding up the company

A disqualification order may be made if a person appears to the court in the course of winding up the company:

1. to have been guilty of an offence (whether convicted or not) of fraudulent trading (s 4(1)(a));
2. to have otherwise been guilty, while an officer or liquidator of the company or receiver or manager of its property, of any fraud in relation to the company or of any breach of his duty as such officer, liquidator, receiver or manager (s 4(1)(b)).

This section applies to fraud, and so on, whenever it occurred. It is the discovery of fraud that must be in the course of the winding up, not the fraud itself. The court with jurisdiction to make the order is 'any court having jurisdiction to wind up the company'. Disqualification is discretionary and the maximum period is 15 years. It is not necessary for the purposes of section 4 that the company should be insolvent.

Under section 4(1)(a), anyone guilty of fraudulent trading may be disqualified. This offence may be committed by any person who was knowingly a party to the carrying on of the fraudulent business. By contrast, those liable to be disqualified under section 4(1)(b) are more uncertain. Sealy (*Disqualification and Personal Liability of Directors*, 5th edn (CCH, 2000)) lists the officers caught and possibly caught under section 4(1)(b). Those who are certainly caught are:

- a director
- a shadow director
- a secretary
- a 'manager' (see below)
- a liquidator
- a receiver.

There is a great deal of uncertainty surrounding the definition of a 'manager'. In *Re A Company No 00996 of 1979* [1980] Ch 138, at p. 144, Shaw LJ said:

> [A]ny person who in the affairs of the company exercises a supervisory control which reflects the general policy of the company or which is related to the general administration of the company is in the sphere of management. He need not be a member of the board of directors. He need not be subject to specific instructions from the board.

Those less certainly included (depending on the construction of the term 'officer') are:

- an auditor
- the supervisor of a voluntary arrangement (made under the Insolvency Act 1986, ss 1–7)
- an administrator (appointed under the Insolvency Act 1986, s 8).

Note that the disqualification order under the above provisions is discretionary. The court does not have to make such an order even if the facts that would enable it to do so are proved.

9.7.2 Duty to disqualify

There is a duty to disqualify imposed on the court under section 6(1) of the Company Directors Disqualification Act 1986, which reads as follows:

> (1) The court shall make a disqualification order against a person in any case where, on an application under this section, it is satisfied—
> (a) that he is or has been a director of a company which has at any time become insolvent (whether while he was a director or subsequently), and
> (b) that his conduct as a director of that company (either taken alone or taken together with his conduct as a director of any other company or companies) makes him unfit to be concerned in the management of a company.

9.7.2(a) Insolvency

Insolvency is defined by section 6(2) of the 1986 Act. A company becomes insolvent if:

1. it goes into liquidation at a time when its assets are insufficient to pay its debts, liabilities and winding-up expenses; or

2. an 'administration order' is made (irrespective of the solvency or otherwise of the company at any relevant time); or

3. an 'administrative receiver' is appointed (irrespective of the company's financial state).

The net is spread wide, as every liquidator (or administrator and so on) must report on the conduct of those possibly caught by the statute to a special enforcement unit which then takes the decision whether or not to ask the court for a disqualification order.

9.7.2(b) Unfitness

In *Re Dawson Print Group* [1987] BCLC 601 and *Re Stanford Services* [1987] BCLC 607 the following definitions of 'unfitness' appeared:

(a) a breach of commercial morality;
(b) really gross incompetence;
(c) recklessness;
(d) the director would be a danger to the public if he were allowed to continue to be involved in the management of companies.

Consideration (d) seems to have been ruled out by the Court of Appeal's decision in *Secretary of State for Trade and Industry v Gray and Another* [1995] 1 BCLC 276, where the Court found that only the behaviour alleged to make the defendant unfit could be considered. The future protection of the public was not a relevant consideration. The Court of Appeal approved the decision of Vinelott J in *Re Pamstock Ltd* [1994] 1 BCLC 736, where a disqualification order was made even though '[t]he respondent seemed … to be a man who today is capable of discharging his duties as director honestly and diligently'.

In *Re Bath Glass* [1988] BCLC 329 and *AB Trucking and BAW Commercials* Ch D, 3 June 1987, an objective standard of unfitness was imposed. A director was unfit if his actions were very far from those of a reasonably competent director.

It is difficult to tell whether this legislation will have an effect on the standard imposed on directors under *Re City Equitable Fire Insurance* (see Section 9.3 above). The willingness of the court to disqualify where the director is incapable of understanding his duties may indicate that the excuse of incompetence which is available under *Re City Equitable Fire Insurance* is ripe for review and may have a limited life. This willingness is illustrated by *AB Trucking and BAW Commercials*. The respondent was said to be 'incapable of understanding the commercial reality of accounts' and thus 'incapable of discharging his duty to the public'. Nevertheless Harman J imposed a disqualification order for four years.

A very high standard of behaviour seems to have been required by the court in *Re New Generation Engineers Ltd* [1993] BCLC 435. The factors said to merit disqualification were keeping inadequate accounting records, so that it was not possible to monitor the financial position of the company, and adopting a policy of paying only those creditors who pressed for payment or who needed to be paid in order to keep the company's business going. Each of these was said to provide grounds for disqualification, although the eventual order was only for three years.

Important factors in determining unfitness

1. The amount of debts outstanding and the practice of not paying debts as a method of continuing to trade. See *Secretary of State for Trade and Industry v McTighe and Another (No 2)* [1996] 2 BCLC 477, although Crown debts do not now seem to be particularly significant (see *Re Sevenoaks Stationers* [1991] BCLC 325).

2. The number of companies that the director has been involved in – in particular the number of liquidations with which he has been concerned.
3. The way in which the companies have been managed – in particular to what extent accounts have been kept up to date and returns made to the Companies Registry.
4. The personal circumstances of the director. Here the cases are confusing. Sometimes the youth and inexperience of a director are held to mitigate against a disqualification. The idea of this presumably is that he is growing up. On the other hand, in *Re Majestic Recording Studios Ltd* [1989] BCLC 1, the court was quite adamant that a person could be unfit when he was incompetent. Fraudulent behaviour did not need to be shown. What seems to be happening is that the court is assessing the degree of moral blame to be attached to the director for the company's failures. This will be less if incompetence was the cause of failure rather than fraud. This does not mean that there will be no finding of unfitness, but it will be a factor which the court will take into account when deciding whether to exercise its discretion as to the length of disqualification.
5. The state of mind of the defendant. The relevance of this factor is closely tied to the debate as to the true nature of disqualification. There are two clearly opposing approaches. One is that the imposition of a disqualification order is a penal sanction which may well have the effect of removal of the livelihood of the director in question. The other approach regards disqualification as the removal of a licence to trade using limited liability. Passages in judgments may be found clearly supporting one approach or the other. In *Re Civicia Investments Ltd* [1983] BCLC 456, Nourse J said:

> It might be thought that [consideration of the appropriate period of disqualification] is something which, like the passing of sentence in a criminal case, ought to be dealt with comparatively briefly and without elaborate reasoning ... [N]o doubt in this, as in other areas, it is possible that there will emerge a broad and undefined system of tariffs for defaults of varying degrees of blame ... [T]he longer periods of disqualification are to be reserved for cases where the defaults and conduct of the person in question have been of a serious nature, for example, where defaults have been made for some dishonest purpose.

The quasi-penal nature of disqualification under this section was clearly acknowledged in *Re Crestjoy Products Ltd* [1990] BCC 23, [1990] BCLC 677. In that case the judgment of Browne-Wilkinson VC in *Re Lo-Line Electric Motors Ltd* [1988] BCLC 698 was cited as a 'most useful encapsulation of the current authority'. The passage cited reads:

> The primary purpose of the section is not to punish the individual but to protect the public against the future conduct of companies by persons whose past records as directors of insolvent companies have shown them to be a danger to creditors and others. Therefore, the power is not fundamentally penal. But, if the power to disqualify is exercised ... disqualification does involve a substantial interference with the freedom of the individual. It follows that the rights of the individual must be fully protected.

The court went on to hold that 'since the making of a disqualification order involves penal consequences for the director, it is necessary that he should know the substance of the charges that he has to meet'. The judge in *Crestjoy* agreed with this analysis but nevertheless went on to say:

> It seems to me, however, that when I am faced with a mandatory two-year disqualification if facts are proved, the matter becomes more nearly penal, or, at least, more serious for the individual faced with it than under the former situation where a judge could, in the exercise of his discretion, say that although the conduct had been bad yet he was now convinced that a disqualification should not be made because, for example, the respondent had learnt his lesson.

In view of the seriousness of the matter, an application to bring an action seeking a disqualification order out of time was refused.

The approach in *Crestjoy* has been disapproved by the Court of Appeal in *Secretary of State for Trade and Industry v Gray and Another* [1995] 1 BCLC 276, where the Court held that only past behaviour could be considered. Mitigating factors which arose after the events alleged would not be relevant. However, both in that case (see further discussion below) and in subsequent cases, the quasi-penal nature of the proceedings have been acknowledged. In *Re Living Images Ltd* [1996] 1 BCLC 348, the court determined that although the proceedings were civil proceedings and the standard of proof was therefore on a balance of probabilities, the seriousness of both the allegations and the consequences meant that the court would 'require cogent evidence as proof', thus presumably setting a higher standard than the 'more likely than not' test.

Although it seems that this reason for regarding the matter as serious is less convincing in view of the possibility of permitting the director to continue as such under licence, nevertheless it is still a significant interference with the freedom of the individual if that licence has to be obtained from the court. The disqualification remains mandatory, not discretionary.

Objective (negligence) standard or subjective fault?

In *Re Bath Glass* [1988] BCLC 329 Peter Gibson J said:

> To reach a finding of unfitness the court must be satisfied that the director has been guilty of a serious failure or serious failures, whether deliberately or through incompetence, to perform those duties of a director which are attendant on the privilege of trading through companies with limited liability. Any misconduct of the respondent qua director may be relevant.

Since the 'serious failure' could occur because of the incompetence of the director, this means that the test imposed is an objective one, in that the standard may be breached by someone who, through no fault of his own, is incapable of performing the duties of a director. This is a clear divergence from the *Re City Equitable Fire Insurance* approach (see Section 9.3 above).

A similar view was taken by Harman J in *AB Trucking and BAW Commercials* (see above). The respondent was said to be 'incapable of understanding the commercial reality of accounts' and thus 'incapable of discharging his duty to the public'. Harman J imposed a disqualification order for four years.

It seems clear that an objective standard of 'fitness' is being imposed. The exact nature of the test is still unclear though. As we have seen, various tests appear in the cases (see Dine, 'The disqualification of company directors' (1988) 9 *Company Lawyer* 213). All or any of these could be at least partially objective in nature. Analysis of the standard has been poor. The view that 'incompetence' is sufficient seems to be growing, but in the absence of a definition of the ability to be expected of a 'reasonable director' such a standard is still necessarily vague. The one thing that does seem clear is that this mythical creature can both understand and keep accounts. If he cannot, he is unfit. Even if he employs a professional who should be competent to deal with the necessary paperwork, this will only be a matter to take into consideration when determining the length of disqualification.

This approach was taken by Harman J in *Re Rolus Properties Ltd & Another* (1988) 4 BCC 446. He said:

The privilege of limited liability is a valuable incentive to encourage entrepreneurs to take on risky ventures without inevitable personal total financial disaster. It is, however, a privilege which must be accorded upon terms and some of the most important terms that Parliament has imposed are that accounts be kept and returns made so that the world can, by referring to those, see what is happening. Thus, a total failure to keep statutory books and to make statutory returns is significant for the public at large and a matter which amounts to misconduct if not complied with and is a matter of which the court should take account in considering whether a man can properly be allowed to continue to operate as a director of companies, or whether the public at large is to be protected against him on the grounds that he is unfit, not because he is fraudulent but because he is incompetent and unable to comply with the statutory obligations attached to limited liability. In my view that is a correct approach and the jurisdiction does extend and should be exercised in cases where a man has by his conduct revealed that he is wholly unable to comply with the obligations that go with the privilege of limited liability.

The disqualification order was reduced from a four-to-six-year period to two years because of the reliance by the director on professional advice. In *Re Continental Assurance Co of London plc* [2001] BPIR 733, the court held that 'the degree of competence required … extended at least to a requirement that a director who was a corporate financier should be prepared to read and understand the statutory accounts of the holding company'.

One thing seems clear. An unfit director is worse than merely incompetent. He is guilty of 'gross negligence or total incompetence' (*Re Lo-Line Electric Motors Ltd* (1988) 4 BCC 415), or of being 'wholly unable to comply with the obligations that go with the privilege of limited liability' (*Re Rolus Properties* – see above). The merely incompetent or those guilty of commercial misjudgment will not be considered unfit (*Re McNulty's Interchange Ltd & Another* (1988) 4 BCC 533). In *Secretary of State for Trade and Industry v Hickling and Others* [1996] BCC 678, the court held that directors who had been guilty of naivety, over-optimism and misplaced trust should not, in the absence of dishonesty, commercial immorality or gross incompetence, be disqualified. There is, however, a rather opaque reference to disqualification being nearer to a 'negligence' standard than a determination of 'reasonable financial provision' in *Secretary of State for Trade and Industry v Gray and Another* [1995] 1 BCLC 276. However, the reference was in the context not of setting the standard for disqualification but of determining whether or not the Court of Appeal should interfere with the judge's findings. It seems to indicate that there is a standard for disqualification which the Court of Appeal can impose on every case. Until the courts have settled the standard of competence of a 'reasonable' director, it will continue to be uncertain whether a particular director has been incompetent. Further uncertainty is added by the requirement that the director should have been totally or wholly incompetent. It would be helpful if the courts addressed the definition of the degree of competence required of a 'fit' director. However, discussion of the meaning of 'unfitness' may be discouraged by the Court of Appeal's dicta in *Re Sevenoaks Stationers* [1991] BCLC 325, where it was held that such 'judicial paraphrases should not be construed in lieu of the words of the statute'. Unfitness was to be regarded as a 'jury question'.

As mentioned above, the Court of Appeal had a further chance to consider the setting of standards in *Secretary of State for Trade and Industry v Gray and Another* [1995] 1 BCLC 276, but again failed to determine the relationship between moral culpability and incompetence, or to set some measure of competence. In view of the latter failure, it is the more surprising that the Court felt able to overturn the lower court's finding that the directors were not unfit and should therefore be disqualified. The Court held that the respondents' conduct fell below the 'standard appropriate' for directors. The three allegations in this case were that the companies involved had (i) been trading while insolvent, (ii) failed to keep proper accounting records, and (iii) failed to file accounts on time. This behaviour had also involved the giving of preferences. Other remedies had been pursued in respect of the preferences, so that the judge discounted them. The Court of Appeal held that she was wrong to do so. The language in the case gives support to the argument that this is a penal measure. As described above, the Court held that only past conduct was relevant. The present state of affairs was irrelevant to the issue of disqualification, as was the future protection of the public. This attitude certainly seems to indicate that the thrust is punishment for past misdeeds. Deterrence is also an aim. Thus Hoffman LJ approved the statement by Sir Donald Nicholls VC in *Secretary of State for Trade and Industry v Ettinger; Re Swift 736 Ltd* [1993] BCLC 896: 'Those who make use of limited liability must do so with a proper sense of responsibility. The directors' disqualification procedure is an important sanction introduced by Parliament to raise standards in that regard.'

In *Re Barings plc* [1999] 1 BCLC 433, Parker J held that a disqualification would be imposed where there were no allegations relating to honesty and integrity. However, the alleged incompetence must be of a 'high degree'. Failure to exercise adequate management control fell into that category.

9.7.3   The length of the disqualification and 'mitigating factors'

9.7.3(a) The period of disqualification

In *Re Sevenoaks Stationers* [1991] BCLC 325, the Court of Appeal held that in determining the length of a disqualification under section 6 of the Company Directors Disqualification Act 1986, the top bracket of disqualification should be reserved for serious cases. This would involve disqualification of 10 years or more. The Court of Appeal suggested that cases in this bracket might well include cases of imposition of a second disqualification order on a director. Unhelpfully, Dillon LJ suggested that the 'middle bracket of disqualification from 6 to 10 years should apply for serious cases which do not merit the top bracket' (at 328). The minimum bracket of two to five years' disqualification 'should be applied where, though disqualification is mandatory, the case is, relatively, not very serious'. Unfortunately the Court did not analyse or discuss the matters which were likely to place a case within one of the 'brackets', with the exception of Crown debts. These were said to be of especial significance only where they had caused suffering over and above that caused by other creditors. It is unfortunate that the Court of Appeal did not seize the opportunity to carry out a more comprehensive review of the matters which would cause a case to fall within each bracket. More particularly, the matters which may be viewed as 'mitigating factors' are even more unclear.

9.7.3(b) The mitigating factors

There are a number of factors which have caused the court to impose a shorter order than would otherwise be the case. In cases decided under section 300 of the Companies Act 1985, the same factors led the court to exercise its discretion not to disqualify. Among those factors are:

1. the effect on a company's employees;
2. the director's having acted on professional advice; and
3. the youth of the director.

Effect on employees

The court may be reluctant to impose a disqualification order where jobs are at stake. In *Re Majestic Recording Studios Ltd* [1989] BCLC 1, the judge made a clear finding that the director was unfit, but then went on to permit him to continue to be director of one company under certain conditions, partly because of the hardship that this would otherwise cause to employees. However, this situation is sometimes dealt with by imposing a disqualification and subsequently granting leave to act as a director on certain conditions (see *Secretary of State for Trade and Industry v Rosenfield* [1999] BCC 413 and Section 9.7.4 below).

Acting on professional advice

This was a significant factor in reducing the period of disqualification in *Re Rolus Properties Ltd & Another* (see Section 9.7.2(b) above).

The youth of the director

The youth of the director at the time of the failure of the company and evidence that he has learnt from past mistakes may be mitigating factors (see *Re Chartmore* [1990] BCLC 673).

Only past behaviour should affect the decision whether to disqualify?

Nevertheless, the status of these cases and factors set out above seems very doubtful in view of the Court of Appeal's clear ruling in *Secretary of State for Trade and Industry v Gray and Another* (see Section 9.7.2(b) above) that only past behaviour should affect the decision to disqualify. Hoffman LJ, however, recognised that 'whether or not he has shown himself unlikely to offend again' will be relevant to whether or not there will be a grant of leave to act while disqualified (see Section 9.7.4 below). He went on to say: '[I]t may also be relevant by way of mitigation on the length of disqualification, although I note that the guidelines in *Re Sevenoaks Stationers* [1991] BCLC 325 are solely by reference to the seriousness of the conduct in question.'

9.7.4 Leave to act while disqualified

A curious light is thrown on the mandatory nature of the disqualification under section 6 of the 1986 Act by the power of the court to exercise a discretion to permit a director to act as such during the period of disqualification. This could amount to a reversal of the duty to impose a disqualification order, but it seems that the court will often impose quite stringent conditions on the grant of such permission (see *Re Lo-Line Electric Motors Ltd* [1988] BCLC 698). Another example is *Re Chartmore* (see Section 9.7.3(b) above). In that case a disqualification for two years for 'gross incompetence' was imposed. However, the director was permitted to continue to act for a named company for one year despite these misgivings expressed by Harman J:

> The only matter that bothers me is that the failure of the company for which I have disqualified Mr Buckingham, Chartmore Limited, was primarily due to Mr Buckingham having started it with

quite inadequate capitalisation and having carried it on unrealising that he was in effect trading on the creditors' backs in such a manner as to show that degree of inadequacy warranting disqualification.

This new company has one hundred pounds paid up share capital and no other equity on its balance sheet at all. There are no other directors' loan accounts which could be subordinated to the trade and other creditors or converted into equity. There is a statement by Mr Buckingham that he and his fellow director have paid fifteen thousand pounds into the company. That worries me because the accounts show no trace of the sum and they therefore cast considerable doubt on Mr Buckingham's sworn statement.

It is to be hoped that the courts will exercise caution in using this discretion.

9.7.5 Disqualification after investigation

Section 8 of the Company Directors Disqualification Act 1986 gives power to the court to make a disqualification order, on the application of the Secretary of State, if it appears from a report made to him or from information or documents obtained by him that it is expedient in the public interest that an order should be made against a director or former director of any company. The court must be satisfied that the conduct of the director in relation to the company makes him unfit to be concerned in the management of a company.

It is to be noted that not only must the unfitness test be satisfied (see Section 9.7.2 above), but also the Secretary of State may make the application only if it appears to be expedient in the public interest that a disqualification order should be made. This gives a very wide discretion to the Secretary of State as to whether he should apply for an order. Presumably he may take into account all such matters as would be considered by the Director of Public Prosecutions when considering whether to exercise his discretion to prosecute. Such matters might well include the wisdom of prolonging an already drawn-out affair, as well as the chances of the application's being successful. It must be noted that the power of the Secretary of State is limited to application to the court. Contrary to the thrust of some press reports at the time of publication of the House of Fraser report, the power to disqualify lies with the court and not with the Secretary of State. There is a discretion to disqualify under this section. The maximum disqualification period is 15 years.

9.7.6 Conclusion

The legislation has been widely used and disqualification is made more significant because a register of disqualified directors is kept and may be consulted. Two major difficulties remain in the operation of section 6 of the 1986 Act: the first is the exact degree to which the penal nature of the provisions should lead to care in protecting the rights of director defendants; the second is the definition of the standard of care to be expected from a reasonable director. The latter needs to be ascertained in order to identify deviancy more clearly. It is to be hoped that care will be taken to define this standard in future cases.

9.8 Insider dealing

The practice of 'insider dealing' or 'insider trading' occurs when a person with information makes use of that information for his own gain or to enable another to gain. Opinions differ as to whether the defendant should have gained the information in some privileged capacity. This aspect makes a fundamental difference to the philosophical basis of the laws forbidding the practice.

In respect of insider dealing or insider trading, UK law applies penal sanctions. There may be other constraints on company directors who contravene insider trading legislation using information gained as a director. They will be in breach of their duties to their company (see Section 9.2 above).

The implementation of the EC Market Abuse Directive (2003/6/EC) (there are amendments proposed in 2014) led to the Financial Services and Markets Act (FSMA) 2000 (see Chapter 6). It had proved extremely difficult to prosecute cases of insider dealing under the criminal law, so the FSMA 2000 included provisions giving the Financial Services Authority (FSA) power to impose civil sanctions, including fines on persons engaging in 'market abuse', which includes insider dealing. The criminal sanctions continue in force. This section should be considered with Chapter 6. The (now) FCA imposes requirements on listed companies, whose directors and senior executives must follow a Model Code which restricts their share dealings so as to reduce suspicion of insider dealing (FSMA 2000, s 102A(2); FCA Handbook, Glossary). The restrictions are more stringent than are required by law, because its purpose is to ensure that insiders do not abuse their powers and do not invite suspicion of abusing insider information.

First, the content of the EU and UK rules will be examined.

9.8.1   The offence of insider dealing

The UK legislation, as well as much of the legislation in force in other Member States, is driven by the EC Directive on Insider Dealing (89/592/EEC), which was implemented in the UK by the Criminal Justice Act 1993 which came into force on 1 March 1994. Part V of the Act implemented the EC Directive. Section 54 and Schedule 2 define the securities to which the insider trading provisions apply (see Section 9.8.1(a) below).

9.8.1(a) Securities

There is a double test. The relevant securities must appear in the list in Schedule 2 to the 1993 Act (which the Treasury may amend by order (s 54(2))) and must satisfy such other conditions as shall be laid down by Treasury order. The FCA imposes additional regulations. The Financial Services Act 2012 also forms part of this set of regulations. The most important securities covered are:

- stocks and shares,
- debt securities,
- warrants,
- depositary receipts,
- options,
- securities futures, and
- contracts for differences.

Having established that the securities in question are within the definition and that the defendant knew this, the prosecutor must show that the defendant knew that the information was inside information and that the defendant 'has [the information] and knows that he has it, from an inside source' (s 57(1)(b)).

9.8.1(b) Inside information

'Inside information' must be information relating to securities as defined for the purposes of Part V of the Act (as discussed in Section 9.8.1(a) above). It must also relate to particular securities or a particular issuer of securities, and not to securities or issuers in general. It must be specific or precise, must not have been made public and would be likely to have had a significant effect on the price of securities if made public.

Uncertainty must exist over the meaning of 'specific or precise' and 'significant effect' on price. Whether or not the facts of an individual case fit within these definitions will be for the jury to decide. They may well be in considerable difficulties in determining these matters, which may involve considerations outside their normal day-to-day experience.

Further difficulties may arise concerning the moment of 'publication', since information may well become available in widening circles rather than to everyone simultaneously. This problem is addressed in section 58 of the 1993 Act. This provides a non-exhaustive definition of the meaning of 'made public'. Information is made public if it is published in accordance with the rules of a regulated market for the purpose of informing investors and their professional advisers, is in any record open to public inspection, can readily be acquired by those likely to deal in relevant securities or is derived from information which has been made public. The section goes on to permit a wide construction of 'made public' in that information may be treated as made public even though it can only be acquired by persons exercising diligence or expertise, it has been communicated only to a section of the public, it can be acquired only by observation, is communicated on payment of a fee or it is published only outside the UK.

9.8.1(c) Insider

It will be remembered that the prosecutor must prove not only knowledge that the information was inside information but also that the defendant has the information from an inside source and knows that he has it from an inside source (s 57 – see Section 9.8.1(a) above).

An insider is defined by section 57 as a person who has the information through being a director, employee or shareholder of an issuer of securities; or having access to the information by virtue of his employment, office or profession or the direct or indirect source of his information is a director, employee or shareholder.

This definition replaces the notion of a person 'knowingly connected with a company' under section 9 of the Company Securities (Insider Dealing) Act 1985 and those abusing information obtained in an official capacity (s 2 of that Act). The wording follows Article 2 of the EC Directive on Insider Dealing, which defines a person prohibited from trading as any person who:

(i) by virtue of his membership of the administrative, management or supervisory bodies of the issuer,
(ii) by virtue of his holding in the capital of the issuer, or
(iii) because he has access to such information by virtue of the exercise of his employment, profession or duties,
possesses inside information.

This formulation may catch, say, a waiter who gleans the information from overheard conversations as he serves a meal to insiders, since he gains the information by virtue of his employment. The loosening of the 'connection' with the company may make the offence too wide. It also puts in doubt the philosophical basis of making this behaviour a criminal offence. If the 'connection' was important, an argument based on breach of trust by individuals was credible. A widening of the offence reduces this credibility. However, it is also arguable that the wording imports a causal link between the employment, etc and the acquisition of the information. (On this point see Takis Tridimas, 'Insider Trading in Europe', 40 *ICLQ* 919.) By requiring that the 'access' to the information was 'by virtue' of the employment, etc, the link required is stronger than in the Commission proposal which defined an insider as any person who 'in the exercise of his employment, profession or duties, acquires inside information'. The wording of the Act follows the wording of the adopted text. However, the wording of both the Directive and the Act is ambiguous, and now the EU will amend the legislation in 2014, tightening the loopholes.

The defendant must know that he 'has' the information as an insider, or that the direct or indirect source of the information was an insider (Criminal Justice Act 1993, s 57). It is clear that unsolicited information is covered. It is clear that positive actions or omissions by the defendant can lead to his prosecution (*Attorney-General's Reference (No 1 of 1988)* [1989] BCLC 193).

9.8.1(d) Liability of individuals

The offence set out in section 52 of the 1993 Act makes it plain that only individuals can be liable. The exclusion of criminal liability for companies may be explained by reference to the provisions of the Directive, which clearly contemplates that companies can be insiders but also expressly provides (Article 2(2)) that when the status of insider is attributable to a legal person, the prohibition applies to the natural persons who decided to carry out the transaction for the account of the legal person concerned. It was therefore not possible to exclude companies from the definition of insiders, but they can and will be excluded from liability as they are not considered to be in a position to commit the offence.

9.8.1(e) Requirement for a 'dealing', disclosure or encouragement to deal

The prosecution must show that there was a 'dealing' in the securities, a disclosure of the information or an encouragement of another to deal (Criminal Justice Act 1993, s 52). It should be noted that unlike the other matters we have examined, these are three alternative methods of committing the offence. All other matters pose cumulative hurdles for the prosecution.

Dealing or encouraging dealing

'Dealing' is further defined by section 55, and includes acquisition and disposal as principal or agent, or the direct or indirect procurement of an acquisition or disposal by any other person. In *Attorney-General's Reference (No 1 of 1975)* [1975] 2 All ER 684 at 686, 'procure' was held to mean 'produce by endeavour'. The defendant must therefore have caused the prohibited result by his actions. In that case the defendant charged with the procurement had added alcohol to the drink of another without that other's knowledge. It was held that if the defendant knew that the other man intended to drive and that the ordinary and natural result of the added alcohol was to cause him to have an alcohol concentration above the limit for drivers, the defendant had procured him to commit the drink-driving offence.

The meaning of an 'indirect procurement' must therefore remain rather obscure, particularly so far as the mens rea to be proved. Must it be proved that the defendant foresaw, or that it was reasonably foreseeable, that the defendant's actions would lead to another acquiring or disposing of securities? The relationship between this provision and section 52(2)(a), which prohibits the encouragement of another to deal, is also somewhat obscure. Could there be an indirect procurement which was not an encouragement to deal or vice versa?

Dealing will amount to an offence only if it takes place in the circumstances set out in section 52(3).

Section 52 states as follows:

(1) An individual who has information as an insider is guilty of insider dealing if, in the circumstances mentioned in subsection (3), he deals in securities that are price-affected securities in relation to the information.

(2) An individual who has information as an insider is also guilty of insider dealing if—
   (a) he encourages another person to deal in securities that are (whether or not that other knows it) price-affected securities in relation to the information, knowing or having reasonable cause to believe that the dealing would take place in the circumstances mentioned in subsection (3); or
   (b) he discloses the information, otherwise than in the proper performance of the functions of his employment, office or profession, to another person.

(3) The circumstances referred to above are that the acquisition or disposal in question occurs on a regulated market, or that the person dealing relies on a professional intermediary or is himself acting as a professional intermediary.

It is clear that the offence happens when the 'the acquisition or disposal in question occurs on a regulated market'. This wording follows Article 2(3) of the EC Directive which permits Member States 'to exempt deals not involving a professional intermediary'. 'Professional intermediary' is defined in section 59. Essentially it is a person who holds himself out to a section of the public as being someone willing to engage in the acquisition or disposal of securities, or to act as an intermediary between persons taking part in any dealing in securities.

Disclosing

Section 52(2)(b) of the 1993 Act provides that it is an offence for an individual to disclose information to another 'otherwise than in the proper performance of the functions of his employment, office or profession'. This provision deals with the simple disclosure of information and is perhaps the most likely offence to be limited by the concept of 'taking advantage'.

Encouraging others to deal

The third way of committing the offence is by encouraging others to deal (Criminal Justice Act 1993, s 52(2)(a)). It must be shown that the defendant knows or has reasonable cause to believe that the deal will occur on a regulated market or would be effected through a professional intermediary.

9.8.2 The defences

If the factors discussed so far can be proved, the defendant is guilty of insider dealing unless he can take advantage of the defences set out in section 53 of the Criminal Justice Act 1993 or specific defences which appear in Schedule 1. The Act is specific about the burden of proof, in that each defence requires that the defendant should 'show' the relevant facts. This will presumably mean that a defendant must establish the defences on a balance of probabilities.

9.8.2(a) Defences to a dealing charge

Under section 53(1) of the 1993 Act:

(1) An individual is not guilty of insider dealing by virtue of dealing in securities if he shows—

    (a) that he did not at the time expect the dealing to result in a profit attributable to the fact that the information in question was price-sensitive information in relation to the securities; or

    (b) that at the time he believed on reasonable grounds that the information had been disclosed widely enough to ensure that none of those taking part in the dealing would be prejudiced by not having the information; or

    (c) that he would have done what he did even if he had not had the information.

This exception replaces section 3 of the 1985 Act and is apt to cover the situation where the profit motive is present but is not a primary purpose. The problem posed by the Directive was to retain this and other exceptions while implementing the Directive which contains no parallels. Use has been made of the 'taking advantage' approach in the Directive to achieve this (see Section 9.8.1(e) and *Attorney-General's Reference (No 1 of 1975)* [1975] 2 All ER 684).

The special trustee exceptions (Insider Dealing Act 1986, s 7) will also be covered by this exception in the Act.

9.8.2(b) Defences to charges of encouraging another to deal or disclosing information

Section 52(2) provides exactly similar defences to the offence of encouraging another to deal as are provided for the offence of dealing (see Section 9.8.2(a) above).

Section 53(3) provides a defence to the offence of disclosing information under section 52(2)(b) (see Section 9.8.1(e) above). It is a defence for a defendant accused of insider dealing by disclosure of information to show either that he did not expect anyone to deal as a result of the disclosure, or that he did not expect the dealing to result in a profit attributable to the fact that the information was price-sensitive. In all cases the notion of profit includes avoidance of a loss (s 53(6)).

9.8.2(c) Other specific defences

There are also specific defences for:

- market makers dealing in good faith in the course of business or employment;
- dealers whose information is market information concerning the acquisition or disposal of certain securities, who deal in good faith in circumstances where it was reasonable for them to deal; and
- price stabilisation operations, provided that the individuals carrying them out have acted in conformity with price stabilisation rules made under section 137Q of the Financial Services and Markets Act 2000.

Article 2(4) of the 2003 Directive provides an exemption for transactions carried out by Member States or their agents 'in pursuit of monetary, exchange rate or public debt-management policies'. This general exemption is reflected in section 63 of the Act.

One concern which may be felt is the reversal of the burden of proof in all the above circumstances, save for the general exemption in section 63. The presumption against a defendant and the defence based on motive may be of little comfort where criminal charges are in prospect.

9.8.3   Jurisdiction

By Article 5 of the Directive on Insider Dealing, the Member States are to apply the prohibitions 'at least' to actions undertaken within their territory, 'to the extent that the transferable securities concerned are admitted to trading on a market of a Member State'. This provision appears to be of impenetrable obscurity, but an attempt has been made to reflect the Directive in section 62 of the Criminal Justice Act 1993, which restricts jurisdiction to acts done within the UK or on markets declared by Treasury order to be a market 'regulated in the United Kingdom'. It is not necessary that the dealing should have occurred within the UK: 'any act constituting or forming part of the alleged dealing' will be sufficient to found jurisdiction (s 62(1)(a)).

Article 13 of the Directive provides that the Member States shall determine the penalties to be applied for infringement of the prohibitions. The only proviso to this discretion is that the 'penalties shall be sufficient to promote compliance'. The maximum penalty provided for in the 1993 Act is seven years' imprisonment and an unlimited fine for a conviction on indictment. The UK would seem to have ignored both the criticism of the use of the criminal law and the possibility of substituting civil remedies. (See Hopt and Wymeersch (eds), *European Insider Dealing* (Butterworths, 1991) and Naylor, 'The Use of Criminal Sanctions by the UK and US Authorities for Insider Trading' (1990) 11 *Company Law* 53.) Although the implementation provisions reflect the Directive well, the use of the criminal law probably does not promote compliance with the prohibitions as it is well known to be ineffective.

The sum total of the matters which the prosecution must prove has been set out above, and it is plain that the offence of insider dealing is still complex and difficult to prove. It is arguable that putting in place an ineffective convoluted criminal offence is at the same time a misuse of the criminal law and an ineffective implementation of the EC Directive.

9.8.4   Should insider dealing be a crime?

Some argue that this is a 'victimless crime' in that it is not clear if there is actually a loser; others claim that the practice of insider trading increases the volume of sales on a market, so that overall the market gains.

9.8.4(a) Theories behind control of insider trading

In the USA, regulation of insider dealing dates from the 1930s. A comprehensive ban on dealing passed into UK law in the 1980s. Prior to this, insider dealing by directors might have given rise to an action for breach of fiduciary duties, provided that the misfeasance was not ratified by the company's general meeting.

The controversy surrounding the regulation of insider trading starts from a number of theoretical standpoints:

▶ *Misappropriation.* Perhaps the simplest is the misappropriation theory, which regards non-public price-sensitive information as a valuable commodity which is the property, or akin to the property, of a company. The information does not belong to the individuals who make up the company. It is therefore inequitable and akin to theft for those individuals to make use of that information for their own gain. This theory does not require any loss to have been suffered in real terms – the offensive behaviour is seen as the unjustifiable gain or avoidance of loss. This equation of insider trading with misappropriation is perhaps the strongest argument in favour of criminal sanctions. It is to be noted, however, that at this stage practical considerations have not been taken into account. The most compelling practical consideration is that both the offence and the transactions which constitute the actus reus are complicated. This makes proof of all of the elements of an offence to the criminal standard extremely difficult.

▶ *Fairness and confidence in the market.* This argument in favour of the regulation of insider trading rests on the perception that if, of two potential players in a market, one has price-sensitive information available and the other has not, that is unfair.

The argument may be bolstered by, or include reference to, the misappropriation theory, and its proponents may or may not assert that the 'victims' suffer loss as opposed to making a profit. The unfairness is said to lead to loss of confidence by investors in the markets and will lead to a diminution in trading.

In fact, there are three closely related approaches which may overlap. The inherent unfairness approach, the misappropriation theory and the idea that insider trading may lead to loss of confidence in the market are all distinct reasons for regulating insider trading. They may be used together as above, but the loss of confidence in the market may not necessarily be related to the perception that the market is unfair.

▶ *Market efficiency.* If it could be shown that insider dealing created a more efficient market then there would be a benefit to all investors at the expense of no one. Manne ('The Economics of Legal Relationships', *Readings in the Theory of Property Rights* (St Paul, 1975)) sought to establish that the effect of insider dealing is to produce a gradual change in prices as more and more people receive and rely on the information in question. Only speculative dealers on the market would suffer from insider dealing. The long-term investor will not be interested in the timing of the disclosure but will reap his reward in due course. When such an investor sells, Manne argues that even if he sells in ignorance of information which is causing insiders to trade, the very fact that they are trading increases the price he receives for his shares. Suter (*The Regulation of Insider Dealing in Britain* (Butterworths, 1989), p 22) has the following to say about that proposition:

> Arguments as to the seller's gain will be of little comfort to a seller who argues that had he known what the insider knew, he would not have sold. In deciding to sell, he sells at a lower price than if the information had been disclosed. He is also deprived of information relevant to his investment decision. The fact that the seller's loss is contingent does not mean that the insider's gain is not made at the expense of anyone.

The gap between the two positions can perhaps be explained by the difference between the economists' approach, which focuses on the efficiency of the market and would regard the improved efficiency of the market and the consequent gain to all investors as outweighing any notions of inequities between individual participants, and the other approaches. This attitude leads to the extreme theory which holds that the ability to use price-sensitive information before it is made public is a legitimate reward for those in a position to be able to do so.

9.8.4(b) The government's view

The view current at present in official circles in the UK is that insider trading undermines confidence in the probity of the market and is unfair. It is a practice also condemned on the ground that it has parallels with those who use information or property belonging to a company to make gains on their own account.

Summary

9.1 Directors' duties can be divided into fiduciary duties and duties of care and skill.

9.2 The duties of care and skill contain an objective and a subjective element.

9.3 Directors are under an equitable duty to act in good faith to promote the success of the company. If they put themselves into certain positions, they are in danger of breaching this duty.

9.4 Those positions are: where they act outside their powers, do not exercise independent judgment, do not act with appropriate care and skill, where their interests and duty conflict, and where they accept benefits from third parties or fail to declare an interest in a transaction with the company.

9.5 The courts may permit the company, acting by a majority in general meeting, to forgive directors who have acted in any of the ways described above. The ease with which this will be allowed depends on the view taken by the court of the seriousness of the behaviour.

9.6 The company may define in advance behaviour which will not be regarded as a breach of duty.

9.7 The general fiduciary duties of directors are backed up by specific duties and prohibitions set out in the statutes.

9.8 These prohibitions include limitations on transactions between the company and directors or their families.

9.9 There is also a general prohibition on the misuse of price-sensitive information about shares obtained by or from a person in a privileged position. The rule against insider dealing attracts criminal and civil penalties.

Exercises

9.1 To whom does a director owe duties?

9.2 What factors make it difficult to impose one standard on all directors?

9.3 Does the duty of directors not to bring themselves into a situation where their personal interest conflicts with the duty they owe to the company cease to exist when they resign?

9.4 Explain the evolution of the standard employed to assess whether there has been a breach of a director's duty of care and skill.

9.5 John and Mary are directors of Wash Ltd. They become suspicious of the behaviour of Joe, the third director of the company. He has recently bought a Porsche and has taken several foreign holidays. John and Mary know that his salary as director would not be sufficient to pay for these luxuries. John discovers that Joe has been buying raw materials for Wash Ltd from a company in which he, Joe, owns all but one of the shares. The price of these materials appears to be excessive. John tells Mary that she is better off knowing nothing about what is going on. She agrees. John then uses his powers under the articles to issue enough shares to friends to ensure that Joe is voted out of office. The company becomes insolvent. It has paid no VAT, PAYE or NICs for many months. What breaches of duty have been committed? Is it likely that any of the directors will be disqualified?

9.6 Would the transactions prohibited by statute be a breach of directors' duties according to the case law?

9.7 Should insider dealing be a criminal offence?

Further reading

Bourne, *Bourne on Company Law* (Routledge-Cavendish, 2011)

Talbot, *Critical Company Law* (Routledge-Cavendish, 2008)

Caspar, 'Stakeholder orientation versus shareholder value: a matter of contractual failures' *European Journal of Law and Economics*, 2004

Chapter 10

Shareholders' remedies

Key terms

▶ **Derivative action** – an action brought by shareholders on behalf of the company (deriving from the company's right to sue).
▶ **Personal act** – remedy when a shareholder suffers a loss separate and distinct from that suffered by the company.
▶ **Section 994** – the company is run in a way unfairly prejudicial to the interests of the shareholders.
▶ **Ratification** – voting by the general meeting to forgive directors' breaches of duty.
▶ **Winding-up order** – the shareholder seeks the dissolution of the company.

10.1 Suing the company

One of the reasons for conferring legal personality on a company was to enable it to sue and be sued in its own name. Consequently, a company may be sued for a wrong perpetrated by it, either by a member or by a third party who has been harmed by the company's action. Where a member is aggrieved by something in the articles, for example, when the articles do not allow him to vote in a general meeting, then he can sue the management directly. This is a personal right. As a general rule, however, where the wrong has been done to or by a company, the company itself will sue or be sued. Thus, if a director is in breach of his duties to the company, the company can sue him for redress.

However, corporate personality has caused problems as well as solving them. Without controls arrived at by the courts and those now in the Companies Act 2006, if the majority of the shares in a company were held by those controlling that company (and they often were), those controllers could perpetrate all kinds of wrongdoing to the detriment of the minority and then vote that the company should not take legal action to gain compensation. Suppose, for example, that a director sells to the company land worth £10,000. He and his cronies, who together hold a majority of the shares in the company, pay £20,000 for the land. They then pass a resolution to the effect that the company should not take action to get back the money that has been taken unnecessarily from the company. The minority shareholders in the company have seen the assets of the company diminished, and thus the value of their shareholding in the company goes down. What can they do? In theory it is the company's money to give away, and it has done so. This is the type of situation as regards which the courts made an exception to the corporate personality rule. This was known as the 'exception to the rule in *Foss v Harbottle*' (see further Section 10.2 below).

10.2 The derivative action

10.2.1 The rule in *Foss v Harbottle*

The duties which a director owes to the company are useful only if they can be enforced effectively. If a right has been infringed which is in law a right belonging to a company (for example, the misapplication of company property – or indeed any other breach of directors' duties) the only proper claimant is the company itself. This rule was known as 'the rule in *Foss v Harbottle*' after the case in which it was first clearly established (*Foss v Harbottle* (1843) 2 Hare 461). In *Bamford v Bamford* [1970] Ch 212, Russell LJ said:

> [I]t would be for the company to decide whether to institute proceedings to avoid the voidable allotment: and again this decision would be one for the company in general meeting to decide by ordinary resolution. To litigate or not to litigate, apart from very special circumstances, is for decision by such a resolution.

As a general principle this was admirable, because it had the advantage of avoiding the problem of proceedings being commenced simultaneously by all members who believed themselves to be aggrieved by a particular action of the management. However, real problems occurred when the alleged perpetrators of the wrong against the company also controlled the general meeting. In those circumstances, of course, it was most unlikely that the members of the general meeting would resolve to sue themselves. When this happened, if the wrong done was serious enough, a shareholder might have been permitted to sue on behalf of the company. However, four major difficulties confronted such a plaintiff:

1. The standing of the plaintiff and his entitlement to sue had to be settled as a preliminary matter before the substantive complaint was heard. This involved the plaintiff in establishing that the alleged wrongdoers were 'in control' of the company. Further, the action had to have been brought bona fide for the benefit of the company for wrongs to the company for which no other remedy was available and not for an ulterior purpose. In *Barrett v Duckett and Others* [1995] 1 BCLC 243, the action was brought to harass an ex son-in-law and thus was not permitted.
2. The plaintiff had to show that the company suffered a wrong of such an order that it would be unfair to permit the general meeting to ratify the wrong. The ambit of this requirement was most uncertain. It seems clear that actions wholly outside the power of the company to perform could not be ratified by ordinary resolution, only by the special procedures under section 35 of the Companies Act 1985 (which provided for ratification of ultra vires acts by special resolutions). It is certain that minor wrongs against the company could be ratified. There remained an enormous area of uncertainty providing a potential pitfall to a plaintiff in this sort of action.
3. The plaintiff had to prove the actual commission of the serious wrong against the company by those controlling it. This in itself was a difficult task, since the plaintiff was not, by definition, a controller of the company and so he would in all likelihood have limited access to information concerning the internal management of the company.
4. If the plaintiff could surmount these three not inconsiderable hurdles, he would succeed in his action. However, during the course of the case, he was always at peril as to costs. Even if he succeeded, the principal beneficiary of the action was the company in whose favour judgment was given. The actual gain to the plaintiff might

thus be very small. His only gain might be the right to participate in the fortunes of a better-managed company.

It is perhaps not surprising that this type of action was brought only infrequently, particularly in view of the remedy introduced in 1980 and now to be found in sections 994–999 of the Companies Act 2006. This whole area is now covered by the Companies Act 2006, although it is not wholly clear how much of the case law will remain relevant.

10.2.2 Derivative claims

The Companies Act 2006 retains the need for the claimant to apply for permission to bring the claim, and the scales seem to be quite heavily weighed against him. There are certainly relics of the need to prove that the wrongdoers were in control to be found in section 263, especially in section 263(4), but it will be a matter for the courts to determine how much of the pre-existing case law will be regarded as relevant.

In section 260 of the 2006 Act, a derivative claim is defined as an act raised by an individual shareholder:

1. in respect of a cause of action vested in the company; and
2. seeking relief on behalf of the company.

Section 260(2) provides:

> (2) A derivative claim may only be brought—
>   (a) under this Chapter, or
>   (b) in pursuance of an order of the court in proceedings under section 994 (proceedings for protection of members against unfair prejudice).

Section 260(2) provides us with a very helpful clarification, as it establishes the Companies Act 2006 and the relevant sections (ss 260–264) as the only rules setting out the procedure in accordance with which a derivative claim may be raised, rendering ineffective other regulations and provisions which applied previously.

The scope of application of the derivative claim is thoroughly presented in section 260(3):

> (3) A derivative claim under this Chapter may be brought only in respect of a cause of action arising from an actual or proposed act or omission involving negligence, default, breach of duty or breach of trust by a director of the company.

According to section 263, the court may refuse permission to proceed where the cause of derivative claim arises from an act or omission which has been ratified by the company since it occurred. Therefore the issue of the ratification of directors' breaches is important at this stage.

10.2.2(a) Ratification

Ratification is now covered by the 2006 Act, but that Act has failed to solve some of the more fundamental issues which stem from the whole concept of ratification. The statute covers the issue in a single section. Section 239 provides:

239 Ratification of acts of directors

(1) This section applies to the ratification of a company of conduct by a director amounting to negligence, default, breach of duty or breach of trust in relation to the company.

(2) The decision of the company to ratify such conduct must be made by resolution of the members of the company.

[Subsections (3) and (4) prevent the director or a connected person from voting on such a resolution.]

(7) This section does not affect any other enactment or rule of law imposing additional requirements for valid ratification or any rule of law as to acts that are incapable of being ratified by the company.

It is section 239(7) which appears to open the interpretation of the statute to all the uncertainties which existed under the case law as to what actions could or could not be ratified. This used to require a 'fraud on the minority', and whether or not this had occurred was one of the most difficult questions in company law. First, however, the claimant must show that he has a right to sue.

The right to sue: who is in control of the company?

Under the case law which preceded the Companies Act 2006, in *Birch v Sullivan* [1958] 1 All ER 56 the court said that when an individual plaintiff instituted a derivative action to enforce a right belonging to the company, he must specifically allege in his pleadings, and be prepared to prove, that those in control of the company would prevent the company from suing in its own name. If there was any challenge to that allegation, the matter had to be determined as a preliminary issue (*Prudential Assurance Co Ltd v Newman Industries Ltd (No 2)* [1982] Ch 204). The great difficulty was in determining an effective test which would embrace all circumstances in which the persons complained about were 'in control' of a company. In *Prudential Assurance Co Ltd v Newman Industries Ltd (No 2)*, the judge at first instance believed that the court should examine the realities of the situation. He said:

> [I]f the defendants against whom relief is sought on behalf of the company control the majority of votes, the action will be allowed to proceed whether a resolution that no action should be brought by the company has been passed or not; so also, if the persons against whom relief is sought do not control a majority of the votes but it is shown that a resolution has been passed and passed only by the use of their votes … But there are an infinite variety of possible circumstances … If shareholders having a majority of votes in general meeting are nominees, the court will look behind the register to the beneficial owners to see whether they are the persons against whom relief is sought: see *Pavlides v Jensen* [1956] Ch 565. There seems no good reason why the court should not have regard to any other circumstances which show that the majority cannot be relied upon to determine in a disinterested way whether it is truly in the interests of the company that proceedings should be brought.

The judgment of the Court of Appeal in that case left matters most unclear. The suggestion was made that if 'control' was an issue, the court should grant an adjournment 'to enable a meeting of shareholders to be convened by the board, so that the court can reach a conclusion in the light of the conduct of, and proceedings at, that meeting'. This would seem to imply rejection of the idea that all matters which might in fact affect control of the company should be investigated. The approach suggested by the Court of Appeal would to some extent confine the court to taking into account matters which appeared, so to speak, 'on the face of' the meeting. However, the judgment offers no very clear guidance as to what matters should be taken into account. Even if it did, the Court of Appeal's words would be of doubtful value, since the issue of the *Foss v Harbottle* rule had become irrelevant to the outcome of the case by the time it was heard in that court. The judges had refused to hear counsel's arguments on the proper scope of *Foss v Harbottle* and were careful to point out that they were not expressing a 'concluded' view on the scope of that rule. The extent to which a court can probe the reality of the situation to determine control thus remains uncertain. What is clear from *Smith v Croft (No 2)* [1988] Ch 114 (see Case note 2, at the end of this chapter) is that a minority shareholder who would otherwise be able to sue on behalf of the company, under an established exception to the rule in *Foss v Harbottle*, may nevertheless be prevented from doing so if a majority of the members, independent of the wrongdoers, is opposed to the litigation. If a majority of the oppressed minority is not prepared to support the action, it cannot go ahead.

Serious wrongdoing by those in control

An essential distinction made in the case law was between actions by the controllers of the company which could not be 'ratified' by the majority of the company voting in a general meeting and those that could be ratified. It seems that section 239(7) of the 2006 Act retains this case law's relevance. Ratification is a concept borrowed from agency law, where it is used to describe the process of retrospective validation of an agent's acts. If an agent acts outside the authority conferred upon him by his principal, the principal can at a later date approve the action of the agent and agree to be legally bound by any transaction entered into by that agent. In company law, if the directors of the company have acted in breach of their duties, it is open to the shareholders, on some occasions but not on others, to vote that such directors will not be sued in respect of those breaches of duty. The major difficulty is in identifying what breaches are ratifiable and may be forgiven and which are not ratifiable and will therefore found a claim, provided the wrongdoers are in control of the company in the sense discussed above. However, there is another curious feature of ratification which must be noted. Under the old law, a breach of duty was ratifiable notwithstanding that the wrongdoers made up part or all of the vote in favour of ratification. This is no longer the case under section 239(3) and (4).

10.2.2(b) What actions make up a wrong which may not be ratified?

The categories that are identifiable from the cases are where there is a 'fraud on the minority'. It is clear in the aftermath of the *Prudential* case (see Section 10.2.2(a) above) that there is to be no exception to the rule in *Foss v Harbottle* simply 'where the interests of justice so require'. Under case law, ratification was not available if the action amounted to a 'fraud on the minority'. It should be noted that 'fraud' in this context has a special meaning unconnected with any considerations of deceit or of criminal law notions of fraud. Some actions may involve crimes, others may not. Over the years commentators have discerned various categories of fraud on the minority from the cases, but all agree that the cases are difficult to reconcile with one another, and in some cases behaviour may be found which fits more than one of the categories. Perhaps the proper way to regard the cases is to extract the total wrongdoing of the controllers and ask whether this is behaviour that is able to be condoned by a majority vote, which would now exclude the wrongdoing director and connected persons.

Categories of wrongdoing which have been identified are:

1. expropriation of the company's property;
2. mala fide breaches of duty;

3. negligent acts from which the directors benefit;
4. use of powers for an improper purpose (but also see below).

To some extent these categories are merely a way of saying that where there has been a breach of duty by directors, the court will examine all the facts to determine whether it is such a serious matter that it cannot be 'forgiven' by ratification. Obviously, taking the company's property is the clearest example of such a situation, so that is an identifiably separate category. With regard to the other instances of breach of duty, it is doubtful whether there is value in attempting to do more than look at the sum total of the behaviour of the controllers in order to assess whether a proper case can be made for a derivative claim being permitted to go ahead. For that reason, breaches of duty not involving expropriation of company property are divided into non-ratifiable acts which are then distinguished from ratifiable acts. Among the latter are:

▶ bona fide incidental profit-making;
▶ use of powers for an improper purpose (but also see point 4. above); and
▶ negligence which does not benefit the directors.

Expropriation of company property

In *Menier v Hooper's Telegraph Works* (1874) LR 9 Ch D 350, a rival company had a controlling interest in the company concerned. It used this controlling interest to settle an impending action between the two companies in its favour. The judge said that the majority had 'put something into their pockets' at the expense of the minority. This fell squarely within the fraud on the minority exception and would not be permitted. Similarly, in *Cook v Deeks* [1916] 1 AC 554, the directors diverted to themselves contracts which they should have taken up on behalf of the company. It was held that directors holding a majority of votes would not be permitted to make a present to themselves. The exact facts of this case could not reoccur today as the interested directors would now not be permitted to vote.

A case falling on the other side of the line, where the behaviour was held to be mere incidental profit-making by the directors so that the breach of duty could have been ratified, is *Regal (Hastings) Ltd v Gulliver* [1942] 1 All ER 378. Regal (Hastings) Ltd owned a cinema. The directors decided to acquire two other cinemas with a view to the sale of the whole concern. They formed a subsidiary company. The owner of the cinemas demanded that the subsidiary should have a paid up capital of £5,000 before he would grant a lease. The directors subscribed for £3,000 of the shares and Regal (Hastings) for £2,000. The concern was then sold and the directors ultimately made a profit on their shares. The court said that the directors were in breach of their duties. As this had involved making a profit out of the fiduciary position in which they stood as regards the company, they were bound to repay the profits they had made.

Breaches of duty

Here, as elsewhere, the only clear distinction between breaches of duty which are ratifiable and those which are not lies in the extent to which the behaviour is regarded as villainous. In *Atwool v Merryweather* (1867) 5 Eq 464, a company was formed to acquire a mine from Merryweather. In fact the mine was worthless, and the formation of the company and its subsequent flotation were nothing more than a conspiracy to defraud the public. It was held that the company could get back the money it had paid for the worthless mine, despite the fact that the majority had voted against this course of action.

Other examples include *Alexander v Automatic Telephone Co* [1900] 2 Ch 56, where the directors holding the majority of the shares tried to avoid paying the full price for their shares, while requiring all other members to do so; and *Estmanco (Kilner House) Ltd v GLC* [1982] 1 WLR 2. The latter case is interesting, since the judge seemed to take an overall view of the wrongdoing without seeking to put it carefully into categories. The court came to the conclusion that a derivative action would lie where the end result of the breaches of duty was to 'stultify the purpose' for which the company had been formed (see Case note 4, at the end of the chapter).

Negligent acts which benefit a director

In *Daniels v Daniels* [1978] Ch 406, the court held that a minority shareholder who has no other remedy may sue where directors use their powers intentionally or unintentionally, fraudulently or negligently in a manner which benefits themselves at the expense of the company.

This case shows that benefit to themselves provides a dividing line between ratifiable and non-ratifiable actions of the directors, because it was held in *Pavlides v Jensen* [1956] Ch 565 that an individual plaintiff would not be permitted to sue where the claim was based on negligence alone. No exception to the rule in *Foss v Harbottle* would be made in such a case. Section 260(3) of the Companies Act 2006 permits a derivative claim where a director is negligent and says nothing about the additional requirement of personal profit. However, it is possible that the court may refuse permission in such a case.

Use of powers for an improper purpose

Clear instances of actions that are ratifiable occur where powers given to the directors for one purpose are misused. An example of this is when shares are issued to fend off a takeover or otherwise to alter the balance of voting power within a company. The courts have held that the power to issue shares must be used only where the primary purpose of the issue is to raise capital (*Bamford v Bamford* [1970] Ch 212). However, where the directors have misused these powers, the courts have consistently allowed ratification by a majority vote at a general meeting, provided that the holders of the newly issued shares were not allowed to exercise votes attached to the new shares (*Bamford v Bamford* above; and *Hogg v Cramphorn Ltd* [1967] Ch 254).

10.2.2(c) Further fraud on the minority

One last category of cases must be mentioned. They are concerned with the alteration of articles. It has been held that an individual may prevent the alteration of articles of association where that alteration was not made bona fide for the benefit of the company. However, the cases do not make it clear on what basis the claim is brought. If it is brought on the basis that a personal right has been infringed then it could be argued that the preservation of the integrity of the articles is the concern of every shareholder and any breach of those articles could be remedied by a personal action. However, this would allow the multiplicity of suits which the rule in *Foss v Harbottle* (see Section 10.2.1) was invented to prevent. Nevertheless, that rule is rarely mentioned in that series of cases, so it may be that the upholding of the articles can be achieved by a personal claim (see Section 10.2.3 below). However, if that is not so, another category must be added to the 'fraud on the minority' cases. That is where alteration of the articles is attempted by a majority in control of the company but that alteration is not bona fide for the benefit of the company (see cases discussed in Chapter 3).

10.2.3 Personal act in case of 'a loss separate and distinct from that suffered by the company'

A shareholder may raise a claim against the company for a loss which should, however, be viewed as separate and distinct from the loss suffered by the company. Case law sheds light on the remedy in question.

In *Johnson v Gore Wood & Co* [2000] UKHL 65, Lord Bingham underlined three propositions stemming from previous case law:

(1) Where a company suffers loss caused by a breach of duty owed to it, only the company may sue in respect of that loss. No action lies at the suit of a shareholder suing in that capacity and no other to make good a diminution in the value of the shareholder's shareholding where that merely reflects the loss suffered by the company. A claim will not lie by a shareholder to make good a loss which would be made good if the company's assets were replenished through action against the party responsible for the loss, even if the company, acting through its constitutional organs, has declined or failed to make good that loss. So much is clear from *Prudential*, particularly at pp 222–3; *Heron International v Lord Grade* [1983] BCLC 244, particularly at pp 261–2; *George Fischer (Great Britain) v Multi Construction Ltd, Dexion Ltd* [1995] 1 BCLC 260, particularly at pp 266 and 270–1; *Gerber Garment Technology Inc v Lectra Systems Ltd and Another* [1997] RPC 443; and *Stein v Blake* [1998] 1 BCLC 573, particularly at pp 726–9.

(2) Where a company suffers loss but has no cause of action to sue to recover that loss, the shareholder in the company may sue in respect of it (if the shareholder has a cause of action to do so), even though the loss is a diminution in the value of the shareholding. This is supported by *Lee v Sheard* [1956] 1 QB 192, at pp 195–6; *George Fischer*; and *Gerber*.

(3) Where a company suffers loss caused by a breach of duty to it, and a shareholder suffers a loss separate and distinct from that suffered by the company caused by breach of a duty independently owed to the shareholder, each may sue to recover the loss caused to it by breach of the duty owed to it but neither may recover loss caused to the other by breach of the duty owed to that other. We take this to be the effect of *Lee v Sheard*, at pp 195–6; *Heron International*, particularly at p 262; *RP Howard Ltd & Richard Alan Witchell v Woodman Matthews and Co* [1983] BCLC 117, particularly at p 123; *Gerber*; and *Stein v Blake*, particularly at p 726. We do not think the observations of Leggatt LJ in *Barings plc and Another v Coopers and Lybrand and Others* [1997] 1 BCLC 427 at p 435B and of the Court of Appeal of New Zealand in *Christensen v Scott* [1996] 1 NZLR 273 at p 280, lines 25–35, can be reconciled with this statement of principle.

In *Walker v Stones* [2001] BCC 757, the court followed the *Johnson* line and stated that when the shareholder in question had suffered a personal loss which is distinct from a loss incurred by the company in which he had a financial stake, he is justified in making a personal claim. Thus, an individual shareholder has a right to bring a personal claim when his loss is separate and distinctive from the losses suffered by the company in cases where a director has breached his fiduciary duty causing damage. If, on the other hand, his losses are just an aspect of the general losses of the company then the former are recoverable only with a derivative claim (see Section 10.2.2 above). This appears to be consistent with the line and the argumentation that the court had previously adopted in *Prudential Assurance Co v Newman Industries* [1982] Ch 204 (see Section 10.2.2(a) above). In that case it was respectively stated that 'what a shareholder cannot do … is to recover a sum … [when] such a loss is merely a reflection of the loss suffered by the company … [H]is loss is through the company, in the diminution in the value of the net assets of the company.' This line was also followed in *Day v Cook* [2001] EWCA Civ 592.

In *Giles v Rhind* [2002] EWCA Civ 1428, the principles laid down by Lord Bingham evolved slightly. In this case the two people involved, G and R, were former directors of a company which had become insolvent after R set up a new business to which he diverted employees and contracts. With these actions he effectively breached a previous shareholder agreement to which himself and G were both parties. Since the company was insolvent, its action against R was discontinued. In the light of this development, G decided to pursue personal claims for damages. The question arising was whether G was entitled to bring a claim on the loss of value of his shareholding and his future losses of remuneration. At first instance it was held that the aforementioned losses of G were reflective of the general losses of the company, thus preventing a personal claim on his part. The company was the legitimate source of action in this case, irrespective of the fact that the company had not been able, because of insolvency, to pursue the recovery of such losses. Still, the losses in question could be legitimately claimed solely by the company.

The Court of Appeal had a different opinion. It stated that G was indeed entitled to pursue his own personal claim against R, since his personal loss was not merely reflective of the company's loss but constituted a separate cause of action. In such a case there will not be a double recovery against R since the company itself, because of its state of insolvency, could not recover the losses itself. Therefore, it was justified to let an individual shareholder take action, especially in the light of the recognition that the inability of the company to act was attributed to R's wrongdoing. So, although a company in this case does have a cause of action, an individual shareholder is allowed to pursue a personal action because the company is in no position to exercise its rights and make its own claims for the losses incurred. This seems to depart from the first proposition laid down by Lord Bingham in *Johnson*.

Moreover, the Court in *Giles v Rhind* went a step further by stating that even in respect of those losses of G which were reflective of the losses of the company, he could still bring a personal claim because the company had been prevented from proceeding with its own claim because of R's wrongdoing. Thus, G's claims for loss of future earnings, especially in relation to his remuneration, were not treated as expected, which is losses reflective of the company's losses which prevent any personal claim from being raised. The company ceased to exist and therefore G was left unemployed, with no future earnings coming from his remuneration. Even if the company had been able to pursue its claims against R, any recovered sums would not have compensated G for the loss of employment. He was allowed, therefore, to raise a personal claim, which seems also to depart from the spirit of the three propositions of *Johnson*.

10.2.4 Unfair prejudice petition under section 994

Sections 994–996 of the Companies Act 2006 replaced sections 459–461 of the Companies Act 1985, providing a remedy for a member when 'the company's affairs are being or have been conducted in a manner which is unfairly prejudicial to the interests of its members generally or of some part of its members' (for the full text of sections 994–996, see Legislation, at the end of the chapter). The extension may have the effect of including nearly all behaviour which could be litigated under a derivative claim, although it is as yet not clear that the two are co-extensive. By section 260, a derivative claim for unfair prejudice can be brought only in pursuance of an order of the court made under section 994. There is little difference between the Companies Act 2006 text and the preceding text of the 1985 text. The case law is therefore assumed to remain relevant.

10.2.4(a) Unfair prejudice

Consideration was given to the meaning of 'unfair prejudice' in *Re Bovey Hotel Ventures* (31 July 1981) unreported, quoted in *Re RA Noble & Son (Clothing) Ltd* [1983] BCLC 273. Slade J said:

> [A] member of a company will be able to bring himself within the section if he can show that the value of his shareholding in the company has been seriously diminished or at least seriously jeopardised by reason of a course of conduct on the part of those persons who do have de facto control of the company, which was unfair to the member concerned.

He suggested that the test should be an objective one: '[W]ould the reasonable bystander observing the consequences of their conduct ... regard it as having unfairly prejudiced the petitioner's interest?' This test was adopted by the court in the *RA Noble* case. There, a clear distinction was drawn between the prejudice which was held to have occurred and the unfair element which was not shown. In the case, one of the directors had been deliberately and systematically excluded from the running of the affairs of the company. This was conduct which the judge found could have come within the section. However, the circumstances of each particular case had to be examined, and in this case the director had brought his exclusion upon himself by disinterest. The conduct was therefore not unfair. This approach was adopted in *Re London School of Electronics Ltd* [1986] Ch 211.

In *Re Macro (Ipswich) Ltd* [1994] 2 BCLC 354, the court held that where conduct was unfairly prejudicial to the financial interests of the company then it would also be unfairly prejudicial to the interests of its members. In assessing the fairness of the conduct, the court had to perform a balancing act in weighing the various interests of different groups within the company. The court did not interfere in questions of commercial management, but where the mismanagement was sufficiently significant and serious to cause loss to the company then it could constitute the basis for finding unfair prejudice. The concept of unfairness is thus capable of being a very broad one indeed.

A number of possible limitations have been raised:

1. What is the 'conduct of the company's affairs'?
2. Must there be infringement of a legal right in order to show unfair prejudice?
3. What interest in the company must the petitioner have?
4. In what capacity must the defendant be complaining?

10.2.4(b) Conduct of company affairs

In *Re A Company (No 001761 of 1986)* [1987] BCLC 141, the court held that the acts of a shareholder in a personal capacity outside the conduct of the company's affairs were irrelevant. Thus the court was not interested in 'an attempt to blacken the respondent's name and to make the court look on her with disfavour as an immoral and attractive woman'. See also *Re Leeds United Holdings plc* (discussed in Section 10.2.4(c) below).

In *Re Red Label Fashions Ltd* [1999] BCC 308, the respondent was alleged to be subject to disqualification proceedings as a 'de facto' director. Although she had been in business with her director husband, the court held that there was no evidence that she had assumed the role of director and exercised management responsibilities. She had acted 'as a dutiful wife' rather than as a director.

10.2.4(c) The infringement of legal rights

The concept of unfair prejudice is larger than the idea of infringement of legal rights. In *Re A Company* [1986] BCLC 376, Hoffman J said that in a small company, 'the member's interests as a member may include a legitimate expectation that he will continue to be employed as a director and his dismissal from that office and exclusion from the management of the company may therefore be unfairly prejudicial to his interests as a member'. The same view was taken in *Re Sam Weller & Sons Ltd (Re A Company (No 823 of 1987)* [1990] BCLC 80, where the court refused to strike out a petition alleging unfair prejudice by a failure to declare an adequate dividend. The court emphasised that 'interests' should be considered wider than 'rights'. It should be noted that this wide view seems to be more easily adhered to in cases where a small company is involved (see *Re Carrington Viyella PLC* (1983) 1 BCC 98), but it has been litigated in a number of sporting contexts. In *Re Tottenham Hotspur plc* [1994] 1 BCLC 655, Terry Venables, the chief executive of Tottenham Hotspur, and Alan Sugar, its chairman, originally had a 50/50 interest in the company. Sugar later obtained control and Venables was removed as chief executive. Venables claimed that this removal was contrary to a legitimate expectation that he would be involved in managing the company. The court found that there was little, if any, evidence to support the allegation, and did not make any order. In *Re Leeds United Holdings plc* [1996] 2 BCLC 545, the court held that '[t]he legitimate expectations which the court has to have regard to under s 459 [now s 994] must relate to the conduct of the company's affairs, the most obvious and common example being an expectation of being allowed to participate in the affairs of the company'. However, the court went on to dismiss the action in that case because it was based on an expectation that a particular shareholder would not sell his shares without the consent of the other shareholders. This was held not to relate to the company's affairs and therefore fell outside the provision.

The important case of *Re Saul D Harrison & Sons plc* [1995] 1 BCLC 14 contains an extensive analysis of the operation of what was section 459 of the 1985 Act (now section 994 of the 2006 Act) to protect 'legitimate expectations'. Hoffman LJ said:

> In deciding what is fair or unfair for the purposes of s 459, it is important to have in mind that fairness is being used in the context of a commercial relationship. The articles of association are just what their name implies: the contractual terms which govern the relationships of the shareholders with the company and each other … Since keeping promises and honouring agreements is probably the most important element of commercial fairness, the starting point on any case under s 459 will be to ask whether the conduct of which the shareholder complains was in accordance with the articles of association … Although one begins with the articles and the powers of the board, a finding that conduct was not in accordance with the articles does not necessarily mean that it was unfair, still less that the court will exercise its discretion to grant relief. There is often sound sense in the rule in *Foss v Harbottle* (1843) 2 Hare 461. In choosing the term 'unfairly prejudicial', the Jenkins Committee (para 204) equated it with Lord Cooper's understanding of 'oppression' in *Elder v Elder and Watson* (1952) SC 49: 'A visible departure from the standards of fair dealing and a violation of the conditions of fair play on which every shareholder who entrusts his money to a company is entitled to rely.' So trivial or technical infringements of the articles were not intended to give rise to petitions under s 459.

Hoffman LJ goes on to point out that technically lawful actions may also be unfair:

[T]he personal relationship between a shareholder and those who control the company may entitle him to say that it would in certain circumstances be unfair for them to exercise a power conferred by the articles upon the board or the company in general meeting. I have in the past ventured to borrow from public law the term 'legitimate expectations' to describe the correlative 'right' in the shareholder to which such a relationship may give rise. It often arises out of a fundamental understanding between the shareholders which formed the basis of their association but was not put into contractual form, such as an assumption that each of the parties who has ventured his capital will also participate in the management of the company and receive the return on his investment in the form of salary rather than dividend.

The judgment emphasised the fact that because the company is small, this is not sufficient to find that there are legitimate expectations above and beyond those in the articles. 'Something more' was needed and was absent in this case. It is clear that some evidence must be brought of an understanding between the parties separate from the articles. In *Re BSB Holdings* [1996] 1 BCLC 155, the court made it clear that *Re Saul D Harrison* did not mean that section 459 was limited to cases of breaches of the articles or other agreements and that the categories of behaviour for which relief could be given were not closed. However, the court followed *Re Saul D Harrison* in emphasising that 'fairness' meant fairness in a commercial context, which meant that directors had a duty to exercise their powers fairly between different classes of shareholders.

This decision was affirmed in *O'Neill and Another v Phillips* [1999] 2 BCLC 1, which was the first case concerning the then section 459 to come before the House of Lords. Lord Hoffman held that the existence of a quasi-partnership did not, of itself, give a right to a member to have his shares purchased; 'fairness' usually required some breach of the terms on which the member had agreed that the affairs of the company should be conducted.

O'Neill established the mainstream approach towards the interpretation of section 459, and its reasoning was found in the basis of other court rulings as well. In *Larvin v Phoenix Office Supplies Ltd* [2002] EWCA Civ 1740, a company appealed against a decision ordering its two remaining directors to purchase at a full price the shares of the third departing director. The latter's decision to leave the company was personal. The remaining directors had refused to buy his shares and did not consent to the provision of any access by him to the accounts of the company. The Court of Appeal held that a director leaving his place on the board on his own volition was not entitled to demand to have his shares bought at their full undiscounted value. The Court underlined that not every quasi-partnership entitled directors to a 'no fault divorce'. Section 459 had a very clear function, and that was to protect shareholders against a breach of terms on which they had initially joined the company or from inequity in the sense noted by *O'Neill*. In this case the departing director had taken the decision to leave the company for his own personal reasons. His departure was not a result of actions performed on the part of the rest of the directors or shareholders of the company. Hence, the remaining directors had not been found to have treated him in an unfairly prejudicial manner just because they excluded him from the company's affairs. The court wanted to prevent the application of section 459 to all directors who decide of their own free will to leave a certain company. If that decision entailed an obligation on behalf of their company to buy their shares, this would mean a severe burden for small companies across the country. The principles applied in *O'Neill* were, therefore, further illuminated.

Another important element in understanding the function of section 459 was clarified in *Re Legal Costs Negotiators Ltd* [1999] BCC 547. There it was revealed that section 459 remains essentially a minority claim. In this case two partners turned their business into a limited company in which the first possessed 75 per cent of the shares while the other held the remaining 25 per cent of the shareholding. The minority shareholder was accused of inefficiency in carrying out his duties towards the company. The majority shareholder managed to obtain his resignation and removal from the board. In addition to that, the majority shareholder actually managed to dismiss the minority shareholder from the company. The holder of the 75 per cent of the company subsequently wanted to rely on section 459 in order to force the removed director to sell him the remaining shares. The court did not consent to these demands, and stated that the majority shareholder, by possessing 75 per cent of the shares, was capable of passing any resolution in the company and could terminate any existing prejudicial state of affairs, which he did since he effectively removed the minority shareholder from the board and dismissed him from the company. Because of his initiatives the minority shareholder did not have any say in the company's affairs. Thus, further relying on section 459 to force the minority shareholder to sell his shares to him would constitute an inappropriate use of the relevant provisions.

10.2.4(d)   What interest in the company must the petitioner have?

In *R & H Electric and Another v Haden Bill Electrical Ltd* [1995] 2 BCLC 280, the court held that a broad view should be taken of the capacity in which a petitioner complained for the purposes of section 459. In that case, a company controlled by P was a major creditor of Haden Bill Electrical (HB). P was a director and chairman of HB until relationships broke down and he was removed at short notice. The court held that P could rely on his interest in having been instrumental in raising the loan through his company and the understandings that flowed from that, and was not just confined to his interest as shareholder.

Section 994(2) of the Companies Act 2006 allows those to whom shares have been transferred or transmitted by operation of law (for example, by inheritance) to petition. Section 995 gives the same right to the Secretary of State. In *Re A Company* (1986) 2 BCC 98 & 952, it was held that those who were not registered as shareholders but who were entitled to the benefit of owning the shares (beneficial owners) could not petition.

In *Gamlestaden Fastigheter AB v Baltic Partners Ltd* [2008] 1 BCLC 468, the appellant alleged that the affairs of the company had been conducted in a manner that was unfairly prejudicial to the interests of some of its members. He held 22 per cent of the company's shares and, having provided it with a loan, he resented the way in which the three directors had conducted the company's affairs. He aimed at forcing the directors to compensate the company for the damage they caused due to their breaches of duty. However, the company in question was insolvent, and would remain so even if the order were made. Therefore, the remedy that he sought would confer no financial benefit on him as a shareholder, but only as a creditor. The court stated that when the affairs of a company had been conducted in a manner that was unfairly prejudicial to a shareholder who provided loans to the company, he was not precluded from relief that would benefit him only as a creditor but not as a shareholder.

In *Re EAP Securities Ltd* [2010] EWHC 2421 (Ch), Geoffrey Lionel Holman presented a petition under section 994 of the Companies Act 2006, alleging that the affairs of EAP Securities Limited were being and had been conducted in a manner which was unfairly prejudicial to the interests of members generally and, in particular, to himself as a minority shareholder. The court noted that this was not a quasi-partnership company. Accordingly, if unfair prejudice was to be found, it must lie in some form of abuse by the directors of their fiduciary powers and duties or in the conduct of the affairs of the company in breach of its articles of association or the Companies Act 2006 requirements.

In *Re Phoenix Contracts (Leicester) Ltd* [2010] EWHC 2375 (Ch), the petitioner sought an order under the Companies Act 2006, section 994, that his shares in the company be bought by the respondent at a fair value. They were the only executive directors and shareholders of the company, and they were both also employees of the company. The articles of association set a fixed price at which shares were to be sold to existing shareholders when a shareholder ceased to be an employee or a director. It was common ground that the respondent was engaged in unlawful collusive practices in which the petitioner had not been directly involved. The respondent was investigated by the Office of Fair Trading. The petitioner left an anonymous voicemail with a potential customer of the company, informing him that the respondent was under investigation. The respondent found out about the phone call and fired the petitioner from the company while offering to buy his shares at a fair value. The offer was not accepted. The petitioner was later hired back to work, but he had been effectively denied participation in the management of the company for a year and he missed a bonus which he had been awarded but did not receive. He was later fired. Employment proceedings were commenced and an employment tribunal made findings of fact, including that the call had been made with the intention of protecting the company. The petitioner relied on section 994 of the 2006 Act while the company was placed in administration.

The court noted that the essential element of unfairness is a breach of the agreement between the members regarding the conduct of the affairs of the company. Such a breach of duty by a director does not of itself amount to unfair prejudice, as the previous case of *Re Saul D Harrison* (Section 10.2.4(c) above) established. That question again depends on whether the conduct is contrary to the underlying agreement between the members in relation to the company. Thus conduct for an ulterior purpose, or conduct in breach of duty which causes the company loss, or a diminution in value in the shares, may be unfairly prejudicial. A member's interests will be prejudiced where the respondent's conduct causes, or threatens to cause, damage to the value of his shareholding.

However, the fall in the value of the company's shares is not the only test. The exclusion of the petitioner from his legitimate expectation of participation in a quasi-partnership situation is a classic instance of prejudice. There is no concept of 'no fault divorce' in a section 994 petition. A petitioner who cannot show that he has been the victim of unfair prejudice is not entitled to a remedy even if, in the context of a quasi-partnership, there has been a breakdown in trust and confidence between the members as it was established in *Re Phoenix Office Supplies* [2003] 1 BCLC 76.

In *Grace v Biagioli* [2006] 2 BCLC 70, Patten J, giving the judgment of the Court of Appeal, said (at [77]):

> Lord Hoffmann's remarks on no-fault divorce in *O'Neill v Phillips* [Section 10.2.4(c) above] were not directed to the case where fault amounting to unfair prejudice was found to exist on the part of the respondents. He was concerned only to exclude the possibility of a buy-out order being made simply because the parties found it difficult to co-exist, although nothing amounting to unfair prejudice could be made out.

Quite importantly, the Court emphasised that it is wholly artificial to draw a distinction between the petitioner's roles as an employee on the one hand and as a director and shareholder on the other. As Lord Hoffmann said in *O'Neill* (at 1107B), the removal of a shareholder from substantially all his functions as a director may be unfairly prejudicial conduct. There was thus prejudice to the petitioner in his exclusion from management. That prejudice was by its nature unfair, and all the more so because of the contrived procedures adopted to dismiss him, procedures which were designed to appear fair while the outcome was intended to be a foregone conclusion. The Court concluded that his exclusion from the company was prejudicial to his interests as a member. It also concluded that the company was a quasi-partnership and that participation by both director-shareholders in its business was part of its agreed operation. The petitioner's expulsion prevented him from participating in the company's management and from contributing to the prosperity of its business which could lead to profits in which he was entitled, as a member, to share.

The court has a very wide discretion as to the relief it grants under section 994, and this discretion extends to a very important issue in this context, that is, the date of the valuation of the price of the shares. The overriding consideration is that the court must select a valuation date that is fair on the facts of the particular case. In *Profinance Trust SA v Gladstone* [2001] EWCA Civ 1031, the Court of Appeal said that there were two competing considerations that the court must bear in mind in deciding what is a fair valuation date. The first is that the shares should be valued at a date as close as possible to the actual sale so as to reflect the value of what the shareholder is selling. That consideration militates in favour of valuation at the date of the court's order. The second is that a valuation at the date of the petition may be appropriate, because that is the date on which the petitioner has elected to treat the unfair conduct as destroying the basis on which he continued to be a shareholder. Thus it may be appropriate to specify an early valuation date where it is simply unclear whether the respondent's conduct after the date of unfairly prejudicial conduct has caused the diminution in the value of the shares, on the basis that it is unfair for the petitioner to assume the burden of the risk.

In *Re Flex Associates Ltd* [2009] EWHC 3690 (Ch), the petitioner issued an unfair prejudice petition and sought an order that the respondents purchase his minority shareholding. The company brought an action against him, however, for a breach of contract and fiduciary duty as an employee and director. In the meantime, the petitioner had been conspiring to divert business away from the company to a rival company in which he had an interest. The petitioner was invited to a meeting where a resolution was to be passed aimed at his removal, but before that could happen he began the instant proceedings. The respondents made a further offer, subject to affordability, to purchase his shares at a fair value to be determined by an expert. The court noted that the petitioner's actions in relation to the company were in breach of his fiduciary obligations as a director and of his employment contract. More directly for present purposes, they ran fundamentally counter to the cooperative understanding on which the company had been operated and on which the petition was based. Whether taken separately or together, those actions made it, in the judgment of the court, wholly inequitable that the respondents should have been required to accept his continued participation in the management of the company. They would, in other words, have justified the defendants in excluding him from such participation. Any such exclusion would not have constituted *unfair* prejudice and would *not* have constituted a proper basis for an order under section 994.

The court also emphasised that in *O'Neill v Phillips*, Lord Hoffman stressed (at 1107C):

> [T]he unfairness does not lie in the exclusion alone but in exclusion without a reasonable offer. If the respondent to a petition has plainly made a reasonable offer, then the exclusion as such will not be unfairly prejudicial and he will be entitled to have the petition struck out.

Since it was therefore very important that 'participants in such companies should be able to know what counts as a reasonable offer', he set out its necessary components. In essence, the defendant must have offered to purchase the shareholding at a fair value to be determined, if not agreed, by a competent expert. The court concluded that the petition would accordingly be dismissed.

In *Croly v Good* [2010] EWHC 1 (Ch), [2011] BCC 105, [2010] 2 BCLC 569, the petitioner alleged that the affairs of the company had been conducted in a manner unfairly prejudicial to his interests as a member, and required the selling of his shares at a value determined as at the date of his exclusion from the management of the company. He had been paid on a commission basis, but had also received shares, ultimately acquiring a 40 per cent holding. After he acquired those shares, the company had become a quasi-partnership between himself and another member. He argued that it had been agreed that he would participate in managing the company's affairs and that the profits would be distributed equally between them, drawing equal amounts of cash as payments on account of dividends to be declared at the year end. However, he was expelled from the company, with no dividends having been declared. The other member who ran the company in the meantime continued to draw money from it and alleged that the petitioner's position was that of an employee to whom various concessions had been granted for motivational purposes.

The court noted that to succeed, the petitioner must establish that the conduct complained of is both prejudicial to his interests and unfair. Further, the necessary element of prejudice must be suffered in his capacity as member rather than in any other capacity, such as employee. The element of unfairness is generally established by reference to a breach of the basis upon which he agreed that the affairs of the company would be conducted. In establishing what that basis is, the starting point is that the company is a separate legal entity established under and required to be operated in accordance with the Companies Acts and its constitution, most particularly its articles of association which form the basis of the contract between the members. The court underlined that if it is found that the company falls into this quasi-partnership category, it is more likely to conclude that it is unfair to fail to give effect to, or bring to an end, arrangements which have been made on an informal basis, even though they do not give rise to legal entitlements, or to exclude a participator from the management or conduct of the company's business, if it was part of the arrangement that he should take part in it.

The court, when attempting to form a definition of the term 'quasi-partnership', noted that there is no universal definition. Although the concept has developed from partnership law, it does not require that the company is entered into, or run, as if it were a partnership, or that the members regard themselves as being partners. In *Re Ebrahimi v Westbourne Galleries* [1973] AC 360, Lord Wilberforce said this (at 379):

> [I]t would be impossible, and wholly undesirable, to define the circumstances in which these [equitable] considerations may arise. Certainly the fact that the company is a small one, or a private company, is not enough. There are very many of these where the association is a purely commercial one, and in which it can safely be said that the basis of association is adequately and exhaustively laid down in the articles. The superimposition of equitable considerations requires something more, which typically may include one, or probably more, of the following elements:

(i) an association formed or continued on the basis of a personal relationship, involving mutual confidence – this element will often be found where a pre-existing partnership has been converted into a limited company; (ii) an agreement, or understanding, that all, or some (for there may be 'sleeping' members), of the shareholders shall participate in the conduct of the business; (iii) restriction upon the transfer of the members' interest in the company – so that if confidence is lost, or one member is removed from management, he cannot take out his stake and go elsewhere.

The Court found his expulsion from the company to be prejudicial to his interests as a member, in that it prevented him from participating in the management of the company, and from contributing to the generation of sales which would lead to profits in which he would share by way of dividend, that is to say in his capacity as member. It was unfair given that the company had become a quasi-partnership and that his participation in its business was part of the agreed basis of operation. The Court also determined the date of valuation to be the date of expulsion.

10.2.4(e) In what capacity must the complaint be made?

Under the predecessor section to section 994 of the Companies Act 2006, a member had to make his complaint 'in his capacity as member'. This meant that if his real complaint was, for example, that he had been excluded from the office of director, this complaint would not found an action. The same difficulty arose as that discussed in Chapter 3 concerning the enforcement of the articles as a contract. In *Re A Company* [1983] Ch 178, the court seemed at first sight to adopt this line. However, the contrast that was being made in that case was between the interests of a person as a shareholder in a company and totally incidental interests that the same shareholder might have which could be affected by the company's actions. An example might be if the company gained permission to establish a rubbish tip in close proximity to the private house of someone who happened to own shares in that company. It seems that in the light of the number of cases which have taken into account the 'legitimate expectations' of the members to partake in the management of the company, the courts will be most reluctant to return to the strict division between a member's interest as a member and his interest as an active participant in the management of the company.

Which members?

In a number of cases (see, for example, *Re Carrington Viyella PLC* (1983) 1 BCC 98; and *Re A Company* (1988) 4 BCC 506) the court ruled that the behaviour would adversely affect all shareholders. Section 994 clearly states that when 'the company's affairs are being or have been conducted in a manner that is unfairly prejudicial to the interests of members generally or of some part of its members (including at least himself)', a member of a company may apply to the court by petition for an order on this ground.

10.2.4(f) The relief that may be granted

Section 996 of the Companies Act 2006 provides that if a court is satisfied that a petition on the ground of unfairly prejudicial conduct is well founded, 'it may make such order as it thinks fit for giving relief in respect of the matters complained of'. Section 996(2) particularises a number of actions which the court might take (see Legislation, at the end of the chapter). The particularisation of these potential actions is expressly 'without prejudice' to the general discretion contained in section 996(1) and so in no way limits the court's powers.

The courts have freely used their powers to order the sale of shares. This has the virtue of breaking the deadlock in a company where the behaviour complained of is exclusion from management, which has caused the shares held by the complainant to lose value. In *Re Brenfield Squash Racquets Club Ltd* [1996] 2 BCLC 184, the court even ordered the majority to sell their shares to the minority shareholders where that (exceptionally) seemed to be the best solution for the company. In such cases the valuation will be backdated to the time before the behaviour complained of commenced.

10.3 Procedure for bringing a derivative claim

10.3.1 Application to continue a derivative claim

Section 261 of the Companies Act 2006 provides:

(1) A member of a company who brings a derivative claim … must apply to the court for permission … to continue it.
(2) If it appears to the court that the application and the evidence filed by the applicant in support of it do not disclose a prima facie case for giving permission, the court—
   (a) must dismiss the action …
(3) If the application is not dismissed under subsection (2), the court—
   (a) may give directions as to the evidence to be provided by the company, and
   (b) may adjourn the proceedings to enable the evidence to be obtained.
(4) On hearing the application, the court may—
   (a) give permission (or leave) to continue the claim on such terms as it thinks fit,
   (b) refuse permission (or leave) and dismiss the claim, or
   (c) adjourn the proceedings on the application and give such directions as it thinks fit.

Section 261 lays down the procedure to be followed when raising a derivative claim and sets out the rules for the derivative claim to proceed. The member of the company who is bringing the derivative claim must apply to the court for permission to continue it. The court will determine whether it is going to allow the derivative claim to proceed in accordance with the criteria laid down in section 263 (see below). Section 261(2) clarifies that during the first stage of the application, the court is interested mainly in the evidence provided by the applicant, to help it decide whether a prima facie case is established; if it is, the court will grant permission to proceed. Basically, the court will examine, on a prima facie basis, whether the directors have committed the wrong against the company and whether the criteria of section 263 are fulfilled so as to allow the case to proceed. During the second stage of the procedure, section 261(3) clarifies that the court can give further directions as to the evidence to be provided, this time by the company. The third stage of the process includes the hearing provided for by section 261(4). If the court is convinced that the criteria of section 263 are met, it may give permission to continue with the claim. Section 261(4) provides for the courses of action left to the discretion of the court, namely, to give permission to proceed, to refuse such permission or to adjourn the proceedings and give directions as it thinks fit.

In *Kleanthous v Paphitis* [2011] EWHC 2287 (Ch), the court refused permission for a shareholder to continue a derivative claim on behalf of a company mainly because redress was more appropriate by other means and more specifically on the basis of section 994 of the 2006 Act.

In *Kiani v Cooper* [2010] EWHC 577 (Ch), permission to continue with a derivative action under section 261 was granted where the director whose actions had been complained about failed to come up with any reliable evidence supporting his defence to allegations that he had breached his fiduciary duties.

The approach of the court under section 263 ('Whether permission to be given') was examined by Lewison J in *Iesini and Others v Westrip Holdings Limited and Others* [2009] EWHC 2526 (Ch). He said (at [78]):

> The Act now provides for a two-stage procedure where it is the member himself who brings the proceedings. At the first stage, the applicant is required to make a *prima facie* case for permission to continue a derivative claim, and the court considers the question on the basis of the evidence filed by the applicant only, without requiring evidence from the defendant or the company. The court must dismiss the application if the applicant cannot establish a *prima facie* case. The *prima facie* case to which section 261(1) refers is a *prima facie* case 'for giving permission'. This necessarily entails a decision that there is a *prima facie* case both that the company has a good cause of action and that the cause of action arises out of a directors' default, breach of duty (etc).

The court concluded that a director acting in accordance with his duty would wish to continue the claim down to disclosure.

In *Mission Capital Plc v Sinclair* [2008] EWHC 1339 (Ch), the court stated that permission to continue with a derivative claim on the basis of section 261 was refused where the fictional director acting on the basis of section 172 (duty to promote the success of the company – see Section 9.2.1(b)) was unlikely to attach much importance to the claim in question and the alleged damaged was speculative. On this basis the court found that the case fitted exactly into section 263(3)(f) (see below), as the acts and omissions in respect of which the claim was made were ones which the members could pursue in their own right. They could rely also on the unfair prejudice petition under section 994 of the Act.

10.3.2   Application for permission to continue claim as a derivative claim

Section 262 of the Companies Act 2006 provides:

262 Application for permission to continue claim as a derivative claim

(1) This section applies where—
    (a) a company has brought a claim, and
    (b) the cause of action on which the claim is based could be pursued as a derivative claim under this Chapter.
(2) A member of the company may apply to the court for permission (in Northern Ireland, leave) to continue the claim as a derivative claim on the ground that—
    (a) the manner in which the company commenced or continued the claim amounts to an abuse of the process of the court,
    (b) the company has failed to prosecute the claim diligently, and
    (c) it is appropriate for the member to continue the claim as a derivative claim.
(3) If it appears to the court that the application and the evidence filed by the applicant in support of it do not disclose a prima facie case for giving permission (or leave), the court—
    (a) must dismiss the application, and
    (b) may make any consequential order it considers appropriate.
(4) If the application is not dismissed under subsection (3), the court—
    (a) may give directions as to the evidence to be provided by the company, and
    (b) may adjourn the proceedings to enable the evidence to be obtained.
(5) On hearing the application, the court may—
    (a) give permission (or leave) to continue the claim as a derivative claim on such terms as it thinks fit,
    (b) refuse permission (or leave) and dismiss the application, or
    (c) adjourn the proceedings on the application and give such directions as it thinks fit.

This section refers to those cases where it is the company which assumes the initiative to raise such a claim. At first sight it may be argued that this procedure will be safer for the minority shareholder, as the costs and efforts to resort to the court are now taken by the company itself. However, in reality the directors might be motivated to undermine the whole process and prevent the claim from ever being granted permission by the court by, for example, deliberately failing to provide the court with the necessary evidence to fulfil the criteria laid down by section 263. In such a case, section 262(2) provides for the ability of the individual shareholder to apply to the court for permission to continue the claim as a derivative claim on the grounds that the manner in which the company has continued the claim amounts to an abuse of the court process, or because the company has simply failed to prosecute the claim diligently. However, although the law now provides for the basis on which an individual member of the company can continue a claim initially raised by the company but undermined by the directors, it sets an additional requirement for the individual member to qualify for the continuation of the claim, that is, to prove that it is 'appropriate for the member to continue the claim as a derivative claim'. Fulfilling this all-encompassing requirement may be difficult. In addition, the member who wishes to continue the claim initially raised by the company has to be granted permission to proceed on the same basis and in accordance with the same procedure as if the claim had been originally raised as a derivative claim. Thus, although the 2006 Act paves the way with section 262 for a more enhanced means of shareholder protection, it sets an additional requirement which might remove what was initially perceived as an extra layer of protection for shareholders.

10.3.3 Whether permission to be given

Under section 263 of the Companies Act 2006:

(1) The following provisions have effect where a member of a company applies for permission (in Northern Ireland, leave) under section 261 or 262.
(2) Permission (or leave) must be refused if the court is satisfied—
    (a) that a person acting in accordance with section 172 (duty to promote the success of the company) would not seek to continue the claim, or
    (b) where the cause of action arises from an act or omission that is yet to occur, that the act or omission has been authorised by the company, or
    (c) where the cause of action arises from an act or omission that has already occurred, that the act or omission—
        (i) was authorised by the company before it occurred, or
        (ii) has been ratified by the company since it occurred.
(3) In considering whether to give permission (or leave) the court must take into account, in particular—
    (a) whether the member is acting in good faith in seeking to continue the claim;
    (b) the importance that a person acting in accordance with section 172 (duty to promote the success of the company) would attach to continuing it;
    (c) where the cause of action results from an act or omission that is yet to occur, whether the act or omission could be, and in the circumstances would be likely to be—
        (i) authorised by the company before it occurs, or
        (ii) ratified by the company after it occurs;
    (d) where the cause of action arises from an act or omission that has already occurred, whether the act or omission could be, and in the circumstances would be likely to be, ratified by the company;
    (e) whether the company has decided not to pursue the claim;

(f) whether the act or omission in respect of which the claim is brought gives rise to a cause of action that the member could pursue in his own right rather than on behalf of the company.

(4) In considering whether to give permission (or leave) the court shall have particular regard to any evidence before it as to the views of members of the company who have no personal interest, direct or indirect, in the matter.

(5) The Secretary of State may by regulations—

(a) amend subsection (2) so as to alter or add to the circumstances in which permission (or leave) is to be refused;

(b) amend subsection (3) so as to alter or add to the matters that the court is required to take into account in considering whether to give permission (or leave).

(6) Before making any such regulations the Secretary of State shall consult such persons as he considers appropriate.

(7) Regulations under this section are subject to affirmative resolution procedure.

Section 263(2) sets out the requirements which, if fulfilled, will render highly unlikely the granting of permission to continue the derivative claim. Section 263(2)(a) introduces a rather difficult hurdle for a minority shareholder to clear. The questions to be asked here would be: Is raising a derivative claim for the benefit of the company as a whole? Would a director acting under his duty to promote the success of the company (s 172) raise a derivative claim? The court must assess whether the derivative claim will contribute to the promotion of the success of the company or not. This is a result of the separate corporate personality principle which also defines the nature of the derivative claim. The latter is raised by a minority shareholder but on behalf of the company, so if resorting to it is not for the benefit of the company then the minority shareholder should be prevented from continuing with the claim.

In accordance with section 263(2)(b) and (c), if the alleged wrong has been either authorised or ratified by the company then permission to continue will not be given. This provision should be viewed in conjunction with section 239, which now makes it more difficult for directors to ratify their own wrongs against the company, as their votes cannot count in the final result (see Section 10.2.2(a) above). But if this threshold is indeed passed and a director manages to convince the rest of the shareholders to ratify his alleged wrong then, in accordance with section 263(2)(c)(ii), the court will refuse permission to proceed with the derivative claim – a choice which sets a considerable burden on the shoulders of minority shareholders. In the case of authorising an act which has yet to occur, the relevant sections to be taken into account at this stage are, for example, section 175 on the authorisation of the conflict of interests or section 180(4) on 'consent, approval and authorisation by the members' (see Chapter 9), which specifically provides that the general duties 'have effect subject to any rule of law enabling the company to give authority, specifically or generally, for anything to be done (or omitted) by the directors, or any of them, that would otherwise be a breach of duty'.

Section 263(3) includes a non-exclusive list of other factors and parameters to be taken into account when the court is to decide whether to allow the derivative claim or not. From the wording of this subsection, it may be deduced that even if the requirements set by section 263(2) are not fulfilled, and therefore the derivative claim could be allowed to proceed, the court could still put a halt to the derivative claim when taking into account the factors included in section 263(3).

Section 263(4) provides that 'particular regard' should be given to the views of those members who have no personal interest in the case. *Smith v Croft* (see Section 10.2.2(a) above) had previously introduced the requirement that in order for a derivative action to proceed, the minority shareholder in question had to prove that he enjoyed the support of the majority of independent-minded shareholders. Before the 2006 Act, the *Smith v Croft* requirement was relevant only for derivative actions raised against breaches of fiduciary duty, and not for breaches of the duty of care and skill. Now, however, it appears that the requirement will have universal application, especially if we take into account that the requirement set by *Pavlides v Jensen* that the director has to benefit personally from his negligence has effectively been removed by the 2006 Act.

In *Stainer v Lee* [2011] 1 BCLC 537, the applicant alleged that two directors were in breach of their duties by reason of the circumstances surrounding the lending of very substantial sums of money by the company to Eldington, a company of which one of the two directors was the sole shareholder and director. The latter, either on his own or through Eldington, came to possess around 87 per cent of the issued shares of the company. The complaints concerned the terms on which those loans were made and, as regards part of the monies, the fact that the loans were made at all. As regards the lending that was the subject of the latter complaint, it was alleged that Eldington held that money as constructive trustee for the company and so should repay it to the company. The court stated that the applicant commenced the proceedings not only in his own interests but for the benefit of a large number of minority shareholders. He secured letters of support and a financial contribution from 35 other small shareholders. The applicant's conduct in seeking and obtaining that support was perceived by the court as strong evidence that he was acting in good faith.

10.3.4 The symbiosis between derivative claims and the unfair prejudice petition

The court in *Stainer v Lee* (see Section 10.3.3 above) stated that this was a case that the applicant could pursue by an 'unfair prejudice' petition under section 994 of the 2006 Act (see Section 10.2.4 above); a relevant consideration under section 263(3)(f) (see Section 10.3.3 above). As Lewison J observed in *Iesini* (Section 10.3.1 above), the availability of the alternative remedy is included under section 263(3) not section 263(2), and is accordingly a discretionary consideration.

In many cases, an allegation of breach by directors of their fiduciary duties could found an unfair prejudice petition as well as a derivative claim. But that should not disguise the fundamentally different nature of the two forms of proceedings. As Millett J explained in *Re Charnley Davies Ltd (No 2)* [1990] BCLC 760 at 784:

> The very same facts may well found either a derivative action or a s [994] petition. But that should not disguise the fact that the nature of the complaint and the appropriate relief is different in the two cases. Had the petitioners' true complaint been of the unlawfulness of the respondent's conduct, so that it would be met by an order for restitution, then a derivative action would have been appropriate and a s [994] petition would not. But that was not the true nature of the petitioners' complaint. They did not rely on the unlawfulness of the respondent's conduct to found their cause of action; and they would not have been content with an order that the respondent make restitution to the company. They relied on the respondent's unlawful conduct as evidence of the manner in which he had conducted the company's affairs for his own benefit and in disregard of their interests as minority shareholders; and they wanted to be bought out. They wanted relief from mismanagement, not a remedy for misconduct.

In *Stainer v Lee*, the applicant was not seeking to be bought out. He commenced the proceedings, with the support of 35 other minority shareholders, seeking financial remedies for misconduct against the two directors personally, and sought an order for restitution from Eldington. Such orders cannot be made on an unfair prejudice petition, therefore a derivative claim is entirely appropriate. However, it should be noted that the availability to the applicant of proceedings by way of an unfair prejudice petition is not a reason to refuse permission.

In *Iesini v Westrip Holdings Ltd* [2009] EWHC 2526 (Ch), [2010] BCC 420; [2011] 1 BCLC 498, the court stated that section 263(2)(a) applied only where a court was satisfied that no director, acting in accordance with the duty to promote the success of the company on the basis of section 172, would seek to continue a derivative claim. If some directors would seek to continue it but others would not, then section 263(3)(b) applied. The judges made a reference to previous case law, and more specifically to *Airey v Cordell* [2007] BCC 785, 800 and *Franbar Holdings Ltd v Patel* [2009] 1 BCLC 1, 11, to state that there are many cases in which some directors, acting in accordance with section 172, would think it worthwhile to continue a claim at least for the time being, while others, also acting in accordance with section 172, would reach the opposite conclusion. In *Franbar*, the court stated that if the claimant could not demonstrate that the fictional director acting on the basis of section 172 would continue with the derivative claims in question then he should proceed on the basis of the remedy under section 994 instead.

There are a number of factors that a director, acting in accordance with section 172, would consider in reaching his decision. They include:

- the size of the claim;
- the strength of the claim;
- the cost of the proceedings;
- the company's ability to fund the proceedings;
- the ability of the potential defendants to satisfy a judgment;
- the impact on the company if it lost the claim and had to pay not only its own costs but the defendant's as well;
- any disruption to the company's activities while the claim is pursued;
- whether the prosecution of the claim would damage the company in other ways (eg by losing the services of a valuable employee, or alienating a key supplier or customer) and so on.

The weighing of all these considerations is essentially a commercial decision, which the court is ill-equipped to take, except in a clear case. Therefore, the court concluded that section 263(2)(a) will apply only where the court is satisfied that no director acting in accordance with section 172 would seek to continue the claim. If some directors would, and others would not, seek to continue the claim, the case is one for the application of section 263(3)(b).

10.4 Winding-up orders

10.4.1 Winding-up orders and the unfair prejudice petition

Section 122(1)(g) of the Insolvency Act 1986 provides that a company may be wound up by the court if the court is of the opinion that it is just and equitable that it should be wound up. This is qualified by section 125(2) of the 1986 Act, where it is provided that the company should not be wound up if some other remedy is available to the petitioners and the court is of the opinion that they are acting unreasonably in seeking to have the company wound up instead of pursuing that other remedy. This proviso is likely to be of much greater importance in the light of the wide jurisdiction exercised by the courts under section 994 of the Companies Act 2006 (see Section 10.2.4 above). It is a drastic move to destroy the company completely as a remedy for unfairness. It is far better to allow an aggrieved party to buy his way out at a fair valuation. The cases prior to 1980 can therefore afford only guidance about the availability of the winding-up remedy now.

In the light of section 994, petitioners might be prevented by section 125(2) of the Insolvency Act 1986 from obtaining a winding-up order which they could have obtained before the section 994 remedy appeared on the statute book. But the 'other remedy' under section 125(2) need not necessarily be a section 994 remedy. In *Re A Company* [1983] 1 WLR 927, the court emphasised that the power to grant a winding-up order on the just and equitable ground was discretionary, and should certainly be refused where a reasonable offer to buy the petitioner's shares had been turned down.

A petition for section 994 relief may be combined with a petition to wind up on the 'just and equitable' ground. It should be noted that unfair prejudice or malpractice need not be alleged in order to show that there is a case for winding up (see, for example, *Re German Date Coffee Co* (1882) 20 Ch D 169, where the purpose for which the company was formed was no longer attainable). In *Re RA Noble & Son (Clothing) Ltd* [1983] BCLC 273, the judge held that malpractice need not be shown, provided that the conduct of those in control had been the 'substantial cause' of the lack of mutual confidence between the parties. In that case the judge dismissed the petition for section 994 relief and made an order for the winding up of the company on the just and equitable ground.

10.4.2 When a winding-up order is likely to be made

The leading case on 'just and equitable' winding up is *Re Ebrahami v Westbourne Galleries Ltd* [1973] AC 360. In that case the petition was brought by Mr Ebrahami, who for many years had been an equal partner with Mr Nazar in a business dealing in Persian carpets. In 1958 it was decided to incorporate the business, and Ebrahami (E) and Nazar (N), who were both appointed directors, each held 500 shares. Soon after this N's son was made a director, and E and N each transferred 100 shares to the son. After this the Nazars held a majority of the votes. In 1965, the relationship between the Nazars and E began to break down. In 1969, the Nazars used their majority to remove E from his directorship. Thereafter he was unable to take any part in the management of the business and he received no money, since all payments were made to the participants in the business by way of directors' salaries rather than dividends. The Court held that the removal of E had been lawful. Nevertheless, because the company was in essence an incorporated partnership, the Nazars had abused their power and were in breach of the good faith partners owed to one another. E was therefore entitled to a winding-up order. This may well now be a situation in which section 994 relief could be granted, and thus a winding-up order would be refused. (For a detailed look at the judgment in this case, see Case note 6, at the end of the chapter.)

Other situations in which the remedy has been granted are where deadlock has been reached because shares were equally divided between two factions at odds with each other (*Re Yenidje Tobacco Co Ltd* [1916] 2 Ch 426) and where the whole purpose or substratum of the company had failed. An instance of the latter situation is to be found in *Re German Date Coffee Co* (1882) 20 Ch D 169, where the company (mercifully?) failed to obtain a patent to make coffee from dates. That activity had been the major purpose for which the company was formed.

In order for a petition to succeed, a shareholder must show that he has an interest in the winding up: that is, that there is a probability that the company is solvent and so, after the winding up, there will be assets to be distributed to the shareholders (*Re Expanded Plugs Ltd* [1960] 1 WLR 514).

10.5 Department for Business, Innovation and Skills (BIS) investigations

The Department for Business, Innovation and Skills (BIS) is the government department concerned with the conduct of companies and the law which governs them. By legislation, BIS is given various powers to investigate the affairs of companies. BIS has a brief to investigate:

- bankruptcy offences
- company officer malpractice offences
- offences under the Insolvency Act 1986
- offences under the Fraud Act 2006
- 'phoenix company' offences relating to re-use of a liquidated company name by a successor company
- breach of directors' disqualification orders, bankruptcy orders and bankruptcy restrictions orders
- fraudulent trading

One way in which this can be done is by the appointment of an inspector to look into the affairs of a company. The appointment may be instigated in a variety of ways, as discussed below.

10.5.1 On the order of the court

BIS may appoint an inspector to investigate the affairs of a company if the court so orders.

10.5.2 On the application of the company

Sections 1034 and 1035 of the Companies Act 2006 provide that inspectors may be appointed on the application of the company. The application must be accompanied by evidence showing a good reason why the company's affairs should be investigated, and even then the Department has a discretion as to whether or not an inspector will be appointed.

10.5.3 Fraud, unfair prejudice or withholding of information

The Department also has a discretion to appoint inspectors where there is evidence of a company's affairs being conducted in a fraudulent or unfairly prejudicial way, that it proposes to act unlawfully or that 'its members have not been given all the information with respect to its affairs which they might reasonably expect' (Companies Act 2006, ss 1034 and 1035).

Although some inspectors have been appointed under this section, there is grave danger that the mere announcement of the appointment of inspectors will bring lasting damage to the reputation of the company which cannot be reversed even if the allegations prove to be unfounded. BIS can now use powers under the 2006 Act to discreetly determine whether allegations of misconduct were soundly based, to require the production of books and papers, to ask for a search warrant if there are grounds for suspecting that articles requested have not been forthcoming and to search premises in respect of which a warrant is issued. Criminal penalties are available for providing false statements and for falsifying, mutilating or destroying documents. It is a defence to show that there was no intention to conceal the state of affairs of the company or to defeat the law. The Department's officers are acting in a police capacity when they require the production of books and papers. They are not acting in a way similar to judges. The court will therefore not exercise its power to review decisions taken by those who act in a judicial or quasi-judicial capacity. However, the notice requiring the production of books and papers must not be unreasonably or excessively wide (*R v Secretary of State for Trade, ex parte Perestrello* [1981] QB 19). The Companies Act 2006, sections 1034–1039 give sweeping powers to the Secretary of State to make regulations concerning the conduct of inspections.

10.5.4 When inspectors have been appointed

In *Re Pergamon Press* [1970] 3 WLR 792, the Court of Appeal held that inspectors were not acting in a judicial or quasi-judicial way. Nevertheless, they have a duty to act fairly. This is important, as they have very wide-ranging powers to examine on oath the officers and agents of the company, to require documents and even to require a person who is not connected with the company to attend before them and assist in their inquiry (Companies Act 2006, ss 1034–1039). Obstruction of officers is treated as contempt of court.

Following the investigation, the inspectors make a report which will be admissible as evidence in any subsequent legal proceedings. The report is evidence only of the opinion of the inspectors with regard to matters investigated by them, not as to the existence of facts.

10.5.5 Human rights and investigations

The whole procedure of investigations may give rise to questions under the Human Rights Act 1998. *Saunders v UK* (Case 43/1994/490/572) [1977] BCC 872 was a judgment by the European Court of Human Rights concerning the use of statements made to the then DTI inspectors during an investigation. These statements had subsequently been used in a criminal prosecution against Saunders. The Court in Strasbourg held that Saunders had been deprived of the right to a fair hearing under Article 6 ECHR by the use of these statements.

10.5.6 Following investigations

After an investigation by inspectors or by the Department using its powers to require books and documents, BIS must decide if it is in the public interest to take legal proceedings. If it decides that the public interest will be best served by so doing, it can bring any action the company itself might bring, including petitioning for a winding-up order (Companies Act 2006, ss 1034–1039).

Summary

10.1 Directors owe their duties to the company, and the company is therefore the proper plaintiff in an action to enforce such duties. This was usually known as the 'rule in *Foss v Harbottle*'. It is now enshrined in the Companies Act 2006, sections 260–263.

10.2 If such a rule was absolute, the majority would have an absolute right to defraud the minority. This is now prevented by the rule that a director (and connected persons) may not vote on a resolution to sue him.

10.3 Exceptions to majority rule were made first by the courts and subsequently by the Companies Act 2006. Whether the individual shareholder can sue or, on the other hand, whether the majority can prevent the action and forgive the directors (ratification of the directors' actions) depends on the gravity of the wrongdoing in question.

10.4 An oppressed minority has a wide and flexible action which is procedurally simpler in sections 994–996 of the Companies Act 2006.

10.5 An aggrieved member may also petition the court to wind up a company on the ground that it would be just and equitable to do so.

10.6 BIS has wide powers to inspect the books of companies where malpractice is suspected.

Exercises

10.1 Discuss the advantages and disadvantages of the courses of action open to an aggrieved minority shareholder.

10.2 What purpose did the rule in *Foss v Harbottle* serve? To what extent has section 994 replaced derivative claims?

10.3 Olivia holds 10 per cent of the shares in Unknown Ltd, a private company. Sian, the chair and managing director of Unknown Ltd, owns 60 per cent of the shares, and the remaining 30 per cent are held by Lynne and Cynthia, the company's other directors. Olivia is not a director. Sian's conduct of the company's business over the past two years has caused heavy losses. She has undertaken a number of contracts at a loss, and has bought untested equipment which has proved mechanically unsound. At meetings of the board and at general meetings Sian has attributed this conduct to the need to build up goodwill. Sian is very slow both in paying the company's debts and in presenting its bills. Sian has explained this behaviour as being the result of pressure of work, and has given repeated assurances of improvement. Olivia has now had enough. She is not supported by Lynne and Cynthia when she voices her criticisms of Sian at general and board meetings. Olivia seeks your advice on the remedies (if any) which may enable her to:

(a) compel Sian to compensate Unknown Ltd for the losses she has caused;
(b) force a change of company policy;
(c) retrieve her investment in Unknown Ltd.

Advise Olivia.

Case notes

1. *Foss v Harbottle* (1843) 2 Hare 461

The Vice Chancellor [Sir James Wigram] said:

'It was not, nor could it successfully be, argued that it was a matter of course for any individual members of a corporation thus to assume to themselves the right of suing in the name of the corporation. In law the corporation and the aggregate members of the corporation are not the same thing for purposes like this; and the only question can be whether the facts alleged in this case justify a departure from the rule which, prima facie, would require that the corporation should sue in its own name and in its corporate character, or in the name of someone whom the law has appointed to be its representative.'

2. *Smith v Croft (No 2)* [1988] Ch 114

The plaintiff's action claimed that certain payments to directors had been excessive and were therefore ultra vires. The court held:

(i) that although excessive remuneration paid to directors might be an abuse of power, where the power to decide remuneration was vested in the board, it could not be ultra vires the company;
(ii) that although a minority shareholder had locus standi to bring an action on behalf of a company to recover money paid away wrongfully, the right was not indefeasible even if the transaction was ultra vires. It was proper to have regard to the views of the independent shareholders, and their votes should be disregarded only if the court was satisfied that they would be cast in favour of the defendant directors in order to support them rather than for the benefit of the company, or if there was a substantial risk of that happening; accordingly since the majority of the independent shareholders' votes would be cast against allowing the action to proceed, the statement of claim should be struck out.

3. *Nurcombe v Nurcombe* [1985] 1 All ER 65

The husband and wife were respectively the majority and minority shareholders in a company. They were divorced in 1974 and in the course of matrimonial proceedings it was disclosed that the husband had breached the fiduciary duty which he owed as a director to the company. The wife continued the matrimonial proceedings after that information came to light and the improper profit made by the husband was taken into account in the matrimonial proceedings. The wife subsequently sought to bring a derivative action. The court would not permit her to do so on the grounds that it would be inequitable to permit the wife to pursue the derivative action when the amount of improper profit had been taken into account in other proceedings.

4. *Estmanco (Kilner House) Ltd v GLC* [1982] 1 WLR 2

A block of flats was in the process of being sold by the Greater London Council (GLC). Once a flat had been sold, the purchasers of the flats became shareholders of the Estmanco company. When all the flats had been sold the company would function to manage the flats and the shareholders would have voting rights. The policy of selling the flats was discontinued after the political control of the Council changed. Twelve flats had been sold. The new Council resolved upon a new housing policy and decided to break the terms of the agreement and use the unsold flats to accommodate the needy. A shareholder sought to bring a derivative action on the company's behalf against the Council to enforce the covenant. The Council held the only voting shares in the company at that time and had voted that no action should be taken in respect of the breach of the agreement. The action succeeded. Megarry VC said:

'There can be no doubt about the twelve voteless purchasers being a minority; there can be no doubt about the advantage to the Council of having the action discontinued; there can be no doubt about the injury to the applicant and the rest of the minority, both as shareholders and as purchasers, of that discontinuance; and I feel little doubt that the Council has used its voting power not to promote the best interests of the company but in order to bring advantage to itself and disadvantage to the minority. Furthermore, that disadvantage is no trivial matter, but represents a radical alteration in the basis on which the Council sold the flats to the minority. It seems to me that the sum total represents a fraud on the minority in the sense in which "fraud" is used in that phrase, or alternatively represents such an abuse of power as to have the same effect.'

5. *Daniels v Daniels* [1978] Ch 406

A husband and wife were the two directors of a company and also the majority shareholders. They caused the company to sell to the wife land owned by the company. Four years later she sold the land for over 28 times what she had paid for it. The judge permitted minority shareholders to claim against the directors. He said:

'[A] minority shareholder who has no other remedy may sue where directors use their powers, intentionally or unintentionally, fraudulently or negligently, in a manner which benefits themselves at the expense of the company.'

6. *Re Ebrahami v Westbourne Galleries Ltd* [1973] AC 360

Lord Wilberforce said:

'[T]he foundation of it all lies in the words "just and equitable" and, if there is any respect in which some of the cases may be open to criticism, it is that the courts may sometimes have been too timorous in giving them full force. The words are a recognition of the fact that a limited company is more than a mere legal entity, with a personality in law of its own: that

there is room in company law for recognition of the fact that behind it, or among it, there are individuals, with rights, expectations and obligations inter se which are not necessarily submerged in the company structure. That structure is defined by the Companies Act and by the articles of association by which shareholders agree to be bound. In most companies and in most contexts, this definition is sufficient and exhaustive, equally so whether the company is large or small. The "just and equitable" provision does not, as the respondents suggest, entitle one party to disregard the obligation he assumes by entering a company, nor the court to dispense him from it. It does, as equity always does, enable the court to subject the exercise of legal rights to equitable considerations, that is, of a personal character arising between one individual and another, which may make it unjust, or inequitable, to insist on legal rights, or to exercise them in a particular way.

It would be impossible, and wholly undesirable, to define the circumstances in which these considerations may arise. Certainly the fact that a company is a small one, or a private company, is not enough. There are very many of these where the association is a purely commercial one, of which it can safely be said that the basis of association is adequately and exhaustively laid down in the articles. The superimposition of equitable considerations requires something more, which typically may include one, or probably more, of the following elements: (i) an association formed or continued on the basis of a personal relationship, involving mutual confidence – this element will often be found where a pre-existing partnership has been converted into a limited company; (ii) an agreement, or understanding, that all, or some (for there may be "sleeping" members), of the shareholders shall participate in the conduct of the business; (iii) restriction upon the transfer of the members' interest in the company – so that if confidence is lost, or one member is removed from management, he cannot take out his stake and go elsewhere.'

Companies Act 2006, sections 994–996

PART 30

PROTECTION OF MEMBERS AGAINST UNFAIR PREJUDICE

Main provisions

994 Petition by company member

(1) A member of a company may apply to the court by petition for an order under this Part on the ground—
   (a) that the company's affairs are being or have been conducted in a manner that is unfairly prejudicial to the interests of members generally or of some part of its members (including at least himself), or
   (b) that an actual or proposed act or omission of the company (including an act or omission on its behalf) is or would be so prejudicial.

(1A) For the purposes of subsection (1)(a), a removal of the company's auditor from office—
   (a) on grounds of divergence of opinions on accounting treatments or audit procedures, or
   (b) on any other improper grounds,
   shall be treated as being unfairly prejudicial to the interests of some part of the company's members.

(2) The provisions of this Part apply to a person who is not a member of a company but to whom shares in the company have been transferred or transmitted by operation of law as they apply to a member of a company.

(3) In this section, and so far as applicable for the purposes of this section in the other provisions of this Part, 'company' means—
   (a) a company within the meaning of this Act, or
   (b) a company that is not such a company but is a statutory water company within the meaning of the Statutory Water Companies Act 1991.

995 Petition by Secretary of State

(1) This section applies to a company in respect of which—
   (a) the Secretary of State has received a report under section 437 of the Companies Act 1985 (inspector's report);
   (b) the Secretary of State has exercised his powers under section 447 or 448 of that Act (powers to require documents and information or to enter and search premises);
   (c) the Secretary of State, the Financial Conduct Authority, the Prudential Regulation Authority or the Bank of England has exercised his or its powers under Part 11 of the Financial Services and Markets Act 2000 (information gathering and investigations); or
   (d) the Secretary of State has received a report from an investigator appointed by him, the Financial Conduct Authority, the Prudential Regulation Authority or the Bank of England under that Part.

(2) If it appears to the Secretary of State that in the case of such a company—
   (a) the company's affairs are being or have been conducted in a manner that is unfairly prejudicial to the interests of members generally or of some part of its members, or
   (b) an actual or proposed act or omission of the company (including an act or omission on its behalf) is or would be so prejudicial,
   he may apply to the court by petition for an order under this Part.

(3) The Secretary of State may do this in addition to, or instead of, presenting a petition for the winding up of the company.

(4) In this section, and so far as applicable for the purposes of this section in the other provisions of this Part, 'company' means any body corporate that is liable to be wound up under the Insolvency Act 1986 or the Insolvency (Northern Ireland) Order 1989.

996 Powers of the court under this Part

(1) If the court is satisfied that a petition under this Part is well founded, it may make such order as it thinks fit for giving relief in respect of the matters complained of.

(2) Without prejudice to the generality of subsection (1), the court's order may—

(a) regulate the conduct of the company's affairs in the future;
(b) require the company—
    (i) to refrain from doing or continuing an act complained of, or
    (ii) to do an act that the petitioner has complained it has omitted to do;
(c) authorise civil proceedings to be brought in the name and on behalf of the company by such person or persons and on such terms as the court may direct;
(d) require the company not to make any, or any specified, alterations in its articles without the leave of the court;
(e) provide for the purchase of the shares of any members of the company by other members or by the company itself and, in the case of a purchase by the company itself, the reduction of the company's capital accordingly.

Further reading

Bourne, *Bourne on Company Law* (Routledge-Cavendish, 2011).
Talbot, *Critical Company Law* (Routledge-Cavendish, 2008).

Chapter 11

Lending money and securing loans

Key terms

- **Debenture** – the document which sets out the terms of a loan to the company.
- **Floating charge** – when a loan is secured by a floating charge it is possible to deal with the property over which the charge 'floats' without the consent of the lender, until the charge 'crystallises'.
- **Crystallisation** – the moment at which a floating charge becomes fixed, that is, attaches to specific items owned by the company.
- **Fixed charge** – a charge on a specific asset.

11.1 Debentures

11.1.1 What is a debenture?

A company can finance its activities by selling shares, or by raising money from banks or other money-lending institutions. If the company is granted a loan, the lender may become a debenture-holder. A debenture has never been satisfactorily defined. The Companies Act 2006 provides (s 738):

> In the Companies Acts 'debenture' includes debenture stock, bonds and any other securities of a company, whether or not constituting a charge on the assets of the company.

In *Levy v Abercorris Slate and Slab Co* (1883) 37 Ch D 260, Chitty J said: 'In my opinion a debenture means a document which either creates a debt or acknowledges it, and any document which fulfils either of these conditions is a "debenture".'

Shareholders are members of the company and their rights have been described in Chapter 5 of this book. Debenture-holders are creditors of the company, and their rights are normally defined in the contract made between them and the company. It is interesting to note that debentures may be issued at a discount unless they are convertible into shares, when such an issue at a discount would be an invitation to evade the rule that shares may not be issued at a discount (*Mosly v Koffyfontein* [1904] 2 Ch 108).

The lender may wish to secure his position by taking a charge over the property of the company, that is, creating a legal relationship between himself and the company which will ensure he is paid in priority at least to some of the other claimants against the company. Charges are considered in Section 11.2 below.

11.1.2 Debenture-holder's receiver

The power of a debenture-holder to appoint a receiver will be determined by the terms of the debenture itself. In the circumstances in which a receiver may be appointed, he will be appointed to collect the assets of the company with a view to the repayment of the debt due to the debenture-holder. He must, however, pay creditors whose claim should be paid before the debenture-holder, for example a preferential creditor, as set out in Schedule 6 to the Insolvency Act 1986 (see Companies Act 2006, s 754). Preferential creditors are tax authorities, for example HM Revenue and Customs, employee remuneration (4 months' pay), some amount of holiday pay for employees and miscellaneous charges, for example landfill charges and climate change levies.

11.1.3 Judgment creditors and the claim of debenture-holders

Once a receiver has been appointed by debenture-holders, the claim of the debenture-holders will take priority over the claim of the creditor despite the fact that he has obtained judgment in his favour (*Re Cairney v Black* [1906] 2 KB 746).

11.2 Fixed and floating charges

11.2.1 The characteristics of fixed and floating charges

It may be important for the purposes of determining the priority of charges to decide whether a particular charge is a 'fixed' or a 'floating' charge. Essentially, a *fixed charge* gives the holder the right to have a particular asset sold in order to repay the loan that he has given the company. This means that the company may not deal with the property subject to the fixed charge without the consent of the holder of the charge. A *floating charge* gives the holder the right to be paid in priority to others after the sale of the assets subject to the charge, but in this case the assets over which the charge floats are not specified. The company may continue to deal with them without the permission of the holder of the charge, and it is only on the happening of certain events (such as non-payment of an instalment of interest or repayment of capital) that the charge will become fixed. On the happening of the event in question (which will be specified in the contract for the loan), the charge is said to 'crystallise' and will become fixed on the particular assets that the company holds at that moment which answer to the general description of the property over which the charge originally 'floated'. It then becomes indistinguishable in form from a fixed charge. Thus, if the original charge 'floated' over all stock-in-trade and a crystallising event occurred, the goods subject to the crystallised charge would be the stock the company owned on that particular day. After the crystallisation, the company would not be able to sell these assets without the permission of the debenture-holder.

The Court in *Re Yorkshire Woolcombers Association Ltd* [1903] 2 Ch 284 (see 'Case note', at the end of the chapter) grappled with the definition of floating charges. In the Court of Appeal, Romer LJ said:

> I certainly do not intend to attempt to give an exact definition of the term 'floating charge' nor am I prepared to say that there will not be a floating charge within the meaning of the Act, which does not contain all the three characteristics that I am about to mention, but I certainly think that if the charge has the three characteristics that I am about to mention it is a floating charge: (1) if it is a charge on a class of assets of a company present and future; (2) if that class is one which, in the ordinary course of the business of the company, would be changing from time to time; and (3) if you find that by the charge it is contemplated that, until some future step is taken by or on behalf of those interested in the charge, the company may carry on its business in the ordinary way as far as concerns the particular class of assets I am dealing with.

Thus, the idea of a 'floating' charge is that the company is unhindered from dealing with its assets despite the fact that an outsider has a legal interest in those assets.

When the charge is created, the nature of the charge as a fixed or floating charge depends on its characteristics and not on whether the parties have described it as a fixed or floating charge. Thus in *Re Armagh Shoes Ltd* [1982] NI 59, the charge being considered by the court was described in the document that created it as a 'fixed' charge but was held by the court to have been a floating charge. The document included the following words:

> [T]he mortgagor pursuant to every power and by force of every estate enabling it in this behalf and as beneficial owner hereby charges in the favour of the bank by way of fixed charge all receivables debtors plant machinery fixtures fittings and ancillary equipment now or at any time hereafter belonging to the mortgagor.

Hutton J said:

> [T]he authorities establish that the description of a charge as a fixed or specific charge does not, in itself, operate to prevent the charge from being a floating charge; and the deed in this case contains no express provision restricting the company from dealing with the assets charged. In my judgment in the present case it is a necessary implication from the deed that the company was to have the right or licence to deal with the assets, comprised within the ambit of the charge, in the ordinary course of its business until the bank decided to enforce the charge. I can see no basis for the implication that it was the intention of the company and the bank that the company would deal with the charged assets in breach of its contract with the bank, to which breaches the bank would turn a blind eye, and that if a third party asked the company if it was entitled to transfer some of the charged assets to him the company would have to tell him to obtain the bank's consent to the transfer.

In *Re Keenan Brothers Ltd* [1986] BCLC 242, the parties tried to create a fixed charge on money that was due to be paid to the company in the future, that is, 'book debts'. This case settled the issue whether it was possible in law to create a fixed charge on future book debts – the court answered in the affirmative. However, there has been significant controversy about what was required to make a charge on book debts and whether book debts were a fixed charge. In *Re Keenan* the second issue was whether the charge that had in fact been created in this case was a fixed charge or a floating charge.

On the latter point, McCarthy J, giving judgment in the Irish Supreme Court, emphasised the term in the agreement that read:

> The company shall pay into an account with the Bank designated for that purpose all moneys which it may receive in respect of the book debts and other debts hereby charged and shall not without the prior consent of the Bank in writing make any withdrawals or direct any payment from the said account.

He said:

> In my view, it is because it was described as a specific or fixed charge and was intended to be such, that the requirement of a special bank account was necessary; if it were a floating charge payment into such an account would be entirely inappropriate and, indeed, would conflict with the ambulatory nature of the floating charge ... In *Re Yorkshire Woolcombers Association Ltd* Romer LJ postulated three characteristics of a floating charge, the third being that, if you find that by the charge it is contemplated that, until some future step is taken by or on behalf of those interested in the charge, the company may carry on its business in the ordinary way as far as concerns the particular class of assets I am dealing with. Counsel for the banks has argued that this latter characteristic is essential to a floating charge and that the banking provision in the instruments here negatives such a characteristic; I would uphold this view.

This case may be contrasted with *Re Brightlife Ltd* [1987] Ch 200, where Hoffman J held that the charge in question was a floating charge. It was a charge over (among other things) future book debts. Hoffman J held that the existence of a floating charge is not dependent on the company over whose property it floats having complete freedom of action. He said:

> It is true that clause 5(ii) does not allow Brightlife to sell, factor or discount debts without the written consent of Norandex [who had the benefit of the charge]. But a floating charge is consistent with some restriction on the company's freedom to deal with its assets. For example, floating charges commonly contain a prohibition on the creation of other charges ranking prior to or pari passu with the floating charge. Such dealings would otherwise be open to a company in the ordinary course of its business. In this debenture, the significant feature is that Brightlife was free to collect its debts and pay the proceeds into its bank account. Once in the account, they would be outside the charge over debts and at the free disposal of the company. In my judgment a right to deal in this way with the charged assets for its own account is a badge of a floating charge and is inconsistent with a fixed charge.

See also *New Bullas Trading Ltd* [1993] BCC 251, in which the Court of Appeal found that the debenture in question in that case had created a fixed charge over book debts which would become a floating charge over the proceeds once they had been collected and paid into a specified account. The debenture-holder had power to give directions as to the application of the money once it had been received, but did not have exclusive control over that money unless a direction had actually been given. There were thus circumstances in which the company could dispose of the money and the charge was a floating charge. Before the money was collected, the company had an absolute obligation to pay any proceeds of book debts into a particular account. At this stage there was therefore a fixed charge over the book debts.

In *William Gaskell Group v Highley* [1994] 1 BCLC 197, the issue of whether the charge was fixed or floating turned on whether a clause requiring payment of the proceeds of debts into an account which could not be drawn on without the consent of the Midland Bank remained valid after the Midland Bank assigned the debenture. The court held that it was still commercially viable to require the Bank's consent, the clause remained valid and the restriction meant that the charge was a fixed charge.

Part of this long controversy was eventually decided in *Re Spectrum Plus* [2005] UKHL 41, [2005] AC 680. Analysing the arguments, the Court said that a debt owed to the company should be analysed into three phases: (a) when the debt was owed to the company and unpaid; (b) payment of the debt and crediting the money to the company's bank account; (c) withdrawal from the bank account of a sum equivalent to the amount of the debt. The House of Lords in *Re Spectrum Plus* rejected the argument that phase (c) is legally separate because money which is paid into a bank account becomes the bank's money, not the account holder's. The Court held that a charge which allowed the company to use the money (phase (c)) without the chargee's permission could not be a fixed charge. Although *Re Spectrum Plus* has settled some issues, the court will still need to look carefully at the substance of the charge and will not be bound by the wording adopted by the parties. In *Re GE Tunbridge Ltd* [1995] 1 BCLC 409, a charge described as a fixed charge which purported to be over all the assets of the company except those covered by a floating charge was held not to create a fixed charge over intangible assets such as book debts or tangible assets which were likely to be changed or sold over time. This was despite the fact that the company was not permitted to dispose of the assets subject to the fixed charge without the consent of the chargee. However, in *Re Climex*

Tissues [1995] 1 BCLC 409, a charge was held to be properly described as a fixed charge despite the fact that the company was apparently permitted to deal with the property subject to the charge 'in the ordinary course of business'. The court held that this wording must be taken to refer to the stock (toilet rolls) and not the capital machinery, but also held that the existence of a limited power to deal with property was not necessarily inconsistent with a fixed charge. Each case therefore turns on its precise facts and the degree of liberty with which the company is able to deal with the property which is subject to the charge. See also *Re Cosslett (Contractors) Ltd* [1998] 2 WLR 131 (CA); *Clark v Mid Glamorgan County Council* [1996] 1 BCLC 407; and *Royal Trust Bank v National Westminster Bank plc and Another* [1996] 2 BCLC 682.

The cases examined above show that the greater the interference with the freedom to use and dispose of the assets affected by the charge, the more likely it is that the courts will hold the charge to be a fixed charge, however the parties have described it. Because of the huge variety of clauses to be found in documents creating charges, it is impossible to arrive at an exhaustive definition of the difference between the two types of charges; the whole of the nature of the restrictions must be examined. The difference is important when the priority of various claimants has to be decided.

11.2.2 Crystallisation of the floating charge

A charge will certainly crystallise on the happening of the following:

1. the appointment of an administrative receiver by the chargeholder;
2. the appointment of an administrator;
3. the commencement of liquidation;
4. the cessation of business.

The document which creates the floating charge will further provide for certain events which will cause the floating charge to become a fixed charge. Prior to the Companies Act 1989 there was much discussion as to whether this 'crystallisation' could be 'automatic', that is, could occur without any action on behalf of the debenture-holders or their agents, merely because an event specified in the debenture had occurred. There was some authority to the effect that this could occur (obiter in *Re Brightlife*, see Section 11.2.1 above). In *Re Woodroffes (Musical Instruments) Ltd* [1986] Ch 366, it was held that the crystallisation of a first floating charge did not occur automatically when a subsequent charge was crystallised. However, it was also held that a floating charge did automatically crystallise on the cessation of a company's business. Whether the cessation of business and the moment at which a business ceases to be a going concern are different was unclear to Nourse J. He said: 'My own impression is that these phrases are used interchangeably in the authorities ... but whether that be right or wrong, I think it clear that the material event is a cessation of business and not, if that is something different, ceasing to be a going concern.' The moment of crystallisation in that case was important, because if the floating charge had crystallised before the appointment of a receiver, the preferential creditors would have lost the priority that they enjoy under section 175 of the Companies Act 1985 over the holders of a 'floating charge' created by the company. The charge would be a fixed charge at the relevant date.

This effect was confirmed in *Re ELS Ltd; Ramsbottom v Luton Borough Council* [1994] BCC 449. The court held that on crystallisation the goods subject to the charge ceased to be goods of the company and became the goods of the chargee. Consequently it was not possible for bailiffs acting for the local authority to seize the goods because of rates owed by the company to the local council.

11.2.3 Legal and equitable charges

The order in which competing claims against company property will be paid will depend on whether the creditor holds a legal or equitable charge. A legal charge will commonly occur only:

1. when there is a charge by way of legal mortgage of land under section 85(1) or section 86(1) of the Law of Property Act 1925; or
2. where the legal interest in the charged property is transferred to the chargee by way of security for an obligation, on condition that the interest will be transferred back to the surety if and when the secured obligation is met.

All other charges are equitable charges. In the absence of registration, equitable charges take priority in order of creation. However, a legal charge created after an equitable charge will take priority over it unless the chargee had notice of the prior charge. For the effect of registration, see Section 11.3 below.

11.2.4 Floating charges and other claims against the company

11.2.4(a) Subsequent fixed charges

In the absence of actual notice of a restriction on the creation of later charges (sometimes called a 'negative pledge clause'), the fixed charge will take priority over a previous floating charge. This, of course, is subject to the effects of non-registration of registrable charges.

11.2.4(b) Subsequent floating charges

A company will not be able to create a second floating charge ranking equally to or having priority over an existing floating charge, in the absence of words permitting this in the instrument creating the first floating charge (*Re Benjamin Cope & Sons* [1914] 1 Ch 800). However, permission to create a subsequent charge ranking equally to or in priority to an earlier one may be construed out of a clause reserving power to create charges over specific property. The theory seems to be that reserving a general power to charge property when a first charge is created will not permit the erosion of the value of the first charge by creation of a second charge. However, such erosion is permitted where the reservation of the right to charge is confined to specific property. In *Re Automatic Bottle Makers Ltd* [1926] Ch 412, Sargant LJ said:

> Great stress has, however, been laid for the respondents on a decision of my own as a judge of first instance in *Re Benjamin Cope & Sons* [1914] 1 Ch 800, and it has been argued that that case decides that a general floating charge is necessarily incompatible with the subsequent creation under a special charging power of a floating charge to rank in priority or pari passu with the earlier floating charge. I have examined that decision with great care, and have no reason to think that it was wrong, particularly in view of the fact that it appears to be in accord with an earlier decision of Vaughan-Williams J in *Smith v England and Scottish Mercantile Investment Trust* [1896] WN 86 and

not to have been questioned since. But the facts in that case were very different. There the original charge was on the whole undertaking and property for the time being of the company, and the reservation of a power to mortgage was in quite general terms; and it was held that such a power could not have been intended to authorise a competing charge on the entirety of the property comprised in the earlier charge. Here the reservation of the power to mortgage is precise and specific in its terms, and extends only to certain particular classes of the property of the company.

In certain circumstances charges may be overturned when a company is liquidated. For a discussion of this, see Chapter 13.

11.2.4(c) Set-offs

If an outsider has a right which is enforceable against the company at the time when a floating charge crystallises, he can resist any claim which the receiver has against him to the extent of his right against the company, that is, he can set off his right against the amount being claimed by the receiver (*Robbie v Whitney Warehouses* [1963] 3 All ER 613).

11.2.5 Retention of title clauses

These clauses are sometimes known as *Romalpa* clauses after the case of *Aluminium Industrie Vaassen BV v Romalpa Aluminium Ltd* [1976] 1 WLR 676, which established their validity. A clause is inserted in a sale of goods contract which provides that the goods purchased shall remain the property of the seller until the purchase price is paid. If a receiver is appointed under the terms of a floating charge before the purchase price is paid, an unpaid purchaser will be able to recover 'his' goods from the company; the receiver may not treat them as the property of the company. The unpaid seller's rights continue only until the goods are identifiable and in the possession of the buyer. Thus in the case of *Borden (UK) Ltd v. Scottish Timber Products* [1979] 3 WLR 672, the material sold under the contract was resin. This was processed with other materials into chipboard. The unpaid seller had no rights over the chipboard.

A simple retention of title clause does not at present require registration (see Section 11.3 below; see also *Clough Mill Ltd v Geoffrey Martin* [1985] 1 WLR 111; and *Specialist Plant Services Ltd v Braithwaite Ltd* [1987] BCLC 1). However, where more complicated clauses have been used, a registrable charge may be created. See *Re Bond Worth* [1980] Ch 228 and *Re Curtain Dream plc* [1990] BCLC 925. A supplier of goods who has stipulated for retention of title to the goods usually wishes to obtain some control over the proceeds of resale of the goods. However, any control might be governed by the legislation on the registration of charges (see the next section) and the purchase price might become a registrable change on the book debt.

11.3 Registration of company charges

For some time the system of registration of company charges has been problematic. Much of the difficulty in this area is that it is difficult to change the system of registration of company charges radically without a complete overhaul of other areas. There have been a number of reviews and recommendations but no legislation which tidies up the issue. Many people thought that the Diamond Report's recommendations (Professor Diamond, *A Review of Security Interests in Property* (HMSO, 1989)) should have been implemented. The Diamond Report's radical proposals called for a review of the whole of the law relating to security over property other than land. If implemented, there would be a single register of security interests created by companies, partnerships and sole traders in the course of business. Determination of priority would be by date of filing. The register would cover retention of title clauses, hire purchase and chattel leases for more than three years. It would replace the present scheme and create a single register for these charges. However, this report was not implemented.

Parliament enacted a revised system for registration of company charges in the Companies Act 2006, section 1180 and Schedule 16 as from 1 October 2009. One issue with which the Diamond Report wanted to grapple was the whole question of whether the date of registration should be changed. In the Companies Act 2006, the charge was to be filed with all of the details, including the original charge contract, after the charge has been created. The charge took priority from the date of creation. The Law Commission recommended that this should be replaced in the same way as suggested in the Diamond Report (see *Company Security Interests* (Law Com No 296, Cm 6654, 2005, available at <www.lawcom.gov.uk>). The Company Law Review Steering Group also suggested the same system (*Modern Company Law for a Competitive Economy: Final Report*, Vol 1 (URN 01/942)). In 2011 the government issued a consultation document (*Registration of Charges Creating by Companies and Limited Liability Partnerships* (URN 10/697)). The relevant law is found in the Companies Act 2006, Part 25, Chapter A1 (sections 859A to 859Q), which came into force on 6 April 2013. This legislation has retrospectively amended the Companies Act 2006. This new system simplifies charges significantly. Any person giving credit to a company only does so if he believes that the company has enough assets. If some of the assets are charged to another creditor, there is a need to make sure that the company is creditworthy. This involves transparency and therefore it is important that there is a register of charges. Copies of a company's charge contracts must be delivered to Companies House and the public may inspect the register. When a company creates a charge, the company (or any interested person) may register it at Companies House within 'the period allowed for delivery', which is 21 days beginning with the day after the date of creation of the charge (s 859A(1), (2) and (4)).

11.3.1 Which charges are registrable?

A company that creates a charge covered by section 860 of the Companies Act 2006 must deliver the prescribed particulars of the charge, together with the instrument by which the charge is created, to the Registrar for registration. The following charges are listed in section 860(7):

(a) a charge on land or any interest in land, other than a charge for any rent or other periodical sum issuing out of land,

(b) a charge created or evidenced by an instrument which, if executed by an individual, would require registration as a bill of sale,

(c) a charge for the purposes of securing any issue of debentures,

(d) a charge on uncalled share capital of the company,

(e) a charge on calls made but not paid,

(f) a charge on book debts of the company,

(g) a floating charge on the company's property or undertaking,

(h) a charge on a ship or aircraft, or any share in a ship,

(i) a charge on goodwill or on any intellectual property.

Of these complicated provisions the most notable factors are:

1. Book debts are registrable although, as we have seen in Section 11.2.1 above, the designation of book debts as fixed or floating charges is highly controversial.
2. Charges over shares are not registrable per se.
3. Registration of the charge in the register of charges constitutes notice to the whole world that a charge of a particular type exists but does not constitute notice of the terms and conditions of the charge.
4. There are some types of charges which are excluded from registration at Companies House (Companies Act 2006, s 859A). They include a charge in favour of a landlord on a cash deposit given as a security in connection with the lease of land (s 859A(6)(a)), a charge created by a member of Lloyd's in the business of underwriting, a financial collateral arrangement entered into the financial markets (SI 2003/3226).

11.3.2 Priorities under the registration system and effect of registration

The date of creation of a charge is the date of execution of the instrument creating the charge or of fulfilment of conditions if executed conditionally, or the date of an enforceable agreement conferring a security interest forthwith or on the acquisition by the company of property subject to the charge.

11.3.2(a) Priorities

The fundamental rule gives priority in accordance with the date of creation of a charge. This is despite the original inadequate protection provided by a system which bases priority on the date of creation of a charge and then permits registration within 21 days. The Diamond Report, the Law Commission Report and the Company Review recommendations, or a system of registration based on date of registration, coupled with a provisional registration system or for a certificate of guarantee from the Registrar, have never been implemented. Although many reports on this issue suggested a system of regulation based on the date of registration, this has not happened. However, section 859D of the Companies Act 2006, inserted by the Companies Act 2006 (Amendment of Part 25) Regulations 2013 (SI 2013/600), sets out the date of creation for each type of security and when the 21-day period starts to run in respect of that security. It is likely that this system will be clearer and more secure for creditors; however, it is early days and until it is tested it is not clear that it is a significant reform.

The regulations followed a series of Government consultations aimed at modernising and streamlining the security registration regime in the UK by providing a single scheme for registration of company charges irrespective of the place of incorporation of the company. The regulations therefore apply to the registration of charges created by companies which are registered in England, Wales, Northern Ireland and Scotland. The main features of the regulations are as follows:

▶ *Registrable securities.* The regulations assume that all charges (as defined in section 859A(7)) may be registered, with the exception of those listed in section 859A(6). BIS had considered excluding charges arising by operation of law, but has instead decided to place the onus on the presenter to determine whether a charge should be registered.
▶ *Filing of a security.* The regulations introduce electronic filing and also provide for the full text of a charge instrument or document to be available on the public register at

Companies House (although some personal information may be redacted). The charge instrument will be accompanied by particulars, the content of which is set out in the regulations. The particulars are intended to improve the ease of searching the register and direct the searcher to any other relevant UK register containing information relating to that charge. A unique reference code (URC) will be designated to each charge, and it is intended that the URC will aid searches and present a more accurate profile of the extent to which the assets of a particular company are encumbered.

▷ *Consequences of non-registration.* The regulations remove the mandatory filing regime enforced by criminal sanction (Companies Act 2006, s 860) but retain the invalidity sanction (currently found in ss 874 and 889 of the 2006 Act) so that a non-registered security will be invalid against an administrator, a liquidator or a creditor of the security provider (but there will be no criminal penalty for non-registration).

▷ *Time limit for delivery and definition of 'date of creation'.* The regulations do not amend the 21-day time limit for the delivery of the charge or security to the Registrar of Companies. They do, however, set out the date of creation for each type of security and when the 21-day period starts to run in respect of that security.

11.3.2(b) Effect of registration

Registration of a charge in the register is notice to everyone that a charge of a particular type exists, but it does not constitute notice of the terms and conditions of the charge (*Wilson v Kelland* [1910] 2 Ch 306).

11.3.3 Duty to register and effect of non-registration

Section 862(2) of the Companies Act 2006 provides that it is the duty of a company which creates a charge, or acquires property subject to a charge, to deliver particulars of the charge, together with a certified copy of the instrument by which the charge is created, to the Registrar for registration. The period allowed for registration is 21 days, beginning with the day after the day on which the charge is created. Anyone interested in the charge may deliver the particulars, and before 6 April 2013 the company and any officer of the company in default had committed an offence. This restriction has been lifted (s 859D, inserted by SI 2013/600).

The most important consequence of failure to deliver, however, is that by section 874(1) the charge becomes void against the liquidator or an administrator and any creditor of the company. This means that a subsequent chargee can ignore an unregistered charge even if he has actual notice of it, unless such subsequent chargee has expressly agreed to be subject to the unregistered charge. These provisions change the situation of a purchaser from the company of the property subject to the charge. Such a purchaser will now take the property free of the charge even if he knew of the charge, provided he has not agreed to take the property subject to the charge.

Section 874(3) of the 2006 Act provides that money secured by an unregistered demand becomes repayable on demand when the charge becomes void to any extent. Such money is automatically repayable at the end of the 21-day period.

Summary

11.1 Money lent to a company will normally be secured by a fixed charge over definite property, or by a floating charge which will enable the company to deal with the assets involved until crystallisation of the floating charge turns it into a fixed charge.

11.2 Crystallisation of a floating charge will normally occur when the lender (debenture-holder) intervenes to assert his rights, often on the appointment of a receiver.

11.3 It is still unclear whether a floating charge can 'automatically' crystallise on the happening of an event specified in the debenture, or whether intervention by the debenture-holder is required.

11.4 Charges must be registered if they are to be valid against others taking security from a company. They must be registered within 21 days of creation, but priority is in order of creation rather than order of registration.

11.5 The registration provisions cover the situations where there is late delivery of particulars of a charge, or errors or omissions in particulars.

Exercises

11.1 Would a system of priority of charges depending on order of registration be better than the present system (which depends on order of creation)? Consider the reform of the system and decide whether the reform has made significant progress in clarifying the issues.

11.2 If a floating charge is created, does (i) a subsequent fixed charge, and (ii) a subsequent floating charge, expressed to rank equally, have priority over it?

Case note

Re Yorkshire Woolcombers Association Ltd
[1903] 2 Ch 284

By a trust deed of 23 April 1890, the Yorkshire Woolcombers Association Ltd specifically mortgaged all its freehold and leasehold properties to trustees to secure its debenture stock, and, as beneficial owner, charged in favour of the trustees 'by way of floating security all its other property and assets both present and future, and its undertaking, but not including capital for the time being uncalled'. The deed contained a power enabling the association to deal with the property and assets which were subject to the charge. The question before the court was whether the charge was a fixed or floating charge, since it had not been registered; if it was a floating charge, it would be void as against the receiver. Farwell J said at first instance:

'The very essence of a specific charge is that the assignee takes possession, and is the person entitled to receive the book debts at once. So long as he licenses the mortgagor to go on receiving the book debts and carry on the business, it is within the exact definition of a floating security.'

The Court of Appeal upheld this judgment: part of the speech of Romer LJ is reproduced in Section 11.2.1 above.

Further reading

McCormack, *Registration of Company Charges* (Jordan, 2009)
Mayson, French and Ryan, *Company Law*, 30th edn, 2013–14, especially Chapter 11

Chapter 12

Takeovers, reconstructions and amalgamations

Key terms

▶ **Offer document** – a company must disclose detailed information concerning the company making the offer and the precise terms of the offer in the document which sets out the takeover proposal. This document is known as the 'offer document'.

▶ **Reconstruction** – a great number of company reconstructions occur as a result of the takeover of one company by another. This will often be achieved by the company which is effecting the takeover offering to buy the shares held by the shareholders in the target company. Such 'reconstructions' are governed by a mixture of rules, some found in the statutes and others to be found in the City Code on Takeovers and Mergers. The rules of the Financial Conduct Authority and the London Stock Exchange also require disclosure of a number of matters when a takeover is attempted and a company listed on the Exchange is involved. Such a company must disclose detailed information concerning the company making the offer and the precise terms of the offer in the document which sets out the takeover proposal.

▶ **Takeover** – this happens when the shares of one company are bought by another company. The two companies continue to exist; what has changed is control in the company whose shares have been bought; the buyer company can use its shares to control the bought company by voting.

▶ **'Bidder' or 'offeror' company** – the company which attempts to acquire control over another company.

▶ **'Target' or the 'offeree' company** – the company which constitutes the target of the takeover bid.

▶ **Takeover Panel** – the body which supervises the takeovers of public and other large companies. It was placed on a statutory footing for the first time by the Companies Act 2006.

12.1 Takeovers

12.1.1 Takeover regulatory framework and rules

The English rules on takeovers cannot be viewed in isolation from the relevant legislative developments at EU level. The latter have created a new landscape in the framework of which the English rules on takeovers are currently operating. Therefore, an examination of the relevant EU law is necessary in order fully to understand the regulatory environment within which takeovers may take place in the UK.

A cross-border element is integral in the regulation of takeovers in every case that one of the companies involved is registered in another country.

The relevant legislative tool is Directive 2004/25/EC of the European Parliament and Council of 21 April 2004 on Takeover Bids ('the Takeovers Directive'). This Directive proved to be controversial throughout the rather long history of its negotiation. Agreement between the Member States of the EU was reached only in December 2003, after 14 years of negotiations that revealed a great divergence between the policies, the aims and targets of the countries involved. The long and rather intense debates to agree on a common text were fuelled by the differences between the corporate governance models adopted by Member States of the EU (analysed in Chapter 2). The UK stood on the one side of the debate, with a corporate governance model marked by public companies with a widely dispersed shareholder basis, and with an emphasis on a liberal approach to the function of the markets and the financial industry as the flagship of the economy. On the other side, Germany championed a corporate governance system marked by the dominance of mostly export-orientated industrial companies with a concentrated shareholder basis, where the existence of shareholders with a significant amount of shares that enable them to block a takeover – namely the blockholders – is common.

The inability to shape a compromise between the two systems of corporate governance was not just the reason behind the failure of the EU to create a corporate governance common at the EU level; it was also the crucial factor behind the debates that delayed the adoption of the Directive for more than a decade and that have led in the end to the adoption of a text with so many optional provisions that has left so much scope to national jurisdictions to keep their distinctive takeover rules, which has rendered it difficult to talk about 'common takeover regime regulation' across the EU.

12.1.2   Takeover bids

Takeovers are one means by which one company, the 'bidder' or 'offeror' company, may acquire control over another company, the 'target' or the 'offeree' company. The process usually involves the purchase of a specific percentage of the shares in the target company to guarantee the establishment of control on the part of the offeror company over the offeree company. The process involves making an offer to the shareholders, and if a certain percentage of the shareholders consent to accept it, the offeror is granted the ability compulsorily to acquire the shares of the remaining shareholders in the offeree company.

The terms 'mergers' and 'takeovers' have sometimes been used interchangeably. 'Merger' is often used to describe a voluntary takeover bid rather than a hostile one. A 'hostile bid' refers to a takeover bid which fuels great opposition from the management board of the offeree company.

The UK has been the principal market for takeovers within the EU framework. This is the main reason why the European Commission used the English institutional and regulatory model as the pattern for the Directive (see Section 12.1.1 above). In the UK, the conduct of takeover bids in public companies has been regulated by the Panel on Takeovers and Mergers ('the Panel' – see Section 12.1.3 below) since 1968. Takeover bids have been subject to the rules contained in the City Code on Takeovers and Mergers (see further Section 12.1.3 below). It was particularly interesting, and also reflective of the country's laissez-faire tradition, that both the Panel and the Code operated on a non-statutory basis. This granted the Panel immense scope of discretion, that allowed a great degree of flexibility over the application of the relevant provisions. On 20 May 2006, the UK brought into force the law implementing the Takeovers Directive – the Takeovers Directive (Interim Implementation) Regulations 2006 (SI 2006/1183) – which placed both the Panel and the Code on a statutory footing. The Regulations were subsequently replaced by the Companies Act 2006 on 6 April 2007, Part 28 of which deals with takeovers. This by itself constitutes a relatively radical reshaping of the takeover regulatory and institutional regime in the UK. In this context the Companies Act 2006 granted to the Code the force of law.

12.1.3 The Panel on Takeovers and Mergers

The Panel supervises takeovers of public and other large companies. As noted in Section 12.1.2 above, the Panel was placed on a statutory footing for the first time by the Companies Act 2006. Sections 942–946 of the Act give the Panel very wide powers and responsibilities. These will be subject to judicial review by the courts. In the past, when the Panel was not a body established by statute, it was argued that turning it into a statutory body would hinder its flexibility and the speed at which it could take decisions. In practice, the powers granted under the 2006 Act are so wide that this outcome has not materialised.

Section 942 of the Companies Act 2006 states:

(1) The body known as the Panel on Takeovers and Mergers ('the Panel') is to have the functions conferred on it by or under this Chapter.

In *R v Panel on Takeovers, ex parte Datafin* [1987] 2 WLR 699, the Court of Appeal held that the decisions of the Panel should be reviewable by the court, although a review was refused in that particular case. The Court was reluctant to hinder the work of the Panel and so held that resort to the courts should not be made during the course of the events on which the Panel was ruling. The courts should allow the Panel to make decisions and allow events to take their course, intervening, if at all, later, in retrospect, by declaratory orders.

In *R v Panel on Takeovers and Mergers, ex parte Guinness PLC* [1989] BCLC 255, the Court of Appeal confirmed that the Panel's decisions would be subject to judicial review only where something had gone wrong with its procedure so as to cause real injustice and require the intervention of the court.

The Companies Act 2006 requires the Panel to make rules to implement the EU Takeovers Directive (s 943(1) and (2)). Rules made by the Panel may also make provision:

(a) for or in connection with the regulation of—
    (i) takeover bids,
    (ii) merger transactions, and
    (iii) transactions (not falling within sub-paragraph (i) or (ii)) that have or may have, directly or indirectly, an effect on the ownership or control of companies.

By section 943(3), the provision that may be made under section 943(2) includes, in particular, provision for a matter that is, or is similar to, a matter provided for by the Panel in the City Code on Takeovers and Mergers as it had effect immediately before the passing of the 2006 Act. It seems, therefore, that the Act does not envisage a significant change in the responsibilities or mode of operation of the Panel, which has operated by issuing the Code mentioned in section 943(3).

The Code sets out general principles 'of conduct to be observed in takeover and merger transactions'. There are also more detailed rules and notes which provide guidance as to the way in which the rules should operate. The Code requires that the spirit of the general principles and rules, as well as the precise wording, should be observed. It seeks to ensure fair treatment of all shareholders, including equal treatment of different classes of shares, as well as equal treatment of members of each class. To this end there is:

- a requirement of disclosure of the financial soundness of the offeror company;
- a duty on directors of both companies to consider their shareholders' interests and not to have regard to their personal interests;
- a requirement that information given to shareholders is sufficient to enable a properly informed decision to be made; and
- a requirement that any information supplied must be available to all shareholders.

There are also rules preventing the use of tactics by an offeree board which would tend to frustrate a takeover bid.

Section 952 of the Companies Act 2006 provides that the Panel rules may contain provisions imposing sanctions on any person who has:

(a) acted in breach of the rules, or
(b) failed to comply with a direction given by [the Panel].

The Panel also has power to apply to the court for an order to secure compliance with its rules (s 955).

12.1.4   Fundamental principles of the Directive and the UK law and implementation

12.1.4(a) *Jurisdictional rules*

Article 4 of the Takeovers Directive deals with two issues of fundamental importance for takeovers: the establishment of a supervisory authority, and the law applicable to the takeover in question. Member States are required to set up an authority which will have as its main function the supervision of the ongoing takeovers. The latter should take place on the basis of the rather flexible rules assumed at the EU level as implemented by national jurisdictions. The authority in question could be a private body or a public body. It is a matter of vital importance that it remains independent and impartial throughout the bid.

Article 4(2) deals with jurisdictional issues. The authority competent to supervise a bid shall be that of the Member State in which the offeree company has its registered office if that company's securities are admitted to trading on a regulated market in that Member State. If the offeree company's securities are not admitted to trading on a regulated market in the Member State in which the company has its registered office, the authority competent to supervise the bid shall be that of the Member State on the regulated market of which the company's securities are admitted to trading.

As proof of the flexible and non-interventionist approach adopted in the UK, the Companies Act 2006 empowers the Panel to introduce the necessary arrangements to comply with the anyway flexible framework set by the Directive. Therefore, instead of introducing hard law solutions at the Companies Act 2006 level, as with the vast majority of the company law-related matters, the Act renders the Panel the institutional authority responsible for the regulation of takeovers. This approach is compatible with the self-regulatory tradition developed in the UK over the years.

Section 943 of the Companies Act 2006 provides:

(1) The Panel must make rules giving effect to Articles 3.1, 4.2, 5, 6.1 to 6.3, 7 to 9 and 13 of the Takeovers Directive.

Therefore, the Act clearly establishes the Panel as the principal authority responsible for the regulation of takeovers in the UK. Therefore, it is clearly understood that this arrangement leaves almost intact the status quo in relation to takeovers in the UK; takeovers continues to operate on the basis of a self-regulatory approach based on a great deal of flexibility, even in the post-Directive era. The granting of statutory status to both the Code and the Panel has had a less radical and far-reaching effect than initially thought or predicted.

12.1.4(b) The mandatory bid

Article 5 of the Takeovers Directive states that where a natural or legal person, as a result of his own acquisition or the acquisition by persons acting in concert with him, holds securities of a company which, added to any existing holdings of those securities of his and the holdings of those securities of persons acting in concert with him, directly or indirectly give him a specified percentage of voting rights in that company, he acquires the control of that company. In this event, Member States shall ensure that such a person is required to make a bid as a means of protecting the minority shareholders of that company. Such a bid shall be addressed at the earliest opportunity to all the holders of those securities for all their holdings at an equitable price. The percentage of voting rights which confers control is to be determined by the rules of the Member State in which the company has its registered office.

In the UK, this is implemented by section 943 of the Companies Act 2006, which essentially gives effect to the relevant rules of the Code. One of the key rules of the Code requires that where 30 per cent or more of the shares in a company have been acquired by one concern, or by a number of concerns or persons 'acting in concert', then, except in exceptional circumstances and with the permission of the Panel, an equivalent offer must be made for the remainder of the shares. This seeks to prevent the situation where there is an acquisition of sufficient shares to ensure control of the company, followed by a much lower offer to remaining shareholders. This rule is backed up by section 793 of the Companies Act 2006, which permits a company to require the disclosure of interests in shares in certain circumstances.

12.1.4(c) Information on bids

Article 6(1) of the Takeovers Directive requires that the decision to make a bid be made public without delay, and that company boards inform employees or their representatives of the bids. Article 6(2) and (3) requires the offeror to draw up and make public an offer document, with information enabling shareholders to reach a decision on the bid. The document should be communicated to shareholders and to employees.

Section 943 of the CA 2006 grants the power to the Panel to implement the rules in question. Therefore, the Code will be the document and the regulatory instrument containing the aforementioned provisions.

Section 947 of the Companies Act 2006 requires the companies involved to provide the Panel with all the necessary information.

947 Power to require documents and information
(1) The Panel may by notice in writing require a person—
  (a) to produce any documents that are specified or described in the notice;
  (b) to provide, in the form and manner specified in the notice, such information as may be specified or described in the notice.

Section 953 of the CA 2006 create a new offence when any of the parties involved does not comply with the aforementioned rule.

953 Failure to comply with rules about bid documentation

(1) This section applies where a takeover bid is made for a company that has securities carrying voting rights admitted to trading on a regulated market in the United Kingdom.

(2) Where an offer document published in respect of the bid does not comply with offer document rules, an offence is committed by—

(a) the person making the bid, and

(b) where the person making the bid is a body of persons, any director, officer or member of that body who caused the document to be published.

(3) A person commits an offence under subsection (2) only if—

(a) he knew that the offer document did not comply, or was reckless as to whether it complied, and

(b) he failed to take all reasonable steps to secure that it did comply.

12.1.4(d) Post-bid defences against a takeover

Article 9 of the Takeovers Directive is its centrepiece. It aims at preventing the frustration of takeover bids by management. Article 9 states that the board of the offeree company shall obtain the prior authorisation of the general meeting of shareholders given for this purpose before taking any action, other than seeking alternative bids, which may result in the frustration of the bid, and in particular before issuing any shares which may result in a lasting impediment to the offeror's acquiring control of the offeree company. Authorisation by shareholders is mandatory from the time the offeree board receives information concerning a bid until the result of the bid is made public or lapses.

This prohibition on post-bid defensive measures fell quite comfortably within the UK regulatory structure, since the Code had already provided for just such a prohibition and the Panel was therefore accustomed to applying such a rule.

In English company law as analysed extensively throughout this book, the shareholders enjoy absolute supremacy within the company context. They are considered as the exclusive members of the company and their interests are viewed as identical to the company's, although the directors owe their duty to the company as a whole and not to the shareholders. Section 172 of Companies Act 2006 (see Chapter 9) confirms the dominance of the principle of enlightened shareholder value in the UK and recognises the shareholders' supremacy within this context. Therefore, the Panel was already accustomed to grant the ability to raise post-bid defences to the shareholders rather than exclusively to managers. The latter are agents of the shareholders, appointed supposedly to represent their rights and promote the success of the company as a whole; however, in practice the reality might be significantly different, with the directors pursuing their personal agenda. The Panel had always been willing to grant this particularly important decision to the shareholders rather than exclusively to the managers. The latter are anyway inclined to prevent a takeover from taking place, as this would almost automatically entail their removal and replacement with a new management, reflecting the new post-takeover reality and ownership status. Therefore, the consent of the shareholders heals this agency rift, confirms the primacy of shareholders within the company and prevents the management for serving their personal agenda to the detriment of the interests of the company.

Examples of post-bid frustration methods are set out in the Code and may include the issuing of new shares which makes the company more expensive. Rule 21 of the Code implements Article 9 of the Directive in the UK and aims at protecting the interests of the shareholders.

12.1.4(e) Disclosure of information on companies

Article 10 of the Takeovers Directive requires the companies involved, both offeror and offeree, to disclose by publishing detailed information, among other things, on:

- the structure of their capital, with an indication of the different classes of shares and, for each class of shares, any restrictions on the transfer of securities, such as limitations on the holding of securities, the holders of any securities with special control rights and a description of those rights
- the system of control of any employee share scheme where the control rights are not exercised directly by the employees
- any restrictions on voting rights, such as limitations of the voting rights of holders of a given percentage or number of votes
- deadlines for exercising voting rights, and
- systems whereby, with the company's cooperation, the financial rights attaching to securities are separated from the holding of securities.

This information must be made public and must also be included in the company's annual report.

Section 992 of the Companies Act 2006 and rule 23 of the Code implement Article 10 of the Takeovers Directive. Failure to comply with this requirement brings about criminal sanctions under section 415(5) of the Act.

12.1.4(f) Pre-bid defences against a takeover provided for by the articles of association

Article 11 of the Takeovers Directive deals with the already existing pre-bid defensive measures and requires their removal. For example, restrictions on voting rights provided for in the articles of association of the offeree company shall not have effect at the general meeting of shareholders which decides on any defensive measures; also multiple-vote securities shall carry only one vote each at the general meeting of shareholders which decides on any defensive measures.

The UK used its right under Article 12 of the Directive, which renders the application of this provision optional, and opted out of Article 11. This is compatible with the contractual nature of English company law. The ability to set aside already assumed contractual obligations and to break through provisions entrenched in the articles of association, which is the constitution of the company and the contractual basis of the agreement among shareholders, would be incompatible with a system where the understanding of the company is founded on a strong contractual element. Therefore, neither the Companies Act 2006 nor the Code has introduced any such requirement, which remains inactive in the UK.

In any case, in the UK the restriction on the transfer of shares can take place only in private companies. Public companies trading on the London Stock Exchange are required under the Listing Rules to have their shares free of any restriction on the right of transfer. Transfer restrictions on shares cannot therefore be used as pre-bid defences in takeover situations in the UK. It should also be noted that any measures that directors may adopt as pre-bid defences are subject to the scrutiny of their statutory duty under the Companies

Act 2006 to act in the interest of the company as a whole. Section 172 therefore would apply in this case, along with section 175 on the conflict between the director's personal interest and the duty he owes to the company (see Chapter 9).

While Article 11 of the Takeovers Directive will not generally apply in the UK, sections 966 to 972 of the Companies Act 2006 provide for the ability of companies with voting shares traded on a regulated market to opt in to Article 11 of the Directive, should they choose to do so.

966 Opting in and opting out

(1) A company may by special resolution (an 'opting-in resolution') opt in for the purposes of this Chapter if the following three conditions are met in relation to the company.

(2) The first condition is that the company has voting shares admitted to trading on a regulated market.

(3) The second condition is that—
    (a) the company's articles of association—
        (i) do not contain any such restrictions as are mentioned in Article 11 of the Takeovers Directive, or
        (ii) if they do contain any such restrictions, provide for the restrictions not to apply at a time when, or in circumstances in which, they would be disapplied by that Article, and
    (b) those articles do not contain any other provision which would be incompatible with that Article.

(4) The third condition is that—
    (a) no shares conferring special rights in the company are held by—
        (i) a minister,
        (ii) a nominee of, or any other person acting on behalf of, a minister, or
        (iii) a company directly or indirectly controlled by a minister, and
    (b) no such rights are exercisable by or on behalf of a minister under any enactment.

(5) A company may revoke an opting-in resolution by a further special resolution (an 'opting-out resolution').

(6) For the purposes of subsection (3), a reference in Article 11 of the Takeovers Directive to Article 7.1 or 9 of that Directive is to be read as referring to rules under section 943(1) giving effect to the relevant Article.

12.1.4(g) Squeeze-out and sell-out rights

Squeeze-out rights enable a successful bidder to purchase compulsorily the shares of remaining minority shareholders who have not accepted the bid. Sell-out rights enable minority shareholders to require the majority shareholder to purchase their shares. The relative threshold set by ss 979 and 933 of the Companies Act 2006 is 90 per cent of the shares. Where the offeror holds securities representing not less than 90 per cent of the offeree company's capital carrying voting rights, he can force the remaining 10 per cent to be sold to him at a fair price. Similarly, the remaining 10 per cent has the right to demand to be bought up by the offeror at a fair price should the offeror reach this level of shareholding.

In the UK, sections 974 to 991 of the Companies Act 2006 implement Articles 15 and 16 of the Takeovers Directive in the national legal order.

'Squeeze-out'

979 Right of offeror to buy out minority shareholder

(1) Subsection (2) applies in a case where a takeover offer does not relate to shares of different classes.

(2) If the offeror has, by virtue of acceptances of the offer, acquired or unconditionally contracted to acquire—

(a) not less than 90% in value of the shares to which the offer relates, and
(b) in a case where the shares to which the offer relates are voting shares, not less than 90% of the voting rights carried by those shares,

he may give notice to the holder of any shares to which the offer relates which the offeror has not acquired or unconditionally contracted to acquire that he desires to acquire those shares.

'Sell-out'

983 Right of minority shareholder to be bought out by offeror

(1) Subsections (2) and (3) apply in a case where a takeover offer relates to all the shares in a company.

For this purpose a takeover offer relates to all the shares in a company if it is an offer to acquire all the shares in the company within the meaning of section 974.

(2) The holder of any voting shares to which the offer relates who has not accepted the offer may require the offeror to acquire those shares if, at any time before the end of the period within which the offer can be accepted—

(a) the offeror has by virtue of acceptances of the offer acquired or unconditionally contracted to acquire some (but not all) of the shares to which the offer relates, and
(b) those shares, with or without any other shares in the company which he has acquired or contracted to acquire (whether unconditionally or subject to conditions being met)—

(i) amount to not less than 90% in value of all the voting shares in the company (or would do so but for section 990(1)), and
(ii) carry not less than 90% of the voting rights in the company (or would do so but for section 990(1)).

12.2 Reconstructions

Sections 902 to 941 of the Companies Act 2006 set out a procedure which envisages major reconstruction of a company. One of the situations in which these sections may be used is where a merger of two companies is proposed. Such a reconstruction will affect the rights of members and creditors. Care must be taken to ensure that all interests are taken into account. The schemes of compromise or arrangement, for merger and division, set out in these sections provide a more streamlined version of previous requirements, permitting the court to dispense with some of the formalities in certain cases and providing exceptions to the requirement to hold meeting of members in some limited circumstances (ss 934, 931 and 932 (division) and 917 (merger)).

A scheme of arrangement, a merger or division requires the consent of 75 per cent in value of the members of each class of shareholders of the affected companies (s 907). If there are conflicting interests within a class, meetings of 'sub-classes' must be held. In *Re Hellenic and General Trust Ltd* [1976] 1 WLR 123, the shares which belonged to the wholly-owned subsidiary of the offeror company were held to belong to a different class from those which belonged to independent shareholders. It was held that where different shareholders have different interests, they must be regarded as belonging to a separate class.

12.2.1 Meetings

Notices summoning the meetings will be sent out to shareholders and (if relevant) creditors. The notices must explain the scheme and the material interests of the directors of the company. The meeting must have draft terms of the scheme, a report by the directors explaining the scheme and an independent expert's report on the financial consequences of the scheme. At the meeting of each class, a majority in number representing 75 per cent in value of those present and voting in person or by proxy must approve the scheme if it is to go further. If the necessary approval is achieved, the approval of the court may be sought under section 939 (see Section 12.2.2 below).

12.2.2 Approval of the court

The court will normally accept the verdict of the substantial majority required at the meetings and approve the scheme. However, the principle that at the meetings the votes must be cast 'with a view to the class as a whole' has evolved to prevent the scheme's being approved because of the vote of someone who had a special interest to protect or further. If such a person is not neutralised by the requirement that persons with different interests should have different class meetings, the scheme may fail at the approval stage because the vote was carried by a voter seeking to further his own interests at the expense of the class as a whole. Thus in *Re English, Scottish and Australian Chartered Bank* [1893] 3 Ch 385, Lindley LJ said:

> If the creditors are acting on sufficient information and with time to consider what they are about and are acting honestly, they are, I apprehend, much better judges of what is to their commercial advantage than the Court can be. I do not say it is conclusive because there might be some blot on a scheme which had passed that had been unobserved and which was pointed out later. If, however, there should be no such blot, then the court ought to be slow to differ from [the creditors].

However, in *Carruth v Imperial Chemical Industries Ltd* [1937] AC 707, Lord Maugham said that '[t]he Court will, in considering whether a scheme ought to be approved, disregard a majority vote in favour of it if it appears that the majority did not consider the matter with a view to the interests of the class to which they belong only'. The situation appears to be that the court has an unfettered discretion to upset a vote if it is unhappy about whether the outcome is fair to the minority.

12.2.3 Reconstruction in a liquidation

Under section s 110 and 111 of the Insolvency Act 1986, a company which is in a member's voluntary liquidation (see Chapter 13) may empower its liquidator by special resolution to transfer a whole or part of its business or property to another company in return for shares in that company. The shares must be distributed amongst the shareholders of the original company in strict accordance with their rights to share in the assets in a winding up. Such a scheme does not require the approval of the court. However, if shareholders with one-quarter of the voting power do not agree with the scheme, they may express their dissent to the liquidator and require him either to abstain from carrying out the scheme, or to purchase their shares at a price agreed or fixed by arbitration. This right could not be excluded by the memorandum of association (see *Bisgood v Henderson's Transvaal Estates* [1908] 1 Ch 743).

Summary

12.1 Takeovers by the purchase of shares are regulated by a code which has a new statutory basis under the Companies Act 2006: the City Code on Takeovers and Mergers, administered by the Panel on Takeovers and Mergers. The UK law both at the Companies Act 2006 level and at the Code level has complied with the EU Directive on Takeovers. The Directive, as a piece of legislation which regulates cross-border takeovers, has been a significant legislative initiative despite the wide ambit of discretion that it left to Member States as to its implementation.

12.2 Submission to the rulings of the Panel is now backed by sanctions which the Panel has authority to impose under the Companies Act 2006.

12.3 The Panel seeks to protect shareholders, in particular by requiring equal treatment of the shareholders in a target company.

12.4 If 90 per cent of the shares in a company have been acquired, the remainder of the shares may be purchased compulsorily (Companies Act 2006, s 994).

12.5 A minority shareholder may require the offeror to purchase his shares.

12.6 The minority whose shares may be purchased in this way may object to the scheme but will generally receive an unsympathetic hearing.

12.7 Sections 110–111 of the Insolvency Act 1986 provide a method of reconstruction of a company through liquidation.

Exercises

12.1 Whose interests are likely to be damaged by reconstructions of companies? Are they all adequately protected?

11.2 What are the advantages and disadvantages of the methods of reconstructing a company?

11.3 Do shareholders have a duty to others when exercising a vote in a shareholders' meeting?

Case study: Kraft's takeover of Cadbury

In 2009, the US food company Kraft launched a takeover bid for the UK-listed company Cadbury for £10.2 billion. Kraft was the world's second-largest food corporation; Cadbury, founded by John Cadbury in 1824 in Birmingham. had a strong presence in the UK. Kraft had a business plan which focused on its splitting into two companies in 2012; namely, a grocery business and a snacks business; Cadbury would fall into the latter category. Cadbury on its part was instrumental in Kraft's snacks business and therefore quite instrumental for the implementation of the new business plan.

The proposed deal would allow up to $625 million a year to be saved in distribution, marketing and product development costs. Despite Cadbury's British origins and listing, approximately 49 per cent of its shares were owned by US investors. Cadbury resisted the Kraft bid. Sir Roger Carr, the chairman of Cadbury, rejected the £7.45 per share offer as 'unattractive' as it undervalued the company. Furthermore, Cadbury clarified that if it had to, it would prefer to be taken over by another company in the same market, such as Nestlé or Ferrero.

However, Kraft's plans to split into two

companies and to focus on the snacks business, generating economies of scale and additional profits for the company and therefore for its shareholders, emerged as an attractive option for Cadbury's shareholders.

Finally, the deal was struck between the two chairmen on 18 January 2010, at £8.40 per share plus a special 10 pence per share dividend, valuing Cadbury at £11.5 billion. The deal was in the end approved by 71 per cent of Cadbury shareholders a couple of weeks later. On 9 February 2010, Kraft announced that it was planning to close the Somerdale Factory in the UK, with the loss of 400 jobs. The union Unite condemned the decision, as it sent the 'worst possible message' to 6,000 other Cadbury workers in the UK and Ireland; the takeover could have been viewed as placing their jobs at risk as well.

Further reading

Bainbridge, 'Director Primacy in Corporate Takeovers: Preliminary Reflections' (2002) 55 *Stanford Law Review* 791

Hannigan, *Company Law*, 3rd edn (Oxford University Press, 2012)

Sealy and Worthington, *Cases and Materials in Company Law*, 10th edn (Oxford University Press, 2013)

Chapter 13

Insolvency

Key terms

▶ **Dissolution** – the 'death' of a company, the moment at which it ceases to exist.
▶ **Liquidation** – the process of collecting in the assets of a company and paying all the debts.
▶ **Preference** – A preferential creditor is a creditor receiving a preferential right to payment upon the debtor's insolvency. That means that certain creditors are given priority over others usually for the whole amount of their claims but potentially also for a certain value of their claims against the company.
▶ **Cash flow insolvency** – when the company is unable to pay debts exceeding £750 as they fall due.
▶ **Balance sheet insolvency** – when the value of the company's assets is less than the amount of its liabilities.
▶ **A fixed charge** – a charge held over specific and pre-defined assets of the company.
▶ **A floating charge** – a charge held over the general assets of the company.

13.1 Definition of insolvency

English insolvency law deals with the insolvency of firms and individuals in the UK. The important statutes are the Insolvency Act 1986, as amended by the Enterprise Act 2002, as well as the Company Directors Disqualification Act 1986 and the Companies Act 2006. 'Insolvency' is a term which encompasses both companies and individuals; however, when referring to individuals the term 'bankruptcy' is preferably used. The term 'insolvency' is therefore reserved for companies in the relevant literature.

'Insolvency' is defined by the Insolvency Act 1986 as the inability of a company to pay off its debts. More specifically, by section 123(1) and (2):

123 Definition of inability to pay debts
(1) A company is deemed unable to pay its debts—
  (a) if a creditor (by assignment or otherwise) to whom the company is indebted in a sum exceeding £750 then due has served on the company, by leaving it at the company's registered office, a written demand (in the prescribed form) requiring the company to pay the sum so due and the company has for 3 weeks thereafter neglected to pay the sum or to secure or compound for it to the reasonable satisfaction of the creditor, or
  (b) if, in England and Wales, execution or other process issued on a judgment, decree or order of any court in favour of a creditor of the company is returned unsatisfied in whole or in part, or
  (c) if, in Scotland, the induciae of a charge for payment on an extract decree, or an extract registered bond, or an extract registered protest, have expired without payment being made, or
  (d) if, in Northern Ireland, a certificate of unenforceability has been granted in respect of a judgment against the company, or
  (e) if it is proved to the satisfaction of the court that the company is unable to pay its debts as they fall due.
(2) A company is also deemed unable to pay its debts if it is proved to the satisfaction of the court that the value of the company's assets is less than the amount of its liabilities, taking into account its contingent and prospective liabilities.

On the basis of section 123, insolvency may be viewed as having two aspects:

1. Cash flow insolvency under section 123(1) – company unable to pay debts exceeding £750 as they fall due.
2. Balance sheet insolvency under section 123(2) – when the value of the company's assets is less than the amount of its liabilities.

A company may be 'balance sheet insolvent' but still 'cash slow solvent' where its liabilities exceed its assets but the flow of revenue keeps it in a position to service its debt. On the other hand, a company may be 'cash flow insolvent' but 'balance sheet solvent' when it has in its possession property or other illiquid assets which still enable it to cover its liabilities.

13.2 Preferences

One of the most distinctive features of insolvency is that there is a list of actors which should be satisfied at the end of the process in priority from others. A preferential creditor is a creditor receiving a preferential right to payment upon the debtor's insolvency. That means that certain creditors are given priority over others, usually for the whole amount of their claims but potentially also for a certain value of their claims against the company. In the UK, creditors with fixed security are prioritised over the preferential creditors generally. The preferences list will be drafted on the basis of the existence of fixed and floating charges.

A fixed charge is a charge held over specific and pre-defined assets of the company, such as a mortgage held over the company's property. The company cannot sell those assets without the consent of the secured creditor unless it repays the amount secured by that charge. A floating charge is a charge held over the general assets of the company. Those assets may indeed change (such as shares) and the company may use them without the consent of the secured creditor – but only until the charge in question crystallises, ie when the floating charge in question becomes fixed. Crystallisation of a floating charge may be brought with the appointment of an administrative receiver (see Section 13.3.1 below) or the announcement of a winding-up petition (see Section 13.3.4 below). In this framework a 'debenture' is usually the document issued as evidence of the debt or a loan from the bank secured by a charge over the company's assets.

In case of insolvency, priority will be given to the following actors as to the distribution of the assets of the company:

- the holders of a fixed charge
- the expenses of the winding up
- the preferential creditors
- the floating charge creditors
- ordinary creditors
- shareholders.

The preferential creditors will include primarily the employees of the company for their wages and up to 15 September 2003 the revenue authorities; after that date the latter will count as unsecured creditors as they were removed from the preferential creditors' list by the Enterprise Act 2002.

There are similar provisions for the upsetting of a preference, which is the doing of anything by the company which has the effect of putting one of its creditors, or someone who is a surety for or guarantor of one of its debts, in a position which, in the event of the company's going into insolvent liquidation, will be better than the position he would have been in if that thing had not been done (Insolvency Act 1986, s 239(4)(b)). The relevant periods during which preferences may be upset are:

1. two years if the other party to the transaction was connected with the company; or
2. six months if the other party was not connected.

The court has the same discretions here as it has with regard to transactions at an undervalue. In *Re MC Bacon Ltd* [1990] BCLC 324, the court (Chancery Division) gave some guidance on the interpretation of the Insolvency Act sections concerning transactions at an undervalue and preferences. In that case a company had carried on business as a bacon importer and wholesaler. It had been profitable until it had lost its principal customer. The company continued trading on a smaller scale for some time, but eventually it had to go into liquidation. During the time when it was trading on a small scale, a debenture was granted to the bank. At this time the company was either insolvent or nearly so. The validity of the debenture was challenged. Miller J held that the debenture was not invalid as a preference under section 239 of the Insolvency Act 1986, because the directors in granting it had not been motivated by a desire to prefer the bank but only by a desire to avoid the calling in of the overdraft and their wish to continue trading. Neither was the debenture invalid as a transaction at an undervalue under section 238 of the Act, because the giving of the security had neither depleted the company's assets nor diminished their value.

In coming to the conclusion about the preference under section 239, Miller J drew a clear distinction between the 'desire' of the directors and their 'intention'. The section requires 'desire', and this was interpreted as synonymous with motive. If intention had been the test, the debenture would surely have been invalid as the court would have needed only to be satisfied that the directors knew that the bank would be put in a better position than before by the debenture. In view of the introduction of objective tests elsewhere (for example, under section 214 of the Insolvency Act 1986, see below), this extremely subjective approach is perhaps surprising.

13.3 Insolvency procedures

When insolvent, the company can enter into several forms of procedures to satisfy its creditors. These are generally categorised as follows:

- administrative receivership
- administration
- voluntary arrangement
- creditors' voluntary winding up
- winding up by the court/liquidation.

Each of these procedures is discussed in further detail below.

All the aforementioned procedures involve the appointment of a qualified insolvency practitioner to the company. These are respectively:

- an administrative receiver
- an administrator
- the supervisor of a voluntary arrangement
- a liquidator
- a provisional liquidator.

The qualified insolvency practitioners involved are normally accountants or solicitors. They must be authorised by the Secretary of State or by one of the recognised professional bodies before they can act as such.

13.3.1 Administrative receivership

Administrative receivership is a procedure that can be initiated only by a secured creditor with a valid floating charge over the assets of the company. This will usually be the company's bank. This charge must have been created prior to 15 September 2003. Secured creditors with floating charges created after 15 September 2003 will appoint an administrator (see Section 13.3.2 below).

An administrative receiver's role is to achieve the best outcome for the appointing charge holder. The floating charge holder will appoint the administrative receiver so as to crystallise his charge. After the appointment of the receiver, the floating charge will become a fixed one and the charge holder will therefore safeguard his interests against the other creditors, as he will achieve advanced ranking in the list of preferential actors for the repayment of their debts (see Section 13.2 above). The appointment will normally be made if the company is no longer in a position to repay a loan; this will trigger the secured creditor's decision to appoint the receiver, turning his floating charge into a fixed one.

During the receivership the directors' power to take decisions in relation to the company's assets basically ceases. The administrative receiver has the power to sell the company's assets covered by the floating charge and apply the proceeds to the debt owed to the holder of the charge. The administrative receiver may sell the assets piecemeal, or sell the whole business as a going concern to pay off the secured creditor and the costs of the receivership. He is, therefore, the manager of the whole of the company's property. The receiver is not, however, able to deal with the other assets of the company, that is, those which are not covered by a crystallised charge. In reality this means that the control of the business will pass from the directors to the administrative receiver. In addition, the receiver will investigate the conduct of the directors of the company and report his findings to the Secretary of State. However, the receiver cannot appoint or remove directors to or from the board.

The shift in the balance of power and the structure of the company is indeed impressive. It is the administrative receiver who will decide whether trading should continue in order to protect the value of the company s assets. He must convene a meeting with the company's creditors within three months of his appointment to assess the measures taken to satisfy the demands of the secured creditors. During the receivership, the company is not protected against creditor action since the creditors can still ask for the company's winding up (see Section 13.3.4 below). The receivership lasts as long as it is necessary to enable the administrative receiver to deal with the assets subject to the appointer's charge.

13.3.2 Administration

An administrator may be appointed in one of three ways:

- by an administration order of the court
- by the company and its directors or
- by a holder of a floating charge.

Before the Insolvency (Amendment) Rules 2003 (SI 2003/549) came into force on 15 September 2003, the only way into administration was by court order appointing an administrator.

The administrator is appointed to manage the company's affairs, business and property for the benefit of the creditors. He must be an insolvency practitioner with the status of an officer of the court, irrespective of whether he was appointed by the court or not. After his appointment the company is officially 'in administration'.

The main duty of the administrator is to rescue the company as a going concern, or to achieve a better result for the creditors than would be possible if the company was wound up immediately; and if the company is eventually wound up, to realise property for the benefit of secured or preferential creditors.

The administrator will effectively take control of the property of the company and be responsible for its affairs and business; the company's documents should bear his name, as he will replace the directors in the running and management of business. The management of the company should not exercise any power without the consent and the approval of the administrator who is in a position to investigate their conduct. The administrator will owe a duty to the body of creditors and the court; therefore he can be removed from his position by the creditors.

During the administration there can be no legal proceedings against the company unless the administrator or the court has granted permission, and any pending winding-up petitions will be suspended. An interim moratorium period is effectively established during which no steps can be taken by a creditor against the company to enforce security or to repossess its assets; a creditor landlord cannot exercise a right of forfeiture during this period and no legal process may be initiated against the company unless the court permits it. In this sense the company is protected against creditor action during administration. The administration will come to an end after 12 months unless extended by the creditors or by the court.

13.3.3 Voluntary arrangement

This is a scheme for making arrangements with creditors which will be legally binding on all creditors, even if not all of them agree. This has the advantage that where a company has sensible plans which are likely to avoid liquidation, those plans cannot be upset by a single creditor insisting on the liquidation of the company. The disadvantage of the scheme under the Insolvency Act 1986 is that the scheme may not be approved for some weeks and there is nothing, until creditor approval is gained, to prevent such liquidation from occurring. For this reason section 1A of and Schedule 1A to the Insolvency Act 1986, which came into force on 1 January 2003, enable an 'eligible company' (basically, a small company) to obtain a moratorium on creditor action while a proposal for a voluntary arrangement is considered.

13.3.3(a) Proposal

The first step towards approval of an arrangement is a proposal to the company and the creditors. The proposal is made by the directors unless the company is in administration or liquidation, when it is made by the administrator or liquidator (Insolvency Act 1986, s 1). A receiver or an administrative receiver is not empowered to propose a voluntary arrangement. The arrangement must be supervised by a qualified insolvency practitioner – the supervisor of the voluntary agreement.

The most likely proposals will be the acceptance by each creditor of a percentage of its claim, or a moratorium on enforcement of claims for a certain period, a freezing of the interest rate or the company's debt, its repayment in monthly instalments, or a writing off of a proportion of the debt, always on the basis of a consensual agreement with the creditors. Therefore, it may involve a voluntary restructuring of the company's debts and a roll over of its obligations to a latest date, further enabling the company to meet its obligations and avoid liquidation. Creditors will support a voluntary agreement when the alternative is liquidation with the potential of little or no return to them.

13.3.3(b) The involvement of the court

If the supervisor of the scheme is someone other than the liquidator or administrator, he must report to the court within 28 days whether the proposal should be considered and, if so, the dates and times when he would call the relevant meetings (Insolvency Act 1986, s 2(2)). He is then obliged to summon those meetings.

13.3.3(c) Contents of the proposal

The rules lay down the matters which must be set out in the proposal. As might be expected, the company's assets and liabilities must be set out in detail, as must the proposed arrangement itself.

13.3.3(d) Meetings

Meetings of the company members and the creditors must be summoned. For the members' meeting, the requisite majority for any resolution is more than one-half of the members present in person or by proxy and voting (Insolvency Rules 1986, r 1.20(1)).

As far as the creditors' meeting is concerned, there are two requisite majorities: (i) more than 75 per cent for the resolution to pass any proposal or any modification of the proposal, and (ii) more than 50 per cent for other resolutions. The percentages are of votes of creditors present in person or by proxy and voting. There are detailed rules by which certain votes must be ignored in order to prevent the majorities being made up of persons connected with the company. If the arrangement is approved, it binds everyone who was entitled to have notice of and vote at the meeting.

13.3.3(e) Challenges

An arrangement may be challenged on the grounds of unfair prejudice or material irregularity at either of the meetings mentioned in Section 13.3.3(d) above (Insolvency Act 1986, s 6(1)).

13.3.4　Voluntary winding up by members or creditors

13.3.4(a)　Two types of voluntary winding up

The voluntary winding up may be one of two types:

1. *Voluntary winding up by members when the company is still solvent.* A company may be wound up voluntarily when the members resolve by special resolution to wind it up. If the directors, after a full investigation, believe that the company will be able to pay its debts in full (with interest) within 12 months from the commencement of the winding up, the liquidation is a 'members' voluntary winding up' (Insolvency Act 1986, s 89). Therefore, to initiate a voluntary winding up by members, the company needs to have passed a special resolution and to have produced a statutory declaration of solvency, that is, a declaration signed by the directors confirming that the company will pay back its creditors in 12 months. It is essentially a voluntary procedure to wind up the affairs of a solvent company. The reasons behind that may vary from the members' intention to retire and withdraw from business life altogether, to a decision to re-orientate the business in a different direction, the winding up of the company therefore being necessary to disengage it from one project and re-invest in another.

2. *Voluntary winding up by creditors when the company is insolvent.* If no declaration of solvency is made, the liquidation becomes a creditors' voluntary winding up. In this case a creditors' meeting must be summoned which the liquidator must attend, giving a report on any exercise of his powers. To initiate a voluntary winding up by creditors, the company needs to have passed an extraordinary resolution that it cannot, by reason of its liabilities, continue its business and that it is advisable to wind it up (Insolvency Act 1986, s 84). The company calls the creditors' meeting because it cannot continue its business due to the size of its liabilities.

Section 107 of the 1986 Act provides that in a voluntary winding up, the property of the company is to be applied, first, in paying the preferential debts, then in satisfaction of its liabilities. Lastly, it is to be distributed among the members according to their rights and interests as determined by the articles.

The directors of the company may petition for its winding up, as may a receiver. The Secretary of State may also petition for a winding up if it appears that it may be in the public interest to do so (Insolvency Act 1986, s 124A).

13.3.4(b)　The liquidator

With the commencement of the winding up of the company, the directors cease to control its affairs and the liquidator manages the company with a view to collecting all the assets of the company. The winding up will normally commence at the time of the presentation of the petition for winding up. However, where a resolution for voluntary winding up has been passed, the date of the resolution will (in the absence of fraud or mistake) be the relevant date (Insolvency Act 1986, s 129).

The liquidator must be an insolvency practitioner (Insolvency Act 1986, s 390(1)). His eventual aim will be to pay the costs of the winding up, pay the debts of the company and distribute any surplus among the members (Insolvency Act 1986, ss 107 and 143). He has a considerable array of powers conferred for this purpose.

In a winding up by the court, the liquidator is subject to the control of the court. All liquidators are subject to substantial duties, both equitable and statutory.

If, during a members' voluntary winding up, the liquidator forms the opinion that the company will be unable to pay its debts within the period specified in the directors' declaration of solvency, he is obliged to summon a creditors' meeting, and from the date of that meeting the liquidation becomes a creditors' voluntary winding up (Insolvency Act 1986, ss 95 and 96).

13.3.4(c) Dissolution

A company ceases to exist when it is dissolved. On completion of a voluntary winding up, the liquidator presents his final accounts to meetings of the company's creditors and/or members. Within a week after that has been done, the liquidator must send copies of the accounts and a return of the holdings of the meetings to the Registrar of Companies. The Registrar registers them, and the company is normally deemed to be dissolved three months later (Insolvency Act 1986, ss 94 and 205).

Sections 201 and 205 of the 1986 Act contain provisions which permit the delaying of dissolution on the application of an interested party. By section 651, the court has a discretion to declare a dissolution void at any time within 12 years. Section 652 provides that dissolution does not affect the liability of officers and members of the company to be sued.

13.3.5 Winding up by the court – compulsory liquidation

A company will cease to exist by being liquidated and struck off the register of companies. The assets of the company will be collected in and realised, its liabilities discharged, and if there is a net surplus this will be distributed to the persons entitled to it.

A company may be wound up by the court or voluntarily by the members. A company may be wound up by the court if:

1. the company has by special resolution resolved that the company should be wound up by the court;
2. the company was originally registered as a public company but has not been issued with a certificate that it satisfies the minimum capital requirement, and more than a year has passed since its registration;
3. it is an old public company within the meaning of the Consequential Provisions Act 1985;
4. the company does not commence its business within a year from its incorporation, or suspends its business for a whole year;
5. the number of members is reduced below two (unless the company converts itself into a single member company in accordance with the Companies (Single Member Private Limited Companies) Regulations 1992 (SI 1992/1699));
6. the company is unable to pay its debts;
7. the court is of opinion that it is just and equitable to wind up the company.

The court will wind up a company after the successful presentation of a winding-up petition, which may be presented by the company, the directors, any creditor or any person liable to contribute to the assets of the company in the event of a winding up (contributory), the supervisor of a voluntary arrangement or in some circumstances by a receiver. All shareholders are contributories, even if they have no further money to pay on their shares and are not actually liable to contribute to the assets of the company.

A member's petition will succeed only if the member can show that he has a tangible interest in the winding up. He must show that he would gain an advantage, or avoid or minimise a disadvantage.

A creditor, contributory, the Official Receiver or the Department for Business, Innovation and Skills may seek a compulsory winding-up order even if the company is in voluntary liquidation.

13.3.5(a) Liquidator

The liquidator will be in a fiduciary relationship with the company; therefore he should not be found to have a conflict of interests and make any unauthorised profit. He will also be able to be found liable for negligence, especially during the collection and realisation of the company's assets. Importantly, his duties are owed to the company, and he is deemed to act as its agent; this further means that he is in a position to represent and bind the company. Any contracts entered into and signed by the liquidator will bind the company as if signed and agreed upon by the directors.

The liquidator's principal aims are to wind up the company, to collect and realise its assets, to make the distributions to creditors and return any surplus to the shareholders. During liquidation, he largely replaces the directors as regards the nature and extent of these functions and duties.

13.3.5(b) Dissolution

A company ceases to exist when it is dissolved. This can happen only when its affairs are completely wound up.

In a winding up by the court, the liquidator sends notice of the final meeting of creditors and vacation of office by him to the Registrar of Companies, the notice is registered and the company is normally dissolved at the end of the period of three months from the date of registration.

13.4 Directors' duties and insolvency

The directors of an insolvent company have a duty to protect creditors' interests. As mentioned in Section 13.3 above, their conduct is subject to investigation by an administrator, an administrative receiver and a liquidator. The liquidator will report to BIS and on the basis of their findings the directors may be disqualified (see Chapter 9 for disqualification of directors).

The types of actions or claims that may be brought against the directors are for:

1. misfeasance;
2. fraudulent trading;
3. wrongful trading;
4. transactions at an undervalue;
5. transactions defrauding creditors;
6. illegal distributions;

7. preferences; and
8. extortionate credit transactions.

Each of these is examined in further detail below.

13.4.1 Misfeasance

Section 212 of the Insolvency Act 1986 may be used as the legal basis for actions brought by liquidators against directors for a breach of duty to the company. That would include breaches both of fiduciary duties (see Section 9.2 above) and duties of care and skill (see Section 9.3 above). Therefore, section 212 will cover a very wide range of directorial actions as it will encompass all the statutory breaches of duty on the part of directors. Basically, the liquidator will replace the shareholders as the party appropriate to raise such an action, since the company is in liquidation and it cannot take any decision by itself. The directors are under the monitoring and potential investigation of the liquidator, who can now exercise the powers reserved exclusively to the shareholders in the pre-liquidation period. In this framework the court may order any director in breach of duty to make a contribution to the assets of the company.

Section 212 of the Insolvency Act 1986 thus provides a means by which any person concerned in the management of a company may be made liable if it can be shown that he has 'misapplied or retained, or become accountable for, any money or other property of the company, or been guilty of any misfeasance or breach of any fiduciary or other duty in relation to the company' (s 212(1)).

This section was given a wide interpretation by Hoffman LJ in *Re D'Jan of London Ltd* [1993] BCC 646, where he held a director liable for a breach of the duty of skill and care, using as a standard that imposed in respect of wrongful trading (see Section 13.4.3 below).

13.4.2 Fraudulent trading

Fraudulent trading is actionable both as a civil offence (Insolvency Act 1986, s 213) and as a criminal offence (Companies Act 2006, s 993). In both cases it is necessary to establish trading with 'intent to defraud'. This requires the court to find that the directors were acting dishonestly, not just that they were acting unreasonably (*Re L Todd (Swanscombe) Ltd* [1990] BCC 125). The difficulty of establishing this has made this remedy little used. It is wider than wrongful trading (see Section 13.4.3 below), however, in that it is available against 'any persons who were knowingly parties to the carrying on of the business' of the company. For a comprehensive discussion of the law concerning fraudulent trading, see *R v Smith* [1996] 2 BCLC 109. It basically refers to carrying on trading with the intention to defraud the creditors or for a fraudulent purpose.

Only a liquidator may apply for the civil remedy, but criminal proceedings may be instituted for fraudulent trading outside the insolvency context, regardless of whether a company is wound up or not. The court has power when awarding the civil remedy to make an order that the respondent 'make such contribution (if any) to the company's assets as the court thinks proper'.

13.4.3 Wrongful trading

In essence, wrongful trading consists of continuing to trade when the company is known to be insolvent. The remedy is a civil claim. It may, if successful, lead to the same order for a contribution as under the fraudulent trading provisions (see Section 13.4.2 above).

In the case of wrongful trading, an application may be made only by the liquidator when the company has gone into an insolvent liquidation (Insolvency Act 1986, s 214(2)), that is, liquidation at a time when its assets are insufficient for the payment of its debts, other liabilities and the expenses of its winding up. An application can be made only against a director or shadow director. In *R v Farmizer (Products) Ltd* [1995] 2 BCLC 462, it was held that a claim under section 214 was subject to section 991 of the Limitation Act 1980, which imposes a six-year limitation period for bringing a claim. Time runs from when the company goes into insolvent liquidation.

13.4.3(a) Standard of knowledge and skill expected of a director

The contrast with fraudulent trading (see Section 13.4.2 above) is clear when it is realised that with regard to wrongful trading the director is judged by what he ought to have known as well as by what he did know, and there is no question of having to establish dishonesty. Civil liability could arise without proof of fraud or dishonesty, in contrast to fraudulent trading. Thus, wrongful trading occurs when a director, at some time prior to the commencement of the winding up, continues to trade, when he knows, or ought to have concluded, that there is no reasonable prospect that the company will avoid going into insolvent liquidation. There is a defence: the relevant person escapes where, by the standard of the 'reasonably diligent person', he satisfies the court that he took every step with a view to minimising the potential loss to the company's creditors after he had the first knowledge of the insolvent state of the company.

The standard of knowledge and skill required of a director is a cumulative blend of the subjective and objective, and includes:

1. the general knowledge, skill and experience that may reasonably be expected of a person carrying out the same functions as are carried out by that director in relation to the company; and
2. the general knowledge, skill and experience that director has (Insolvency Act 1986, s 214(5)).

The thinking of the courts was well explained by Knox J in *Produce Marketing Consortium Ltd* [1989] 1 WLR 745:

> It is evident that Parliament intended to widen the scope of legislation under which directors who trade on when the company is insolvent may in appropriate circumstances be required to make a contribution to [a company's creditors] ... [T]he test to be applied by the Court has become one under which the director in question is to be judged by the standards of what can reasonably be expected of a person fulfilling his functions and showing reasonable diligence in doing so ... The general knowledge, skill and experience postulated will be much less extensive in a small company in a modest way of business with simple accounting procedures and equipment than it will be in a large company with sophisticated procedures. Nevertheless certain minimum standards are assumed to be attained ... [Wrongful trading is] an enhanced version of the right which any company would have to sue its directors for breach of duty – enhanced in the sense that the standard of knowledge, skill and experience required is made objective.

Although much academic discussion has focused on wrongful trading, it is not used frequently by practitioners, who usually consider that the money which will be clawed back will not be worth the time and effort involved in proceedings.

13.4.4 Transactions at an undervalue

An administrator or a liquidator may apply to the court where the company has entered into a transaction at an undervalue (Insolvency Act 1986, s 238). The court has an unfettered discretion to make such order as it thinks fit. The Act lays down the time limits within which the transaction must have occurred for it to be vulnerable to this application (s 238). So far as a company going directly into liquidation is concerned, these periods are: (i) the period counted back from the date of the resolution to wind up, or (ii) the date of the presentation of the winding-up petition. The liquidator must establish that at the time of the transaction the company was unable to pay its debts.

Under section 241 the court has a wide discretion to make orders to transfer property in order to correct the situation, but may not affect the rights of a bona fide purchaser of property. This latter restriction was clarified and extended by the Insolvency (No 2) Act 1994, which came into force on 26 July 1994 in relation to interests acquired and benefits received by third party purchasers after that date. It applies both to transactions at an undervalue and to preferences (see Section 13.4.7 below), and protects a subsequent purchaser if he has acted in good faith for value. This extends protection to those who knew that there had been a transaction at an undervalue or a preference at some time but nevertheless acted in good faith at the time of the transaction. However, where the purchaser has knowledge both of the preference or undervalue transaction and 'relevant proceedings', there is a rebuttable presumption that the purchaser is not acting in good faith. Lack of good faith is also presumed where the subsequent purchaser is connected with or is an associate of the company. 'Relevant proceedings' means an administration or a liquidation within certain time-scales set out in the Act.

13.4.5 Transaction defrauding creditors

A transaction at an undervalue may also be challenged under section 423 of the Insolvency Act 1986. Under this provision there are no time limits and the company need not be in liquidation or even insolvent. It is necessary to show that the transaction was entered into for the purpose of putting assets beyond the reach of a creditor or potential creditor, or of prejudicing the interests of such a person. In *Arbuthnot Leasing International Ltd v Havelet Leasing Ltd (No 2)* [1990] BCC 636, a company's business and assets had been transferred on legal advice to an off-the-shelf company shortly before it went into receivership. The court ordered the reversal of the transaction. In *Chohan v Saggar and Another* [1994] 1 BCLC 706, the court held that the proper purpose of an order under section 423 was both to restore the position to what it would have been if the transaction had not been entered into and to protect the interests of the victims of the transaction.

13.4.6 Illegal distributions

Distributions are covered by Part 23 of the Companies Act 2006 (ss 829–853). Under section 830(1), a company may only make a distribution out of profits available for the purpose. Therefore, when a distribution to shareholders has been made at a time when the company has insufficient profits to make the distribution, that distribution may be challenged and a request can be made for repayment of the monies.

In addition, section 847 of the 2006 Act provides:

847 Consequences of unlawful distribution

(1) This section applies where a distribution, or part of one, made by a company to one of its members is made in contravention of this Part.

(2) If at the time of the distribution the member knows or has reasonable grounds for believing that it is so made, he is liable—

(a) to repay it (or that part of it, as the case may be) to the company, or

(b) in the case of a distribution made otherwise than in cash, to pay the company a sum equal to the value of the distribution (or part) at that time.

Therefore, if at the time of the distribution the member knows or has reasonable grounds for believing that a distribution was unlawful, he is liable to repay it to the company.

13.4.7 Preferences

One of the main objectives of winding up is to ensure that the creditors will be treated on an equal basis. The court is particularly vigilant about that, and can exercise its powers under section 239 of the Insolvency Act 1986 to set aside transactions entered by the company during the period of insolvency which have the effect of preferring a creditor ahead of others. The outcome of the agreement complained against on the basis of preference is that a creditor is now in a better place than he would have been had the agreement not taken place.

13.4.8 Extortionate credit transactions

Section 244 of the Insolvency Act 1986 permits companies to set aside credit transactions which are deemed to be extortionate. This can occur only when the company is in liquidation or administration. The transaction must have been entered into at any time during the three-year period ending with the day on which an administrator was appointed or the day on which the company goes into liquidation (either the date on which the winding-up resolution is passed or the date on which a winding-up order is granted).

A credit transaction is extortionate if it either:

1. requires grossly exorbitant payments to be made, whether unconditionally or only in certain events in exchange for credit; or
2. it grossly contravenes ordinary principles of fair dealing.

The court must, however, take account of the risk that was taken by the creditor in providing credit. This may be important, as companies in this situation may have been bad risks even some considerable time previously.

The court may set such an agreement aside in whole or in part, or vary the terms.

13.4.9 The destination of the money

Assets recovered by the liquidator in connection with transactions at an undervalue, voidable preferences, extortionate credit transactions, wrongful and fraudulent trading, and misfeasance proceedings under section 212 of the Insolvency Act 1986 are paid into the general pool of the company's assets. They are not available for the payment of particular creditors. However, where a floating charge is invalidated, the effect will often be to give priority to another charge which has been validly created over the same assets (*Capital Finance Co Ltd v Stokes* [1968] 1 All ER 573).

13.5 Disqualification of directors

A disqualification order is made by the court under the Company Directors Disqualification Act 1986 (see further Chapter 9). The Act applies not only to de jure directors, but also to de facto directors and to shadow directors. The individual in question will be disqualified from acting as a director of a company, taking part, directly or indirectly, in the formation or management of a company, being a liquidator or an administrator of a company, or a receiver and manager of a company's property. The period of disqualification will vary between two and 15 years, during which the person in question cannot exercise any of the aforementioned duties or perform in any of the aforementioned capacities. The directors are investigated by the liquidator and on the basis of his report the Secretary of State might find it appropriate to seek a disqualification order.

The most usual types of directorial behaviour that lead to disqualification are:

- failure to keep proper accounting records;
- failure to cooperate with or to facilitate the actions of insolvency practitioners in the conduct of their duties;
- continuing to trade to the detriment of the creditors' interests.

Summary

13.1 Voluntary arrangements are schemes for coming to an arrangement with creditors. By a majority agreeing to the scheme, it becomes binding on all the creditors. The purpose is to prevent a minority of creditors from precipitating a liquidation where there is a hope that the company can be saved.

13.2 A company may be wound up by a court or by a voluntary creditors' or members' winding up. The last course is available only where the company is solvent.

13.3 So far as the distribution of property is concerned, holders of fixed charges have a right to enforce their security. After that, other property is distributed as follows:

(a) for the proper expenses of the winding up;
(b) to preferential creditors, who take priority over floating chargeholders where there is not enough money to satisfy them in full;
(c) to creditors with floating charges by way of security;
(d) to ordinary creditors; and
(e) to members.

Summary cont'd

13.4 There are a number of provisions for avoiding transactions which took place before the liquidation. In certain circumstances the following may be avoided:

(a) transactions at an undervalue;
(b) preferences;
(c) extortionate credit transactions; and
(d) floating charges.

13.5 Anyone may be liable to criminal or civil penalties if they have been involved in fraudulent trading. Directors or shadow directors may be liable for wrongful trading if they continued to trade when they knew or ought to have concluded that the company was insolvent.

Exercises

13.1 Describe the roles of liquidators and receivers.

13.2 Consider the possible liabilities of directors on a winding up of a company. In what circumstances and over what time-scale may transactions prior to a liquidation be avoided?

Further reading

Hannigan, *Company Law*, 3rd edn (Oxford University Press, 2012)

Sealy and Worthington, *Cases and Materials in Company Law*, 10th edn (Oxford University Press, 2013)

Chapter 14

Multinational companies

Key terms

▶ **Multinational companies** – a group of companies linked by shared shareholders or contractual arrangements in a number of countries.

▶ **Transnational companies** – a group of companies linked by shared shareholders or contractual arrangements in a number of countries where the management of the company arranges the business in a global context.

▶ **Enterprises** – groups of companies which manage their affairs together.

14.1 Groups of companies

14.1.1 A group of companies as one entity

We have seen how shareholders are separate from the company (see *Salomon v Salomon* (Section 1.5)). In this chapter we consider whether companies can by linked into a group. Legally, each company is a separate entity; however, they may be linked either by having the same shareholders or directors or by contractual arrangements.

The courts have sometimes had to make difficult decisions about the circumstances in which a group of companies is to be regarded as one entity. Different jurisdictions have reached different answers. In UK case law there is no formal or informal recognition of group interests.

Do companies with a significant cross-shareholding have a special relationship? In the UK, while for many tax and accounting purposes groups of companies are treated as one unit, the courts are reluctant to admit the reality of interrelated companies acting in any way other than as a number of separate entities tied together by their relationship as significant shareholders in each other. Thus in *Scottish Co-operative Wholesale Society Ltd v Meyer* [1959] AC 324, three directors of a subsidiary company were also directors of the parent company. Lord Denning said:

> So long as the interests of all concerned were in harmony, there was no difficulty. The nominee directors could do their duty by both companies without embarrassment. But, so soon as the interests of the two companies were in conflict, the nominee directors were placed in an impossible position. It is plain that, in the circumstances, these three gentlemen could not do their duty by both companies, and they did not do so. They put their duty to the co-operative society above their duty to the textile company …

The approach of the UK courts is epitomised by that of Templeman LJ in *Re Southard & Co Ltd* [1979] 3 All ER 556:

> English company law possesses some curious features, which may generate curious results. A parent company may spawn a number of subsidiary companies, all controlled directly or indirectly by the shareholders of the parent company. If one of the subsidiary companies, to change the metaphor, turns out to be the runt of the litter and declines into insolvency to the dismay of its creditors, the parent company and the other subsidiary companies may prosper to the joy of the shareholders without any liability for the debts of the insolvent subsidiary.

The approach is confirmed by the cavalier treatment by the courts of 'letters of comfort'. Thus in *Re Augustus Barnett & Son Ltd* [1986] BCLC 170, the company was a wholly owned subsidiary of a Spanish company. The subsidiary traded at a loss for some time, but the parent company repeatedly issued statements that it would continue to support the subsidiary. Some of the statements were made in letters written to the subsidiary's auditors and published in the subsidiary's annual accounts for three successive years. Later the parent company allowed the subsidiary to go into liquidation and failed to provide any financial support to pay off the debts of the subsidiary. In deciding that this did not constitute fraudulent trading on the part of the parent company, Hoffman J accepted that the assurances of the parent were without legal effect.

The treatment of groups in the UK is examined in further detail in Section 14.1.5 below.

14.1.2   EU law and concepts of 'undertaking' or 'enterprise'

The 'economic unit' approach is exemplified by a number of cases concerning Article 85 of the EEC Treaty of Rome (later Article 81 of the Treaty establishing the European Community (TEC) and now Article 101 of the Treaty on the Functioning of the European Union (TFEU)) which tried to control unfair competition by, amongst other things, outlawing 'agreements between undertakings, decisions by associations of undertakings' the object or effect of which is distortion of competition. It has become necessary on occasion to determine the nature of an 'undertaking', and it is clear that the EU (through the European Court of Justice (ECJ)) will not adopt the somewhat simplistic approach of the UK courts and will investigate the reality of the economic unit rather than relying on the technical boundaries drawn by incorporation. Thus the definition includes non profit-making associations, and the reality of the parent–subsidiary relationship will always be investigated by the Court. In *Centrafarm BV et Adriaan de Peijper v Sterling Drug Inc* (Case 15/74) [1974] ECR 1147, the ECJ said:

> Article 85 [now Art 101 TFEU], however, is not concerned with agreements or concerted practices between undertakings belonging to the same concern and having the status of parent and subsidiary, if the undertakings form an economic unit within which the subsidiary has no real freedom to determine its course of action on the market, and if the agreements or practices are concerned merely with the internal allocation of tasks as between undertakings.

Similarly, in *Viho Europe BV v Commission of the European Communities (supported by Parker Pen Ltd, Intervener)* (1996) *The Times*, 9 December, (92/426/EEC of 15 July 1992), the ECJ held that where a company and its subsidiaries formed a single economic unit, Article 85 EEC (now Art 101 TFEU) did not apply. The subsidiaries enjoyed no autonomy and were obliged to follow the instructions of the parent company.

14.1.3   German law

In Germany there is a law which links companies together making a group of companies. This German law has been for some time on a statutory footing. It is this *Konzernrecht* which formed the model for the draft EC Ninth Directive on Company Law (now defunct). The *Konzernrecht* is applicable only to stock corporations, although a vigorous body of developing law applies it to other companies.

Under this law a distinction is made between contractual and de facto groups of companies. In contractual groups, the creditors of the subsidiary are protected by a legal obligation of the parent towards the subsidiary to make good any losses at the end of the year. Shareholders other than the parent company have a right to periodic compensation payments and must be offered the opportunity of selling their shares to the parent at a reasonable price. They have a right to an annual dividend which is calculated according to:

1. the value of their shares at the time of the formation of the contractual group; and
2. the likelihood of such dividends without the formation of the group.

The board of the subsidiary has to give a report on all transactions, measures and omissions during the past year which result from its membership of the group. The conclusion of the contract between members of the group is encouraged by the ability of the parent company to induce the subsidiary to act against its own interests, thus legitimising the concept of the interests of the group as a whole. However, the concept has been little used. Hopt (Schmittoff and Wooldridge (eds), *Groups of Companies* (Sweet & Maxwell 1991)) observed that most groups have chosen 'cohabitation without marriage certificates'.

Despite problems experienced in the operation of the German law, the draft proposal for an EC Ninth Company Law Directive took a similar route. The proposal would have affected groups of companies and public limited companies controlled by any other undertaking (whether or not that undertaking was itself a company). The proposal was that there should be a harmonised structure for the 'unified management' of groups of such companies and undertakings. Under the proposal, rules would be laid down for the conduct of groups which were not managed on a 'unified' basis. Unless an undertaking which exercised a dominant interest over a public limited company formalised its relationship and provided for some prescribed form of 'unified' management', it would be liable for any losses suffered by a dependent company, provided the losses could be traced to the exercise of the influence or to action which was contrary to the dependent company's interest. Although loosely based on the German *Konzernrecht*, the proposal would have been less effective. Not only did it rely on a satisfactory definition of 'dominance' or 'control' being found, it also failed to give adequate incentives to persuade companies to adopt a formal 'unified management' approach. The German law on which it was based, as mentioned above, permits a parent company to induce a subsidiary to act against its own interests if the contractual 'unified management' approach is adopted.

14.1.4 Approaches in the United States of America

In the USA it is recognised that dominant shareholders have fiduciary duties towards both the company and other shareholders. Thus dominant shareholders are distinguished from other shareholders. The latter, as in the UK, are permitted to vote their shares according to their own selfish interests. In *Southern Pacific Co v Bogert* (1919) 250 US 483, the Supreme Court stated:

> The rule of corporation law and of equity invoked is well settled and has been often applied. The majority has the right to control; but when it does so, it occupies a fiduciary relation toward the minority, as much so as the corporation itself or its officers or directors.

The principle is widely, if not unanimously, accepted by States. However, the implications of the doctrine vary widely. Two States have adopted by legislation a general principle which authorises contracts between parent and subsidiary companies subject to certain conditions of fairness and procedural requirements for adoption or ratification. In other States a voluminous body of case law is evidence of the different and uncertain effects of the doctrine. Part V of the American Law Institute's Principles of Corporate Governance: Analysis and Recommendations deals with the duties of dominating shareholders. Ability to control over 25 per cent of the voting equity would give rise to a presumption of control. It is a strange feature of the definition of 'control' that it focuses solely on control of shareholder votes. In Tentative Draft No 5, 'control' is defined as:

> the power directly or indirectly, either alone or pursuant to an arrangement or understanding with one or more other persons, to exercise a controlling influence over the management or policies of a business organization through the ownership of equity interests, through one or more intermediary persons, by contract or otherwise.

Transactions between a dominating shareholder and the corporation are valid if:

1. the transaction is fair to the corporation when entered into; or
2. the transaction is authorised or ratified by disinterested shareholders, following disclosure concerning the conflict of interest and the transaction, and does not constitute a waste of corporate assets at the time of the shareholder transaction.

If the transaction is ratified according to 2. above, the burden of proving unfairness is on the challenging party. Otherwise it is for the dominant shareholder to prove the fairness of the transaction. A transaction is 'fair' if it falls 'within a range of reasonableness'.

Conflicting duties of loyalty owed by directors who sit on boards of parents and subsidiaries are also judged on a 'fairness' scale: 'In the absence of total abstention of an independent negotiating structure, common directors must determine what is best for both parent and subsidiary.' This rule is intended to reflect the decision in *Jones v HF Ahmanson & Co* (1993) 1 Cal 3d, in which a majority of shareholders had enhanced their investments in a scheme which was not open to the minority investors. Delivering the judgment of the Supreme Court of California, Chief Justice Roger Traynor determined that the conduct of the majority had been unfair. Although he emphasised the duty of the majority towards the corporation as well as to minority shareholders, in fact the relevant opportunity would not have been available to the corporation so that, on the facts, only the majority's duty to the minority was an issue. What is interesting, and may provide further insight into a way forward, is that the minority did not suffer a loss but were denied an opportunity which was available exclusively to the majority.

14.1.5 In the United Kingdom

14.1.5(a) Lifting the veil of incorporation

In many circumstances, statutes dictate where groups should act as if they were one enterprise (see Section 7.6.8: group accounts). Where there are no statutory rules, the principles that will guide the court are to be found in *Smith, Stone & Knight v Birmingham Corporation* [1939] 4 All ER 116. Atkinson J reviewed previous cases on the point and said:

I find six points which were deemed relevant for the determination of the question: Who was really carrying on the business? In all the cases, the question was whether the company, an English company here, could be taxed in respect of all the profits made by some other company, being carried on elsewhere. The first point was: Were the profits treated as the profits of the company? – when I say 'the company' I mean the parent company – secondly, were the persons conducting the business appointed by the parent company? Thirdly, was the company the head and brain of the trading venture? Fourthly, did the company govern the adventure, decide what should be done and what capital should be embarked on the venture? Fifthly, did the company make the profits by its skill and direction? Sixthly, was the company in effectual and constant control?

Where these questions can be answered in the affirmative, it is likely that the group will be treated as a single entity. However, the answers to these questions can provide only guidelines and the court will determine each case according to its own facts and the context in which the case arises.

The background to such cases can be varied. One involved the determination of the residence of a company registered in Kenya but managed by a parent in the UK. The company was held to be resident in the UK (*Unit Construction Co v Bullock* [1960] AC 351). In *Firestone Tyre Co v Llewellin* [1957] 1 WLR 464, an English subsidiary was held to be the means whereby the American parent company traded in the UK. A similar decision was arrived at in *DHN Food Distributors v Tower Hamlets Borough Council* [1976] 1 WLR 852. In *Lonrho v Shell Petroleum* [1980] 1 WLR 627, it was decided that documents could not be regarded as in the 'power' of a parent company when they were in fact held by a subsidiary. In *National Dock Labour Board v Pinn & Wheeler Ltd & Others* [1989] BCLC 647, the court emphasised that it is only in 'special circumstances which indicate that there is a mere façade concealing the true facts that it is appropriate to pierce the corporate veil'. Similarly, the rule in *Salomon* (Section 1.5) was approved and relied on in *JH Rayner (Mincing Lane) Ltd v Department of Trade and Industry (Court of Appeal Judgment)* [1988] 3 WLR 1033. This approach was upheld by the House of Lords in *Maclaine Watson & Co v DTI (International Tin Council)* [1990] BCLC 102 and applied in *Adams v Cape Industries PLC* [1990] BCLC 479. *Adams v Cape Industries* provides a particularly stark example of the application of the *Salomon* principle. Several hundred employees of the group headed by Cape Industries had been awarded damages for injuries received as a result of exposure to asbestos dust. The injuries had been received in the course of their employment. The damages had been awarded in a Texan court. The English Court of Appeal held that the awards could not be enforced against Cape, even though one of the defendants was a subsidiary of Cape and there was evidence that the group had been restructured so as to avoid liability. Slade J said:

> Our law, for better or worse, recognises the creation of subsidiary companies, which, though in one sense the creation of their parent companies, will nevertheless under the general law fall to be treated as separate legal entities with all the rights and liabilities which would normally attach to separate legal entities … We do not accept as a matter of law that the court is entitled to lift the corporate veil as against a defendant company which is the member of a corporate group merely because the corporate structure has been used so as to ensure that the legal liability (if any) in respect of particular future activities of the group … will fall on another member of the group rather than the defendant company. Whether or not this is desirable, the right to use a corporate structure in this way is inherent in our law.

A similar approach was taken in *Re Polly Peck International Plc (in administration)* [1996] 2 All ER 433, where the court held that where companies were insolvent, the separate legal existence of each within the group became more, not less, important. The courts consistently repeat the finding in *Cape* that the veil of incorporation cannot be lifted 'simply because the consequences of not doing so are unfair or even absurd' (*Graphical Paper and Media Union v Derry Print and Another* [2002] IRLR 380; see also *Trustor AB v Smallbone and Others (No 2)* [2001] 3 All ER 987).

14.1.5(b) Agency and trust

Other cases that are often cited on this issue are sometimes put into categories such as 'agency' or 'trust' cases. This can give the impression that the reason for lifting the corporate veil in those cases was that the court made a finding that an agency or trust relationship had developed between the company in question and some other body. In fact it may well be that, as in the *Malyon* (*Malyon v Plummer* [1963] 2 All ER 344) and *Lee* (*Lee v Lee's Air Farming* [1916] AC 12) cases, the interests of justice required the court to ignore the corporate veil. In both of those cases the judges assessed widows' entitlements without any reference to the doctrine of separate company personality. This was for the benefit of the widows but against doctrinal concepts.

The finding of agency or trust may be a convenient excuse for a refusal to follow the rule in *Salomon*. Thus, in *Abbey Malvern Wells v Minister of Local Government* [1951] Ch 728, the company owned a school which was managed by a board of trustees who were bound by the terms of the trust to use the assets of the company for educational purposes. The company applied to the Minister for Town and Country Planning for a ruling that the land they held was exempt from development charges because it was held for charitable (educational in this case) purposes. The Minister ruled against the company, but on appeal from that decision the court held:

1. that the land was occupied by the company for the educational purposes of the school;
2. that the trusts in the trust deed were charitable;
3. that the company was controlled by trustees who were bound by the trust deed;
4. thus the property and assets of the company could only be applied to the charitable purposes of the trust deed.

Accordingly, the company's interest in and use of the land were charitable and fell within the exemption provisions of the tax statute. In this case it was because the very strict control over the use of the land that was imposed by the trust deed bound the controllers of the company both as trustees and directors. In consequence, the legally separate nature of the trust and the company could safely be ignored. Similarly, in *Littlewoods Stores v IRC* [1969] 1 WLR 1241, it was held that a subsidiary company held an asset on trust for the holding company, Littlewoods, because Littlewoods had provided the purchase price. Littlewoods could therefore not take advantage of the separate legal identity of its subsidiary to avoid the tax consequences of ownership of the asset.

The decision in *Re FG Films* [1953] 1 WLR 483 is sometimes regarded as an instance of lifting the veil where the company concerned is acting as an agent for another. Although the judgment mentions agency, the true basis for the decision is that the interests of justice required the court to have regard to the realities behind the situation. The case concerned an application to have a film registered as a British film. To succeed, the applicant company had to show that they were the 'makers' of the film. Vaisey J said:

The applicants have a capital of £100 divided into 100 shares of £1 each, 90 of which are held by the American director and the remaining 10 by a British one ... I now understand that they have no place of business apart from their registered office and they do not employ any staff ... [I]t seems to me to be contrary, not only to all sense and reason, but to the proved and admitted facts of the case, to say or to believe that this insignificant company undertook in any real sense of that word the arrangements for the making of this film. I think that their participation in any such undertaking was so small as to be practically negligible, and that they acted, in so far as they acted at all in the matter, merely as the nominee of and agent for an American company called Film Group Incorporated ... The applicant's intervention in the matter was purely colourable.

A similar motive lies behind the decision in *Daimler v Continental Tyre Co* [1916] AC 307, where an English company was held to be an enemy alien because of the nationality of its shareholders.

It is impossible to find a legally consistent basis for the cases in which the courts have decided to ignore the separate legal personality of the company. All that can be said with certainty is that unless there are compelling considerations of justice and fairness, the courts will follow *Salomon* and respect the doctrine which declares a company to be a body quite distinct from its members.

14.2 Why multinational companies became so powerful

There are three principal reasons why multinationals became so powerful:

1. the veil of incorporation;
2. large-scale production; and
3. extraterritoriality.

14.2.1 The veil of incorporation

We have seen that each company is considered as a separate enterprise in many jurisdictions, including the UK (see Section 14.1 above). We have also seen examples where the courts have been very reluctant to lift the veil between a parent company and a subsidiary (*Adams v Cape Industries PLC* [1990] BCLC 479, allowing the parent company to avoid liability for tortious behaviour – see Section 14.1.5(a)).

Limited liability was a device invented by lawyers to shift risk between investors (shareholders) and creditors and other stakeholders. In company governance in the UK and the US, the shareholders are the most powerful stakeholders in the company. The only risk that they run is losing a stake of the money that they invested; they are protected from losing their other assets including their houses, etc. At the same time they might get dividends from the company. The protection of shareholders gives them a cushion, which can be used to speculate, perhaps founding other businesses. This is the basic tenet of capitalism. Often the investment fuels other businesses, which will be linked with the original company; often this is the reason for the foundation of multinational companies. Once the linked companies are established, they become powerful, often pushing smaller companies into insolvency.

14.2.2 Large-scale production

Having a number of companies linked together allows them to consolidate their business, making them more efficient. For example, if a parent company and several subsidiaries merge their administration and their chain of production, the product that they manufacture will be cheaper because the costs will be less. They will not employ as many people and in the chain of production their transport costs will be shared. This means that their competitors will be at a disadvantage, and eventually they will either have to cut their prices or reduce expenses in their business. Otherwise they will be become insolvent.

14.2.3 Extraterritoriality

As a company group grows, it will often export its products into other jurisdictions. If this happens, often the parent company will incorporate a subsidiary in the countries where the business is to be found. This will allow the group to expand, and this will mean further efficiency savings. Such savings will be not only in the business itself but also in tax advantages. Within a group, assets can be switched between companies, allowing them to trade between themselves. This is known as 'transfer pricing'. Theoretically the asset should be evaluated by an 'arm's length' evaluation. However, there is a serious conflict of interests in these negotiations and the tax authorities in each jurisdiction need to regulate such transactions. In a poor country this is problematic because the local authorities might not have the resources to police the transfers adequately. In all countries in these situations there is a serious risk of corruption. This may amount to simple bribery, but more subtle conflicts of interests can occur, for example where a government wishes to promote a company for regional or national advantages, it might change the tax rate for that particular company.

The EU tries to prevent these abuses, but multinational companies are global now. Frequently, in the case of environmental hazards or labour abuses including health and safety violations, a parent company can hive out risky or dirty business abroad. Problematically, the subsidiary company will generally not be sued, either because the venture is in a state which is politically unstable and/or lacking in effective environmental regulation or enforcement practices, or because the subsidiary can be starved of finance by the parent and placed in danger of insolvency. Meanwhile, suing the parent company is problematic because each company in the multinational company group is construed as completely separate. Each jurisdiction, moreover, has a limited jurisdictional reach, whilst, in effect, each company in the multinational company group is insulated by the operation of the 'corporate veil', isolating the companies making up the group. In this sense, the multinational company makes a particularly complex target for the imposition of liability: there is no single multinational company 'entity' as such.

As we have seen in Section 14.1 above, German law (via the *Konzernrecht*) and EU law have made some progress in constructing an enterprise system, but more comprehensive provisions could be useful for labour rights and the environment. Constructing a form of 'enterprise liability' is politically controversial because the pre-eminent model of companies in the western world is the 'nexus of companies'. However, if such a form of liability could be enacted, it would potentially mean that the whole multinational company enterprise might be sued simultaneously, making it simpler to force the directors of each company to respect standards of environmental probity and good standards for employees, and to strengthen the relevant fiduciary duties.

14.3 Company groups in action

According to Blumberg and Blumberg ('The American Law of Corporate Groups' in *Corporate Control and Accountability*, McCaherty, Picciotto and Scott (eds) (Clarendon Press, 1993)), '[e]ffectively, law performs a conjuring trick in order to disguise the power concentrations and opportunity for manipulation in corporate groups'. Tracing this distorted perception back to classic economic analysis:

> Economic analysis was predicated on the role played by the individual entrepreneur in organising production. Classical economists assumed that 'entrepreneurs' headed firms which they personally owned; and they could see no obvious reason to modify this view when analysing the behaviour of the modern, large scale business corporation. (Blumberg and Blumberg, p 292)

The authors identified two other reasons for the power concentrations and opportunity for manipulation in corporate groups in the context of US law:

1. the fact that it was not possible until 1888–93 for one corporation to become a shareholder in another corporation, allowing linked companies to form a group of companies; and
2. that when the issue of the liability of parent corporations first came before the courts, not only had the limited liability of shareholders been accepted for decades but that at the time:

> American law was experiencing the high tide of formalism, or conceptualism, as the only legitimate form of legal analysis. Shareholders were not liable for the obligations of the corporations of which they were shareholders. A parent company was a shareholder. [Therefore], a parent corporation was not liable for the obligations of its subsidiary corporations of which it was a shareholder. (Blumberg and Blumberg, p 308).

So the courts determined that there was no difference between a solitary individual owning a few shares in a giant company and one company owning shares in another, even if it owned a majority of the shares and could consequently appoint the directors and manipulate the finances of the other company.

Despite what Blumberg and Blumberg called the 'dramatic change in the underlying relationship', which occurs when companies form themselves into groups, this analysis prevailed and is still evident today in both US and UK jurisprudence. What this does is create a legal pretence which completely ignores and disguises the cumulative power which a group of companies may exert over suppliers, consumers, employees and the political system. Suppliers will be frightened that if they are put on a 'black list', they will have no destination for their produce; consumers may get less choice and may be subject to price fluctuations at the will of the group; employees will fear loss of a job as alternative possibilities shrink; and politicians will be subject to the threat of increasing unpopularity if a group of companies threatens to take its operations elsewhere causing a collapse in local economies.

Economists sometimes describe companies as a series of individual contracts – between suppliers and the buyer (in the company), between employees and the person (in the company) who employs them, and so on (the 'nexus of contracts', see Chapter 2). This vision also misrepresents the cumulative power of the company by reducing its operations to the individual transactions which make up the operation. It also carries the suggestion of equality – these individual transactions look as if real bargains are being struck, but you (as an employee) try telling Gap or Nike what terms of employment you would like! Possible if you are Tiger Woods promoting Nike products, but not for the rest of us (<www.youtube.com/nikegolf>).

Thus the reality of corporate power is rather different from the fragmented vision of the economists. Very few inhabitants of the planet are untouched by the activities of companies, and some argue that they are taking over the world at the expense of the nation state and to the detriment of developing nations and the environment. As Pettet writes, '[a]t the heart of the ... capitalist system, the free market economy, lies company law' (see 'Further reading' below).

It is through the medium of companies that wealth is created. More than this, the way in which companies are regulated says a great deal about the values to which each society and the global community gives preference.

The concept of a company carrying on business in several countries is far from new. However, the scale of this activity has increased enormously in recent years, and current statistics contain a rather frightening message. According to the UN's *World Investment Report 2011*, the world has about 45,000 transnational firms controlling 280,000 foreign affiliates. Worldwide sales of the latter amounted to about $7 trillion. The largest 100 companies own about $1.7 trillion of foreign assets – a fifth of the estimated global total. Multinational companies account for 51 of the world's largest economic entities (the other 49 are nation states).

The important characteristic of the multinational phenomenon is that management is increasingly responsible for activities on an *international basis*. Their horizons are no longer limited by national or local considerations. A useful definition is that put forward by the Commission of Transnational Corporations in its draft code of conduct for Transnational Corporations. The emphasis is on 'a system of decision making, permitting coherent policies and a common strategy through one or more decision-making centres' (United Nations Economic and Social Council, *Work on the Formulation of the United Nations Code of Conduct on Transnational Corporations - Outstanding Issues in the Draft Code of Conduct on Transnational Corporations* (E/C10/1985/5/2, 22 May 1985)). Unfortunately this initiative was stopped by the hostility of the business community. Recently, the UN has revisited the issue in the UN Guiding Principles on Business and Human Rights, 16 June 2011. This initiative is welcome but it will be very difficult to implement a human rights agenda into the way business is transacted. The Guiding Principles have three pillars, deriving from Professor John Ruggie's work for the UN. The framework is simple, using a 'respect, protect and remedy' concept. This framework is taken from human rights law which uses a framework of 'respect, protect and fulfill'. The new part of this framework is the focus on 'remedies', ie the UN wants to strengthen rules on corporate social responsibility and eventually put into hard law the accountability of businesses.

These are the Principles:

These Guiding Principles are grounded in recognition of:
(a) States' existing obligations to respect, protect and fulfil human rights and fundamental freedoms;
(b) The role of business enterprises as specialized organs of society performing specialized functions, required to comply with all applicable laws and to respect human rights;
(c) The need for rights and obligations to be matched to appropriate and effective remedies when breached.

The Guiding Principles apply to all States and to all business enterprises, both transnational and others, regardless of their size, sector, location, ownership and structure.

As we have seen, this is going to be a fraught plan. The tensions between the human rights community and the business world are enormous. This, coupled with the reason for the existence of companies, which is often seen to be to make the maximum profit for shareholders, creates a system which opens up poorer countries to exploitation, often involving human rights violations by multinational companies.

Where all the component companies of a group are situated in one legal jurisdiction, it is open to the laws of that country to treat the group as a single entity where the formal legal structure is being used for fraudulent purposes. This is often termed 'lifting the corporate veil', and many jurisdictions (including the Member States of the EU) collect tax from groups of companies on this basis. However, where companies use group structures but spread themselves across different legal jurisdictions, many problems arise. Because many developing states are desperate for foreign direct investment, they will offer tax holidays and lax regulatory regimes in order to entice the powerful multinationals to invest. Take an example where a parent company is situated in a rich OECD country (as most of them are). It has control over a subsidiary in a developing country because of its shareholding in that subsidiary. The parent and its associated group have a turnover which is greater than that of the state where its subsidiary is located, and they have therefore been able to bargain for a very loose regulatory regime in the subsidiary's host state. The subsidiary is causing environmental degradation and imposing terrible working conditions on its labour force. What legal results follow from this scenario?

1. The poor country is in breach of its duty to protect its citizens, who are forced to work in poor conditions and endure the environmental damage. It will be reluctant to try to enforce higher standards if the parent company is likely to withdraw the subsidiary from the country. This is the 'race to the bottom' in regulatory standards. Remember, the parent can cause the subsidiary to vanish (liquidate), transfer all its funds to the parent or simply stop doing business.
2. In the poor country the parent company will be viewed as a separate entity from the subsidiary, and because it owes its existence to the laws of a foreign country (the rich state), it has no legal presence in the poor country state and can incur no liability, even if the courts of that country were functioning fairly and effectively.
3. In the extremely unlikely event that the legal system of the poor country 'lifts the veil' and finds the parent liable, it will be difficult for those damaged to enforce judgment against a parent situated in a foreign country, and funds may also be diverted elsewhere in the group and/or the company may liquidate.

To turn attention to the legal results of this scenario in the home state of the parent (the rich country):

1. The separate legal status of the parent company will very likely allow the parent corporation to escape from any liability for the actions of its subsidiary.
2. The subsidiary has no legal presence in the rich country so cannot be subject to any liability there.

No prizes for guessing the winners and losers in this international legal game.

In terms of the globalisation debate, the problems associated with multinational companies are compounded because they may not even be shareholders in the companies which they use to supply their component parts. Many companies are linked only by contracts of supply, so that although they are effectively entirely dependent on retaining the goodwill of the central management of the multinational, they are legally not connected to them by structural ties. This problem is made worse when the suppliers contract out work to home-workers whose conditions are impossible to monitor or inspect. There is a multitude of Codes of Conduct (well over 700) which seek to impose control over the operation of multinational corporations, but none of these have any legal remedies for breach. Monitoring the compliance of corporations with these Codes is extremely difficult, not least because much of the relevant information is under the control of the company itself.

Let us look at one more example: the worst industrial disaster in history, a massive leak of toxic gas on the night of 2–3 December 1984 in the city of Bhopal, India. At the time of writing we are 30 years on, and in addition to the approximately 25,000 killed (no one knows the exact number as many families were simply wiped out) and 500,000 injured that night, we must add current-day victims. The plant has never been cleaned up, children still play with the poisons that remain and pollution due to the plant is poisoning the water. Respiratory problems, persistent coughs, fevers, depression, deaths from cancer, deformations at birth and anorexia remain significantly higher in this blighted city. Some 15,000 people are still chronically ill as a result of the tragedy and on-going pollution. Samples taken by Greenpeace from local water supplies showed a carbon tetrachloride level 682 times higher than the acceptable maximum, a chloroform level 260 times higher and a trichloroethylene level 50 times higher. (See Lapierre and Moro, *Five Minutes Past Midnight in Bhopal* (Scribner, 2003), translated from the French by Kathryn Spink.)

The plant from which the devastation emanated was owned by Union Carbide India, a subsidiary of the mighty US company Union Carbide, a company with 130 subsidiaries in 40 countries, 500 production sites and 12,000 employees at the time. Forty tons of methyl isocyanate exploded that night, because the safety systems had been shut down to save running costs and the alarms disconnected. Union Carbide was sued in the United States for US$15 billion. The case was never decided. Instead, Union Carbide offered US$470 million in compensation without admission of liability, and the official line is that the accident was caused by sabotage, not negligence. Further, that the plant was designed and built by Indian engineers and thus not the responsibility of the US parent. Facts are still emerging to contradict this version of events, but official figures show that about half a million survivors eventually received compensation in the region of £1,000 for the death of relatives and about half of that for serious injury. Union Carbide no longer exists, taken over in 1999 by the Dow Chemical Group. Warren Anderson, Chairman of Union Carbide, resides in New York and Miami in comfortable retirement, despite an Indian and Interpol arrest warrant for 'culpable homicide' issued in 1992 and never served. Recently, some victims received some compensation from the Indian government, but the giant, profitable companies have been able to walk away.

Further reading

Dine, *Companies, International Law and Human Rights* (Cambridge University Press, 2005)

Korten, *When Corporations Rule the World* (Kumarian, 1995)

Muchlinski, *Multinational Enterprises and the Law*, 2nd edn (Oxford University Press, 2007)

Pettet, *Company Law* (Pearson Education, 2001)

Zerk, *Multinationals and Corporate Social Responsibility* (Cambridge University Press, 2006)

Index